Imperial Desire

Imperial Desire

Dissident Sexualities and Colonial Literature

Philip Holden and Richard J. Ruppel, Editors

University of Minnesota Press
Minneapolis
London

Chapter 1 is adapted by permission of New York University Press from *Rum, Sodomy, and the Lash: Piracy, Sexuality, and Masculine Identity* by Hans Turley (New York: New York University Press, 1999). In chapter 10, extracts from E. M. Forster's "The Feminine Note in Literature" and "The Locked Journal" (Volume 4/4) are reprinted by permission of the Society of Authors as agent for the Provost and Scholars of King's College Cambridge.

Published by the University of Minnesota Press
111 Third Avenue South, Suite 290
Minneapolis, MN 55401-2520
http://www.upress.umn.edu

Library of Congress Cataloging-in-Publication Data

Imperial desire : dissident sexualities and colonial literature / Philip Holden and Richard J. Ruppel, editors.
    p.   cm.
Includes bibliographical references and index.
ISBN 0-8166-3764-4 (HC : alk. paper) — ISBN 0-8166-3765-2 (PH : alk. paper)
    1. English literature—History and criticism.   2. Homosexuality and literature—Great Britain.   3. Homosexuality and literature—Great Britain—Colonies.   4. Imperialism in literature.   5. Colonies in literature.   6. Desire in literature.   7. Sex in literature.   I. Holden, Philip, 1962–   II. Ruppel, Richard R., 1953–
PR408.H65 I47 2002
820.9'353—dc21   2002154449

Printed in the United States of America on acid-free paper

The University of Minnesota is an equal-opportunity educator and employer.

12 11 10 09 08 07 06 05 04 03   10 9 8 7 6 5 4 3 2 1

Contents

Introduction

Philip Holden and Richard J. Ruppel

"My book," writes Gayatri Spivak in her preface to *A Critique of Post-colonial Reason*, "charts a practitioner's progress from colonial discourse studies to transnational cultural studies."[1] The path Spivak has taken is one that has been followed by many cultural theorists working in post-colonial studies[2] through the 1990s and into the new millennium. Colonial discourse analysis's relentless deconstruction of colonial texts written by Europeans has been replaced with a more nuanced understanding of colonial social structures, and an emphasis on diasporic histories that intersect with, but are not contained by, colonialism. Queer theory, similarly, has exceeded the careful examination of the specification of male homosexuality in the late nineteenth century, which was a feature of early work in gay and lesbian studies, to examine a myriad of practices, subjectivities, and readings. Queer and diasporic studies have, indeed, come together in recent work on queer diasporas, interstitial spaces of identity that resist solidifying into coherent identities. The notion of a queer diaspora, in its focus on a community beyond the nation, destabilizes nationalist ideologies that attempt to interpellate respectable sexual citizen-subjects; simultaneously, in its stress on a queer, multiply inflected identity, it questions globalizing discourses of gay or lesbian sexuality.[3]

If there is a danger in such new work, it is perhaps that colonialism itself, precisely specified by scholars such as Spivak, Homi Bhabha, Ann Laura Stoler, Robert Young, and other analysts of colonial discourse, here becomes only a metaphor for any regime of unequal power. Mindful of a need for specificity, this collection of essays thus attempts to revisit colonial texts understood as the product of a particular historical series of regimes of power with the hindsight enabled by the growth of queer theory, and to see colonial texts as important factors in the formation of metropolitan[4] sexualities, sexualities that then might be appropriated, with subtle modifications, by an emergent nationalist bourgeoisie in the colonies during the first stirrings of national, anticolonial struggles.[5] If our chronological range is wide—Daniel Defoe to Doris Lessing—the center of gravity of the collection is the time of the so-called New Imperialism in the second half of the nineteenth century, a time of the urgent production and regulation of national citizen-subjects.

In this process of regulation, the circulation of specifically literary texts had an important place. In the twentieth century, for example, we commonly see *Robinson Crusoe* as a textual embodiment of the rise of a Protestant work ethic that would provide the motor for the rise of industrial capitalism. Yet we might also plausibly see the novel as a nineteenth-century text; it was vitally important in the subject formation of nineteenth-century readers. As Richard Altick notes, *Robinson Crusoe* was one of the most widely read books in Victorian England, rivaled in popularity only by Bunyan's *Pilgrim's Progress*.[6] The popularity of both tales, indeed, is more than coincidental: both are concerned with the cultivation of a Protestant sensibility, with what the French philosopher Michel Foucault has called "technologies of the self"[7] that provide a means to bourgeois subjectification. This process of self-construction is also relational: Crusoe's relationship with Friday establishes a paradigm for other relationships between colonizer and colonized in Victorian adventure fiction, fiction that served as a series of conduct books for the creation of a certain style of colonial—and metropolitan—masculinity.

If paradigmatic, however, the relationship between Friday and Crusoe is also paradoxical. Much of the work of empire was routine, and most relationships between colonizer and colonized would involve colonial officials and nonofficials on the one hand, and members of compradore classes on the other. Friday does of course become anglicized through his submission to Crusoe's government, becoming one of a class whom, as Thomas Babington Macaulay famously expressed it, "may be interpreted between us and the millions whom we govern; a class of persons, Indian in blood and colour, but English in taste, in opinions, in morals and in intellect."[8] The initial intimacy between Friday and Crusoe,

however, seems to be predicated not on mimicry but on absolute difference, on the production of Friday as a noble savage uncontaminated
by Europe. Other relationships "between men" in the fiction of colonialism also show desire for an exorbitant or wayward masculinity outside nineteenth-century heterosexual norms: one thinks of Dain Waris in
Lord Jim, Umbopa in *King Solomon's Mines*, Bukta, Peroo, and Billy Fish
in Kipling's "The Tomb of His Ancestors," "The Bridge Builders," and
"The Man Who Would Be King."

Such relationships between the colonizer and the not-yet-quite colonized cannot be simply read as "queer": they may, indeed, represent a
longing for a nostalgically conceived heteronormative "real masculinity" preserved in the raw in a natural state on the frontier. Much writing
of the New Imperialism mourns the passing of such a stage and indulges
in misogynist scapegoating of European women in the colonies as en-
forcers of respectable bourgeois, and debilitating, morality. The binarism of gender, however, clearly does not map easily onto that of colonization: the colonized may be either hypermasculine, or feminized,
while the colonizer may either be a protector of bourgeois virtue or a
seeker awaiting the revitalization of primitive gender energy. Such textual dissonance offers the possibility of queer reading if the text is read
not just in terms of gender but of sexuality, and if we do not define
"queer" as merely a search for homoeroticism but a capacity, in Arlene
Stein's and Ken Plummer's words, "to interrogate areas which normally
would not be seen as the terrain of sexuality, and to conduct queer 'readings' of ostensibly heterosexual or nonsexualized texts."[9]

A starting point for such a reading, then, might be to look at the simultaneous need for, and yet disavowal of, relationships between the
colonizer and the colonized. This paradox may be approached through
Homi Bhabha's notion of mimicry. In a ground-breaking essay that has
suffered by being read out of its immediate and very specific context,
Bhabha suggests that colonialism is haunted by an ambivalence arising
from the colonized's mimicry of the colonizer. Mimicry, Bhabha notes,
is not merely a "narcissistic identification" on the part of the colonized;
rather, it menaces colonialism through a "*double vision* which in dis-
closing the ambivalence of colonial discourse also disrupts its authority."[10]
Colonialism thus both requires successfully colonized subjects and works
to dismiss them; it requires them, impossibly, to be "almost the same but
not white" (89). Intimate relationships between colonizer and colonized,

relationships normatively between men, are thus necessary for the success of the colonial enterprise, and yet the intimacy of the relationship must be continually disavowed. Colonial texts both require mimicry as a mark of the success of the colonizing project and yet feel the menace of that mimicry when its impersonation of the colonizer becomes too acutely observed, too accurate.

The need for, and yet constant disavowal of an Other, is constitutive not only of the colonial subject but also the heterosexual male subject in the second part of the nineteenth century. Eve Sedgwick's seminal work suggests that "the radically disrupted continuum, in our society, between sexual and nonsexual male bonds" results in a state of panic for men performing heterosexual masculinity.[11] There is a need, Sedgwick notes, for strong homosocial bonds between men in patriarchal society, but such relationships remain haunted by the possibility of moving further down the continuum, of crossing over a barrier and becoming definably homosexual. In her later work, *Epistemology of the Closet,* Sedgwick concentrates more closely on the nineteenth century as a time when, after the specification of the homosexual, such panic became a crucial element in the construction of masculinity. Just as the colonized in the colonial narrative must be both acknowledged and disavowed, then must be seen as similar and yet also different, so the homosexual must be excluded within heterosexual masculinity.[12] Heterosexuality, David Halperin notes, comes into the English language after homosexuality: normative heterosexual masculinity is only possible in contrast to a constitutive homosexual other.[13] Similarly, as Etienne Balibar has pointed out, "European" subjectivity begins in the colonies: it is in spaces entered by non-European Others that the need for differentiation becomes most acute.[14]

Parallels, of course, do not necessarily make symmetries. In the last decade, areas of inquiry such as postcolonial studies and queer studies have moved to a more closely historicized analysis. We need to distinguish different kinds of colonialisms, and different noncolonial cultural presences that already mark a landscape that is phantasmically constructed in the adventure narrative as *terra nullius.* Modern gender regimes and normative sexualities are complex and many-faceted, and different social and political factors influence each writer. Tales of adventure generated by imperial experiences might reflect these internal and external forces in different ways—and might be read differently, and put to new uses, by their readers in both colonies and the metropole. Such "queer reading," in its widest sense, might take many forms. If we have stressed the heteronormative masculinity of tales of imperial adventure, it is surely germane to note that such tales, despite Rider Haggard's polemics,[15] were read by women as well as men, by the colonized as well as the colonizers. In turn, adventure stories were written by women, and these might, as both Alison Blunt and Sara Mills have argued,[16] exhibit a clear difference from those of men, thematizing homoeroticism and dissident sexualities in different ways. The adventure story might also be appropriated by the colonized: *Mhudi* (1930), the epic novel written by Sol Plaatje, the first general secretary of the African National Congress, for example, was produced under the acknowledged influence of Haggard.[17]

Much of the literature of colonialism, then, attempts to provide a series of gendered technologies of the self. From the eighteenth century to the early twentieth century, gender regimes in Europe underwent a radical transformation, or, more properly, a series of transformations. R. W. Connell, adopting a longer historical perspective, sees these changes as reflecting the "formation of the modern gender order"[18] that maintains hegemonic status in industrialized societies throughout the world today. Individualizing practices from Protestantism, visible in such writings as *Robinson Crusoe* and Benjamin Franklin's *Autobiography,* gradually began to assume importance, and masculinity came to be seen as an act of self-governance, a series of technologies of the self applied to an unruly body. In the late eighteenth century, Catherine Hall and Leonore Davidoff have noted, masculinity was often expressed as excess, while by the middle of the nineteenth century it was associated with sobriety and the application of self-discipline. Heavy drinking was discouraged,[19] language became "more formal, more differentiated and more careful of gender connotations" (401), while men's clothing gradually became tighter fitting and more monochromatic (412–13). In mid-century, books such as A. P. Stanley's *Life and Correspondence of Thomas Arnold, D. D.,* and Samuel Smiles's *Character* stressed masculinity as self-governance.[20] Fiction and poetry, James Eli Adams argues, produced a series of models of masculinity, each "understood as the incarnation of an ascetic regimen, an elaborately articulated program of self-discipline" (2).

Any discussion of masculinity cannot ignore the social position of and the representation of women. Cultural codings of femininity were also transformed in relation to the new technologization of masculinity under a modern gender regime. Victorian representations of femininity were dichotomous, Mary Poovey notes: based on a conflict "between the image of the woman as a sexual creature that flourished in the seventeenth century and the domestic, idealized woman that gradually repressed this image in the eighteenth century."[21] If women were responsible for ordering and arrangement within the home, then, for making supporting contributions toward the government of the male self, they also carried within them the potential to cause the abdication of such responsibility, of the technologies of the self that enabled domestic bourgeois discipline. Thus the domestic gender regime was neither uncontested nor innately secure. In the late nineteenth century, anxieties regarding degeneration rose in Europe, concomitant with fears that the over-regulation of masculinity might result in the depletion of vital racial energy. Manliness underwent changes: from the earnest self-restraint of the early nineteenth century it became transformed into the so-called "muscular Christianity," demanding "neo-Spartan virility as exemplified by stoicism, hardiness and endurance."[22] In a sense, therefore, the tensions within the framework of masculinity were drawn tighter: primitive masculine energy, Charles Kingsley's manly *thumos*, was revitalized, only to be subject to new, reinforced technologies of control.

Parallel to this history of gendered subjectification is a history of sexuality. Michel Foucault's account of the specification of the homosexual by medical discourses in the mid- to late nineteenth century, part of a larger Western *scientia sexualis*, remains influential but incomplete. Certainly, identifiable sexual minorities did exist in eighteenth-century England: London's molly houses and the Romantic fascination with Greek love are evidence of this. Contrary to Foucault's assertions that the homosexual subject was summoned by medical discourses and then proceeded to answer back, Joseph Bristow has noted that "Uranians" such as Karl Heinz Ulrichs elaborated their identities through a notion of individual rights before the specification of the homosexual.[23] Nonetheless, Foucault's account remains essential to our discussion. By the end of the nineteenth century, homosexuality would certainly have been established as Fuss's "indispensable interior exclusion" within a normative heterosexuality.

Interestingly for our subject here, Connell also writes of colonialism and imperialism as a major factor in the formation of the modern gender order. Imperialism, Connell notes, was a "gendered enterprise" (187), and the frontier produced a new "masculine cultural type" (187). So gendered was the imperial space, we have noted, that when white women did come to the colonies they were subject to criticism and caricatured as interrupting an idyllic golden age of free contact between cultures.[24] Yet few European men or women would actually have voyaged to the colonies, and the centrality of colonialism to metropolitan sexuality and gender formations cannot have been achieved through direct individual experience. Rather, adventure narratives set in the colonies, successors to *Robinson Crusoe*, provided conduct books to produce normative masculine subjects. Such narratives, Martin Green argues, were "the energizing myth of British imperialism."[25] In adventure tales, the protagonist overcomes a hostile environment not only through superior technology but by "keeping a diary and keeping accounts," by adopting a "puritan examination of conscience," and in the discipline of developing "rationalized and systematized and demystified habits of thought" (23). These processes, Joseph Bristow notes, were not only protocapitalist but also gendered. Boys and young men read adventure stories with the knowledge that their "narrative dimensions clearly bore close relations (admittedly complex ones) with the way men would learn to live their lives— *as men*."[26] The adventure narrative was widely read as a conduct book by both metropolitan and colonial audiences as a way of producing a normative masculine subject.

Many of these narratives feature an interracial homoeroticism that at times enables, and at other times interrupts, the processes of subjectification that the novels and travelogues incite. It may, indeed, be possible to plot changes in the content of such writing as European constructions of gender and sexuality change. As homosexuality becomes specified and individualized through the second half of the nineteenth century, the latent homoeroticism in much nineteenth-century adventure fiction becomes more manifest, and then, after the trials of Oscar Wilde, begins to haunt the disciplining powers of narrative. In Joseph Conrad and Ford Madox Ford's *Romance*, for example, the homoeroticism has become detached from the colonialist adventure tale, and, along with other colonialist adventure tropes, becomes subject to parody. The pursuit of colonial mastery follows a similar development: from the triumphant self-creation through colonial mastery represented in *Robinson Crusoe* to suspicions concerning the degradation of character that *results* from colonial mastery in works like *Heart of Darkness*. For a writer such as

E. M. Forster, closeted queer sexualities become a metaphor for the incommensurability of the colonizer/colonized divide in a morally bankrupt system: it is the simultaneous desire and inability of Fielding and Aziz to be together at the end of *A Passage to India* that gives the novel its tantalizingly modernist indeterminacy.

In response, and at times in opposition to, this chronological movement, *Imperial Desire: Dissident Sexualities and Colonial Literature* consists of five sections. The first, titled "Frontiers and Discoveries," examines three texts with widely different geographical and political locations. Hans Turley's essay reads Defoe's *Robinson Crusoe* (1719), a text that has paradigmatic status in both colonial discourse analysis and studies in the novel, in parallel with its two sequels, *The Farther Adventures of Robinson Crusoe* (1719) and *The Serious Reflections of Robinson Crusoe* (1720). Many previous readings of Defoe's novel, Turley notes, focus exclusively on the first volume and see the island as a microcosm of an incipient capitalist and colonialist world order. Reading the three volumes together produces a different emphasis—the island becomes a utopian, homoerotic space, marked by a stress on mutuality and economic development. In contrast, once Crusoe leaves his island and Friday is killed, Crusoe's worldview is dominated by a violent, dissenting Christianity that incites colonial conquest in the later volumes. Turley's strategy of queer reading thus opens up contradictions in the colonial text, contradictions that are explored in subsequent essays. Justifications of colonialism—economic development, a civilizing mission—are contrasted with scenes of violent suppression and conquest, while the celebration of the colonies as a space of homoerotic mutuality outside normative European sexuality collides with the continued enforcement of colonial power.

John C. Beynon's discussion of Lady Mary Wortley Montagu's *Turkish Embassy Letters* also indicates the possibilities of queer reading to disrupt the apparently straightforward binarisms of a colonial discourse. Other critics have argued that Montagu's vision of the harem reflects a colonial division of space, a feminized area of darkness and overt sexuality observed by a rational, fully clothed European spectator who, though female, explicitly aligns herself with the cartographic vision of male painters. Such readings, Beynon notes, are common, and yet they do not do Montagu's representation of Turkish women justice. Responding to orientalist depictions of the harem as a space of perverse lesbian desire, Montagu reimagines it as a community of women outside patriarchal control. Her visual representation of the harem is thus less through a petrifying male gaze than through a series of exchanged, desiring glances: Montagu is simultaneously both subject and object, spectator and spectacle. Montagu's praise of the veil also celebrates the possibility of transgression of hierarchies of rank, of public space, and indeed in desire; rather than solidifying a home/harem binarism, Montagu's "pursuit of a Sapphic vision" tends to problematize it.

In contrast to Turley and Beynon, Terry Goldie interrogates a text that, although clearly colonial, has also been retrospectively understood as the origin of a distinctly autonomous literary tradition. John Richardson's *Wacousta,* Goldie notes, has been viewed as both the first Canadian novel and as paradigmatic for Canadian literature in its celebration of the frontier garrison. Like many contributors to this collection, Goldie employs Sedgwick's notion of erotic triangles to describe the manner in which the homosocial relationship between the Cornishman-become-Native-American Wacousta and his erstwhile friend, Colonel de Haldimar, is mediated through the common desire for a woman. Rereading *Wacousta* in a Sedgwickean frame produces other insights, since the garrison itself is a homoerotic space marked by manly comradeship. De Haldimar opts for heterosexual union, patriarchy, and the stability of military command, while Wacousta, as a "white Indian," is sexually and politically vagrant: heterosexuality and European identity are thus constituted by the presence of their Others just over the horizon, "an outside," in Fuss's terms again, "inside interiority making the articulation of the latter possible, a transgression of the border which is necessary to constitute the border as such."[27] If the trajectory of Richardson's plot aims to erase these contradictions, they are clearly made visible again by Goldie's reading strategy.

Fiction and travel narratives also feature in the second section of *Imperial Desire,* which explores texts written under the "New Imperialism" in the second half of the nineteenth century. Mark Forrester's close examination of Anthony Trollope's short story "The Banks of the Jordan" demonstrates the insights a queer reading of a colonial text may bring. Trollope's story might seem to reproduce a heterosexual gender order, feminizing the Holy Land's landscape and opening it to the surveillance of and penetration by a male protagonist. Contemporary objections to the story, indeed, as Forrester notes, focused on its breaches of heterosexual propriety, not on its homoerotic subtext. Forrester's painstaking disinterring of such a text, however, has wider implications. Commencing from the homoerotic attraction between the two main characters, Forrester continues to demonstrate how the landscape itself is inscribed with a fluid sexuality. If Jones and Smith penetrate crowds and tourist attractions in celebratory imperialist style, Jones himself is penetrated by the Dead Sea and swallows its salty fluids. Mappings of colonial power onto landscape are thus disrupted, "questions of complicity and consent become hopelessly blurred," and the twin symbols of colonial dominance that Jones gives to Smith, the pistol and the purse, become symbols of interchangeable sexual activity and passivity and a concomitant inability to separate oneself from the landscape.

Forrester's insights thus demonstrate the extent to which the colonial landscape has always been a contested territory in terms of sexuality in colonial texts; the queering of the colony clearly does not begin with E. M. Forster's Marabar caves.[28]

Anjali Arondekar's essay introduces a new theme, one that will become increasingly central to the later essays in *Imperial Desire*. Under New Imperialism, concern moved from idealizing the frontier as a space of challenge and transgression to the production of regimes of respectable sexuality in the colonies. Thus Arondekar provides a carefully nuanced reading of the production of a new colonial masculinity in Kipling's short stories, and its maintenance through a homosociality focused not on bodies but on the interchange of texts. Kipling's "new narrative of colonial masculinity," Arondekar notes, attempts to erase the trauma of the Mutiny by producing an exoticized Anglo Indian subject who represents an ideal of English manliness, a virile imperial type. The English author's texts, however, are littered by the bodies of failed strong men who have suffered madness, injury, or death. Refuge for these men comes in the transmission of stories to other men, in the passing on of secrets to their male readers, editors, and commentators. This transmission, Arondekar suggests, is marked by a "lingering" on male bodies in uncompleted stories in which reading pleasure is generated not by the completion of grand narratives of empire but in companionship. In Kipling's stories, scenes of writing and reading are central, figured as moments of bonding between men that occupy shifting positions on the continuum between homosociality and homoeroticism.

Arondekar's essay is significant in that it resists a temptation to apply the full Sedgwickean template but rather adapts Sedgwick's structures to a particular historical situation. Indian women, she stresses, do not provide a means of transmission of male characters' mutual desire in Kipling's fiction, as an application of Sedgwick's notion of triangular desire would suggest—rather, their "management" and domestication signifies an imaginative control over the Indian landscape. Her insight that the text itself provides a means of homosocial mediation, furthermore, allows her to make use of psychoanalytic theory—in particular Leo Bersani's linking of the "perversions" of uncompleted narratives to challenges to dominant heterosexuality—while at the same time maintaining historical specificity.

Christopher Lane's *The Ruling Passion* is a pioneering work that draws together queer theory and colonial discourse analysis; it is therefore fitting that his essay concentrates on imperial pioneers, here women writers, exemplified by Mary Kingsley. In a wide-ranging introduction, Lane argues for a queer reading strategy that does not attempt to smooth away the contradictions in Kingsley's writings or to argue that they are merely expressions of colonial discourse. In examining Kingsley's *Travels in West Africa* against the background of critical interest in colonial women's writing, Lane explores the power of fantasy to empty out the African landscape and to "explore where meaning ceases to exist." Women travelers such as Kingsley, who were both pioneers and "ladies," Lane notes, continually negotiated gender roles. They produced texts in which a gap opens between identification and identity, and in which colonial certainties are thrown into question. Lane illustrates this in an analysis of Kingsley's fantasies regarding West African women, in which simultaneous eroticization and stress on the notion of "separate spheres" call attention to the gap between her psychic life as an imperial traveler and her public persona as a lady. Lane's reading of the ambiguity of such eroticization thus has much in common with, and indeed contextualizes, Beynon's account of Sapphism in Lady Mary Wortley Montagu's works. At the same time, Kingsley's dual identification as lady and pioneer indicates her engagement with the association between colonialism and sexual propriety that Arondekar's essay investigates.

Given the debate in many essays concerning the ability of a literary text to challenge the discursive parameters of imperialism, it is perhaps fitting that our third section is a cluster of readings of the fiction of Joseph Conrad. Conrad himself opposed the excesses of imperialism in the Belgian Congo, but commentators such as Chinua Achebe have seen in his writing an acceptance of the racist doxologies of colonialism.[29] The Conrad essays in this collection may be seen, in part, as participants in this ongoing debate. Eschewing a simple model of either complicity with or resistance to colonialism, Tim Middleton, in discussing *The Nigger of the "Narcissus,"* notes that while Conrad was writing the text for publication in W. E. Henley's jingoistic *New Review,* his novel is ultimately dialogic. Middleton employs a familiar theoretical apparatus, deftly combining Homi Bhabha and Eve Sedgwick: Conrad's mimicry of the colonial adventure story—his replaying of colonial masculinity slightly off key— thus reveals tensions in late-nineteenth-century sexuality clustered around the concept of narcissism. Middleton does not conflate queer and postcolonial theoretical notions of ambivalence, avoiding a simplistic reading of Conrad's text as a metonymic representation of "colonial discourse." Rather, like Lane, he resorts to careful historicization of the circumstances of the text's reception and production. Mimicry, in this reading, is a conscious strategy on the part of the author, embedded in the stylistic features of the novel. Contemporary criticism of the novel, indeed, indicates that the novel's openness to many readings was apparent to its first readers, and not merely a matter for readers in our century. Middleton's use of Sedgwick is also nuanced: he draws on *Epistemology of the Closet* to illustrate the anxieties contained in the novel's representation of Wait as "a closeted, dandyesque man with a secret" two brief years after the trials of Oscar Wilde.

Richard Ruppel follows Middleton's example in analyzing a key Conrad text as engaging in ironic commentary upon the genre of which it is an example. *Heart of Darkness,* Ruppel notes, follows conventional imperial adventure stories in its relentless excision of women characters and its production of an all-male, homosocial world. Homoerotic filiations between Marlow, the harlequin, and Kurtz, however, register a certain uneasiness with normative heterosexuality, while Marlow's homoerotic identification with African characters, Ruppel suggests in conclusion, introduces a queerness that may call into question, even if it cannot fully erase, the projection of colonial racism. Like Middleton, Ruppel owes a theoretical debt to Eve Sedgwick, drawing on the notions of homosexual panic and triangular desire elaborated in *Between Men.* Like Lane, however, Ruppel avoids reading off elements of *Heart of Darkness* as manifestations of colonial discourse. Both the form and content of the novella, Ruppel maintains, represent a critical engagement with colonialism by an author who explicitly critiqued imperial excess, even if the frame narrative works to return us to "a world of conventional thinking and morality that tolerates no queer lapses."

Ford Madox Ford and Conrad's collaborative novel, *Romance*, Sarah Cole notes, initially seems less experimental in form than either writer's best-known works. The text's imperial setting, however, Cole notes, means that it directly confronts questions of imperial masculinity and queers them through dual competing narratives. The first of these is implied by the novel's title: a romantic plot based on a nostalgic investment in a primordial masculinity symbolized by the Reigeo family. In this plot, homoeroticism has free rein, but romance also at times betrays itself as fantasy, even parody, a "calcified" representation of masculine self-fashioning that has no place in a modern, capitalist world order. The second plot is thus a heterosexual love story between Kemp and Seraphina, which embeds Kemp within capitalist modernity, in allegiance to a state, and in devotion to labor. While complementing Ruppel's and Middleton's analysis in its focus on triangular desire and traffic in women, Cole's essay extends their arguments to a consideration of how heterosexuality is embedded in processes of subject formation in capitalist modernity.

Our fourth section is perhaps the most diverse thematically. Lois Cucullu's wittily titled "Only Cathect" explores a text that might be thought scrupulously domestic: E. M. Forster's *Howards End*. Colonialism enters the novel, however, not so much as a disavowed presence in the imperial activities of the Wilcoxes as through a series of incisive parallels Cucullu draws with Forster's essay "The Feminine Note in Literature." In this essay, composed at the time he was writing *Howards End*, Forster negotiates between the heteronormativity of the "feminine" nineteenth-century domestic novel and the masculinity of the colonial adventure story. His representative of masculine writing is Conrad's *Lord Jim*, in which homophilia is preserved but the violence of conquest muted. In *Howards End*, in Cucullu's argument, Forster imports the fruits of his imperial inquiry, the imperial adventurer becoming the English yeoman, and the country house itself forming a repository of a new, bourgeois masculinity based on homoeroticism and homophilia.

Maria Davidis, in contrast to Cucullu, examines a text that maintains the genre of imperial adventure fiction into the twentieth century: John Buchan's *Prester John*. Buchan confronts growing unease regarding imperial rule and metropolitan degeneration, Davidis argues, with a return to a Victorian notion of imperialism as a civilizing mission, maintained by Calvinist disciplinary practices. The empire thus becomes a place for national regeneration. In *Prester John*, Davie Crawfurd's Calvinist imperialism confronts its mirror image: the syncretic, revolutionary religion of the African preacher Laputa. Despite the text's efforts to abject Laputa, Davidis notes, Crawfurd clearly sees him as an embodiment of masculine energy, his appreciation of the preacher drenched in a febrile mixture of homoeroticism and religious devotion. Much of the energy of the narrative is thus exerted in an effort to reverse the terms of a Platonic homophilic relationship, Davie moving from the position of student to master through his appropriation of Laputa's vital energy.

If adventure fiction seems to reflect doxological constructions of late-Victorian masculinity, aestheticism, as Dennis Denisoff notes, constituted a means of self-construction for sexual minorities from Pater onward. Denisoff's study of the Russian writer Mikhail Kuzmin extends and questions the scope of colonialism that many of our essays take as a starting point. Russian aestheticism, Denisoff notes, saw Russia very much as part of Europe. At the same time, much contemporary literature in Western Europe produced Eastern Europeans in general, and Russians in particular, as exotic Others. A further complicating factor in these shifting notions of European identity is Kuzmin's use of Egypt, and in particular Alexandria, as an unconventional place in which homosexual desire might be expressed. Such a flux of identity positions, suggests Denisoff, extending Harish Trivedi's notion of colonial dialogism—and in the process borrowing from a Russian theorist whose work is central to postcolonial theory—might be properly called polyphonic. Denisoff proceeds to explore the intertextual links between Kuzmin's novel *Wings* and his *Alexandrian Songs*, and the manner in which the invocation of Alexandria as a disembodied "Eastern" city imbued with infinite sexual possibility is allied to the formal properties of the *Songs*, which often evade gender specificity when describing affection for a beloved. Such maneuvers, Denisoff suggests, may ultimately reinforce orientalist discourse and seem unable to construct a lesbian, as opposed to male homosexual, identity, yet they do allow the construction of a wider queer community.

Finally, Joseph Allen Boone provides a startling rereading of a seminal work by an author whose work has an important place in both early postcolonial and feminist criticism: Doris Lessing's *The Golden Notebook*. While Lessing's narrative, Boone notes, aims to draw parallels between women's oppression and the oppression of colonialism through its linked narratives, it is marked by homosexual panic. Its female characters thus project rage from the "sex wars" onto nonheterosexual men, who often become scapegoated as unnatural and unmanly. Such projection, and a disavowal of lesbian eroticism, Boone notes, compromises powerful critiques of gender and colonial oppression in *The Golden Notebook;* its identification of homosexuality as inauthentic masculinity in the colony, we might add, provides a disturbing link back to the heteronormative adventure tradition that many contributors to this volume have discussed. Boone's study, concluding our series of critical essays, also exemplifies the possibilities of queer reading, revisiting a canonical text and making it impossible ever again to read it in quite the same way.

In a concluding coda, Philip Holden's single essay provides a genealogy of both queer theory and colonial discourse analysis, and of efforts to bring the two modes of analysis together, followed by a polemical account of the future courses the application of queer theory to colonial texts might take. Rather than relying on methodological parallels, Holden argues, practitioners should aim for more thorough attention to historicity, to the need for colonial regimes to deploy the apparatus of sexuality to produce "respectable" subjects, and to the appropriation and retooling of such respectability by bourgeois elites among the colonized. If the contours of such an apparatus can be mapped, colonial discourse in its widest sense may be "queered." Looking beyond the scope of this collection, Holden argues for a widening of the application of the phrase "colonial text" beyond European literature with colonial themes, while simultaneously urging clear specification of colonialism itself.

Despite their disciplinary functions, then, the colonial (and, in one case, postcolonial) narratives explored in the volume reveal themselves as flawed, containing contradictions that are available to the leverage queer theory provides. In *Imperial Desire,* each of our contributors uses the discursive analysis provided by queer theory—and indeed defines queer theory itself—in different ways. A common concern of many essays, however, is not merely to throw deconstructive light into the prison-house of colonialism but to consider how such queer reading enables a reflexive consideration of the genealogy of normative sexualities today, and the possibility of imagining other futures in what we—perhaps too precipitately—call a postcolonial world.

Notes

1. Gayatri Chakravorty Spivak, *A Critique of Postcolonial Reason: Toward a History of the Vanishing Present* (Cambridge: Harvard University Press, 1999), ix–x.

2. The phrase is taken from the title of Spivak's *The Post-Colonial Critic,* ed. Sarah Harasym (London: Routledge, 1990). Spivak herself has expressed some dissatisfaction with the description.

3. Recent work that explicitly uses the phrase includes Gayatri Gopinath's 1998 Columbia Ph.D. dissertation, "Queer Diasporas: Gender, Sexuality, and Migration in Contemporary South Asian Literature and Cultural Production"; Cindy Patton and Benigno Sánchez-Eppler's edited collection *Queer Diasporas* (Durham: Duke University Press, 2000); and Jasbir Puar's essay "Transnational Sexualities: South Asian (Trans)nation(alism)s and Queer Diasporas" in *Q & A: Queer in Asian America,* ed. David Eng and Alice Hom (Philadelphia: Temple University Press, 1998).

4. The distinction between "colonial" and "metropolitan" is here used in the absence of a more satisfactory alternative terminology. Such a division erases the colonial metropolis, itself the site of generation of colonial modernity and globalization.

5. For an exemplary account of this process, see Mrinalini Sinha, "Nationalism and Respectable Sexuality in India," *Genders* 21 (1995): 30–57. Sinha's *Colonial Masculinity: The "Manly Englishman" and the "Effeminate Bengali" in the Late Nineteenth Century* (Manchester: Manchester University Press, 1995) shows how the stereotypes mentioned in her title were mutually supporting in the creation of two separate versions of respectable sexuality. For the British, the stereotype of the effeminate Bengali served to reinscribe a contested line between colonizer and colonized: for the Bengali bourgeoisie "the degeneration of the body of the elite Hindu male became the symbol of the negative impact of colonial rule on indigenous society as a whole" (7).

6. Richard D. Altick, *The English Common Reader: A Social History of the Mass Reading Public, 1800–1900* (Chicago: University of Chicago Press, 1957): 258.

7. Michel Foucault, "Technologies of the Self," in *Technologies of the Self: A Seminar with Michel Foucault,* ed. Luther H. Martin et al. (Amherst: University of Massachusetts Press, 1988): 16–49.

8. Thomas Babington Macaulay, "Minute on Indian Education," in *Selected Writings,* ed. John Clive (Chicago: University of Chicago Press, 1972), 249.

9. Arlene Stein and Ken Plummer, "'I Can't Even Think Straight': 'Queer' Theory and the Missing Sexual Revolution in Sociology," *Sociological Theory* 12, no. 2 (July 1994): 182.

10. Homi Bhabha, *The Location of Culture* (London: Routledge, 1994), 88.

11. Eve Kosofsky Sedgwick, *Between Men: English Literature and Male Homosocial Desire* (New York: Columbia University Press, 1985), 23.

12. Diana Fuss, "Inside/Out," in *Inside/Out: Lesbian Theories, Gay Theories,* ed. Fuss (London: Routledge, 1991), 3.

13. David Halperin, *One Hundred Years of Homosexuality and Other Essays on Greek Love* (London: Routledge, 1990).

14. Etienne Balibar, "Es Gibt Keinen Staat in Europa: Racism and Politics in Europe Today," *New Left Review* 186 (March–April 1991): 5–19.

15. See Henry Rider Haggard, "About Fiction," *Contemporary Review* 51 (February 1887): 172–80. Haggard here argues that "there are still subjects that may be handled . . . if the man can be found bold enough to handle them" (180). Ironically, Haggard's fiction was at times condemned because of its barbarism and lack of manly self-restraint. See Philip Holden, *Modern Subjects/Colonial Texts: Hugh Clifford and the Discipline of English Literature in the Straits Settlements and Malaya, 1895–1907* (Greensboro: ELT Press, 2000), 116.

16. See, in particular, Mills, *Discourses of Difference: An Analysis of Women's Travel Writing and Colonialism* (London: Routledge, 1991), and Blunt and Gillian Roses's "Introduction: Women's Colonial and Postcolonial Geographies," in *Writing Women and Space: Colonial and Postcolonial Geographies,* ed. Blunt and Rose (New York: Guildford, 1994), 1–25.

17. Sol[omon] T[shekisho] Plaatje, *Mhudi: An Epic of South African Native Life a Hundred Years Ago* (Lovedale: Lovedale Press, 1930).

18. R. W. Connell, *Masculinities* (London: Polity, 1995), 186. Connell amplifies his discussion in his recent *The Men and the Boys* (Berkeley: University of California Press, 2001).

19. Leonore Davidoff and Catherine Hall, *Family Fortunes: Men and Women of the English Middle Class, 1780–1850* (Chicago: University of Chicago Press, 1987), 400.

20. James Eli Adams, *Dandies and Desert Saints: Styles of Victorian Masculinity* (Ithaca: Cornell University Press, 1995), 65–75.

21. Mary Poovey, *Uneven Developments: The Ideological Work of Gender in Mid-Victorian England* (Chicago: Chicago University Press, 1988), 50.

22. J. A. Mangan and James Walvin, "Introduction," in *Manliness and Morality: Middle-Class Masculinity in Britain and America, 1880–1940,* ed. Mangan and Walvin (Manchester: Manchester University Press, 1987), 1.

23. Joseph Bristow, *Sexuality* (London: Routledge, 1997), 12–46.

24. See Beverly Gartrell, "Colonial Wives: Villains or Victims?," in *The Incorporated Wife,* ed. Hilary Callan and Shirley Ardener (London: Croom Helm, 1984), 165–85, and Vron Ware, *Beyond the Pale: White Women, Racism, and History* (London: Verso, 1992).

25. Martin Green, *Dreams of Adventure, Deeds of Empire* (New York: Basic, 1979), 3.

26. Joseph Bristow, *Empire Boys: Adventures in a Man's World* (London: Harper Collins Academic, 1991), 48.

27. Fuss, "Inside/Out," 3.

28. See Sara Suleri's reading in *The Rhetoric of English India* (Chicago: University of Chicago Press, 1992), in which *A Passage to India* is introduced as "an allegory in

which the category of 'Marabar Cave' roughly translates into the anus of imperialism" (132).

29.   Chinua Achebe, "An Image of Africa: Racism in Conrad's *Heart of Darkness,*" *Massachusetts Review* 18 (1977): 782–94. Reprinted in *Heart of Darkness,* 3rd ed., ed. Robert Kimbrough (New York: Norton, 1988), 251–62.

Part I
Frontiers and Discoveries

CHAPTER ONE

The Sublimation of Desire to Apocalyptic Passion in Defoe's Crusoe Trilogy

Hans Turley

> Taboos and the divine are opposed to each other in one sense only, for the sacred aspect of the taboo is what draws men towards it and transfigures the original interdiction. The often intertwined themes of mythology spring from these factors.
>
> —Georges Bataille

In Michel Tournier's *Friday* (1967)[1]—an extraordinary retelling of Daniel Defoe's *Robinson Crusoe* (1719) and of the mythology of Crusoe—Robinson consummates his desire to control the island completely:

> He buried his face in the grass roots, breathing open-mouthed a long, hot breath. And the earth responded, filling his nostrils with the heavy scent of dead grass and the ripening of seed, and of sap rising in new shoots. How closely and how wisely were life and death intermingled at this elemental level! His sex burrowed like a plowshare into the earth, and overflowed in immense compassion for all created things. A strange wedlock, consummated in the vast solitude of the Pacific! (120)

Tournier's insight responds to two intertwined themes often found by critics of Defoe's novel: Crusoe's burgeoning faith, his intermittent sense of providence and belief in God, and his taming of the island, a mercantile investment in all that the island can produce. In other words, these twin themes are spiritual profit and economic profit, each, in good Protestant fashion, reflecting and affirming the sacredness of the other. Crusoe—almost mythological in Western literature—is *homo economicus,* to use Ian Watt's memorable phrase, a man whose very identity is defined by his ability to accumulate capital.

But a third theme, a taboo theme, lies buried within the text. Crusoe's sexual desires in Defoe's novel are silent, sublimated by unstable faith and unspendable wealth. The silence, paradoxically, speaks loudly, as Tournier explicitly demonstrates. The island, the feminized incarnation of Crusoe's desire for economic profit and wealth, implicitly gives all of herself to Crusoe in Defoe's novel. What is more logical, then, that—as Tournier reimagines it—Crusoe consummates his relationship with the literal manifestation of that desire? By fucking Speranza—his name for the island—Crusoe symbolically owns her totally. He has married the island; his erotic relationship to her shows what Georges Bataille calls "the other side of a façade of unimpeachable propriety." Unimpeachable propriety for Crusoe is his economic and religious identity, his ability to colonize the island and to profit both spiritually and economically as the signs of providence show him. The other side of the façade? "The feelings, parts of the body and habits we are normally ashamed of."[2] He eroticizes the island and by implication reveals his own unspoken erotic desires.

This essay responds to the dual themes of alienation and desire that I see in *Robinson Crusoe* (1719), as well as in the two sequels, *The Farther Adventures of Robinson Crusoe* (1719) and *The Serious Reflections of Robinson Crusoe* (1720).[3] Crusoe is alienated from society—particularly from the middle-class mercantile life that his father desires for him. I intend to argue that this alienation reveals Crusoe's anxiety toward domesticity and thus normative sexuality. This essay will look at the homoerotic desire he shows toward his man Friday, and to a certain extent toward his young companion Xury. Homoerotic desire—be it sexually explicit or represented as homosocial affection—is masked by Crusoe's passion for spiritual and economic profit. After he leaves his island, his homosocial stronghold, and Friday dies, leaving Crusoe finally and inevitably alone, I will show that implicit sexual deviance is displaced by extraordinary Christian zeal. His identity becomes based solely on his religious faith. This Christian zealotry is motivated by a radical, dissenting Puritanism that is in complete opposition to the elaborately hierarchical Anglican and Roman Catholic churches. Further, in his zealotry, Crusoe advocates violence against all those who do not profess his own vision of Christianity.

The appraisal of *Robinson Crusoe* as an early masterpiece of the modern novel has relied on criticism that takes into account only the events that lead up to and include Crusoe's stay on the island. The incidents that occur after his rescue and in *Robinson Crusoe*'s two sequels are dismissed as tangential to Defoe's first and greatest attempt at fiction.[4] In the last lines of volume one, Crusoe writes that he has more to tell of his life after his rescue. "All these things," he notes, "with some very surprizing incidents in some new adventures of my own, for ten years more, I may perhaps give a farther account of hereafter." That "farther account" demonstrates that in all three volumes Crusoe is on a quest to determine his identity. Throughout the first two volumes, Crusoe's "wandring inclination" (*Robinson Crusoe*, 27) demonstrates the extent of his alienation. Wandering seems to become the repressive mechanism for his unarticulated desires, his undetermined identity. Crusoe, in both parts one and two of *Robinson Crusoe*, travels the world in order to discover who he is. His travels show him trying to find some way to negotiate the conflicting demands of society that equate identity with the desire for domestic stability through property and marriage. These hallmarks of an identity predicated on heterosexuality, however, never really satisfy Crusoe after he is rescued from the island, as his inability to settle anywhere for long demonstrates. The third volume of the trilogy finally brings together all the disparate elements of property, trade, and middle-class domesticity—represented by the colonization of his island, his profit from trade, and his barely mentioned marriage—implicit in the first two volumes. The representation of Christianity in both the end of the *Farther Adventures* and in the *Serious Reflections* becomes a means to understand his alienation and, significantly, his seeming lack of any sexual desire that is often seen as a fundamental part of a person's sense of self.

How then do we uncover the source for his alienation and the desires repressed by Crusoe? Further, how do we make sense of his always unstable sense of identity? His marriage late in life, contrasted with his homosocial relationship with Friday, is suggestive here. Crusoe has never thought about marriage and "settling down" before being rescued in the first volume. When his wife dies at the end of *Robinson Crusoe*, he dismisses not only her death but the marriage as well in one famous sentence:

> In the meantime I in part settled myself [in London]: for first of all I marry'd, and that not either to my disadvantage or dissatisfaction; and had three children, two sons and one daughter: but my wife dying, and my nephew coming home with good success from a voyage to Spain,

my inclination to go abroad, and his importunity, prevailed and engaged me to go in his ship, as a private trader to the East Indies. (*Robinson Crusoe,* 298)

There is no sense in this passage—nor elsewhere in the novels—that "love," "romance," or even affection for his wife is a part of Crusoe's marriage into the domestic economy late in his life. One point of middle-class domesticity, as Michel Foucault would argue, is to control deviance, to legitimate nondeviant sexuality through marriage, and authorize the flow of capital throughout society.[5] Entrance into middle-class marriage, in other words, is based on the exchange of capital. If heterosexual domesticity holds no interest for Crusoe, what does? Crusoe's relationship with Friday is delineated much more clearly and at much greater length than his marriage. The lack of affection that Crusoe shows for his wife stands starkly against his affection for Friday. In part because I see homoerotic connotations in their relationship, the desire exhibited by Crusoe toward Friday is different from a master/slave dichotomy that critics often observe.[6] After Crusoe rescues Friday from cannibals in part one and teaches him English and about Christianity, the two men return to England. They have built a life together bound by, as he says, "affection ... ty'd to me" (*Robinson Crusoe,* 211). Indeed, Crusoe uses variations on the word "affection" to describe his relationship with Friday no fewer than ten times in the next twenty-nine pages. There is no question that Friday is an essential part of Crusoe's life. In fact, his status as "companion" and "servant"—never "slave"—is taken for granted throughout the *Farther Adventures* until he is killed off midway through the novel.[7]

Affection between men is, of course, not necessarily about sexual intercourse, as George E. Haggerty has noted: "Often emotion determines the terms of a relationship, the context for sexual activity as well as the ground for interpersonal attachment. The emotion matters so much because it is undefined."[8] And undefined emotion is exactly the way that Defoe represents the relationship between Friday and Crusoe. In Crusoe's world, conventions of religion and master/slave relationships mask and discipline the love and affection that are explicit and the eroticism that is implicit within their relationship.

In Defoe's novels, Friday and Crusoe develop a relationship based, in part, on masculine affection through a mutual understanding of Christianity. I am not, of course, denying that their relationship is also one of power: Crusoe is, after all, the colonizer of his island, and, indeed, the colonizer of Friday himself. However, their affection is mutual (at least in Crusoe's mind), and Crusoe depends on Friday in ways that go beyond a typical master/slave dichotomy. Indeed, Crusoe admits that Friday's understanding of Christianity is complex and that Friday is "a good Christian, a much better one than I" (*Robinson Crusoe*, 222).

With the exception of his great and abiding affection for Friday and the emotional context it offers, Crusoe is silent concerning other relationships that might suggest affection or some kind of sexual desire. Part of the fascination with the Crusoe story, I would argue, is the "silent" side of the protagonist's life. We hear about his relationship to God, we read in great detail about his taming of the island, a feminized place with, in Tournier's vision, a cave that is a womb and a combe that is a vagina. But if we are reading a fully "psychological" human being through Defoe's depiction of Crusoe, much is also left out. Crusoe, willing to discuss anything ad infinitum, is strangely silent about any sexual feelings he might have. Bataille argues that "eroticism is that within man ... which calls his being into question," asserting that religion and eroticism are but two sides of private experience: one sacred and one profane. "Private experience"—and what else do we get in *Robinson Crusoe* but the title character's own account of his private experience?—and religion and eroticism are inextricably dialectical and linked together.[9]

The affection Crusoe shows toward Friday is quite different from the affection he professes when he introduces the boy Xury in part one. As a young man, years before he is initially shipwrecked on his island, Crusoe is captured by a Sallee or Turkish pirate while on a trading voyage. The pirate keeps Crusoe "as his proper prize, and made [him] his slave, being young, and nimble and fit for his business" (*Robinson Crusoe*, 41). It is unclear what the pirate's " business" is with Crusoe, beyond making him "look after his garden, and do the common drudgery of slaves about his house" when his master goes away to sea (41). In an intriguing analysis of his relationship with the Turk, Minaz Jooma points out that "the Turk's pointed separation of Crusoe from the crew, and his deliberate selection of [very young] Crusoe for domestic and personal uses are described in terms that connote their invasiveness."[10] Defoe's language is implicitly sodomitical, Jooma argues. The Turk "builds a little state-room or cabin in the middle of the long boat ... and had in it room for him to lye with a slave or two," in other words, with young Crusoe himself

(42–43). As he says, the Turk "ordered me to lye in the cabin" (41). In this episode we see the first indication of implicit homoeroticism that, while unspoken, continues throughout the novel.

Eventually Crusoe makes his escape with Xury, an even younger man than Crusoe, a "Maresco" from Spain for whom Crusoe shows some fondness. Xury, along with the Turkish pirate, the Brazilians, the Cannibals, and Friday himself all show what Suzanne Wheeler identifies as the "racial multiplicity" in Defoe's novel, the different and complex representations of race that complicate an eighteenth-century reader's response to Crusoe and his servants.[11] After they've made their escape and are sailing along the coast of Africa, Xury offers to go on shore, to risk certain death from "savages" or "lyons and tygers" (*Robinson Crusoe*, 47). "I asked him why he would go," Crusoe recollects, "why I should not go and he stay in the boat; and the boy answered with so much affection that made me love him ever after" (47). The "affection" that Xury shows and the "love" that Crusoe asserts contrast sharply with Crusoe's reaction to Friday's death: Crusoe ends up selling Xury after the two are rescued by the Portuguese captain. Even though he protests that he is "loath to sell the poor boy's liberty," sell him he does, for sixty pieces of eight (54). And except for two brief references later in the novel, that is the last the reader hears of Xury.[12]

Crusoe's homosocial relationship with Friday is much more complex than that with Xury despite assertions of "affection." There is no indication that actual sexual relations take place between Friday and Crusoe, nor is that important for my argument. As Jonathan Goldberg has argued, "homosociality suggests a continuum of male-male relations, one capable of being sexualized, though where and how such sexualization occurs cannot be assumed a priori." Goldberg points out that the representation of sexuality is frequently incoherent but that we can still focus on "male-male sexual possibilities."[13] It is more significant, then, that Crusoe lives in a homosocial world in which affection—indeed love—for Friday causes a tension in an analysis of the novel between notions of master and slave and notions of the colonization or domestication of the island and Friday himself. Crusoe describes Friday physically in terms of idealized European beauty:

> He was a comely fellow, perfectly well made; with straight strong limbs, not too large; tall and well shaped, and as I reckon, about twenty six years of age. He had a very good countenance, not a fierce and surly

aspect; but seemed to have something very manly in his face, and yet he had all the sweetness and softness of an European in his countenance too, especially when he smiled. (208)

Here Friday is made to conform with European standards of male beauty: a "good countenance," a "manly" face, "the sweetness and softness of an European." But Crusoe goes on to describe Friday in contradistinction to other natives of the Caribbean and Africa as well:

His hair was long and black, not curled like wool; his forehead very high and large, and a great vivacity and sparkling sharpness in his eyes. The colour of his skin was not quite black, but very tawny: and yet not of an ugly yellow nauseous tawny, as the Brasilians, and Virginians . . . but of a bright kind of dun olive colour, that had in it something very agreeable, tho' not very easy to describe. His face was round and plump; his nose small, not flat like the negroes, a very good mouth, thin lips, and his fine teeth well set, and white as ivory. (208–09)

Friday, then, is contrasted to both Europeans (he is as handsome as they although darker) and people of color. Indeed, the language anatomizes and feminizes Friday as well: "round and plump," a small nose, "fine teeth . . . white as ivory." Friday is racially different from his fellow natives, but not so different from Crusoe and other Europeans. As Roxann Wheeler argues, Friday is both a slave and has an "upgraded" status as a Christian. Defoe, writes Wheeler, makes "an ideological compromise [that] constructs Friday as an exceptional savage and silences the issue of racial difference."[14] I would not go quite that far, however; like Xury, a Spanish Moor, it seems that it is Friday's religion and physicality, his heathenism and implied femininity, that position him oppositionally to Crusoe rather than his race. Furthermore, Friday's and Crusoe's relationship is deepened and eroticized by the foregrounding of Christianity as a means of constructing a "new" identity for Friday not entirely dependent on race. Friday's Christianity positions him as less oppositional to and more correctly bivalent with Crusoe. Yes, he is still Crusoe's servant, yes, he never really learns to speak English correctly (always adding "two e's" at the end of words), but he becomes a Christian, indeed a better Christian than Crusoe. Their religion and Friday's beauty, in fact, bring them closer and complicate an affectionate, reciprocal relationship originally based on racial difference.

Of course, when Crusoe and Friday live together in England, the terms of their relationship change because Crusoe's acquaintances in London would perceive them doxologically as a "civilized" man and a "savage." However, the island is a world where different rules apply and Crusoe attributes his friendship with Friday to providence (*Robinson Crusoe*, 206). The transgressive nature of their relationship—not entirely subordinated by notions of servitude and slavery—is in fact sanctioned by the signs of providence. That is, theirs is a sacred relationship that is one more sign from providence that justifies Crusoe's protracted colonization of the island and his economic success as a gift from God. Indeed, Crusoe continues to flourish after he rescues Friday. First Crusoe and Friday rescue honorable Spaniards, and then Crusoe is able to create his own little "kingdom," a homosocial world in which gendered difference is entirely absent from representations of human relationships (240–41). Difference becomes defined by religion (the Spanish Catholics versus the dissenting Protestant), national origin (Spain versus England), and race (Friday's distinctive physical appearance that is neither black, Native American, nor white European.) By looking closely at Friday and Crusoe, one can see how their relationship is capable of being sexualized, and how Crusoe's own alienation from society is symptomatic of his repressed, unsure, and unspoken sexual identity.

Because their affection for one another develops through the novel, Friday's death in the *Farther Adventures* comes as a horrible shock to Crusoe and a surprise to the reader as well. His grief is startling compared to the matter-of-fact way that he announces his wife's death at the end of the first volume. Friday's death scene begins as an amusing episode. Crusoe and his ship are sailing down the eastern coast of South America and are set upon by "a hundred and six and twenty" canoes (*Farther Adventures*, 178) filled with furious natives. Neither side can communicate with the other, until Crusoe sends Friday to "go out upon the deck and call out aloud to them in his language, to know what they meant" (179). Friday attempts to talk to the natives. They pay no attention to Friday's efforts; instead, Defoe writes, "six of them, who were in the foremost or nighest boat to us, turned their canoes from us, and stooping down, showed us their naked backsides; just as if, in England, saving your presence, they had bid us kiss—" (179). Unfortunately, Friday is killed in the ensuing fusillade: "Friday cried out they were going to shoot; and unhappily for him, poor fellow, they let fly about three hundred of their arrows, and to my inexpressible grief killed poor Friday" (179).

As the scene opens the situation is, admittedly, humorous with its striking image of a canoe full of mooning natives. That is, the humorous image is a spectacle that could overwhelm the tragic dimension of the event. However, I would argue that the contrast of the mooning natives to Crusoe's reaction—his "inexpressible grief"—unmasks the effect that Friday's death has on Crusoe. Defoe goes from comedy to tragedy, and that narrative contrast makes Crusoe's grief all the more compelling. Crusoe, so nonchalant when his wife dies, becomes, he says, "so enraged with the loss of my old servant, the companion of all my sorrows and solitudes, that I immediately ordered five guns to be loaded with small shot, and four with great, and gave them such a broadside as they had never heard in their lives before, to be sure" (179).

Friday's death has an indelible effect on Crusoe, an effect that permeates the entire second half of the novel, just as his father's presence is never completely out of Crusoe's—or the reader's—consciousness in *Robinson Crusoe*. Crusoe becomes more and more alienated from his fellow men. At the same time, he finds solace in a violent, zealous dissenting Christianity. Unlike in the *Farther Adventures* and the *Serious Reflections*, we see that religion serves two purposes in volume one, neither of which is defined by violence. Religion has been the means to justify a working society and economic stability on his island both when Crusoe is alone and when it is "peopled," by Friday, Friday's father, the Spaniards, and pirates. Further, Friday and Crusoe seal their affection through Christian faith. Religion has made their relationship deeper than a master/slave dichotomy and, indeed, has been the means for Crusoe to connect with another human being.

For Crusoe, violence is not a part of his burgeoning faith on the island. Indeed, his reaction when he runs across some bones from a cannibal feast is quietly reflective: he goes away from the horrible sight not wanting to take revenge on the cannibals for their heathen ways. Instead, he says, "I entertained such an abhorrence of the savage wretches ... and of the wretched inhuman custom of their devouring and eating one another up, that I continued pensive and sad, and kept close within my own circle for almost two years after this" (*Robinson Crusoe*, 173). "Pensive and sad" suggests reflection—certainly not the emotions of violence and unrepressed hatred toward non-Christians we find after Friday's death. However, his death provides the catalyst for Crusoe's new way of looking at non-Christian people. From now on in the *Farther Adventures*, Christianity manifests itself as a violent hatred of "heathens" and "pagans." Crusoe's reaction to Friday's death can help us see the linkage between homoeroticism and violent radical Christian zeal within the context of Crusoe's identity.

Crusoe makes a point of saying it is not "the ill manners of turning up their bare backsides to us" that aggrieved him. Instead, the natives "killed my poor Friday, whom I so entirely loved and valued, and who, indeed, so well deserved it, I not only had been justified before God and man, but would have been very glad, if I could, to have overset every canoe there, and drowned every one of them" (*Farther Adventures*, 180). Crusoe's response to the natives' actions contrasts sharply with his reaction to the massacre of an entire town by his sailors, a few pages later in the novel. When Crusoe and his ship land on Madagascar to supply the ship, one of the sailors rapes a Madagascar woman. In retribution, the natives execute the man. The other sailors on Crusoe's ship are so angry that they set the Madagascar village on fire and in the holocaust kill every one of their adversaries. Here Crusoe is horrified by his men's actions. While angry that one of his men had been killed he understands the native reaction. "I thought of Jacob's words to his sons Simeon and Levi," Crusoe says, "'Cursed be their anger for it was fierce; and their wrath for it was cruel'" (204). Again Crusoe is, as he says, "pensive and sad" after he observes the horrible remains of the villagers (205). For weeks he berates his crew because they have overreacted to the killing of one of their own by a group of Madagascar natives. When Friday is killed, however, Crusoe only considers such extreme violence. For him, faith is still relatively benign. However, with his repressed urge to "overset every canoe" the natives are in, we see the beginning of his need for violence as a means to give him a sense of identity (180).

Memories of Friday keep intruding into Crusoe's thoughts. When he speaks of him, Crusoe can barely repress the welling up of emotions that come through the prose. He describes the way that the "natives . . . always add two *e*'s at the end of the words where we make one . . . nay, I could hardly make Friday leave it off, though at last he did" (182). This memory sets Crusoe off once again in a digression about his late friend: "And now I name the poor fellow once more, I must take my last leave of him, poor honest Friday! We buried him with all the decency and solemnity possible, by putting him into a coffin, and throwing him into the sea; and I caused them to fire eleven guns for him; and so ended the life of the most grateful, faithful, honest, and most affectionate servant that ever man had" (182).

After Friday's death, Crusoe's journey loses the purpose that it had as means to an end: to return to England. Crusoe has no companion or partner with whom to share his life. Coupling provides closures for certain other Defoe novels: think of *Captain Singleton* (1720)[15] or *Moll Flanders* (1722). The end of the *Farther Adventures* is left ambiguous, like the conclusions of the open-ended novels *Roxana* (1724) and *Colonel Jack* (1722). Instead, religion—what Crusoe calls "true Christianity" in the *Serious Reflections*—accompanies all of his actions throughout the remainder of the *Farther Adventures*. This religion becomes increasingly zealous, culminating in the destruction of the Asian idol in the *Farther Adventures,* and his call for a holy war at the end of the *Serious Reflections.* Religious zealotry replaces any other center of identity for Crusoe: aimless wandering, economic profit, religious sharing with and affection for Friday, implicit homoeroticism.

In this final section of this essay, I will show how religion becomes proxy for all of the unspoken and uncertain desires that Crusoe has carried with him his whole life. One of Bataille's great insights is to demonstrate that religion serves as a mechanism—a "moving force," in his words—"behind the breaking of taboos."[16] Bataille argues that religion works not merely to repress the desires to break taboos but, through its rituals and its rules, allows for the breaking of taboos during certain festivals and rites. Catholicism, for example, has the confession and its rites of penitence. Puritanism, professed by Crusoe, has the signs of providence that tell Crusoe that his faith is justified (the huge profits that Crusoe accrues on his island). By the end of the *Farther Adventures,* the signs tell Crusoe that the world must be colonized into the Christian, Puritan faith. Crusoe no longer desires economic profit. As he joins a caravan and goes deeper and deeper into Asia, west from China toward Russia and home, he becomes increasingly appalled by people he sees. The "heathens" begin to look as they act: dirty, ill-clothed, belligerent, and, Crusoe believes, ignorant and "stupid" (285). The more heathenish these people are to Crusoe, the angrier he becomes. His newfound zeal causes him to become more intolerant. Finally, giving in to the kind of outrage shown by the sailors who wipe out the Madagascar village, Crusoe decides something must be done to teach these "worst and most ignorant pagans" a lesson (282). We see Crusoe's beliefs evolve from a providential reliance on the wisdom of God's ways in part one—"How do I know what God himself judges in this particular case?" (*Robinson Crusoe*, 177)—to a conviction at the end of part two that he himself is entitled to play God by asserting his faith and resorting to violence.

Soon after Crusoe and his caravan cross into "the Muscovite dominions" (*Farther Adventures*, 283), they stop for the night in a village. There Crusoe comes upon "an idol made of wood, frightful as the devil, at least as anything we can think of to represent the devil can be made" (284). For the first time since he left his island many years before, Crusoe has a profound and immediate conversion; he decides he must do something about these heathens and their "devil worship." His behavior seems extreme because at the same time that he spouts "Christianity" the reader sees Crusoe behaving exactly the way that his men in Madagascar did. He is horrified by this "scarecrow" figure worshiped by the "heathens" and is "resolved to go and destroy that vile, abominable idol" (287). This Crusoe is not the man who decides to spare the cannibals and who patiently teaches Friday the tenets of Christianity and in the process develops a close and affectionate relationship with him. Nor is he the Crusoe who is able to repress his most violent tendencies when even Friday is killed. Instead, this man is a religious fanatic who "resolves" that a violent course of action is necessary (286).

Crusoe sees no irony in his determination to destroy the heathens' idol. "So I related the story of our men at Madagascar" to a Scotsman, Crusoe says, "and how they burnt and sacked the village there, and killed man, woman, and child for their murdering of one of our men, just as it is related before; and when I had done, I added that I thought we ought to do so to this village" (286). Completely forgotten are Crusoe's "pensive and sad" reactions to both the remains of the cannibal feast in part one and his sailors' horrific massacre of the Madagascar village in part two. That night, Crusoe and the Scotsman creep into the village, surprise the villagers, tie them up, and burn down the idol. They pull some of the "pagans" out of their huts. "We supposed," Crusoe says, they "had been about some of their diabolic sacrifices" (292). Crusoe and his companions force the "heathens" to watch their "monstrous idol" blow up, and, satisfied with a job well done, they return to their encampment. In a shift of belief confusing to the reader, Crusoe decides that he can be judge and executioner of "heathens" who are ignorant of

Christianity. He has no island, no family, no friends, no Friday; instead, newly found religious belief gives him a sense of identity, a sense of place in a world in which he really has no home.

The destruction of the "idol" is the last major adventure in the novel. Crusoe notes at the end of the *Farther Adventures* that "I am preparing for a longer journey than all these, having lived seventy-two years a life of infinite variety, and learnt sufficiently to know the value of retirement, and the blessing of ending our days in peace" (323). Unlike the island, which he is able to colonize and control, the whole world is a vast place that needs religious colonization. On the island Crusoe has previously found some stability in his affectionate relationship with Friday. Now that he is finally headed home, he no longer desires profit or cares to wander, because he believes he has found what he has been looking for since he first left home as a young man. The reader discovers that "true Christianity" displaces all of Crusoe's unfulfilled economic and sexual desires. Crusoe's sense of identity—based on "true Christianity"—enables him to return home with a newfound purpose.

In the *Serious Reflections*, Defoe finally demonstrates the alarming repercussions of that purpose.[17] But what began as a questioning of his own faith in *Robinson Crusoe* and became an intellectual and spiritual battle for "souls" in the *Farther Adventures* turns into a plan for an out-and-out war "against the kingdom of the devil" (*Serious Reflections*, 239). In the midst of the common pieties that Crusoe repeats in the *Serious Reflections* comes a violent, narrowly defined Christianity that advocates killing and war "in behalf of the Christian worship" (239). In the *Serious Reflections* Crusoe asserts that if "talk" and persuasion do not work, then force must be used. He advocates burning temples and pagodas—which he has already done—and "destroying" "priests and dedicated persons of every kind" (239). In an understatement, Crusoe says "This is all the coercion I propose . . . yet I insist that we may by force . . . suppress paganism, and the worship of God's enemy the Devil" (239). Christianity will be spread over the world, and Crusoe himself—who never felt at home in England—will finally feel at home in the world because all of the world will be reconstructed, indeed, colonized, in the terms of his own religious beliefs, just as his time alone reconstructed the island into his own "kingdom."

In the *Serious Reflections* religion displaces all the masked emotions and desires that are implicit in Crusoe's character. "Profit" and property as they define personal psychological stability—in the terms that make Crusoe happy on the island—are an ideal that eludes him when he returns to England at the end of the first volume. When Friday dies, he continues to travel the globe, both trying and avoiding to return home. Religion displaces his own desires, whatever they may be. The displacement becomes clear in the final lines of the *Serious Reflection:*

> All I can add is, I doubt no such zeal for the Christian religion will be found in our days, or perhaps in any age of the world, till Heaven beats the drums itself, and the glorious legions from above come down on purpose to propagate the work, and to reduce the whole world to the obedience of King Jesus—a time which some tell us is not far off, but of which I heard nothing in all my travels and illuminations, no, not one word. (243)

This is an extraordinary passage. Crusoe is doubtful that "man" can do much good prior to the millennium, but he finds what amounts to an apocalyptic identity. Even though he is uncertain anyone will show the religious zeal he has shown, he still offers suggestions for bringing the whole world into his Christian belief. In fact, Crusoe tries to "play God" by waging war on the heathens; he has thus done what Charles Gildon— one of Defoe's harshest contemporary critics—accused Defoe of doing in part one of *Robinson Crusoe.* Gildon argued that Defoe himself tried to "play God" by claiming that *Robinson Crusoe* is "a just history of fact" (*Robinson Crusoe,* 25). On the contrary, Gildon argued, "the impiety of this Part of the Book, in making the truths of the Bible of a Piece with the fictitious Story of *Robinson Crusoe,* is so horribly shocking that I dare not dwell upon it ... and [the book should be] held in Abhorrence by all good Christians."[18]

Ironically, Gildon was right to find *Robinson Crusoe* "horribly shocking." Crusoe found "happiness" on the island: the great profit he accrued, and the domestic satisfaction that came with it, were the result of his colonization and transformation of the island into an ideal state. To his own regret, however, Crusoe is unable to colonize the world. In the *Serious Reflections,* the protagonist's belief transfers his resistant passion for travel and dissatisfaction with middle-class domesticity into a system that allows him to "play God" and impose his "true Christianity" on the rest of the world. Sexuality and economy drop out of Crusoe's life, but religious passion—an obsession with Christianizing the world— replaces those needs. All three parts of *Robinson Crusoe* suggest that the only way to transcend sexual and economic desire—to break away from *any* transgressive position that questions a normative identity based on heterosexuality—is through an unshakable belief in God and "true Christianity." Crusoe, after all of his wandering, finds a kind of peace in his old age when he believes that the millennium approaches. Writing his *Reflections*—and granting that his persona is a character—gives him the discursive means to assert his own identity not dependent on ideal or illegitimate profit or middle-class domesticity. The ultimate narrative to Crusoe is a belief in the apocalypse.

In *The Rise of the Novel* Ian Watt writes that "Romantic love has certainly no greater antagonist among novelists than Defoe."[19] Certainly if one is looking at heterosexual love, at normative conventions of marriage and domesticity, Watt is correct. With the exception of *Captain Singleton* and its homosocial piratical milieu that suggests homoerotic attraction between the title character and his companion Quaker William, other Defoe protagonists inevitably have relationships more correctly described as economically sexual. Watt goes on to argue that in *Robinson Crusoe* "even the temptations of sex are excluded from the scene of his greatest triumphs, the island. . . . Then, with Friday, he enjoys an idyll without benefit of woman—a revolutionary departure from the traditional expectations aroused by desert islands from the *Odyssey* to the *New Yorker*."[20] I hope I have demonstrated that the Crusoe character is much more complicated sexually than Watt and others suggest, that the nexus of sexuality, alienation, religious zealotry, and homosocial affection can open a different reading of the novel that embraces and, in a strange way, legitimates deviant sexuality. If, as has been argued, Crusoe is an Everyman, at least in the economic and psychological terms of modern criticism, then he is an Everyman who challenges conventional norms in all sorts of ways.

Notes

1. Michel Tournier, *Friday* (1967), trans. Norman Denny (Baltimore: Johns Hopkins University Press, 1997). Further citations noted in the text.

2. Georges Bataille, *Erotism: Death and Sensuality* (1962), trans. Mary Dalwood (San Francisco: City Light Books, 1986), 109.

3. Although dismissed as tangential to *Robinson Crusoe*, the two sequels enable a reading of Crusoe's desires that goes beyond the narrow analyses of the novel that examine Crusoe as a merging of *homo economicus* and a man of faith. Furthermore,

of course it can be and has been argued that the narrative voice of the *Serious Reflections* represents a persona for Defoe. We cannot read the *Serious Reflections* as a continuation of the kind of story that Defoe has been writing in the first two Crusoe books. However, let us accept that Defoe was not working toward an "invention" of the novel—Ian Watt's assumption in *The Rise of the Novel*. Instead, Defoe wrote the book as a continuation of the kind of moral instruction that he asserts is the purpose of the first two books. *Serious Reflections* does not contain the "entertaining" diversions found in the first two volumes that might divert the reader from the book's overtly didactic purpose. However, one can also argue that the "persona" is Crusoe's voice, since for two volumes we have seen the development of a mutable character: Robinson Crusoe himself. If read as a second sequel, the *Serious Reflections* is the culmination of all the stories and "incidents" that Defoe relates in the first two volumes of *Robinson Crusoe*. For more on challenging criticism of Defoe and the origins of the novel, see Robert Markley, "'So Inexhaustible a Treasure of Gold': Defoe, Credit, and the Romance of the South Seas," *Eighteenth-Century Life* 18 (1994): 147–68. *The Life and Adventures of Robinson Crusoe* (1719), edited and introduction by Angus Ross (London: Penguin Books, 1965); *The Farther Adventures of Robinson Crusoe* (1719) (New York: The Jenson Society, 1905); *The Serious Reflections of Robinson Crusoe* (1720) (New York: The Jenson Society, 1905). All citations noted in the text.

    4. In *The Reluctant Pilgrim,* for example, J. Paul Hunter writes that the *Farther Adventures* and the *Serious Reflections* "seem . . . to have been separately conceived." *Robinson Crusoe,* on the other hand, has a definite form that contributes to the book's continued power: "*Robinson Crusoe* is constructed on the basis of a familiar Christian pattern of disobedience-punishment-repentance-deliverance, a pattern set up in the first few pages of the book . . . Crusoe's continual appraisal of his situation keeps the conflict at the forefront of the action throughout, for his appraisal is not the superficial, unrelated commentary some critics have described, but rather an integral part of the thematic pattern set up by Crusoe's rebellion and the prophecy of his father that Crusoe 'will be the miserablest Wretch that was ever born'" (*Reluctant Pilgrim,* 19–20). Hunter is correct, as far as he goes, but he sells Defoe—and Crusoe—short by limiting his discussion to *Robinson Crusoe*. Like other critics, Hunter argues that Crusoe's "deliverance" ends with his rescue, and that the last section of the book does not count or is reduced to an epilogue. The tidy package that can explain Crusoe's behavior, and allows Hunter and other critics to find the "thematic pattern" in the novel, necessitates ignoring the *Farther Adventures* and the *Serious Reflections*. Hunter, *The Reluctant Pilgrim: Defoe's Emblematic Method and Quest for Form in* Robinson Crusoe (Baltimore: Johns Hopkins University Press, 1966), x. See also Ian Watt, *The Rise of the Novel* (Berkeley: University of California Press, 1957), 60–92. Paula Backscheider, Maximillian E. Novak, and John J. Richetti, among others, all tend to focus on the island. Backsheider, *Daniel Defoe: His Life* (Baltimore: Johns Hopkins University Press, 1989); Novak, *Realism, Myth, and History in Defoe's Fiction* (Lincoln: University of Nebraska Press, 1983); Richard Phillips, *Mapping Men and Empire: A Geography of Adventure* (London: Routledge, 1997); Richetti, *Defoe's Narratives* (Oxford: Clarendon Press, 1975); Michael Seidel, *Robinson Crusoe: Island Myths and the Novel* (Boston: Twayne, 1991).

    5. See, for example, Michel Foucault, *The History of Sexuality,* vol. 1, *An Introduction,* trans. Robert Hurley (New York: Vintage Books, 1978), esp. 103–14.

6. See the following critics who often observe a master/slave dichotomy in *Robinson Crusoe:* Timothy Blackburn, "Friday's Religion," *Eighteenth-Century Studies* 18, no. 1 (spring 1985); Richard Braverman, "Crusoe's Legacy," *Studies in the Novel* 18, no. 1 (spring 1986): 1–28; Edith Clowes, "The Robinson Myth Reread in Postcolonial and Postcommunist Modes," *Critique* 36, no. 2 (winter 1995): 145–59; Markman Ellis, "Crusoe, Cannibalism, and Empire," *Robinson Crusoe: Myths and Metamorphoses,* ed. Lieve Spass and Brian Simpson (New York: St. Martin's Press, 1996), 45–61; Andrew Fleck, "Crusoe's Shadow: Christianity, Colonization, and the Other," *Christian Encounters with the Other,* ed. John C. Hawley (New York: New York University Press, 1998), 74–89; Christopher Flint, "The Orphaning of the Family," *ELH* 55, no. 2 (summer 1988): 381–419; Minaz Jooma, "Robinson Crusoe Inc(orporates): Domestic Economy, Incest, and the Trope of Cannibalism," *Lit: Literature Interpretation Theory* 8, no. 1 (June 1997): 61–81; Maximillian E. Novak, "Friday, or the Power of Naming," *Augustan Subjects: Essays in Honor of Martin C. Battestin* (Newark: University of Delaware Press, 1997), 110–22; my own *Rum, Sodomy, and the Lash: Piracy, Sexuality, and Masculine Identity* (New York: New York University Press, 1999); Roxann Wheeler, "'My Savage,' 'My Man': Racial Multiplicity in *Robinson Crusoe,*" *ELH* 62, no. 4 (winter 1995): 821–61.

7. In an amusing little pornographic novel from the 1960s titled *The Secret Life of Robinson Crusoe,* the author plays with the idea of the implicit sexuality in Crusoe's world. "Humphrey Richardson" (surely a pseudonym) writes in the introduction: "And the tale that follows is nothing more or less than an attempt to visualize and to recapture the secret side, the neglected aspect of Robinson Crusoe's life, a life led in a world perhaps less devoid of at least the thought of women (in the practical absence of their carnal presence) than an XVIIIth Century journalist's version of the story has led us to suppose" (9). What follows is an at times hilarious retelling of the Crusoe story. Toward the end of the short novel, after Crusoe has tired of fantasies and onanism, he sets his eyes on Friday and "he would possess the unhappy lad. Possess him furiously" (176). Each night, Friday lies awake and waits for a drunken Crusoe to come into his bed: "Robinson staggers over to the bed. He reaches down, grabs the undershorts, pulls. His fumbling hands find their way to the fly. . . . Finally pulls the garment off. Friday hides his timid nudity. 'Hey, by God! Turn over, d'ye hear!' Robinson bellows. Shocking scenes like that" (176). Crusoe and Friday here act out what is implicit in the Crusoe character: sexual desire made manifest by its very silence in Defoe's novels. Of course, this "secret history" is soft-core porn, and thus (however amusing) is a vulgar reduction of the complications within their relationship. In fact, historically in the late seventeenth and eighteenth centuries, "secret histories" of the sort written by Delarivier Manley were enormously popular. Manley's *New Atlantis* (1709), for instance, tells the secret, or sexual, exploits of some of the most important Whiggish men and women in British government. It is not too far off the mark to imagine that readers of *Robinson Crusoe,* explicitly a "history of fact" in the words of the book's "editor," might wonder about the secret history of Crusoe (*RC,* 25). Humphrey Richardson, *The Secret Life of Robinson Crusoe* (Covina, California: Collectors Publications, 1967).

8. George E. Haggerty, *Men in Love: Masculinity and Sexuality in the Eighteenth Century* (New York: Columbia University Press, 1999), 174.

9. *Erotism,* 23, 35.

10. Jooma, "Robinson Crusoe Inc(corporates)," 68.

11. In the excellent article "'My Savage,' 'My Man': Racial Multiplicity in *Robinson Crusoe*," Roxann Wheeler examines Crusoe's "various relationships to non-British Men" in order to show how complex Defoe's representation of racial difference is and to argue that Crusoe's and Friday's relationship, while one of colonizer and colonized, actually highlights Crusoe's own difference from his countrymen once he has settled on his island (821–61).

12. As Crusoe is building his first boat, he says "I wished for my boy Xury, and the long boat with the shoulder of mutton sail" to ease the effort building his boat entails (*Robinson Crusoe*, 136).

13. Jonathan Goldberg, *Sodometries: Renaissance Texts, Modern Sensibilities* (Stanford: Stanford University Press, 1992), 23.

14. Wheeler, "'My Savage,' 'My Man,'" 845.

15. See my "Piracy, Identity, and Desire in *Captain Singleton*," *Eighteenth-Century Studies* 31, no. 2 (winter 1998–99): 199–214. *Captain Singleton* is Defoe's other novel that has tensions of homoerotic affection; indeed, the ending of the novel leaves the reader with the title character and his companion living together disguised as Greeks in England and speaking their own private language.

16. *Erotism*, 69.

17. Most of this little-read book is filled with chapters such as "Of Solitude" or "Of Honesty in Promises." Defoe writes in the preface, "here is the just and only good end of all parable or allegoric history brought to pass, viz., for moral and religious improvement" (*Serious Reflections*, xii). All of Crusoe's anecdotes about spiritual improvement are conventional, until, as we have seen, his chapter "Of Religion." The distinctions he makes between "negative religion" and the "true Christian" highlight Crusoe's change from self-serving profiteer and a man with a "wandering inclination" to religious crusader. For a recent postcolonial (but brief) account of religion and sexuality in *Crusoe*'s two sequels, see Srinivas Aravamudan, *Tropicopolitans: Colonialism and Agency, 1688–1804* (Durham: Duke University Press, 1999), esp. 98, 275. See the following few examples that talk about the *Serious Reflections*: Fakrul Alam—in "Religious and Linguistic Colonialism in Defoe's Fiction," *North Dakota Quarterly* 55, no. 3: 116–23—discusses "religion" in the trilogy, but without any of the historical context I am trying to provide. Novak makes a similar argument in *Realism, Myth, and History in Defoe's Fiction*. Otherwise, in books about Defoe such as Backscheider's or Hunter's, the *Serious Reflections* is noted as one of Defoe's works but never commented on except as subordinate to *Robinson Crusoe*.

18. Lennard Davis notes this. For Davis, however, the point is Defoe's ability to construct a "reality" based on accretion of detail and thus creating a new kind of "novel" that imitates "reality" in ways that frighten Gildon. "Defoe's works seem still plainly to bear the marks," Davis argues, "of their intimate connection with the news/novels discourse." In *Factual Fictions: The Origins of the English Novel* (New York: Columbia University Press, 1983), 152–75, esp. 155.

19. Watt, *Rise of the Novel*, 67.

20. Ibid., 68.

CHAPTER TWO

Lady Mary Wortley Montagu's Sapphic Vision

John C. Beynon

Shortly after leaving Constantinople on her return voyage to England, Lady Mary Wortley Montagu passed through Greece in July of 1718 and wrote to her friend, the Abbé Conti, of the sites of classical antiquity she visited during her journey. While roaming through the Grecian countryside, Lady Mary ruminated on the land of the *Iliad* and tried to imagine the feats of Menelaus, Paris, and Ajax as she passed through Homeric landscapes. Yet, in the midst of such heroic raptures, she writes, "I can-not forebear mentioning Lesbos, where Sapho sung."[1] Later as she scans the islands of the Aegean from her ship, she writes of her impatience to take in all of the ancient world as it passes by, complaining,

> I am so angry at my selfe that I will pass by all the other Islands with
> this general reflection, that 'tis impossible to imagine any thing more
> agreeable than this Journey would have been between 2 and 3,000 years
> since, when, after drinking a dish of tea with Sapho, I might have gone
> the same evening to visit the temple of Homer in Chios, and have pass'd
> this voyage in takeing plans of magnificent Temples, delineateing the
> miracles of Statuarys and converseing with the most polite and most gay
> of humankind. (423)

Lady Mary's desire to visit the Lesbian poet of antiquity is wholly understandable when one considers that she has just spent the past year among the women of Turkey, whose incomparable beauty and pleasant company she never tired of extolling throughout her *Turkish Embassy Letters*.

Lady Mary's letters were originally composed while she accompanied her husband, Edward Wortley, in his new appointment as England's

Ambassador Extraordinary to the Court of Turkey, although she would later revise and prepare them for publication.[2] While Wortley's diplomatic ineptitude would doom his mission to failure within two short years, Lady Mary would thrive among the aristocratic women of the Levant, forming friendships, acquiring a wide array of experience and knowledge, and learning how successfully to perform smallpox inoculations—knowledge that she would disseminate upon returning to England. For the purposes of this essay, however, I will focus on Lady Mary's efforts to reenvision the Near East in such a way as to enable her to develop an erotics of female vision that challenged both masculinist norms of female sexuality and orientalist assumptions about Islamic culture. Although many of these revisions of the female gaze in a cross-cultural encounter rely on Montagu's capacity for fantasy, which entailed its own version of eighteenth-century orientalism, I will explain how these fantasies might in turn have served more liberatory, even subversive, ends, for they can be understood to play an important role in the history of sapphism in eighteenth-century literature and culture.[3]

Although Montagu's position in the history of sapphism has largely been unexplored, her life and writings provide useful illustrations of how the figure of Sappho was often deployed in ways that designated lesbian erotics, if not fully fledged lesbian identities.[4] Indeed, Lady Mary circulated in an upper-class, literate society fascinated with the possibilities of same-sex desire among women. Her friendship with the feminist Mary Astell, who envisioned an all-female community in her own *A Serious Proposal to the Ladies* (1694), provides one reason to consider Lady Mary's writings in relation to the history of all-female communities and same-sex desire. One of Montagu's earliest readers of the revised *Turkish Embassy Letters* was an enthusiastic Astell, who, in her 1724 preface to the then privately circulated letters, writes, "I confess I am malicious enough to desire that the World shou'd see to how much better purpose the LADYS Travel than their LORDS," and that "a *Lady* has the skill to strike out a New Path and to embellish a worn-out Subject with variety of fresh and elegant Entertainment" (467). In her 1725 coda to the preface, Astell is even more laudatory of Montagu's ingenious insights into Turkish culture and customs. "You see, Madam, how I lay every thing at your Feet," she writes, marveling at "the extent of your Empire over my Imagination" (468). Astell found in Lady Mary's letters a feminist project complementary to her own that not only promoted the public circulation of women's experience and women's writing but described the forms of female intimacy that Astell so desired to enjoy. Astell's feminist visions of exclusively female spaces in which women might delight in intellectual and moral improvements together finds its counterpart in the visions of harems and women-only baths that Montagu describes in her letters. Both Astell's and Montagu's literary explorations of freedom for women in all-female spaces contributed to an eighteenth-century sapphic imagination.[5]

Montagu's friendship with Alexander Pope and her admiration for his work (she read Pope's translation of the *Iliad* while in Turkey and Greece) provide yet another valence for understanding her connection to Sappho. Among Pope's earliest translations is his version of "Sapho and Phaon," written in 1707 and published in his *Ovid's Epistles* in 1712. In this version of Sappho's unrequited love for Phaon, Pope describes the Lesbian poet's love of women in terms of a desire specific to women who love other women. Sappho explains to Phaon that "I'm my own Disease: / No more the *Lesbian* Dames my Passion move, / Once the dear Objects of my guilty Love."[6] And as she prepares to throw herself from a promontory in the Ionian Islands, she bids her female lovers adieu:

> Ye *Lesbian* Virgins, and ye *Lesbian* Dames,
> Themes of my Verse, and Objects of my Flames,
> No more your Groves with my glad Songs shall ring,
> No more these Hands shall touch the trembling String:
> My *Phaon*'s fled, and I those Arts resign.
> (lines 232–36)

Despite the fact that Sappho's lament is largely about a man who abandons her, Pope includes references to Sappho's former female lovers that mark her attachment to them as passionate and praiseworthy, notwithstanding his use of the phrase "guilty Love" to characterize desire between women as perverse. Once their friendship had expired, and the two developed a deep animosity toward one another, Pope characteristically attacked Lady Mary in terms of her transgressions of gender and sexual norms, dubbing her a "furious *Sappho*" and a "lewd Lesbia."[7]

Many of the writings about sapphism that would have been familiar to Lady Mary link this supposedly deviant sexual inclination to Middle Eastern women and their presumed erotic proclivities. William Walsh's "A Dialogue Concerning Women" (1699) discusses "amours" among women as a "new Sort of Sin, that was follow'd not only in *Lucian*'s Time, but is practis'd frequently in *Turkey* at this Day."[8] And the French nobleman J. B. Tavernier, Baron of Aubonne, created some of the most famous depictions of the sapphic harem in *Six Voyages . . . through Turkey, into Persia and the East-Indies, for the space of Forty Years* (1676), translated into English in 1684. In his "New Relation of the Inner-Part of the Grand Seignor's Seraglio," Tavernier explains that while their caliphs and sultans are buggering the eunuchs, the women of the seraglio indulge in sexual practices "in a manner naturall to them, though it be against nature." Tavernier also repeats the notorious myth of the oriental woman's perverse appetite for cucumbers, remarking how imperative it is that the women "be served up with Cucumbers cut into pieces, and not entire, out of a ridiculous fear lest they should put them to indecent uses."[9]

Malek Alloula explains such connections between female perversion and the oriental harem in the Western imagination: "What is remembered about the harem . . . are the sexual excesses to which it gave rise and which it promotes. A universe of *generalized perversion* and of the *absolute limitlessness of pleasure,* the seraglio does appear as the ideal locus of the phantasm in all its contagious splendor. . . . Sapphism would thus contribute to further eroticize the idea of the harem."[10] In her own study of Montagu's *Turkish Embassy Letters* Lisa Lowe further explains that "the harem is not merely an orientalist voyeur's fantasy of imagined female sexuality; it is also the possibility of an erotic universe in which there are no men, a site of social and sexual practices that are not organized around the phallus or a central male authority."[11] Such were the imagined connections between sapphism and orientalism that circulated during Montagu's day; in fact, so prevalent were the assumptions that sapphism had its genesis in locations to the south and east of England, that, like sodomy, sapphism was frequently characterized as a foreign vice, "imported" to England by contact with the East through trade and exploration.[12]

That Montagu was familiar with myths about the lesbian erotics of the harem is likely, if not certain. She was well-read in the literature recounting European men's travels in the Middle East, and she took it upon herself to correct certain false accounts of the Orient—particularly the improbable and fantastic stereotypes of oriental women's passive subservience to despotic husbands. Before embarking on her journey to Constantinople, Montagu had tried to familiarize herself with her destination as much as possible. She had read the *Arabian Nights* in French as well as François de la Croix's *Milles et un jours,* and she had studied the Koran. She had also read nearly every account of the Ottoman Empire published in Britain and France, which often included references to oriental sapphism.[13] Even Pope was sure that Montagu would understand his lewd suggestion when he wrote to her in 1717 that she should beware of entering "the Land of Jealousy, where the unhappy Women converse with none but Eunuchs, and where the very Cucumbers are brought to them cutt."[14] Montagu embarked on her journey to the Levant aware that she was traveling to a land where same-sex desire and activity among women were rumored to be rampant. That she refrains from correcting Pope's stereotypes of the sapphic woman of the Near East and the same-sex female erotics of the harem perhaps underscores her own fascination with the possibilities of a world in which women manage to create intimate relationships based on all-female spaces marked by lesbian possibility. My discussion of these letters reveals that what Lady Mary discovered during her experience in Constantinople was a newfound pleasure in looking at women—an at once orientalist and sapphic pleasure in the company of women that enabled her to imagine new possibilities for female beauty and female sexuality, and the more Montagu was willing to understand and even submit to the standards of female beauty and sexuality that she encountered in the Levant, the more "sapphic" her vision of women and female intimacy became.[15]

Lady Mary begins her journey to Constantinople asserting her own received notions of taste and beauty, and these are the standards by which she scrutinizes and evaluates the faces, figures, clothing, and conduct of the women she encounters in Vienna, Prague, Leipzig, and Hanover. But upon entering the Ottoman Empire, Montagu's attitude toward visual pleasure shifts dramatically, and she writes with all the enthusiasm of an explorer: "I am now got into a new World where every thing I see appears to me a change of Scene." Although Montagu's new perspective is owed largely to her actual movement across the European continent, she also emphasizes her ability to see differently as she makes an entrance into this "new World." Her newfound vision is a particularly feminine mode of sight that she first describes when detailing the carriages that transport her through the Ottoman Empire. "They are cover'd all over with scarlet cloth, lin'd with silk and very often richly embroider'd and fring'd," she writes of the Turkish coaches, "This covering entirely hides the persons in them, but may be thrown back at pleasure and the Ladys peep through the Lattices" (312). Here Montagu discovers the luxuries of moving about incognito while retaining the prerogative of looking. This is a practice that fascinates Montagu throughout her stay in Turkey, and, in her subsequent correspondence, she continues to explore the implications of a woman who sees without being seen.

These prerogatives of female vision are complemented by instances in which she is allowed to gaze upon the women of the Levant, who in turn bestow their own appreciative sights on their English visitor. She describes such an experience in an account of her visit to Fatima, the wife of the Kahya, or second officer of the empire. As she enters the Kahya's household in Adrianpole, she is led by "2 black Eunuchs" who guide her down a long gallery lined with "2 ranks of beautifull young Girls with their Hair finely plaited almost hanging to their Feet, all dress'd in fine light damasks brocaded with silver." Montagu must appreciate these beauties while in motion, however, and she laments that "Decency did not permit me to stop to consider them nearer." Her small journey down this corridor bears a synecdochical relationship with Lady Mary's journey to Turkey. She passes a number of beautiful women all of whom she would love to inspect more closely, until she is led by the eunuchs toward the interior where she encounters the incomparable Fatima, "leaning on cushions of white Satin embroider'd, and at her feet sat 2 young Girls" (349). Montagu's has been a journey through various versions of femininity culminating in her invitation to the harem, which, as Melman reminds us, serves as "the *locus* of an exotic and abnormal sexuality [that] fascinated Westerners. It came to be regarded as a microcosmic Middle East."[16] Interestingly, two black eunuchs, in whom racial and sexual codes are conjoined, usher Montagu into this inner sanctum. These ambiguous figures lead Montagu from her husband and the traditional modes of patriarchal and political authority he represents to a world of women and alternative modes of fantasy and desire.[17]

When Montagu enters Fatima's room, she is stunned by the woman's beauty and describes her in enthusiastic terms of adoration:

> her beauty effac'd every thing. I have seen all that has been call'd lovely either in England or Germany, and must own that I never saw any thing so gloriously Beautifull, nor can I recollect a face that would have been taken notice of near hers. . . . I was so struck with Admiration that I

could not for some time speak to her, being wholly taken up on gazing.
That surprizing Harmony of features! that charming result of the whole!
that exact proportion of Body! that lovely bloom of Complexion
unsully'd by art! the unutterable Enchantment of her Smile! But her
Eyes! large and black with all the soft languishment of the bleu! every
turn of her face discovering some new charm! (349–50)

After these apostrophes, Montagu indulges in a close inspection of
Fatima's perfect face and provides an inventory of the woman's apparel.
She justifies her digression into the praises of Fatima's beauties and
charms, claiming, "I think I have read somewhere that Women allways
speak in rapture when they speak of Beauty, but I can't imagine why
they should not be allow'd to do so. I rather think it Virtue to be able to
admire without any Mixture of desire or Envy.... For me, I am not
asham'd to own I took more pleasure in looking on the beauteous Fatima than the finest piece of Sculpture could have given me" (350–51). If
Lady Mary attempts to deny that she experiences desire upon gazing at
Fatima, her excessive pleasure belies the complete absence of ecstasy.
Rather, what Lady Mary appears to denounce here is the sort of relationship that gazing at a statue produces. In other words, rather than
convert Fatima into an object of beauty to be passively desired, Lady
Mary attempts to convey her pleasures by proposing another model of
looking at women, one that ensures an even greater degree of pleasure.
Furthermore, she invites Fatima's appreciative gaze so that the two women
may enjoy the pleasures of mutual admiration: "The lovely Fatima en-
tertain'd me all this time in the most polite agreable Manner, calling me
often Uzelle Sultanam, or the beautifull Sultana, and desiring my Freind-
ship with the best Grace in the World, lamenting that she could not en-
tertain me in my own Language" (352). If language stands in for the cultural barriers that separate these women, the immediate and unmediated
pleasures in looking at one another represent the possibility of overcoming such obstacles, allowing the women to convey pleasurable feelings
to one another that otherwise they could not.

Of course, in this and in other encounters with the women of Eastern
Europe and the Levant, Lady Mary's writings themselves manifest an
orientalist sensibility. She tends to employ the language of exoticism and
hyperbole, exploits the sensuality supposedly intrinsic to the harem and
highlights the wonderful and the curious. Yet Montagu's orientalism is
pointedly different from that of her male counterparts, who, in their

writings, tend to find less to praise in Islamic culture and who submit the supposedly feminine nature of the Orient to a chauvinistic inspection and evaluation rooted in Western norms. Billie Melman, Lisa Lowe, and Srinivas Aravamudan have all attempted to explain how Montagu engages in orientalism with a difference.[18] I locate this difference in her conscious efforts to highlight and revise the *way* she sees the Levant and the women who inhabit it. A sapphic sensibility informs different ways of envisioning the Orient, creating new possibilities for women to see and be seen by one another in an encounter between the "East" and the "West."

Attempting to account for Lady Mary's particular ways of viewing the women she encounters in Constantinople, Bridget Orr has suggested that Lady Mary's practices of looking at other women make her "both subject and object of the gaze" and have little to do with traditional conceptions of how and why women look at one another. According to Orr, Montagu is aware that her enjoyment in looking at women and being seen by them could be construed as one of "two negative poles of predictable enthusiasm or envious detraction by which women's praise of other women is always judged." Nevertheless, what Montagu struggles to represent in her descriptions of how women look at one another is marked by "the sheer difficulty of finding a way of expressing a desiring rather than an envious admiration: trying to find a language of female admiration for femininity."[19] Montagu seems determined to deploy a version of the gaze that refuses to dissect the women she sees, and in so doing discovers pleasures in seeing and being seen by women that had heretofore been unavailable to her.

If her encounter with Fatima entails one version of oriental sensuality that sparks Montagu's heightened admiration of Ottoman women, the veiled woman who circulates in public further incites Montagu's fantasies of female sexual possibility. Montagu's famous revision of the veiled Muslim woman and the liberty she enjoys beneath her veils is among the most notable contributions she makes to the politics and erotics of being able to see without being seen. Thus she prefigures, if not inaugurates, a tradition of feminist revisionist scholarship that interprets the veil as an enabling rather than confining feature of Islamic femininity. Regarding this newly discovered relationship between women, the gaze, and how the veil enables Islamic women to function in public, Montagu describes the veiled woman in terms of increased freedom—both the freedom to see and the freedom to move about. She writes to her sister that "Tis very easy to see they have more Liberty than we have, no Woman of what rank so ever being permitted to go in the streets without 2 muslins, one that covers her face all but her Eyes and another that hides the whole dress of her head" (328). This description of the veil echoes the earlier description of the Turkish coaches that allow a woman to travel incognito and spy through the lattices. In his analysis of postcards depicting orientalized women that were sent from Algeria to France during the early decades of this century, Alloula explains how the veil served as an "obstacle to sight" for photographers. "The Algerian woman does not conceal herself, does not play at concealing herself," explains Alloula. "But the eye cannot catch hold of her. The opaque veil that covers her intimates clearly and simply to the photographer a refusal. . . . the Algerian woman discourages the *scopic desire* (the voyeurism) of the photographer."[20] If the veil frustrates the French colonial photographer in Alloula's account of him, it serves as a surface upon which Montagu can project her fantasies of female sexual license. "You may guess how effectually this disguises them," Montagu continues to explain to her sister, "that there is no distinguishing the great Lady from her Slave, and 'tis impossible for the most jealous Husband to know his Wife when he meets her, and no Man dare either touch or follow a Woman in the Street" (328). Here Lady Mary finds in the veil and the accompanying *ferigée*—a full-length piece of cloth that covers a woman's body—a style of clothing that does not allow for distinctions of social rank. This delight in the indistinguishability of noblewomen from their servants is a far cry from Montagu's earlier praise of Dutch sumptuary laws. It also recalls the moment in which Lady Mary imagines herself as a woman of lower rank, thus permitted to kiss the hand of the Austrian Empress. This mode of rendering women indistinguishable from one another also prevents the men from recognizing their wives, thereby enabling the women to move freely through the streets of Constantinople.[21]

Montagu explicitly connects this freedom of movement to sexual freedom when she explains:

> This perpetual Masquerade gives them entire Liberty of following their Inclinations without danger of Discovery. . . . The Great Ladys seldom let their Gallants know who they are, and 'tis so difficult to find it out that they can very seldom guess at her name they have corresponded with above halfe a year together. You may easily imagine the number of

faithfull Wives very small in a country where they have nothing to fear from their Lovers' Indiscretion, since we see so many that have the courage to expose them selves to that in this World and all the threaten'd Punishment of the next, which is never preach'd to the Turkish Damsels. Neither have they much to apprehend of from the resentment of their Husbands, those Ladys that are rich having all their money in their own hands, which they take with 'em upon a divorce with an addition which he is oblig'd to give 'em. (328–29)

Such observations led Montagu to pronounce, "Upon the Whole, I look upon the Turkish Women as the only free people in the Empire" (329). Of Lady Mary's notions of liberty, Melman writes, "'Liberty' spelled out *sexual freedom*. And it meant one's ability to follow one's 'inclination' and 'indulge' oneself (Montagu's words) in that inclination, regardless of one's sex.... What is novel in [Montagu's] usage of the metaphor of the veil is the notion that 'Liberty'—that is moral-free and natural sexual conduct—is applicable to both sexes"[22] Montagu shunned sexual hypocrisy and prudery, and she felt women should not be required to live by a different standard of sexual behavior than men, as her outspoken views on the subject to Edward Wortley during their courtship and her flirtations with Pope suggest. At the same time, her remarks to her sister on the perceived freedom that veiled women in Turkey enjoy indicate that her attitudes toward sexual morality and conduct were continually challenged and reshaped by her observations of and encounters with Turkish women. Aravamudan further elaborates on Lady Mary's fantasies of female sexual freedom: "Tenuous though this fantasy may be, Montagu invents a female subjectivity existing without subjection, a sexual agency without concomitant object status, and generalized public privileges abiding with few corresponding obligations." I would add that Montagu's fantasy specifically entails a denial of heterosexual and patriarchal privilege on the part of men—a position that further enables her fantasies of sapphic possibilities within Islamic society.[23]

Surely the most complex instance of Montagu's newfound pleasures in looking at Turkish women is found in her most famous and influential letter of April 1717 to an unnamed woman in which she recounts her visit to the hot baths of Sophia. As Montagu enters the women-only baths, she observes the naked bodies that surround her and remarks that "twas impossible to stay there with one's Cloths on," and yet she appears "in my travelling Habit, which is a rideing dress," and refuses to remove her clothing during the visit (313). That Montagu chooses not to undress hardly prevents her own body from being imagined and appreciated by the naked bathers, however. Melman suggests that Montagu's fascination with the dynamics of dress and undress at the baths indicates a "sophisticated usage of dress and undress as both metaphors for and symbols of, varying degrees of freedom and the relation of individuals to Nature," a term which Montagu uses to refer to "human inclination, basically the inclination of the body and senses."[24] Montagu's decision to remain clothed may even heighten the erotic nature of her encounter at the baths, for as Kaja Silverman argues, "Dress is one of the most important cultural implements for articulating and territorializing human corporeality—for mapping its erotogenic zones and for affixing a sexual identity."[25] In fact, Montagu's refusal to undress ultimately necessitates that she partially disrobe. While mingling with the bathers, Lady Mary reveals that "The Lady that seem'd the most considerable amongst them entreated me to sit by her and would fain have undress'd me for the bath. I excus'd my selfe with some difficulty, they being all so earnest in perswading me. I was at last forc'd to open my skirt and shew them my stays, which satisfy'd 'em very well, for I saw they beleiv'd I was so lock'd up in that machine that it was not in my own power to open it, which contrivance they attributed to my Husband" (314). In revealing her corset, Lady Mary affords her audience a sense of the contours of her own body, highlighting the erotic play entailed in her teasing refusals to disrobe. But the bathing women can only imagine the contraption to be a sort of chastity belt imposed on the Englishwoman by her jealous husband. What the Turkish women are allowed to imagine, then, even while they are refused its actual appearance, is the English visitor's body— and even more specifically, its sexual function and significance.

Lady Mary is equally fascinated with the "stark naked" bodies she sees. Summoning Milton, Guido, and Titian as the traditional arbiters of female beauty, Montagu begins to praise the women's figures, but she soon depicts her mode of vision in less mediated terms: "I perceiv'd that the Ladys with the finest skins and most delicate shapes had the greatest share of my admiration, thô their faces were sometimes less beautifull than those of their companions." In fact, Montagu seems more interested in other areas of the body that might be considered beautiful: "I was here convinc'd of the Truth of a Refflexion that I had often made, that if twas the fashion to go naked, the face would be hardly observ'd"

(314).[26] Montagu abandons conventional standards of beauty that require a handsome face and instead allows her eyes to travel over the surfaces of her companions' bodies. She unabashedly explains just where her eye roams, and one can hardly account for her visual pleasure as anything other than erotic appreciation for the women that she regrets abandoning in order to adhere to her husband's schedule.[27] Montagu's admiration for the women is not one-sided, however, and she is pleased when the women repeat "Uzelle, pek uzelle, which is nothing but, charming, very charming" (313). At the baths, Montagu figures herself as a spectacle within a spectacle. She cannot help but describe the baths in terms of novelty and wonderment, yet she finds herself the object of two hundred curious gazes as she wanders through the rooms of the baths in her European riding dress.[28]

Such a complication of subject/object positions is congruent with Lacanian conceptualizations of the gaze in the twentieth century. Elizabeth Grosz glosses Lacan's theory of the gaze as set forth in his *Four Fundamental Concepts of Psychoanalysis* as follows: "The subject is defined as that which is seeable, capable of being shown, being seen without necessarily being able to see either the observer or itself." Thus the gaze is situated outside the subject, and "by this Lacan means that, like the phallus, like desire itself, the gaze emanates from the field of the Other." The gaze is, therefore, predicated on a hierarchical relationship between the viewer and the viewed: "the other's look is justified, legitimized, by the Other. It is the result of being placed in the field of the Other."[29] Kaja Silverman further explains that "at issue here is what Lacan calls the 'inside-out structure of the gaze,' whereby the subject comes to regard itself from a vantage external to itself."[30] Montagu's desire to look is inevitably accompanied by an equally strong desire to be seen. She desires not mastery over the gaze in a unidirectional sense of active spectator who assaults a passive spectacle; instead she desires to be both the spectator and the spectacle—to see and be seen seeing in a mutual transaction of gazes that caress the surfaces of seeing bodies.

Nonetheless, contemporary theories of the gaze have largely depended on Freud's firmly gendered notions of fetishism, scopophilia, and exhibitionism, so that the subject of the gaze is frequently gendered as male or masculine while the spectacle or the object of the gaze is predictably female or feminine. Kristina Straub finds a historical basis for this masculine encoding of the gaze when she examines Restoration and eighteenth-century discussions of spectatorship and spectacle in relation to the stage and the self-presentation of English actors and actresses of Montagu's day. "It is my contention," asserts Straub, "that one can see with particular vividness in eighteenth-century discourse about players the ongoing process of naturalization by which the powerful, gendered tropes of the male spectator and the female spectacle become encoded in modern ideology."[31] That Montagu posed for numerous male portraitists, some of whom depicted her in the Turkish garments with which she returned to England, suggests that she herself not only understood but also participated in this ideology.

Of course, Montagu quite consciously presents herself as a woman looking at other women in her letters, requiring an analysis of the gaze that takes the female viewer and her femininity into account. Feminist explorations of the gaze have grappled with the problem of female spectatorship since both Freud's and Lacan's accounts of the gaze largely insist on a male or phallic spectator and a female object of his gaze. One answer to this problem has been to place the female viewer in a masculine subject-position. Laura Mulvey's pioneering work on what she dubs "fetishistic scopophilia" explains how both women and men might occupy the place of the phallic voyeur when she writes of the "masculinisation" of the female subject.[32] This mode of masculine viewing is precisely how both Lowe and Felicity Nussbaum interpret Montagu's acts of looking at Turkish women. For Lowe, Montagu's appreciation of these women is related from a "subjective position . . . not unlike that of male poets who eulogize the body of the female muse or beloved, regarding her and enumerating her many beauties," and she claims that "it appears that Montagu is able to articulate her affection for Fatima only by means of the established literary tradition that exists for the praise and regard of female beauty, a male tradition of courtly love poetry exemplified by the sonnets of Shakespeare, Sidney, and Spenser. Following this literary convention, Montagu takes up a posture toward Fatima that still expresses love by means of an aestheticizing and anatomizing gaze."[33] In other words, according to Lowe, Montagu cannot escape a mode of masculine vision that places her in the position of a male spectator and the women of Turkey as spectacle. Nussbaum echoes Lowe's assessment of Montagu's gaze, focusing on Lady Mary's remarks that "I had wickedness enough to wish secretly that Mr. Gervase could have been there [at the baths] invisible. I fancy it would have very much

improv'd his art to see so many fine Women naked in different pos-
tures" (314).[34] Nussbaum sees in Montagu's reference to Charles Jervas a
"wish to impersonate a male voyeur," which enables Montagu's "erotically charged vision." "The transvestite gazing may," continues Nussbaum, "be interpreted as an expression of a slippery sexuality with affinities to homoerotic desire and an instance of Oriental sapphism." Montagu
"express[es] homoerotic desire by impersonating men, and imagine[s]
that women's freedom arises from sexual liberty."[35] Surely Nussbaum is
correct to highlight the sapphic erotics involved in the scene at the
baths, but I question the necessity of finding in Montagu a transvestite
viewer in order to locate "an instance of Oriental sapphism."

Although there are many accounts of the ways in which transvestism
enables the pursuit of same-sex desire among women—especially in
eighteen-century Britain—Montagu's experiences in Constantinople,
and her recorded experiences in the letters as a whole, do not entirely
conform to this model.[36] Lady Mary usually highlights her own femininity and that of her female companions—often through a heightened attention to particularly female dress—and she foregrounds intimate situations in which she finds herself in the presence of other
women as they gaze on one another. The model of transvestism that
Lowe and Nussbaum rely on to discuss Montagu's gaze and her sapphic
pleasures fails to account for the ways in which Montagu herself insists
on staging an interaction of pleasurable gazing as occurring between
two *women* independent of male mediation. Sapphic, rather than transvestite, models of visual pleasure between women seem a more appropriate model for understanding Lady Mary's erotic delight in looking at
women.

Straub's discussion of spectatorship in relation to the eighteenth-century stage is interested not only in the female subject of the gaze but
also in the ways in which desire influences how the female gaze operates. "Sexuality crosses the category of gender," she writes, "rendering it
the site of more complex distinctions than the binary opposition of
masculine and feminine." In other words, one's biological sex or identification with one of two genders will not ensure how any subject will
interpolate him- or herself in the field of vision. Desire is one factor
that will complicate the way one assumes a position in relation to the
operations of the gaze. Regarding women whose sexuality might chal-

lenge heterosexual desire between the sexes, Straub asserts that "women may behave in sexually subversive ways that, while not constituting a 'lesbian identity,' demand some articulation in the feminist re-visioning of sexual history."[37] Lady Mary's own attempts to express her exhilaration in looking at other women provide us with an opportunity to understand a feminist as well as a specifically sapphic "re-visioning of sexual history."

According to many contemporary theorists of female spectatorship, the lesbian erotics that seem to accompany Montagu's visual practices are apparent impossibilities for the contemporary female viewer. Mary Ann Doane highlights this problem when she reminds us that "the cinema generates and guarantees pleasure by a corroboration of the spectator's identity. Because that identity is bound up with that of the voyeur and the fetishist, because it requires for its support the attributes of the 'noncastrated,' the potential for illusory mastery of the signifier, it is not accessible to the female spectator, who, in buying her ticket, must deny her sex. There are no images either *for* her or *of* her."[38] Just as Mulvey had announced a decade earlier, only by positioning herself as a normatively developed (i.e., heterosexual) woman or by erroneously self-identifying as a man can a woman experience any pleasure in narrative cinema. Such analyses have led lesbian critics like Judith Mayne to observe that "feminist film theory...has resolutely bracketed any discussion of lesbianism or of the female homoerotic."[39]

But some critics have tried to theorize how the lesbian spectator does indeed enjoy looking at other women. Mayne, for instance, in her discussion of the work of the lesbian filmmaker Dorothy Arzner, finds that "Arzner's look has quite another function...one that has received very little critical attention, and that is to decenter the man's look and eroticize the exchange of looks between...two women." "An assessment of Arzner's importance within the framework of female authorship," continues Mayne, "needs to account not only for how Arzner problematizes the pleasures of the cinematic institution as we understand it—for example, in terms of voyeurism and fetishism reenacted through the power of the male gaze and the objectification of the female body—but also for how, in her films, those pleasures are identified in ways that are not reducible to the theoretical clichés of the omnipotence of the male gaze." One of the ways in which Mayne locates this challenge to "the omnipotence of the male gaze" in Arzner's oeuvre is to highlight Arzner's fascination with female friendship. "Female friendship," writes Mayne, "acquires a resistant function in the way that it exerts a pressure against the supposed 'natural' laws of heterosexual romance. Relations between women and communities of women have a privileged status in Arzner's films."[40]

Investigating female friendship as a means to understand the significance of the gaze between women is also the project of Mieke Bal's essay "His Master's Eye," in which Bal challenges traditional male critiques of female nudes as depicted in Rembrandt's *Danae* and Manet's *Olympia*. Bal's work focuses on painting and art criticism, so her discussion of the gaze is concerned with precinematic modes of representation that are, therefore, more congruous with the practices of viewing that Montagu would have understood. It also makes sense to discuss the gaze in terms of painting, considering Montagu's own comparisons of her vision with that of eighteenth-century painters like Jervas and Joshua Reynolds. Bal offers a model of seeing that is based on the *glance* as opposed to the *gaze*. For her, the gaze is a masculinist version of looking characterized by voyeurism in which "the receiver is totally passive, a container rather than a subject, and the sender is omnipotent," and thus Bal echoes Mulvey's position in "Visual Pleasure and Narrative Cinema." Bal suggests an alternative dynamic of seeing, however, in the glance, which she defines as "the awareness of one's own engagement in the act of looking [that] entails the recognition that what one sees is a representation, not an objective reality."[41] In other words, if the gaze encourages a male/ masculinized spectator to indulge in a fantasy of fetishized scopophilia, the employment of the glance allows a degree of remove in which the spectator can reflect on one's own visual processes and pleasures.[42] Montagu's delight in seeing the naked women of the Turkish baths in Sophia is indeed characterized by self-conscious reflection about her own status as an observer and interest in her own acts of looking. Her invocation of male painters—eighteenth-century representatives of voyeurism—is a means of drawing attention to the very acts of viewing she enjoys among the naked women of the baths. Much as Bal describes, Montagu's mode of vision is one characterized by a high degree of awareness of one's own ability to see and thus to represent. The "painterly" view that Montagu brings to bear on her own practices of seeing also reveals Montagu's recognition that she is constructing her own representation of these women—one informed by her own fantasies and desires.

Bal then turns to an analysis of racial difference and desire between women in Manet's *Olympia*. Her analysis of these female figures focuses on the way the black woman in the painting gazes upon the reclining white woman. In this internal representation of looking, Bal suggests an alternative to voyeuristic viewing: "She really looks at the white woman. If one takes up the clue offered in the internal focalizer, the look is friendly, perhaps erotic, but not in a colonizing way." Although most critics have interpreted the black visitor as a servant, Bal refuses to impose this reading onto the painting, as a colonial reading allows critics to say nothing more of the visitor who directs our gaze at the reclining Olympia. Instead, Bal pays close attention to the black visitor's posture, her direction of vision, and her handling of a bouquet of flowers and notes that "her body suggests a sitting position. She may be not serving, but visiting." Bal further extends this vision of friendship into one that can encompass lesbian passion: "The friendly look enables an erotic, lesbian reading, but does not enforce it."[43] In this reading, Olympia's defiant stare reprimands an intruding voyeuristic gaze that interrupts the friendly, erotic exchange of looks between the black woman and her white friend.

Bal's rereading of *Olympia* is helpful in thinking about Lady Mary's friendships with the Turkish women of Adrianople and Constantinople—friendships that are extraordinarily reliant on the congenial, even erotic exchange of gazes across ethnic and cultural divides.[44] When, for example, Montagu writes to her sister of her visit to the Sultana Hafise, "the favourite of the last Emperour Mustapha," Montagu once again elaborates on this empress's beauty, her elaborate clothing and impressive collection of jewelry, and her kind hospitality. After dining and walking through the Sultana's gardens, she begins, in a by now familiar gesture, to praise the empress's beauty: "I assur'd her that if all the Turkish Ladys were like her, it was absolutely necessary to confine them from public view for the repose of Mankind, and proceeded to tell her what a noise such a face as hers would make in London or Paris. I can't beleive you (reply'd she agreably); if Beauty were so much valu'd in your Country as you say, they would never have suffer'd you to leave it" (380–87). This exchange epitomizes the delight Montagu receives in gazing on her companions and being gazed on with equal relish. Such a mutual ex-

change of looks, pleasures, and praises, like the reciprocal friendly looking that Bal locates in Manet's *Olympia,* allows for erotic visual pleasure
between women of different races that seems largely ignorant and free
of the confines of the gaze as we have come to know it through a heterosexual, patriarchal norm of vision that divides the seer from the seen
along the axes of sexual difference.[45]

Assessing the importance of Montagu's letters to the history of orientalism, Melman argues that "Montagu's letters, in short, may be appro-
priately designated a key text, the corner-stone in the new, alternative
discourse that developed in the West on the Middle-East,"[46] and Lowe
reminds us that Montagu's intervention into orientalist discourse is
largely a feminist enterprise: "An emergent feminist discourse provides
Montagu with the language, arguments, and rhetoric with which to interrogate travel writing about the Orient while furnishing her with a
critical position from which to write."[47] Astell's praises of the letters extol
Montagu's superior perspective on the Middle East, and, as I have demonstrated, Montagu continually explores this perspective in the most literal fashion as she attends carefully to her own practices of seeing and
explores her own place within the complex field of vision she describes.

Lady Mary's revisions of British orientalism and contributions to early
modern feminism are central to understanding the implications of her
letters. Nevertheless, I find Montagu's erotic pleasures in viewing and
being in the company of women—pleasures available to the early eighteenth-century imagination through the cult of Sappho and popular
orientalist fantasies of the harem—essential to understanding and assessing Montagu's re-visioning of oriental femininity. Teresa de Lauretis, in
her own attempt to investigate the connections between lesbian desire
and representation, celebrates attempts by lesbian artists to "alter the
standard of vision, the frame of reference of visibility, of *what can be
seen.*"[48] I would argue that Montagu's attempts at a re-vision of the orient include a project similar to that which de Lauretis describes. Lady
Mary's recording of what she saw on her journey to the Middle East entails an attempt to revise *what can be seen* from a sapphic viewpoint—
from the perspective of a woman who desires both to see the women of
the Orient and to be seen by them. And it is Montagu's pursuit of a
sapphic vision and its concomitant pleasures that at once enables her to
challenge the patriarchal gaze and the narrow version of orientalism it
produced.

Notes

1. Robert Halsband, ed., *The Complete Letters of Lady Mary Wortley Montagu*, 3 vols. (Oxford: Clarendon, 1965), 1:421. All further citations refer to the first volume of the Halsband edition of *The Complete Letters*.

2. Not all of Montagu's fifty-two *Turkish Embassy Letters* were actual letters sent to her friends and relatives. Instead, they are, as Robert Halsband explains in his introduction to *The Complete Letters*, "a compilation of pseudo-letters," and "although they are clearly an accurate record of her experiences and observations during her two-year sojourn abroad, we may still wonder to what extent they are based on real letters." (See Halsband, introduction to *The Complete Letters*, xiv.) Whether Montagu's letters are to be considered more fact than fiction or vice versa is incidental to my study of her letters. If they are indeed largely embellished accounts of her experiences in Turkey, then they serve to record the fantasies and desires that emerged from her encounters with the women of Europe and the Middle East.

3. For a lucid explanation of Lady Mary's deployment of orientalist "fantasy" and its implications for her own practices of "levantinization," see Srinivas Aravamudan, "Lady Mary in the *Hammam*," in *Tropicopolitans: Colonialism and Agency, 1688–1804* (Durham: Duke University Press, 1999), 160–62.

4. Felicity Nussbaum, one of the few critics to carefully explore the sapphic dimensions of the *Turkish Embassy Letters*, usefully points out that Lady Mary's associations with the poet of Lesbos should be read in light of eighteenth-century efforts to link her and many of her female contemporaries with Sappho: "The contemporary allusions to Sappho in reference to Montagu and others clearly connect their poetic genius to their homoerotic sexuality." See Nussbaum, *Torrid Zones: Sexuality and Maternity in Eighteenth-Century English Narratives* (Baltimore: Johns Hopkins University Press, 1995), 143. Other writers who have remarked on the ways in which an association with Sappho served to taint a woman with suggestions of lesbianism include Emma Donoghue, Lisa L. Moore, and Susan Sniader Lanser. See Donoghue, *Passions between Women: British Lesbian Culture, 1668–1801* (New York: HarperPerennial, 1993); Moore, *Dangerous Intimacies: Toward a Sapphic History of the British Novel* (Durham: Duke University Press, 1997); and Lanser, "Befriending the Body: Female Intimacies as Class Acts," *Eighteenth-Century Studies* 32, no. 2 (winter 1998–99): 179–98.

5. At fifteen, Lady Mary herself had entertained fantasies of establishing an all-female English monastery. See Halsband, *The Life of Lady Mary Wortley Montagu* (Oxford: Clarendon, 1956), 7. For a discussion of the mutual admiration that Lady Mary and Mary Astell expressed for one another, see Ruth Perry, *The Celebrated Mary Astell: An Early English Feminist* (Chicago: University of Chicago Press, 1986), 270–71, 273–74, and 275–77. For a recent discussion of Mary Astell's role in the history of female intimacy in eighteenth-century England, see Elizabeth Wahl, *Invisible Relations: Representations of Female Intimacy in the Age of Enlightenment* (Stanford: Stanford University Press, 1999), 77, 168.

6. Alexander Pope, "Sapho and Phaon," in *The Poems of Alexander Pope*, ed. John Butt (New Haven: Yale University Press, 1963), ll. 16–18. Further quotations from Pope's poem are cited in the text.

7. See Halsband's discussion of Pope's attacks on Lady Mary in his *Life*, 130–32, 140–42, 147–48, 149–52.

8. William Walsh, "A Dialogue Concerning Women" (1699), quoted in Donoghue, *Passions between Women*, 255.

9. J. B. Tavernier, Baron of Aubonne, "A New Relation of the Inner-Part of the Grand Seignor's Seraglio" (1684), quoted in Donoghue, *Passions between Women*, 255–56.

10. Alloula, *The Colonial Harem*, trans. Myrna Godzich and Wlad Godzich (Minneapolis: University of Minnesota Press, 1986), 95–96.

11. Lowe, *Critical Terrains: French and British Orientalisms* (Ithaca: Cornell University Press, 1991), 48.

12. For discussions of sapphic desire as originating outside of England, see Moore, *Dangerous Intimacies*, 50–55, and Nussbaum, *Torrid Zones*, 147–49. The pamphlet *Plain Reasons for the Growth of Sodomy* (London: 1730) also suggests that, like sodomy, lesbian passions and practices sprouted in exotic Mediterranean locales.

13. For an account of Montagu's mastery of oriental scholarship, see Billie Melman, *Women's Orients: English Women and the Middle East, 1718–1918: Sexuality, Religion, and Work* (Ann Arbor: University of Michigan Press, 1992), 82–83.

14. *The Correspondence of Alexander Pope*, ed. George Sherburn, 5 vols. (Oxford: Clarendon, 1956), 1: 368.

15. This is not to suggest that the "Orient" is indeed more thoroughly sapphic than the West, only that Lady Mary's understanding of orientalism—howsoever it may differ from that of her male counterparts—relies on certain understandings of the oriental woman's unique opportunities for sapphic pleasure. While Lady Mary relies on this stereotypical understanding of Near Eastern women, she finds such myths liberating and erotically satisfying.

16. Melman, *Women's Orients*, 60.

17. Charles Ancillon's *Traité des eunuques dans lequel on explique toutes les différentes sortes d'eunugues, quel rang ils ont tenu et quel cas on en a fait* (Paris: 1707), which was translated as *Eunuchism display'd* (London: 1718), suggests how one might think about eunuch sexuality. Among the four types of eunuchs that Ancillon delineates, he mentions "those types of men who were so unsuitable or of such a frigid temperament that they were incapable of procreating" (quoted in Lowe, *Critical Terrains*, 63, n. 25). Alloula considers eunuchs "the absolute negation of the male principle" (96).

18. See Melman, *Women's Orients;* Lowe, *Critical Terrains;* and Aravamudan, "Lady Mary in the *Hammam.*"

19. Bridget Orr, "'The Only Free People in the Empire': Gender Difference in Colonial Discourse," in *De-Scribing Empire: Post-Colonialism and Textuality*, ed. Chris Tiffin and Alan Lawson (London: Routledge, 1994), 162, 164. For a discussion of Lady Mary's introduction to the nonverbal "language of flowers" in Turkey and the possible lesbian implications of such coded communication, see Aravamudan, "Lady Mary in the *Hammam,*" 168–69, 179.

20. Alloula, *The Colonial Harem*, 7. For other discussions of the role the veil plays in constructions of Islamic femininity, see Frantz Fanon, "Algeria Unveiled," in *A Dying Colonialism*, trans. Haakon Chevalier (New York: Grove Weidenfeld, 1967), 35–67; Fatima Mernissi, *Beyond the Veil: Male-Female Dynamics in a Modern Muslim Society* (Cambridge: Shenkman, 1975), and *The Veil and the Male Elite: A Feminist Interpretation of Women's Rights in Islam*, trans. Mary J. Lakeland (New York: Addison Wesley, 1991); and Leila Ahmed, "The Discourse of the Veil," in *Women*

and Gender in Islam: Historical Roots of a Modern Debate (New Haven: Yale University Press, 1992), 144–68.

21. I find these instances of Montagu's fantasy of being declassed interesting in light of her own position within British aristocratic culture and her desire to mingle with upper-class and wealthy women of Europe and the Levant. Lowe argues that Montagu's class solidarity enables her to identify with the Turkish women she encounters: "The identification Montagu articulates between herself and Turkish women is established primarily by means of an analogy of gender, but it is also supported by an implicit rhetoric that is based on, and enunciates, an identity of social class." Such identifications with Turkish women allow Montagu to "rhetorically identif[y] her position with that of Turkish women." See *Critical Terrains*, 40, 42. As her meditations on the meaning of the veil suggest, however, not all of Montagu's encounters with Turkish women depend on an absolute solidarity with other noblewomen.

22. Melman, *Women's Orients*, 86.

23. See Aravamudan, "Lady Mary in the *Hammam*," 171.

24. Melman, *Women's Orients*, 89.

25. Kaja Silverman, "Fragments of a Fashionable Discourse," in *Theorizing Feminism: Parallel Trends in the Humanities and Social Sciences*, ed. Anne C. Herrmann and Abigail J. Stewart (Boulder: Westview, 1994), 83.

26. Perhaps Montagu is also challenging traditional norms of feminine beauty because of her own bout with smallpox in 1715 and the scars the disease left on her face. In her 1762 novel *Millennium Hall*, published a year before *The Turkish Embassy Letters*, Sarah Scott would envisage a fantasy of female space that served as a refuge for women, many of whom were afflicted with such scars or were otherwise rendered "ugly." For the sapphic implications of such female communities, see George E. Haggerty, "'Romantic Friendship' in *Millenium Hall*," in *Unnatural Affections: Women and Fiction in the Later Eighteenth Century* (Bloomington: Indiana University Press, 1998), 88–102. For a discussion of how such themes might in turn rely on orientalist fantasies of the harem, see Nussbaum, "Feminotopias: The Seraglio, the Homoerotic, and the Pleasures of 'Deformity,'" in *Torrid Zones*, 135–66.

27. Of the various sexual meanings that the Turkish baths evoke, see Aravamudan, "Lady Mary in the *Hammam*," 174–82. See also Melman, *Women's Orients*, 89.

28. To understand Montagu's desire to engage with the women of Turkey, Bridget Orr evokes Irigaray's notion of wonder: "Irigaray invokes the primary passion of awestruck surprise at the new and unfamiliar as a model for a way in which the two sexes could meet and marvel at each other's difference. In such an encounter there would be no identities, opposites or complements but instead two irreducibly different beings." Orr places Irigaray's notion of wonder in a context of two women admiring one another across the boundaries of race and suggests that "certain moments in [Montagu's] texts suggest the breakdown of that incorporative [appropriative] drive in a moment of wonder, or admiration." Orr, "'The Only Free People,'" 155–56.

29. Elizabeth Grosz, "Voyeurism/Exhibitionism/the Gaze," in *Feminism and Psychoanalysis: A Critical Dictionary*, ed. Elizabeth Wright (London: Blackwell, 1992), 449.

30. Silverman, "Fragments of a Fashionable Discourse," 80.

31. Kristina Straub, *Sexual Suspects: Eighteenth-Century Players and Sexual Ideology* (Princeton: Princeton University Press, 1992), 19.

32. See Mulvey, "Visual Pleasure and Narrative Cinema" and "Afterthoughts on 'Visual Pleasure and Narrative Cinema' Inspired by King Vidor's *Duel in the Sun,*" both collected in *Visual and Other Pleasures* (Bloomington: Indiana University Press, 1989). Although her "Afterthoughts" attempt to account for and celebrate female visual pleasure, it strikes me that this essay is even more insistent on reinscribing the Freudian paradigms of sexual difference that she appears to expose and lament in her earlier essay. She explains that the female viewer of films in which women are featured as protagonists and resist gender expectations experiences "masculinisation" by returning to the phallic stage in which the little girl mistakenly thought of herself as a "little man" à la Freud's 1933 essay "Femininity." "The memory of the 'masculine' phase has its own romantic attraction," writes Mulvey, elaborating on the sort of misguided nostalgia for misogynist Hollywood films that she condemns at the conclusion of her earlier essay, "a last-ditch resistance, in which the power of masculinity can be used as postponement against the power of patriarchy." Of course, this identification with the assertive heroine requires psychic transvestism from the female audience—what Mulvey calls "Trans-sex Identification"—which does not allow for a woman to experience any pleasure in desiring the woman on the screen other than through an evocation of her inner tomboy. See Mulvey, *Visual and Other Pleasures,* 37.

33. Lowe, *Critical Terrains,* 46, 48.

34. In 1710, Lady Mary's friend Charles Jervas depicted her as a shepherdess. Not Jervas, but Ingres, created the most famous painting of the Turkish baths in 1862 with *Le Bain Turc.* His notebooks reveal that he copied passages from Montagu's letters in preparing to execute his work. Notice that in this instance the male painter is influenced by the female traveler, and not the reverse.

35. Nussbaum, *Torrid Zones,* 139–40.

36. See, for instance, Charlotte Charke's *A Narrative of the Life of Mrs. Charlotte Charke* (London: 1755) and Kristina Straub's analysis of it in *Sexual Suspects,* 127–50; Henry Fielding's *The Female Husband: or, the Surprising History of Mrs. Mary, alias Mr. George Hamilton* (London: 1746) and Terry Castle's interpretation of it in *The Female Thermometer: Eighteenth-Century Culture and the Invention of the Uncanny* (Oxford: Oxford University Press, 1995); and Emma Donoghue's discussion of these and other instances of female cross-dressing in *Passions between Women,* 59–108.

37. Straub, *Sexual Suspects,* 16, 22.

38. Doane, "Women's Stake: Filming the Female Body," in *Feminism and Film Theory,* ed. Constance Penley (New York: Routledge, 1988), 216.

39. Mayne, "Lesbian Looks: Dorothy Arzner and Female Authorship" in *How Do I Look? Queer Film and Video,* ed. Bad Object-Choices (Seattle: Bay Press, 1991), 110.

40. Ibid., 112, 118.

41. Bal, "His Master's Eye," in *Modernity and the Hegemony of Vision,* ed. David Michael Levin (Berkeley: University of California Press, 1993), 382–84.

42. Bal's articulation of the glance and the distance a viewer achieves through it is similar to Mayne's discussion of irony in Arzner's films: "I am arguing that it is precisely in its ironic inflection of heterosexual norms, whether by the mirroring gesture that suggests a reflection of Arzner herself or by the definition of the female community as resistant to, rather than complicitous with, heterosexual relations, that Arzner's signature is written on her films." See Mayne, "Lesbian Looks," 120–21.

43. Bal, "His Master's Eye," 399.

44. One must note that Lady Mary was not consistently color-blind or antiracist in her descriptions of the women she encountered on her journey. On her return voyage, she describes women of North Africa thus: "Their posture in siting, the colour of their skin, their lank black Hair falling on each side their faces, their features and the shape of their Limbs, differ so little from their own country people, the Baboons, tis hard to fancy them a distinct race, and I could not help thinking there had been some ancient alliances between them" (427). These gratuitously racist remarks are best understood, I think, in light of Lady Mary's dismay at abandoning her orientalist utopia and the chauvinistic fervor with which she psychically prepares for her return to England. For a compelling discussion of this passage in light of Montagu's nationalism, see Aravamudan, "Lady Mary in the *Hammam*," 183–89. See also Nussbaum, *Torrid Zones*, 91–92.

45. Romantic friendship remains an important model for understanding intimacy between women in eighteenth-century England. Lillian Faderman's elucidations of these relationships have provided the basis for further investigations into the erotic underpinnings of romantic friendship by critics such as George Haggerty and Emma Donoghue, who attempt to understand such friendships in terms of sexual passion. See Faderman, *Surpassing the Love of Men: Romantic Friendship and Love between Women from the Renaissance to the Present* (New York: Quill, 1981), 74–143; Haggerty, *Unnatural Affections*, 73–119; and Donoghue, *Passions between Women*, 109–81. For a discussion of the problems of reading romantic friendships in terms of "lesbianism," see Wahl, *Invisible Relations*, 75–170.

46. See Melman, *Women's Orients*, 78. Hers is a different assessment from that of G. S. Rousseau and Roy Porter, who cursorily dismiss Montagu as a woman with a narcissistic vision of the Levant. See Rousseau and Porter, Introduction, *Exoticism in the Enlightenment*, ed. G. S. Rousseau and Roy Porter (Manchester: Manchester University Press, 1990), 12.

47. Lowe, *Critical Terrains*, 51.

48. De Lauretis, "Sexual Indifference and Lesbian Representation," in *The Lesbian and Gay Studies Reader*, ed. Henry Abelove, Michèle Aina Barale, and David M. Halperin (New York: Routledge, 1993), 152.

CHAPTER THREE

The Guise of Friendship

Terry Goldie

John Richardson's *Wacousta or, The Prophecy: A Tale of the Canadas*[1] has been seen as one of the defining texts of English Canadian culture. While both the date of the action, 1763, and the date of publication, 1832, are well before Canadian confederation in 1867, it has been read as symbolizing various processes through which the country emerged from its colonial status. Gaile McGregor names her thematic study of Canadian literature *The Wacousta Syndrome*[2] and Robin Mathews's highly polemical analysis, *Canadian Literature: Surrender or Revolution*, states that "*Wacousta*, the first major novel to be written by an author born in this country, is at the centre of the Canadian imagination."[3] It is certainly at the beginning of many imaginations. Thus Peter Dickinson's book, *Here Is Queer: Nationalisms, Sexualities, and the Literatures of Canada*,[4] a study of contemporary literature, begins with a few pages on *Wacousta*. Whether or not one accepts Northrop Frye's famous argument that Canada is infected by a fear of the wilderness, what he termed a "garrison mentality," *Wacousta* remains the garrison's most identifiable symbol.

The novel takes much of its form and atmosphere from the gothic romance. Its most extravagant figure is the title character, a Cornish soldier named Reginald Morton who is transformed by his love's rejection into an almost supernatural Native warrior fighting with Pontiac's forces against the British in the wilds of Canada. He has met his inamorata, Clara, in the highlands of Scotland and, as one might expect, she is described as a child of nature and her home as paradise. She abandons Reginald, who is to become Wacousta, for his very staid friend, the cold disciplinarian who is to become Colonel de Haldimar, commander of the garrison.

Recently, critics and theorists have made many attempts to understand the association between sexual desire and colonial rule. In *Colonial Desire: Hybridity in Theory, Culture, and Race*,[5] Robert Young emphasizes heterosexual dynamics, while in *The Ruling Passion: British Colonial Allegory and the Paradox of Homosexual Desire*,[6] Christopher Lane looks at male/male issues. Both texts discuss later periods, Lane beginning with Kipling and Young with Matthew Arnold, but the energies they depict are remarkably similar to those visible in *Wacousta*. Given that it has become almost automatic to consider the gothic romance as a representation of subterranean sexuality, it should not be surprising that setting the genre in a colony does not erase these dynamics but indeed adds more layers.

I take my title from an extensive speech Wacousta makes to de Haldimar's daughter, confusingly also named Clara, about the reason he fights her father: "he who, under the guise of friendship, had stolen into the Eden of my love, and left it barrenless of affection" (491).[7] The reference to Eden puts de Haldimar in a snakelike position, but the power of that friendship as an enabler of such a Satan is also worthy of note. There is a myriad of narratives from the eighteenth and nineteenth centuries that establish one man's absolute bond of affection with another. They are a microcosm of the category Eve Kosofsky Sedgwick analyzes in *Between Men* as "homosocial desire": "To draw the 'homosocial' back into the orbit of 'desire,' of the potentially erotic, then, is to hypothesize the potential unbrokenness of a continuum between homosocial and homosexual—a continuum whose visibility, for men, in our society, is radically disrupted."[8]

When Sedgwick refers to "our society" she might seem to be edging toward the ahistorical, but her idea of a continuum is reasonable, as long as all realize that the continuum varies in different periods and also that there is no period in which "men, in our society" are all in a similar place on that continuum. As George E. Haggerty states in *Men in Love*, "Masculinity is not one thing in the eighteenth century, any more than it is one thing in the twentieth."[9] The possible opposites of masculinity appear in the friendship between Wacousta and de Haldimar, the key homosocial relationship in terms of the structure of the novel.

As Wacousta tells Clara of its beginnings, he emphasizes the "unnatural" blend between his own passion and her father's austerity:

> "An intimacy suddenly sprang up between us which, as it was then to our brother officers, has since been a source of utter astonishment to myself. Unnatural, I repeat, for fire and ice are not more opposite than were the elements of which our natures were composed. He all coldness, prudence, obsequiousness and forethought. I all enthusiasm, carelessness, impetuosity and independence. Whether this incongruous friendship— friendship! no, I will not so far sully the sacred name as thus to term the unnatural union that subsisted between us;—whether this intimacy, then, sprang from the adventitious circumstance of our being more frequently thrown together as officers of the same company,—for we were both attached to the grenadiers,—or that my wild spirit was soothed by the bland amenity of his manners, I know not." (447)

Wacousta first establishes the importance and elevation of "friendship" at the level of the sacred but then denies his friendship with de Haldimar by calling it an "unnatural union," although there is no suggestion why it must be "unnatural."

The term seems to fit Haggerty's portrait of the extravagant possibilities of friendship in the period Richardson is depicting:

> If male-male love is given a voice and the ideals of friendship are described so as to make them indistinguishable from erotic love, then what does this tell us about the parameters of public discourse in the eighteenth century? It would be a mistake to dismiss this love as "simple friendship," not only because in certain cases (such as between Gray and Walpole) it is definitely more, but also because there is no such thing as the "simple friendship" the phrase implies. Friendship can be animated by many things, including rivalry, jealousy, desire and love. (*Men in Love*, 5)

All of these become part of the tortured bonds between de Haldimar and Wacousta, bonds which drive almost all the action of the novel.[10] This is clearly much more than could ever be circumscribed by a phrase such as "simple friendship."

The emotions between de Haldimar and Wacousta contradict rather than enable colonization. The distinction between this intimacy and the fraternity of the officers suggests an opposition between the surprising attachment between the two men and the sustaining homosociality of the military operation. In both *Patterns of Isolation* and *Sex and Violence in the Canadian Novel*, John Moss explores homoerotic relations in *Wacousta* and comes to the assumption that they are part of "the landscape of a troubled dream."[11] Moss notes that "homosexuality, of course, is anathema to the integrative principles of generation"[12] and therefore considers it to be a contribution to the chaos and disintegration in the novel. In *A World under Sentence: John Richardson and the Interior*, Dennis Duffy confronts Moss and replies that the belief that male-male love implies some psychic crisis is mistaken: "Any military unit maintaining high morale and professional standards inevitably involves homoerotic bonding between its members. . . . That was recognized long before Walt Whitman and Wilfred Owen wrote of it."[13] Duffy later makes the point still more emphatically, noting that "this is ultimately what love between military men is about. The (homo)eroticism is not some 'perverse' by-product of a system but the force driving it. Mars revels in the boudoir of Venus in order to renew his energies for the wars to come" (33).

According to Duffy the individual erotic relationship between soldiers is but a part of the collective eros of the military organization. Whitman is a useful reference as someone who was writing in North America in the period just after *Wacousta*, but the most developed contemporary commentary on male friendship in the nineteenth century is probably that found in the philosophy of Whitman's sometime disciple, Edward Carpenter. I am not claiming a uniformity throughout the century and between North America and Britain. However, there are interesting similarities in Richardson, Whitman, and Carpenter that might inform my understanding of their various representations, especially of the bonds found in an idealized military relationship. While I would not state that they are all one, their views of comradeship seem within the historical development of one broad discursive field, to use Foucault's term. Haggerty provides subtle distinctions for these glimpses of coherence in his overview of the eighteenth century: "These are male relations of a kind that, 'gay and graceful' as they are, begin to suggest the male sensibility that later in the next century would begin to cohere, not in the figure of the 'homosexual' as Mowl and other twentieth-century critics caricature him but rather in the writings of Carpenter, Symonds, Wilde, and Forster" (172).[14]

Carpenter's most popular work, *Towards Democracy* (1883), offers a number of effusive poetic descriptions of the ideals of comradeship. In

"Into the Regions of the Sun" he makes a reference to the specifically homosexual legion from Thebes so honored in gay history: "the life-long faithful comradeship now springing on all sides, the Theban band henceforth to overcome the world."[15] In "The Elder Soldier in the Brotherhood to the Younger" he anticipates Duffy in identifying comradeship in a one-to-one bond:

> Through love, faithful love and comradeship, at last emancipating the
> soul into that other realm (of freedom and joy) into which it is
> permitted to no mortal to enter—
> Thus to realise the indissoluble compact, to reveal form of humanity.
> To you, dear comrade, I transmit this charge—bequeathed also to me—
> In love remaining faithful to you, as now, never to change,
> Through all times and vicissitudes faithful faithful to you.[16]

As for many such writers in this period, the specifically sexual nature of Carpenter's ideal bond between men caused him a great deal of trauma. His pamphlet on what he called *Homogenic Love* led to a response from M. D. O'Brien in another pamphlet, *Socialism and Infamy:* "Embrace and Endearment between men. . . . The very thought of such effeminate practice fills one with loathing."[17] And yet, as Whitman and others had shown, "embrace and endearment," as long as it stopped short of the overtly sexual, was a popular ideal for many. As Duffy suggests, it provided the Venus charge for Mars.

The romantic relationship between Wacousta and de Haldimar is based on difference, as in the relationship between Clive and Maurice which the Dean attempts to disrupt in Forster's *Maurice:* "Mr. Cornwallis always suspected such friendships. It was not natural that men of different characters and tastes should be intimate. . . ."[18] It is tempting to see a similar intimation of sexuality in the "unnatural union" between Wacousta and de Haldimar, although there is no specific support for this reading of the novel, and the "unnatural" seems only a reflection of their opposing characters. In *Maurice,* Cornwallis offers the common assumption that homosexual love overcomes the lack of gender difference by eroticizing other differences, such as class. As Whitman says in "I am He That Aches With Love," "I pick out some low person for my dearest friend, / He shall be lawless, rude illiterate, he shall be / One condemned by others for deeds done" (quoted in Rowbotham and Weeks, *Socialism and the New Life,* 34). In the case of de Haldimar there is also a hidden ethnicity. His name and character suggest the aristocratic Norman Englishman, while Wacousta is clearly one of the Celts often depicted in the eighteenth and nineteenth centuries as Britain's resident savages; his Cornish wildness is frequently emphasized.

Of course both Carpenter and Whitman were specifically attracted to a homoerotic comradeship that crossed class barriers, but *Wacousta* consistently accepts division by class. Reginald Morton the younger, Wacousta's nephew who is executed by de Haldimar toward the beginning of the narrative, is troubled by the necessity of assuming a lower class to become a common soldier. The death of Murphy and rumors of the death of Frederick de Haldimar, de Haldimar's son, lead to a comparison of the feelings of their fellow officers. The description of Murphy has an ethnic element, but the implication is that "Irish" is more class than country and that it is this which makes him less worthy of affection:

> Murphy—a rude, vulgar, and illiterate, though brave Irishman—having risen from the ranks, the coarseness of which he had never been able to shake off, was little calculated, either by habits or education, to awaken feelings, except of the most ordinary description, in his favour; and he and Ensign Delme were the only exceptions to those disinterested and tacit friendships that had grown up out of circumstances in common among the majority. If, therefore, they could regret the loss of such a companion as Murphy, how deep and heartfelt must have been the sorrow they experienced when they beheld the brave, generous, manly, amiable, and highly talented Frederick de Haldimar—the pride of the garrison, and the idol of his family. (53)

Thus in this novel class precludes the friendships based on sensitivity and emotion. One of the few instances where an appropriate sentimentality surfaces from the common men is after the execution of the younger Morton: "large tears coursing each other over the furrowed cheeks of some of our oldest soldiers" (214).

Yet there is another instance where the situation of comradeship causes a transposition of male-male relations, in this case where a military connection becomes not homoerotic love but explicitly paternal, within certain limitations, when Charles de Haldimar is once more wallowing in despair: "Old Morrison shed tears also; for his heart bled for the sufferings of one whom he had nursed and played with even in infancy, and whom, although his master, he regarded with the affection he would have borne to his own child" (103). Morrison transforms the role of soldier into the stereotype of the aged and devoted nurse, perhaps best known from *Romeo and Juliet*. Whitman had acclaimed a homoerotic relation across class but Richardson seems to reject this. Instead Richardson offers as a same-sex relation acceptable across military class that which imitates the pseudomaternal relation that lingers from the nursery. Otherwise the homoerotic affection must be between peers and thus is apparently unavailable to the rough-hewn Murphy.

According to Moss, the relationship between Wacousta and de Haldimar is part of "trisexuality," a bond between two men and a woman.[19] The attraction Wacousta felt for Clara, his "child of nature," is a constant reference in the novel. He says to her daughter,

> "oh, what a feeble word is love to express the concentration of mighty feelings that flowed like burning lava through my veins! Who shall pretend to give a name to the emotion that ran thrillingly—madly through my excited frame, when I first gazed on her, who, in every attribute of womanly beauty, realized all my fondest fancy ever painted?" (455)

There seems no question of Wacousta's ardent heterosexual desire here but it is interesting how, just a few lines later, he describes the imperative that drew him to climb various cliffs and precipices where his life hung in the balance: "it was the strong necessity I felt of pouring into some devoted bosom the overflowing fulness of my heart, that made me court in solitude those positions of danger with which the image of woman was ever associated" (455).

Wacousta seems to have been interested less in a person than in some general receptacle for "overflowing fulness." The emphasis is not a potential subject that might respond but rather an object to mirror. Wacousta seeks the "image of woman," preferably with a devoted bosom. This is appropriate to the portrayal of women throughout the novel. The Native woman Oucanasta goes through all the usual games of the stereotypical Indian maid, including cross-dressing as a warrior. Ellen Halloway, the wife of Wacousta's nephew in his disguise as the common soldier Frank Halloway, and later Wacousta's own companion, is similarly proverbial. She is forced to dress as the drummer boy of folklore to follow her husband and then later to live in the woods with Wacousta. In one passage she enables the novel to qualify as a literal bodice-ripper:

Her long fair hair, that had hitherto been hid under the coarse mob-cap, usually worn by the wives of the soldiers, was now divested of all fastening, and lay shadowing a white and polished bosom, which, in her violent struggles to detain the governor, had burst from its rude but modest confinement, and was now displayed in all the dazzling delicacy of youth and sex. (121)

She plays Cassandra in her prophecy of doom for the de Haldimars and is the final sacrifice of the narrative in the last sentence of the novel: "As for poor Ellen Halloway, search had been made for her, but she never was heard of afterwards" (543). Young Clara and her cousin Madeline are constantly represented as fainting flowers, most useful as objects of white desire or Native violence. But the elder Clara is the most extreme example. She seems little more than a vapor, at first Wacousta's muse and then the thing stolen by de Haldimar. Regardless of Wacousta's devotion and the attractions she apparently held for de Haldimar, her representation offers little justification. The circumlocution in Wacousta's comment to Clara about his response to her mother's death is a good example:

"A change now came over the spirit of my vengeance; for about this period your mother died. I had never ceased to love, even while I despised her; and notwithstanding, had she, after her flagrant inconstancy, thrown herself into my arms, I should have rejected her with scorn, still I was sensible no other woman could ever supply her place in my affection. She was, in truth, the only being I had ever looked upon with fondness; and deeply even as I had been injured by her, I wept her memory with many a scalding tear. This, however, only increased my hatred for him who had rioted in her beauty, and supplanted me in her devotedness." (494–95)

The love is a plot device; the hatred is a visceral necessity.

I do not mean to imply that a more vital heterosexuality is not visible in the novel. The relationship between the younger Reginald Morton and Ellen has the star-crossed energy of any of the famous lovers of history. Morton recalls the reason for his fall in class and ultimately for his death: "A marriage of affection—a marriage with one who had nothing but her own virtues and her own beauty to recommend her, drew upon me the displeasure of my family, and the little I possessed, independently of the pleasure of my relations, was soon dissipated" (78). At the moment of his death the dominant image is Ellen's fervent devotion. It seems appropriate that it is in her passionate support for her husband that her breasts are revealed. The combination of both the memory of her husband's death and her extravagantly emotional response is again and again the reason for outpourings by the various sentimental heroes of the novel.

Many critics see Colonel de Haldimar as the antithesis of the various sentimental men of the novel. De Haldimar is rather the logic-bound emissary of relentless duty. Mathews sees the center of the novel provided by de Haldimar as the expression of invasion: "De Haldimar can be seen in the dialectic of the novel as the figure who embodies the thesis—the expression of the 'reasonable' power, the status quo, in the disputed territory where the Indian people must give way to white authority" (*Canadian Literature*, 14). Duffy gives the slightly more psychological interpretation that Richardson "views the colonel as a person ground by the interplay of selfhood and system" (*A World under Sentence*, 30). Yet there are a few glimmers of feeling. Apparently he had felt at least some passion for Clara, which Wacousta recalls: "it has often occurred to me since, although I did not remark it at the time, that while his voice and manner were calm, there was a burning glow upon his handsome cheek, and a suppressed exultation in his eye, that I had never observed on either before" (486).

In *Between Men*, Sedgwick explores the quality Moss labels as trisexuality, but her template is the erotic triangle of René Girard. She notes, "Girard finds many examples in which the choice of the beloved is determined in the first place, not by the qualities of the beloved, but by the beloved's already being the choice of the person who has been chosen as a rival. In fact, Girard seems to see the bond between rivals in an erotic triangle as being even stronger, more heavily determinant of actions and choices, than anything in the bond between either of the lovers and the beloved."[20] Thus it fits that de Haldimar's passion for Clara seems a construction rather than an emanation of his character. There is nothing in the representation of de Haldimar to suggest that his emotional repertoire includes "exultation," even in a "suppressed" form. This is very unlike Wacousta's hatred for de Haldimar, which is a felt presence everywhere. Wacousta replies to Captain de Haldimar that "hell does not supply a feeling half so bitter as my enmity to your proud father" (269). Wacousta sees his passion as reaching the metaphysical: "even now I think I see him withering, if heart so hard can wither, beneath this proof of my undying hate" (270).

The gothic extremes of Wacousta's feelings lead to an ultimate misanthropy, expressed when he tells Clara of how he eluded the soldiers after the false accusations against him by her father and mother:

> "Accustomed, however, as I had ever been, to rocks and fastnesses, I had no difficulty in eluding the vigilance of those who were sent in pursuit of me, and thus compelled to live wholly apart from my species, I at length learned to hate them, and to know that man is the only enemy of man upon earth." (494)

Wacousta focuses this hate on one man, but after Clara's death he decides not to kill de Haldimar: "I no longer sought his life; for the jealousy that had half impelled that thirst existed no longer: but, deeming his cold nature at least accessible through his parental affection, I was resolved that in his children he should suffer a portion of the agonies he had inflicted on me" (495). There are many possible interpretations of this triangle, and a number of them are visible in the critics already mentioned. Here I wish to concentrate on what I see as the way the homoerotic operates in the light of various social constructions. The relationships between Clara and Wacousta and between Clara and de Haldimar seem plot devices rather than reflections of character, assuming there is a character to Clara. That between Wacousta and de Haldimar begins as "unnatural," but it is a perversion of nature that supports the comradeship of the army. Then it is broken by de Haldimar and the scene moves to Canada.

Regardless of the emotional motivation of these actions, they have a number of symbolic effects. Wacousta becomes the ultimate romantic individual, ruled completely by passion. De Haldimar becomes an agent of socialization, but in two directions. He is the authority of government in the wilderness but he is also the father of the family. It is interesting that he is a central foe in both positions for Wacousta, and in the above quotation his value as father is the direct focus of Wacousta's attack.

Carpenter, in his chapter on "The Homogenic Attachment" in *The Intermediate Sex*, suggests the social value of same-sex love: "It certainly does not seem impossible to suppose that as the ordinary love has a special function in the propagation of the race, so the other has its special function in social and heroic work, and in the generation—not of bodily children—but of those children of the mind, the philosophical conceptions and ideals which transform our lives and those of society."[21]

Carpenter quotes from Symonds's *A Problem in Greek Ethics* on such attachment in the Greek military: "unions between man and man no less firm than that of marriage. On such connections a wise captain would have relied for giving strength to his battalions, and for keeping alive the flames of enterprise and daring."[22] Carpenter sees this embodied in the story of Harmodius: "it is difficult to believe that anything can supply the force and liberate the energies required for social and mental activities of the most necessary kind so well as a comrade-union which yet leaves the two lovers free from the responsibilities and impedimenta of family life."[23]

Many aspects of the Wacousta triangle interfere with Carpenter's portrait of the ideal comrade-union. De Haldimar chooses to break the homoerotic bond with Wacousta in order to establish a traditional heterosexual unit of the family. The situation somewhat resembles that described when Carpenter's lover Andrew Beck decided to abandon him for respectable married life:

> The letter in which Beck severed the relationship was more dramatic in its denial of the romance and poetry between them and indicates the strength of masculine bourgeois culture when it came to claim its own:
> I looked at the rising moon unmoved. I wad my mental ears against all manner of sentiments—I will not allow myself to cry out or ache inwardly at any sorrow or any injustice. I systematically train myself into a consistent brutality. I'm utterly changed, it is all the reaction from you. (Rowbotham and Weeks, *Socialism and the New Life*, 33)

Beck's belief that the move to heterosexuality removed sentiment and produced brutality is an interesting comment on both de Haldimar and Wacousta. In the former it produces a rejection of sentiment and a repressed brutality. In Wacousta, however, it produces an excess of sentiment and an unrestrained brutality.

When de Haldimar transposes his family to the garrison, heterosexuality and military repression do not conform. As Carpenter might seem to imply, "the propagation of the race" and the army are not a good mix. The values of governor and family man are in constant conflict. Again and again his children are endangered and Colonel de Haldimar must choose whether he is first a parent or an officer, whether the man at risk is his soldier or his son. Unlike the paternal moment of Old Morrison, in which the imitation of parenting supports the homosociality of the army, de Haldimar's actual fatherhood conflicts with military values. It should be no wonder that his only choice is to become even more repressed and oppressive than before.

The union between de Haldimar and Wacousta may have been "unnatural" but it was of significant value in terms of comradeship. De Haldimar's actions to break the homoerotic link might seem part of the repression of the military but they work in opposition to its viability. They make a complement into an opposition, as each reverts to type: de Haldimar a bloodless figure like Beck, and Wacousta a representation of vengeful hatred without restraint, the unspeakable monster so common in gothic fiction. Just as de Haldimar's character makes Wacousta more and more angry, Wacousta's raucous individualism convinces de Haldimar of the impossibility of freedom and the necessity of tyrannical rather than comradely leadership. Instead of the force for social good envisaged by Carpenter, they become two powers who create enormous destruction in the colony.

Another male friendship that is emphasized in the novel is that between Sir Everard Valletort and the young Clara's brother, Charles de Haldimar. The degree of the affection between them is suggested by yet another of Richardson's typical circumlocutory descriptions: this one of the first encounter between Charles and Sir Everard after an event that seemed to have produced the death of the young Clara's other brother, Frederick:

> We shall not attempt to paint all that passed between the friends during the first interesting moments of an interview which neither had expected to enjoy again, or the delight and satisfaction with which they congratulated themselves on the futility of those fears which, if realized, must have embittered every future moment of their lives with the most harrowing recollections. (106)

Both characters are presented as men of unusual sensitivity, displayed even in their physical appearance: "Never had Charles de Haldimar appeared so eminently handsome; and yet his beauty resembled that of a frail and delicate woman, rather than that of one called to the manly and arduous profession of a soldier" (107). Charles's tears on his contemplation of the death of Frank Halloway startle his colleague Blessington:

> "For God's sake, check this weakness! There are men observing you on every side, and your strange manner has already been the subject of remark in the company."

"When the heart is sick, like mine," replied the youth, in a tone of fearful despondency, "it is alike reckless of forms, and careless of appearances." (210)

Blessington cannot be convinced: "this immoderate grief is wrong—it is unmanly and should be repressed" (215). When Charles gets still more upset, however, Blessington becomes more gentle: "Friendship and interest in your deep affliction of spirit alone brought me here—the same feelings prompted my remark" (216).

The eros here is very much that defined by Haggerty but so is the confusion. Haggerty traces this in the novel of sensibility. He sees an important tension where at first the tear is the eruption of eros into polite society and yet later becomes molded into the absence of eros:

> For the man or, in a very different way, the woman of feeling a sigh, a tear, the touch of a pulse, or the distribution of a charitable coin can carry with it an unmistakably erotic charge, and each of them becomes, in various circumstances, the carefully articulated substitute for sexual activity. By considering the language in which physical and emotional problems are expressed and by relating that "expression" to the larger concern of ideological appropriation, by which language is marked, gestures are coded, and feelings are mediated, I will show how sensibility shifted from a liberating and potentially radical social force to a threateningly repressed and repressive system of control. (*Men in Love*, 82)

Haggerty's comment is precisely applicable to *Wacousta*. The liberating friendship of Reginald Morton meets a threateningly repressed and heterosexualized de Haldimar. The result is the terrifying anger of Wacousta, the emotional problems created by de Haldimar's repression.

Blessington fears the potential dangers of such a man of feeling, dangers already realized in Wacousta. As Haggerty says, in what could be a diagnosis of the young Charles: "Sensibility is the fissure in the bourgeois ideology that emerges in the late eighteenth century. As sensibility's influence became more pervasive, 'sensibility' itself became a 'symptom' of nervous disorders of various kind" (*Men in Love*, 83). But Blessington is also responding to something that might be called display, and he is concerned not just with what it says about de Haldimar but also with what it might mean to observers. Thus it suits one of Haggerty's comments about theater: "A gestic moment of male-male love could bring together the forces of theatrical representation in order to make the sodomite visible to a culture that both celebrates heroic friendship and sees male-male love as monstrous" (37). In this case, presumably Richard-son has no wish to make the sodomite visible but Blessington certainly exhibits the conflicted response of someone who fears the effeminate sodomite but wishes to worship at the altar of the hero of sensibility.

The various delicacies associated with Charles are a reinforcement for another triangular relationship established through Valletort's devo-tion to the as-yet-unseen Clara: "Sir Everard suffered his imagination to draw on the brother for those attributes he ascribed to the sister" (107). Thus in this case the erotic triangle, because one side represents two siblings, maintains the homoerotic within the sanctioned heterosexual and seems to be positive for both society and the military. Carpenter was very clear that homogenic love must not be a jealous love, and that it must especially not be jealous of the heterosexual relations that soci-ety might require.

When Wacousta says to Clara that his revenge is at hand, he claims, "In no other country in the world—under no other circumstances than the present—could I have so secured it" (491). At one level this is sim-ply a statement about the gothic opportunities of the wilderness, the reason why the setting and the gothic romance seem such a perfect combination. But Wacousta is also noting the particular time and place of colonization. He himself, as a "white Indian," has found the space for passion that was impossible in Britain. And while Wacousta appears alien to all socialization, Pontiac's speeches show that a space can be found for him in Native civilization. Similarly, de Haldimar's repression, which might have been functional in Britain, is here a source of doom.

The complexities of this relation are well beyond this brief essay, but Lane's study offers some possible suggestions. He examines some of the common arguments that sexual energy was the force behind imperial-ism and offers a modification in "the failure of self-mastery, the insuffi-ciency and overabundance of drives to colonial sublimation" (*The Rul-ing Passion*, 2). This seems applicable to both Wacousta and de Haldimar, from quite different directions. Wacousta has rejected self-mastery to become a white Indian, the colonizer so beyond colonial sublimation that he is now an active force against colonization. Whatever his sexual-ity, his sexual drive and de Haldimar's thwarting of that drive provide the energy for his anticolonialism. De Haldimar, abandoning Wacousta, stealing Clara, caught between fatherhood and commanding the garri-son, has made much more obvious efforts to control his destiny within various dimensions of the law of the father, in marriage, in parenting, in the military. But in the end his offenses against his homoerotic relationship with Wacousta and his inability to subdue the indigenous cultures reveal the limits of all these controls.

The most obvious homosocial necessity that colonialism creates in *Wacousta* is simply the garrison itself. Military environments are a cliché of narratives of same-sex desire, as are boarding schools and prisons. At the beginning of the novel, the description of Murphy's death seems to reflect this. To follow such an argument, the appearance of the elder Clara in Scotland and then later the arrival of the younger Clara and Madelaine at the fort provide a heterosexual intrusion in the "natural" homosocial environment. The latter two also create a still larger question of family, following that already established by the Colonel and his sons. One might argue that they intrude the colonial, the family of settlement, into the homosocial environment of imperial adventure.

Imperial adventure, of course, does not seem as much of a romp as it used to be, now that it is generally recognized to be a gloss on the harsh reality of invasion. As the imperialist was adventuring, another race was being invaded. Young gives extensive detail to the dynamics of sexuality and race in the mid-nineteenth century, a time only a few years after Richardson's novel was published. Young's observations raise particularly interesting questions about the delicacy of the treatment of the Indian maiden figure, Oucanasta. The other soldiers tease Frederick about her potential as a paramour and, like Ellen, her bosom is in one instance exposed. There is no question that she is a sexual object, but there is also no question that her attractions are not pursued by the officers. And her brother is never given the slightest erotic flavor. The other Native males raise only the usual specter of the sexual predator.

In both the triangles discussed above, however, the homosocial triangle, which I claim to be homoerotic, emphasizes a particular sameness. Reginald Morton's Cornishness, like Clara's Scottishness, offers a variation, and thus both love objects express some difference from de Haldimar, but in both cases there is no suggestion that this variation in British ethnicity is an important distinction, unlike the class associated with the Irish Murphy. As Young suggests, in this period in which the empire was exploding, race was a highly vexed issue, as was the danger of miscegenation.[24] Thus the foundational homosocial couple, Wacousta and de Haldimar, are of the same race, with no comment on the racial difference that one might expect to be the definition of the European invasion and yet provide the extreme oppositions of imperialism. De Haldimar has absolute belief in military rule while Wacousta escapes all vestiges of British civilization. Their romantic failure happens in Britain but the plot is played out in Canada. And de Haldimar goes so far as to bring his children, to intrude the rule of the father in still another sense. The tension is that noted by Young: "an unremitting dread of external defiance *and* internal unmaking propelled Britain's drive for global mastery" (*Colonial Desire*, 16).

The terms used by Young seem to be directly reflected in Dickinson's creative blend of Northrop Frye and Diana Fuss's comments in *Inside/ Out:*

> Fuss's description of homosexuality's necessarily oppositional status in relation to the "compulsory" regime of heterosexuality would seem to apply equally well to the structures of exclusion and interiorization at work in the Canadian "garrison mentality": "an outside which is inside interiority making the articulation of the latter possible, a transgression of the border which is necessary to constitute the border as such." (*Here Is Queer*, 37)

Wacousta represents the potential dangers of both the white Indian and sexuality, particularly in the tradition of sodomy, a sexual deviance that offends the natural order of the state. Besides his homoerotic tension with de Haldimar, at various times he is suggested as a sexual threat to Ellen, his nephew's niece, and to the younger Clara. He seems able to enter the garrison at will, in spite of all the efforts the military makes to keep him out. This intrusion into the garrison is a transgression in the senses of both Frye and Fuss. The terror he might cause de Haldimar the father, de Haldimar the widower, and de Haldimar the commander of the garrison is multiple. And yet if Mathews is correct and the novel calls for a balance between the rigid British civilization offered by de Haldimar and the rampant American individualism offered by Wacousta, then presumably the only answer is exactly Fuss's "outside which is inside interiority." As the wilderness is the threat that necessitates but also indigenizes the garrison, which produces the new world through overcoming the palisades, so the sexual undercurrent disrupts the normative palisades of the heterosexual family.

But at the conclusion of the novel, all the complications are erased, in a quite bold manner. Most of the central characters are dead and we are left with a happy settlement in which Captain de Haldimar's daughters are taught by the apparently celibate but attentive Oucanasta, while Oucanasta's brother trains his sons. If there is a suggestion of miscegenation in the next generation resulting from this obvious gender division, it is well hidden. Rather, any possibility of miscegenation seems nicely displaced through an indigenizing pedagogy. All the dangers of colonization, military obsession, and the white savage, and of a homoerotic conflict with heterosexuality, seem gone in a happily biracial settlement of the new Canada. The rules of Europe were invaded by the id of Europe, but now all those alien tensions have quietly departed and pleasant little Canada remains.

Not that Europe had brought anything that should be labeled "homosexuality" in the novel. All of the male relations are constructed according to that ideal of male friendship that Wacousta esteems as sacred. They live in the idealized world noted by Sedgwick in her study of Melville's *Billy Budd*, where homosociality and the homoerotic are not tainted by homophobia.[25] There is a fear of feminine qualities disrupting the idealized image of soldierly masculinity, and perhaps the sodomite lurks in the wings, as Haggerty suggests, but the homoerotic is a quality that supports rather than interferes with male-male relations. It is also something that need not interrupt heterosexual systems if appropriate balances are maintained. The eros of Valletort and Charles provides the hope of the future, but the heterosexual disruption of that eros between Colonel de Haldimar and Wacousta almost destroys the colony. At this stage, before the homosexual—and before Canada—the potential of homoeroticism remains a positive value but with possible dangers.

It is also more complicated than that. In his conclusion Haggerty states,

> Men have never been allowed to love one another, however, even in studies of the history of sexuality, and it is worth considering the implications of that love before charging it with the abuses of patriarchy. Usually this suppressed and unacknowledged love between men is euphemized as heroic friendship or domesticated as spiritually meaningful; denounced as sodomy or dismissed as paederasty. (*Men in Love*, 173)

But of course the homoerotic homosocial of the garrison is the essence of the "patriarchy," a male bonding that enabled the invasion of the Americas. Still, the thwarted love of Wacousta and de Haldimar represents the danger when these men of sensibility allow the feelings to overwhelm, the problem of which Blessington is all too well aware. And it is telling that the eruption of feeling is played out in the liminal realm of the colony, in the ultimately liminal moment of the garrison. The soldiers of the garrison should have searched a bit harder for "poor Ellen Halloway" if they had hoped for their happy homosocial world to continue. Her prophecy of family disruption was a good assessment of the future of Canadian fiction.

Notes

1. John Richardson, *Wacousta or, The Prophecy: A Tale of the Canadas*, ed. Douglas Cronk (1832; Ottawa: Carleton University Press, 1987). Page references in the text are to this edition.

2. Gaile McGregor, *The Wacousta Syndrome: Explorations in the Canadian Landscape* (Toronto: University of Toronto Press, 1985).

3. Robin Mathews, *Canadian Literature: Surrender or Revolution* (Toronto: Steel Rail, 1978), 13.

4. Peter Dickinson, *Here Is Queer: Nationalisms, Sexualities, and the Literatures of Canada* (Toronto: University of Toronto Press, 1999).

5. Robert J. C. Young, *Colonial Desire: Hybridity in Theory, Culture, and Race* (London: Routledge, 1995).

6. Christopher Lane, *The Ruling Passion: British Colonial Allegory and the Paradox of Homosexual Desire* (Durham: Duke University Press, 1995).

7. The term "barrenless," which was changed to "barren" in later editions, no doubt seems an absurd tautology but it also represents the overreaching emphasis of gothic emotion.

8. Eve Kosofsky Sedgwick, *Between Men: English Literature and Male Homosocial Desire* (New York: Columbia University Press, 1985), 1–2.

9. George E. Haggerty, *Men in Love: Masculinity and Sexuality in the Eighteenth Century* (New York: Columbia University Press, 1999), 5.

10. At least in the case of rivalry these bonds provided the very nexus of the invasion of the Americas, as mercantile, political, and military alliances formed and divided ad nauseam.

11. John Moss, *Patterns of Isolation* (Toronto: McClelland and Stewart, 1974), 50.

12. John Moss, *Sex and Violence in the Canadian Novel: The Ancestral Present* (Toronto: McClelland and Stewart, 1977), 86.

13. Dennis Duffy, *A World under Sentence: John Richardson and the Interior* (Toronto: ECW Press, 1996), 30.

14. Yet of course there are still greater continuities, although scholars such as Haggerty might find them ahistorical. In a recent interview, the British gay activist Peter Tatchell said, "Carpenter was a far-sighted visionary who makes many of today's lesbian and gay rights campaigners look very conservative and un-ambitious. His agenda was way beyond mere equality and civil rights. Carpenter wanted what we would now call queer emancipation." Jack Nichols, "Peter Tatchell: Outrage! In Action," *GayToday.* www.gaytoday.badpuppy.com/interview (2 February 2000).

15. Edward Carpenter, *Towards Democracy* (London: George Allen and Unwin, 1905), 279.

16. Ibid., 278.

17. Sheila Rowbotham and Jeffrey Weeks, *Socialism and the New Life: The Personal and Sexual Politics of Edward Carpenter and Havelock Ellis* (London: Pluto Press, 1977), 89.

18. E. M. Forster, *Maurice* (London: Penguin Books, 1972), 75.

19. While Dickinson does not refer to Moss at all, he briefly notes that *Wacousta* "has striking resonances with Sedgwick's thesis of the triangulation of male homosocial desire" (14). I develop this argument below.

20. Sedgwick, *Between Men*, 21.

21. Edward Carpenter, *The Intermediate Sex: A Study of Some Transitional Types of Men and Women* (London: George Allen and Unwin, 1908), 70.

22. Ibid., 71.

23. Ibid., 74. In his Ph.D. dissertation, "Into the Fire: Masculinities and Militarism in Timothy Findley's *The Wars*" (York University, 1997), Thomas Hastings labels the military leaders as "the fathers" and suggests that Findley's novel shows phallic patriarchy destroying "the sons." *Wacousta* could be read in a similar way although there seems a very specific conflict between de Haldimar as father and de Haldimar as "law of the father" for his troops. He has contradictory socializations, while Wacousta has rejected all socializations.

24. Young points out that the word "miscegenation" was coined after the publication date of Richardson's novel. As he explains, in the early nineteenth century the "problem" of racial mixing was becoming sufficiently perplexing to require this neologism.

25. Eve Kosofsky Sedgwick, *Epistemology of the Closet* (Berkeley: University of California Press, 1990), 91–130.

Part II
Queering the New Imperialism

CHAPTER FOUR

Lingering Pleasures, Perverted Texts: Colonial Desire in Kipling's Anglo-India

Anjali Arondekar

With the arrival of Rudyard Kipling, the Anglo-Indian story of the British empire takes on a new cast. Andrew Lang, one of the foremost literary critics of the 1890s, writes: "Mr. Kipling makes us regard the continent [India] which was a bore as an enchanted land, full of marvels and magic which are real."[1] S. R. Crockett remarked, in 1895, that the "pre-Kipling generation had only to glimpse the word 'Indian' at the head of an article, or upon the title of a book, to retreat with a boredom that verged upon disgust."[2] Even Kipling's toughest critics, such as Robert Buchanan, who identified him with "the voice of a hooligan," acknowledged grudgingly that under Kipling's tutelage India's usefulness as imaginative capital had been recuperated; India had again become a site of pleasurable literary production: "Mr. Kipling's little Kodak-glimpses, therefore, seemed unusually fresh and new... and in the background of them we perceived... the shadow of the great and wonderful national life of India."[3] From boredom and disgust to freshness and marvel, Kipling's fiction is heralded for inaugurating a new range of narrative relationships with Anglo-India.

Further accolades for Kipling come from critics like the popular novelist Gilbert Frankau, who extolled Kipling for a second unusual characteristic: his ability to do a man's work narratively, not to be, as Frankau argued, "women-ridden" in his subject matter and narrative style.[4] In Lang's words, Kipling's was "more of a man's book, than a woman's."[5] To be "women-ridden," Kipling's critics and reviewers repeatedly claimed, is to hinder the true tales of empire by obstructing the flow of masculine representations with an extensive interest in female characters and emotions. Consequently, women need to be simply flattened out, reduced to one-dimensional characters who act as aesthetic foils to the machinations of the men in empire. As one critic said dismissively of the women characters in Kipling's Anglo-India: "Who remembers her? . . . the women are as if they had never been."[6] The critics thus acknowledge the absence of developed female characters but at the same time suggest that the success of Kipling's imaginative structures depends on precisely such an absence. In place of "women-ridden" fiction, we have instead stories about men, such as that of the "Three Musketeers," which an anonymous critic in 1890 described as pertaining to "three private soldiers of the Indian army, linked together by a close and romantic friendship, different as are their races and characters."[7] Virginia Woolf recalls just such a reading experience of Kipling's fiction and describes his fictional landscape as a blissful "world of men"; not a dispassionate, detached world, but a world so permeated with intense masculine emotion that it seemed incomprehensible to women readers: "one blushes at all these capital letters as if one has been caught eavesdropping at some purely masculine orgy."[8]

Yet only few nineteenth-century reviewers, such as Francis Adams, choose to articulate the historical context in which such imaginative shifts are taking place. According to Adams, Kipling's transformative narratives of Anglo-Indian life must be read as a careful colonial reconstruction of the powerful events of the 1857 Indian Mutiny:

> The events of the year 1857 were crowning proof of this [Kipling's success]. In that year we simplified even these simpler theories [about foreign races] into the one simplest theory of all. "We gave 'em hell" to an extent that they have never forgotten, and Mr. Kipling smiles cunningly over the still active native prejudice against being blown away from the mouths of cannons. The foolish person in search of a little disinterested information about things may find the so-called Indian Mutiny an unexplained historical phenomenon. He will get little or no information from Mr. Kipling.[9]

For Adams, Kipling's omission of any references to the 1857 Indian Mutiny is crucial to the story of his success. It is only when sites of such imaginative unrest as the Indian Mutiny are controlled in an altered vision of the landscape, Adams argues, that any comfortable narrative relationship with India can be established. More than a century later, Teresa Hubel writes on the multiple inscriptions of the Indian empire and further clarifies the importance of such imaginative shifts. Hubel argues that such deliberate historical lacunae in colonial narratives are critical to Britain's ownership of India, whereby the "imperialist connotations traditionally implicit in the word 'own' are furthered by the broadening of the epistemic boundaries of India: the potential for appropriating India increases when it is recognized as the [safe] property of the imagination."[10] Kipling's extensive knowledge of and literary monopoly over the Indian landscape provides the perfect backdrop for Britain's economic dominance of the subcontinent, muting as it were the echoes of a disturbed colonial history. Even George Orwell, an avowed Kipling critic, invokes this powerful trope of ownership and admits that "tawdry and shallow though it is, Kipling's is the only literary picture we possess of nineteenth-century Anglo-India."[11]

What Kipling sees and translates, what makes his stories sell, contemporary readers are thus told over and again, is his ability to translate India, to transform it from a space of imaginative boredom, "woman-riddenness," and historical terror to a space of communal enjoyment, masculine achievement, and national celebration. This essay is a story of that transformation. I will argue that the novelty of Kipling can be located in his ability to bridge the volatile gap between the colonial terror of the events of 1857 and a more popular language of colonial celebration. Such a novelty depends, I will suggest further, on a particular eroticized dynamics of narration whereby the rhetorical cohesion of the British empire is made not only plausible but also desirable. As a perfect example of what Susanne Howe in 1949 called "the newly washed face" of post-Mutiny fiction, Kipling refashions the colonial encounter, domesticating it into the facticities of everyday life, such that the confrontation and management of colonial terror becomes a source of extended male articulation—founding imperial presence rather than eradicating it. Kipling's narratives become harbingers of a new model of colonial masculinity, in which attachments between men are detoured through narratives, rather than through bodies. These are narratives into which the incoherencies of colonial rule are secreted as hauntings, as gestures contained by the paradoxical fullness of a defeated masculinity. Such narrative efforts, I demonstrate, uncover the slippages between the desired and feared, the colonizer and the colonized, foregrounding the contradictory efforts that serve as the warp and woof of imperial texts, binding their incoherencies or "perversions" into fictions that are constitutive of late-nineteenth-century efforts to represent India. In the readings that follow, I propose an understanding of Kipling's "perverse" narratives through three overlapping critical sites that must also be distinguished in historical, literary, and political terms. The first explores the role of self-exoticization in producing a new aesthetic model of English masculinity within a post-Mutiny atmosphere of brutal colonial terror. The second decodes the structure of this aesthetic model within Kipling's short stories in which male homosociality sustains and extends the mythology of empire through a precarious evacuation of its homoerotic content. The third links the success of Kipling's model of colonial masculinity to the careful management of his native women characters whose portrayals crucially enable the desirability of Kipling's narrative project.

Historical Incursions, Narrative Inversions

> The rhythm is coarse, and the facture by no means irreproachable; but to read it without emotion is impossible. *It is a man's work done for men;* and it puts before you the feeling of the Anglo-Indian for the Indian Empire in terms so single-hearted and so strong as to make you glory in the name of Briton and exult in the work your race has done.
>
> —W. E. Henley on Kipling in "The New Writer," 1890

The aesthetic production of Kipling's Anglo-Indian empire, as I have pointed out, is linked closely to the aestheticization of a new narrative of colonial masculinity. It is a narrative of a "man's work done for men" that evokes strong "emotion" and a renewed pride in Englishness and empire. For such a transformation to take place, the attachments to empire have to be reinvented, alongside the traditional images of masculinity. While earlier empire-adventure fiction had provided an image of the swashbuckling hero in colonial spaces, by the late Victorian period, with its changing and fraught imperial authority, such images did not have the same cultural purchase they did earlier in the century, as evinced by the references to boredom noted earlier. Not only had India to be re-exoticized but so also had models of English masculinity. Here I use the term "exotic" to provide a sense of something new, different, other, and what better way to realize this need for exoticization than to locate it in the English subject himself. It is thus not the machinations of the natives and their "exotic" customs that animate Kipling's imagination but rather the effects of empire on Englishmen. Ali Behdad brilliantly summarizes this tendency in his reading of "self-exoticization" in Kipling. For Behdad, this process of reinventing the colonial self is integral to the workings of empire, especially at a time when the "Other" no longer provides suitable locations of imaginative pleasure. To maintain what Behdad calls an "epistemic" hold over empire, one must continue to produce the colony as a site of continued regeneration, newness, and affect. Simultaneously, the men of empire also need to be constantly marked as distinct from their counterparts in the mother country, as a kind of representational playing field, if you will, on which Englishness as a characteristic can be measured, weathered, and reproduced. To cite Behdad:

> The desire for self-exoticism consists of both a mimetic code of identification with the exotic Other (i.e. "Thou art that") and a differential or negative mode of identification (i.e. "I am not the Other"—the Other being the "not-I"). The marginalized natives as photographic props mediate the colonizers' identity as "exotic"—the British colonizers wanting to look "different" from the British back home in England—while the colonizer's pensive gaze conveys an unexpected, even violent, flash of uncertainty that undermines his or her self-assured, confident pose.[12]

In this essay I want to use Behdad's notion of "self-exoticization" as a point of departure for my own analysis. Behdad argues that the desire for self-exoticization is always mediated through the split subject positions of the colonizer, a desire that unravels or unpacks only at the level of the unconscious, and in the cracks between the "mimetic code of identification" and a "negative mode of identification." What is potentially disruptive in this desire is its fracturing of the colonizer's identity. While I agree that there is a certain "transgressiveness" in these slippages that betray the colonizer's psychic anxiety, I am not entirely convinced such split mediations of subject positions are always necessarily unconscious. In fact, as I will demonstrate, it is precisely the salability of this anguished, tortured, and indeed constantly isolated colonial male subject that Kipling mines in his popular stories of Anglo-Indian life. Stephen Arata's insightful readings of Kipling's texts foreground the instrumentality of this notion of self-exoticization, contextualizing it more precisely within the growing fears around degeneration and atavism. Arata suggests that Kipling's breed of exotic Englishmen produces a much-needed new model of Britons:

> The Anglo-Indian became the type of this new, reinvigorated Briton.... Part of the developing myth of Anglo-India to rule was that the work of empire attracted the sturdiest of domestic stock, leaving only the dregs behind.... Having emptied England of its best, Anglo-India could provide a space for the exercise and propagation of virtues which had been desiccated by modern life in the West. Anglo-India was what England had been.[13]

Fiction fuels the regeneration of a tired, debauched national spirit, and Kipling steps in with his new construction of Anglo-India, a place of hope and possibility where Britons regain their sense of moral purpose and propriety.

However, before moving to an analysis of Kipling's fiction, it is important to briefly review Britain's fraught political and economic relationship with India at the time of his early writings in the late 1880s. Mrinalini Sinha reminds us that, on the one hand, India was "the lynch pin of Britain's economic and political pre-eminence in the world. India served as a source of raw materials for British manufactures, and as a field for British overseas investments in agriculture, extractive industries, and in public works like the railways that had a guaranteed rate of profit."[14] On the other hand, the traumatic memory of the 1857 Mutiny still echoed within the British psyche as a savage and violent attack on English men, women, and children by India's barbaric native populace. The events of the mutiny had disrupted and derailed earlier notions of how the "natives" needed to be governed. Suddenly, as Jenny Sharpe suggests, the British found themselves without a script they could rely on.[15] Much later, in 1925, the English historian Edward Thompson would publish his powerful tract *The Other Side of the Medal,* an impassioned statement against British rule and for Indian independence. He would single out the Mutiny as the great symbolic event by which the two sides, Indian and British, defined their full and conscious opposition to each other. In his tract, he dramatically suggests that Indian and British history diverge most emphatically on representations of the Mutiny, reinforcing, through this opposition, the difference between the colonizer and the colonized.[16]

The foundation of an economically flourishing Indian empire thus coexisted precariously with the fracturing memories of the Indian Mutiny. Shailendre Dhari Singh's *Novels on the Indian Mutiny* points out that the impact of the Mutiny was so deep that there were over fifty Mutiny novels written in the thirty years following the event. Lewis Wurgaft's work on Kipling and the imperial imagination argues similarly that "although the political aspirations of the Mutineers were contained, the emotional meaning of their revolt was deeply ingrained in the imperial imagination of post-Mutiny India."[17] Accordingly, economic profits from the Indian colony were accompanied by a growing sense of unrest in England over the "India question." India was clearly "the jewel in the crown," but a jewel badly in need of a new setting. A different knowledge of India was sought by an anxious public, eager to restore the sense of imperial complacency that the Mutiny had shattered.

Men at Work: Kipling's Community of Male Readers

> I must seek out this reader (must "cruise" him) without knowing where he is. A site of bliss is then created. It is not the reader's "person" that is necessary to me, it is this site: the possibility of a dialectics of desire, of any unpredictability of bliss: the bets are not placed, there can still be a game.
>
> —Roland Barthes, *The Pleasure of the Text*

In a remarkable scene from "The House of Shadows," the first work of fiction by Kipling to appear in the *Civil and Military Gazette* in 1887, the male narrator describes the experience of being haunted by a male presence whom he can sense but cannot see, a presence he seeks but cannot find. "He," and "he must be a man" (247), we are told, enters the narrator's room every night, casts aside the dividing curtain or "*purdah,*" gazes at the narrator's prone and pliant body, and then retreats into the shadows. His face is never seen, his desires never known: "He will never face me and tell me what he wants." Yet his presence is palpable, his memory unforgettable. Kipling's narrator, bewitched and obsessed with the pursuit of this "he," can do little else but recognize that he "interferes sadly with one's work" (248). As the narrator finally admits in a gesture of acute self-consciousness and hope: "I believe now that if he dared he would come out from the other side of the *purdah* and peep over my shoulder to see what I am writing" (248).[18]

The liminal male presence—intimate but elusive and unsettling—that hovers over the body of this narrator's text, I want to argue, haunts most of Kipling's adult fiction. A crucial link is always made between the writing of a text and its recipient, collaborator, and/or source who, in most cases, is male. It is as if each of Kipling's narrators struggles with the burden of possibility, with the hope that somehow his narrative gesture will be the one to draw the elusive "he" out from the mysteries behind the purdah. The gesture of moving aside the veil to reveal the presence behind it is also a particularly gender-coded gesture. Within the Indian traditions of the *zenana* or harem, the chastity of the female is safeguarded against the gaze of the male, a prize that is only yielded to him as a sign of ultimate surrender. To see the desired object is to consume it. In the scene described above, this ritualized gesture is repeated, albeit between two men. Here, it is Kipling's narrator who takes on the role of the "oriental" female behind the purdah whose body/space/text is invaded by this male presence who gazes at him but does not permit the narrator to gaze back. Yet, by the end of the story, Kipling's narrator is no longer passive and suppliant. Instead, he wants desperately to return the gaze of his intruder.

It is this constitutive ambivalence of presence and absence that creates the very possibility of a Barthesian "dialectics of desire," of a game of pleasurable narrative hide and seek, of an addictive "site of bliss" that Kipling's narrators seem unable to give up. Indeed, in most of his stories the narrators go to great lengths to carefully elaborate the structural psychodynamics behind their individual acts of narration. Despite the cultural injunctions to silence on the subjects the narrators write about, they are still inexorably drawn to them; many of the prefaces to individual collections of short stories emphasize the enormity and danger behind the narrative task being undertaken. In the preface to "The Story of the Gadsbys," Kipling urges his readers to "remember that I wrote this story as an Awful Warning,"[19] a warning that will probably lose him the affection of his very dear friend, Captain Gadsby. The narrator of the collection *Life's Handicap* warns us that "the most remarkable stories are, of course, those which do not appear—for obvious reason,"[20] and the obvious reason, we are told, is that while these stories are true, "not one in twenty could be printed in an English book, because the English do not think as natives do" (*Life's Handicap*, xii). Other individual stories strike similarly alarming notes in terms of the nature of the narrative material they are covering. Even in "The End of the Passage," as Hummil dies, we are told, "in the staring eyes was written terror beyond the expression of any pen" (*Indian Tales*, 191). All we know is that Hummil "spoke in broken whispers for nearly ten minutes" (*Indian Tales*, 188), and that what he says is too harrowing for the reader's ears. In all of these narratives, it is the intrepid narrator who braves cultural obstacles, linguistic barriers, and his own profound fear of what he sees in order to bring home (as it were) the "plain tales" of the Raj. And in all of these narratives, new avatars of a failed, exhausted colonial masculinity are being created, as Englishmen retreat, surrender, and collapse under the pressures of the Raj. The stories are also carefully screened of their unspeakable horror, a horror that only the narrators can wholly see and decipher. Over and over again, the narrators return to scenes of terror and alienation, compelled into narrative by the sights they uncover.[21]

In her work on narrative obsession and its links to fetishism, Emily Apter connects such narrative structures to a particular kind of pleasurable preoccupation. For her,

> the literary psychodynamics of vision: the conceit of seeing . . . heightens erotic atmosphere by placing the reader-viewer at a distance (the suspense of image-suspension) or situating him or her at some transgressively hidden vantage point. The reader is a lonely voyeur, hunched over a keyhole, and the space that separates him or her from the spectacle correlates to the temporality of *lingering* on the way to a sexual aim . . . what Freud called perversion . . . and what Peter Brooks (glossing Freud) has described as the protracted forepleasure of narrative "clock-teasing." [emphasis added][22]

A footnote to the above passage further points us to the section "The Sexual Aberrations" in the *Three Essays on the Theory of Sexuality* (1905), in which Freud places the burden of perversity on the rather elusive notion of "lingering": "Perversions are sexual activities . . . which either (a) extend, in an anatomical sense, beyond the regions of the body that are designed for sexual union, or (b) linger over the intermediate relations to the sexual object which should normally be traversed rapidly on the path towards the final sexual aim."[23] For Freud, these aberrant activities are problematic beginnings, preliminary stages that lose their "abnormalcy" when placed in a strongly teleological model of sexuality that must have as its endpoint the stabilizing space of heterosexual genitality. The founding split in all of Freud's revisions of these essays is his inability to account for the breakdown in such developmental models.

What happens, I want to ask, if this "lingering" or "forepleasure" supersedes the value of genitally defined pleasure, or more interestingly, what if "lingering" becomes, because of and not despite its defined incompleteness, the desired object of narrative focus? Leo Bersani's *Freudian Body* persuasively argues that the distinction between "forepleasures and end-pleasures really amounts to two distinct ontologies of sexuality itself," thus undoing any system of a dominant heterosexual genitality. In fact, for Bersani there is a clear connection between the heterosexual regime of sexuality and the aesthetic ordering of narratives. As he says, "Heterosexual genitality is the hierarchical stabilization of sexuality's component instincts. And the perversions of adults therefore become intelligible as the sickness of *uncompleted narratives.*"[24]

In Kipling's fiction, the narrators perform the role of Apter's hunched-over reader, peering through the keyhole into what they announce is the underbelly of Anglo-Indian life. His tales "linger" on the bodies of "strong men" in different stages of decay and companionship and betray the structural logic of a colonial world that sustains itself only through "uncompleted narratives" of a crumbling masculinity, and/or failed or thwarted heterosexuality. Kipling's world is a self-contained male-only fantasy, with women acting as complicated enablers, aesthetic foils to the inexorable logic of a deferred heterosexuality. The swashbuckling no-nonsense heroes of earlier empire fiction are replaced by self-tortured Englishmen whose only source of pleasure and rationality is neither the business of ruling nor their women nor the countryside, but instead the company of one another and of their native male companions. Kipling's Anglo-India is strewn with the traces of men who are either dead, hovering on the brink of insanity, missing from their homes, or carefully navigating their survival amidst the creaking machinations of a tired English bureaucracy. There is no turning away from the ghosts of these men in Kipling's Anglo-India. Like the obsessed narrator of "The House of Shadows," Kipling's other narrators too share a tormented relationship of loss and recuperation with the male figures that dot their narrative horizon. Men are constantly dying, blowing their brains out, or simply rotting in the savage heat of the Anglo-Indian sun. The only immortality, the only refuge promised to the men, we are told over and over again, lies in the stories of their lives that the different narrators so carefully record. As Wressley of the Foreign Office, one of Kipling's bitterest characters, says when he hands over his "magnum opus . . . the work of [his] life" to the narrator: "Take it and keep it. Write one of your penny-farthing yarns about its birth. Perhaps—perhaps—the whole business may have been ordained to this end" (*Indian Tales*, 678).

Relationships between men in Kipling's India are thus not routed through attachments to women but through an attachment to stories of different shapes and memories: some stories are written, others unwritten, some fragmented, some whole, some stories such as that of Wressley's speak of a life's lost work, while others like that of young Charlie in "The Finest Story in the World" speak of pirate ships and failed literary aspirations. These stories fill the worlds of the men we meet: civilians, subalterns, and, significantly, even natives. East is east, and west is indeed west, as the popular Kipling refrain goes, except when, as the often ignored last line of that stanza tells us, "two strong men stand face to face, though they come from the ends of the earth."[25] When it comes to the circulation of stories, no exchange/liaison between men is taboo; race lines, class lines, and even lines of mortality are crossed and overcome. Creative collaborations and narrative pacts are struck between Englishmen, as well as between the native servants and their English masters.[26] Each narrator plays an active part in each story's unfolding, reminding the reader constantly of his participation and control over the narrative he is crafting. Instead of merely framing what is seen by his eyes, the narrative incorporates the narrator into the very picture it presents, thus eradicating the distant relation of observer and observed. The narrator is as much part of the world he is describing and is privy to its internal rumblings; similarly, the content of the stories is as much about the relationship between the individual narrator and his male subject(s) as it is about the lives of his protagonists.

Yet these stories are no simple records of colonial masculinity surviving against all odds. Instead these are avatars of a colonial masculinity ravaged by doubt and fear, paralyzed by the fragility of its own construction. Eve Kosofsky Sedgwick is almost too gentle in her characterization of the English empire as a "remedial public school, a male place in which it is relatively safe for men to explore the crucial terrain of homosociality."[27] More often than not in Kipling's fiction, the Anglo-

Indian landscape resembles a version of Foucault's asylum, with revolving doors that dizzyingly lead us in and out of the rational order of things:[28] "This stench, combined with that of native tobacco, baked brick, and dried earth, sends the heart of many a strong man to his boots, for it is the smell of the Great Indian Empire when she turns herself for six months into a house of torment" (Indian Tales, 183). However, even as the characters degenerate and collapse into incoherent beings barely performing their roles in the empire's machinery, Kipling's narrators appear to experience quite the opposite effect. Every calamity, every emotional breakdown is turned upside down, emptied of its horror, and regenerated to fuel narratives that smuggle out of the collective torment of everyday life some sense of the personal interior life of its participants. A new kind of masculinity emerges, where the neglected sites of repression and fear become a generating site for what John Kucich has called "libidinal acts, forms of luxuriously self-disruptive and auto-erotic experience."[29] Colonial masculinity is now defined, valued, and understood not through its brazen gestures of conquest, nor through its mastery over the native landscape, but instead through an uncovering of its own dark secrets. The narrative gaze turns inward, as the reader, like Bobby Wick, the young subaltern, begins "to be instructed in the dark art and mystery of managing men" in India. The narrator of "Only a Subaltern" forebodingly reminds us that even something as controlled and ordered as a "regiment [of English soldiers] had as much right to its own secrets as a woman" (Indian Tales, 93).

In "The End of the Passage," one of Kipling's most evocative tales of colonial neurosis, the narrator turns to one of the many "secrets" of colonial masculinity, "the horror, the horror" that exists even as the British empire continues its inexorable journey toward expansion and consolidation. The story depicts a physical landscape of stasis and suffocating despair: "There was neither sky, sun nor horizon—nothing but a brown-purple haze of heat. It was as though the earth were dying of apoplexy" (Life's Handicap, 170). A deadly langorous calm hangs around the men's quarters, a calm that threatens to swallow them up in its final deathly silence. Hummil, the central protagonist of the story, struggles to survive the deranging effects of empire with little success; for him, there is only one end to his passage to India: "A man hasn't many privileges in this country, but he might at least be allowed to mishandle his own rifle. Besides, some day I may need a man to smother up an accident to myself. Live and let live. Die and let die" (*Life's Handicap*, 178). And he is not alone in coming to this realization. Such despair gnaws at most of the Englishmen we meet in Kipling's India—young/old, civilian/subaltern: "They squabbled whenever they met; but they ardently desired to meet, as men without water desire to drink. They were lonely folk who understood the dread meaning of loneliness. They were all under thirty years of age—which is too soon for any man to possess that knowledge" (*Life's Handicap*, 173). Shuddering under the force of the "dread meaning of loneliness," these young men cling to each other for different forms of solace and companionship and, in doing so, discover their own ability to take on roles hitherto repressed in themselves and reserved for women. There is an acute pained poignancy in the bonds that form between men, bonds that not only swing along the continuum between homosociality and homoeroticism but that also deeply emphasize the complex dependency between them.

Men become mothers, wives, doctors, patients on their way to surviving the "house of torment" that is Anglo-India. The relationship that develops between Dormer and young Bobby Wick in the story of "Only a Subaltern" is one such example. In a scene that speaks of complicated longing and loneliness, Dormer pleads with Bobby for comfort as he lays sick on his hospital bed: "Beg y'pardon, sir, disturbin' of you now, but would you min' 'oldin' my 'and, sir?" Bobby does as he is asked and then proceeds to spend the night at Dormer's bedside, Dormer's "icy cold hand closed on his own like a vice" (*Indian Tales*, 106). Later, as Bobby himself lays dying, Dormer appears, crazed in grief, "a hairy apparition in a blue-gray dressing-gown who stared in horror at the bed and cried—'Oh my Gawd! It can't be 'im!'" (108).

In "The Finest Story in the World" we are presented with a gentler version of the bonds that arise between men. This story strikes me as being perhaps the closest to a metanarrative of Kipling's own narrative and heuristic strategies. It recounts the denouement of an intimate relationship between an older male narrator and young Charlie, who encounters and pursues him in a "public billiard room" (*Indian Tales*, 1). Charlie is irresistible in the expression of his devotion for the older man, in a manner that even the most coquettish and sophisticated of women could not replicate: "There are few things sweeter in this world than the guileless, hot-headed intemperate open admiration of a junior. Even a woman in her blindest devotion does not fall into his gait. . . .

Still it was necessary to salve my conscience before I possessed myself of Charlie's thoughts" (5). The scene of writing is indeed the site of bliss here, procuring and sanctioning parameters for a sustained dialectics of desire. The act of writing stories, talking about their conception and their process, sets the stage for the nurturing bond between the two men, with Charlie appearing late at night and asking to spend the night just so that he can "write all evening" (3). There is no room, we are told, for such activity "in his mother's house" (3). The elaborate dynamic that develops between the two men unravels itself over the rituals of writing, resembling often the structure of a carefully managed court-ship (5). The older man cajoles and comforts as the younger one faces despair. It is a mutually generative relationship as the narrator is aware that he has come across a lucrative "Notion among notions" (4). We are reminded of his expertise and of the youth's inexperience, much as Kipling's other narrators remind us of the suitability of their recording position: "It would be folly to allow his idea to remain in his own inept hands, when I could do so much with it" (5). Like a triumphant con-queror, the narrator announces: "I, I alone held this jewel to my hand for the cutting and polishing" (14). He pledges everything, as he tells his "young, fat, full-bodied Bengali friend," Grish Chunder, "for the sake of writing the story. On my honor that will be all" (34). Writing the young man's story becomes his life's "lingering" preoccupation.

What kills this story is what kills most of Kipling's fiction: the appear-ance of a woman. The "Awful Warning" given by the narrator of "The Story of the Gadsbys" holds true yet again, as the script of heterosexual-ity intrudes to end what could have been the "finest story in the world," and the narrative ends with the bitter announcement: "Grish Chunder was right. Charlie had tasted the love of women that kills remembrance, and the finest story in the world would never be written" (48).

"Yet Who Remembers Her?" Women in Kipling's Anglo-India

> According to Kipling, woman kills the man of action and also the action itself.
> —André Maurois, "A French View of Kipling," 1934

> The "duel between the sexes" is Mr. Kipling's theme (which increases his chances of immortality), and there is a woman in most of his stories. Yet who remembers her?
> —J. M. Barrie on "Mr. Kipling's Stories," 1891

As suggested in the introduction to this essay, the management of empire, especially of post-Mutiny India, hinged heavily on the reorganization of India as a fertile landscape, both imaginatively and politically. In Kipling's Anglo-India, such a reorganization requires a careful bracketing of his female characters, both English and Indian, as either peripheral to the story line or as instrumental to the creation of Kipling's brand of ravaged masculinity. For Kipling's stories to work as desirable and desired perversions of a thwarted heterosexuality, the female characters must succumb to a necessary narrative death. Such a delineation of women characters, I will demonstrate, is no easy sleight of the literary hand in which women are merely flattened out within the contours of the text. Like the double-edged treatment of native women in colonial India, where women are granted a subjectivity only to have it erased, Kipling's women too are produced and needed as subjects who must enable and/or invite their own erasure and/or rescue at the hands of their English male counterparts for the story not to be "killed," as in the case of "The Finest Story in the World." Women characters are shuttled across an imaginative spectrum between "harem" and "home," between the roles of daughter, wife, mother, prostitute, each flawed incarnation proving over and over how untenable the presence of women, and thus of normative heterosexuality, is within the landscape of Kipling's Anglo-India. His taxonomy of women's roles, though ostensibly traditional (women are wives and mothers), is hardly conventional: Englishwomen are most desirable as other men's wives (Mrs. Hauskbee, the most charming female character in Kipling's fiction); English mothers are notoriously neglectful (the mother figure in "Baa Baa Black Sheep"), or the subject of men's fantasies (the mother in "Brushwood Boy"); Englishwomen of marriageable age are suspiciously boyish looking and entirely asexual (William in "William the Conqueror"); native women who are objects of Englishmen's desires are mostly either below the age of fifteen (Bisesa in "Beyond the Pale")[30] or prostitutes (Lalun in "On the City Wall"). The English home and the native harem in most of the stories are thus sites of chaos and dysfunctionality, providing no safe haven or closure for the male heroes; instead, the only solace men appear to find is with each other and within the stories they tell.

Deirdre David's *Rule Britannia: Women, Empire, and Victorian Writing* provides us with the historical and political context for understanding Kipling's flattening of women characters, both English and native.

For David, Kipling's revisioning of India and colonial masculinity would be untenable without a careful management of the volatile feminist struggles at the time. She points to two foci of control in mid- to late-nineteenth-century discursive management of the empire: (1) native sites of resistance such as the burgeoning nationalist movement in India, and (2) feminist struggles manifested in growing discussions of the New Woman and in the formation of groups such as the Women's Emigration Society. David writes:

> The issue, then, for Victorian writing about empire produced after mid-century is less one of refashioning the nation to fit the rapid acquisition of colonized territories than it is of securing Britain's continued imperial power. In the later period, the empire is not so much under construction as it is under *a discursive inspection* designed to shore up rocky founda-tions, ward off agitation, and ensure that the cost of imperial power not unbalance the political, social and cultural order of the metropolitan center. [emphasis added][31]

Within a project of "discursive inspection" such as Kipling's the presence of "feminist and colonial agitations" thus has to be carefully renegotiated in the rhetorical repair of the imperial edifice. While David is careful to emphasize the concerted censorship of colonial and feminist agitations in the maintenance of narratives of empire, she is less convincing in her formulation of the two sites of resistance. First, any analysis of native sites of resistance must take into account the uneven developments within the different classes of the disenfranchised colonized masses, a point that the scholars of the Subaltern Studies group have made quite forcefully. Second, David's linking of the colonized body with the female body en masse, without respect to the particular racialized avatar of the female body, risks performing the same kind of negligent reading of empire that it seeks to remedy. In other words, there are clear structural similarities between the feminist struggles of English-women and the nativist struggles for increasing autonomy, but analysis of such parallels excludes the position of Indian women.

Kipling's fiction documents such differences even as his women characters disappear into the margins of his plots. The increasing surveillance of the English memsahib's activities in India (Mrs. Gadsby in "The Story of the Gadsbys") is concurrent with an ostensible movement by the English to "civilize" Eastern women (Lispeth in "Lispeth"). Indeed, as Gayatri Spivak and other feminist postcolonial critics have pointed out, the legitimacy of the "*mission civilisatrice*" came to rest more and more on putatively reformist gestures, such as the official abolition of sati, that the English government made toward the "emancipation" of native women from their despotic Indian traditions. For Spivak, "imperialism's image as the establisher of the good society is marked by the espousal of woman as object of protection from her own kind," and she asks us to "examine the dissimulation of patriarchal strategy, which apparently grants the woman free choice as subject" within the colonial scenario of "white men saving brown women from brown men."[32]

In this scenario, the sites of feminist struggles for Englishwomen were deliberately pushed to the periphery of colonial discourse, while the uplifting of native women took center stage. Kipling's stories frequently record the possible "saving" of their native female characters at the hands of his English characters (Ameera in "Without the Benefit of Clergy"), but rarely do we see independent, unconventional English female characters. Inderpal Grewal reiterates this important distinction in her recently published *Home and Harem* and further explicates the uneven development of English versus native women as it specifically unfolds in colonial India. For her, the domestication of Englishwomen kept them indoors, unreadable, impervious to the threat of the native male, while the "move to 'civilize' Eastern women functioned to make them less opaque, to strip them of their veils, and to remove them from harems where they lived lives hidden from the European male." In a gesture of political irony, the Victorian "home" became a metaphorical native "harem," and vice versa.[33]

My analysis of the enabling role of female characters in Kipling's India extends this political binary of home/harem to focus on one of his most complicated female characters, Lalun, an Indian prostitute. Lalun's portrayal transforms the double threat of Indian nationalism and feminist struggles into a shared peace between male characters. In "On a City Wall" Kipling crafts an alternative narrative space where desire is allowed to exist between men, and racial differences substitute for gender. Wali Dad, the native male character, substitutes for Lalun as the narrative shifts to a description of the burgeoning relationship between him and the English narrator. This is a story whose protagonists find themselves in the interstices of home and harem, within the confines of a native prostitute's salon, where "all the City seemed to assemble in Lalun's little white room to smoke and to talk" (*Indian Tales*, 293). Here, the violence of the Mutiny is tempered through rituals of male kinship that are forged over the carefully desexualized body of the native prostitute. This story is thus compelling not simply because it locates for the first time an influential native female character, Lalun (albeit in the guise of a prostitute), but also because it is the only occasion in which a Kipling narrator overtly addresses the memory of the 1857 uprising. Through Lalun's window on the city wall, the narrator negotiates his reading of the Mutiny, and through her eyes he gains access to the activities of the native mutineers. Lalun enables the narrator to minimize and lay to rest the brutal myth of the rebellion, unveiling in its place the figure of an old warrior, Khem Singh, whose allegiance to the cause of the Mutiny appears as arcane and useless as the wizened body in which it is encased. At the end of the story, we are left with the abject figure of the old mutineer who is rejected by the younger natives and dismissed by the English authorities, both considering him too unimportant for their political purposes. "'57 [may have been] a year that no man, Black or White, cares to speak of" (*Indian Tales*, 310), we are told, but in this version of Kipling's Anglo-India, the horrifying "glamour" of the year is gone, "passed away" (329–30), with the writing on the city wall gesturing to the activities between men in Lalun's salon rather than to the memory of a bygone native insurrection.

In this discursive management of the Mutiny, from a site of horror, to a site of harmlessness, the story displaces the focus of colonial panic from the military threat posed by the natives to the possibility of the sexual threat posed by the native prostitute and the consequences of the activities in her little white room. The narrator reminds us from the outset that the politics of sexual conduct and its consequences are constitutive to the business of empire. We are told, tongue in cheek, that the "beauty of Lalun was so great that it troubled the hearts of the British government, and caused them to lose their peace of mind." And just in case we miss the import of this declaration, the narrator explains further: "By the sublety of Lalun, the administration of the Government was troubled and it lost such and such a man" (295–96). Despite its irony, the mention of the loss of "such and such a man" still directly alludes to the problem of venereal disease that besieged the Indian empire, especially in post-Mutiny India.

Phillipa Levine's illuminating argument on the connections between "sexually transmitted diseases and the business of politics and governance" in post-Mutiny British India is worth summarizing here.[34] For Levine, the success of the script of colonial governance, especially as it skirts the threat of homosexuality within its armed forces in India, depends primarily on its management of the debates around venereal diseases. To explain, Levine points out that the passing of the Contagious Diseases Acts after 1870 had very different repercussions for women in the metropole and in the colonies. While the three British acts (1864, 1869, and 1869) exercised control only over Englishwomen who were registered as prostitutes, such control in India was more arbitrary and exercised on any woman suspected of being a prostitute. The logic behind such a difference in rule, Levine argues, was based on a colonial understanding of native morality as endemically depraved and fallen, especially in the female. Kipling's narrator corroborates this line of thinking, albeit humorously, even as he introduces the story:

> In the West, people say rude things about Lalun's profession, and write lectures to young persons in order that Morality may be preserved. In the East where the profession is hereditary, descending from mother to daughter, nobody writes lectures or takes any notice; and that is a distinct proof of the inability of the East to manage its own affairs. (*Indian Tales*, 293)

Levine further suggests that such an understanding of native women's morality in a post-Mutiny era of deadly venereal diseases firmly locates the racialized prostitute's body as the purveyor of a threat so deadly that the English soldier's body is no match for its effects. Because native prostitution is so widespread, so also is the onslaught of venereal diseases, which are understood as being transmitted primarily through the body of the native prostitute. In other words, the frequent contact between the native prostitutes and the English troops conveniently becomes an issue of less import, as more public attention is paid instead to the so-called unnatural and debilitating effects of the prostitute's sexual labor. Levine adds that such a shift of focus to the effects of venereal disease as the emerging threat to the empire is particularly critical to understanding the "centrality of sexual politics in the maintenance of empire":

> Without available women, soldiers unable to control their passions in the tropical heat of the East would turn to rape—or worse to one another. The constant haunting fear of homosexuality, the presence of which would undermine the manly adventure of imperial conquest,

underscores the whole debate on prostitution in this era, despite a conspicuous reluctance to discuss the question in official circles. ("Venereal Disease," 596)

The problem of venereal diseases, finally, is narrowed down to the disease-transmitting body of the native prostitute who is read as symptomatic of the dubious moral core of India that assaults the fine and civilized corps of the British army. Such conceptualizations bury that "haunting fear of homosexuality" within the space of colonial panic around hygiene and native amorality. And Kipling's story is no exception.

In Kipling's "On the City Wall," the problem of the native prostitute and her disease-producing body is carefully rearranged and recast in another order of things. Lalun's salon, the potential producing location for disease and death, is transformed instead to a space where the real work of the colonial civilizing mission takes place. Gone is the threat of army barracks, disease, and immorality; in its place, we have an idyllic and diverse melting pot of cultures where men of all races gather to exchange intellectual views and to enjoy each other's company:

> In the long hot nights of latter April and May all the City seemed to assemble in Lalun's little white room to smoke and to talk. Shiahs of the grimmest and most uncompromising persuasion; Sufis who had lost all belief in the Prophet and retained but little in God; wandering Hindu priests passing southward on their way to the Central India fairs ...
> M.A.'s of the University, very superior, very voluble—all these people and more also you might find in the white room. (*Indian Tales*, 300)

It is here, in Lalun's salon, that the English narrator is truly able to colonize, putatively to understand and educate the native mind, as he bustles around busily lending books to Wali Dad, the main native male voice in the story. There is hardly a hint of the sexual activities that presumably go on in such a venue, the story's attention focusing more on the filial relationship developing between Wali Dad and the English narrator. Lalun's potential to bury "such and such a man" is thus never put to test, as the story suggests that in the company of the right men such a threat can be quietly put to rest.

Thus Lalun's body is carefully recast and desexualized, made to produce information on the underground workings of a native resistance movement. We are told repeatedly that to know and understand Lalun is to know and understand the native mind: "Lalun is Lalun, and when you have said that, you have only come to the Beginning of Knowledge" (299). There is no threat of disease emanating from Lalun in this story. Instead, the narrator is more intent on demonstrating the extent of her knowledge in matters close to the ruling of empire. "Lalun knows everything," the narrator acknowledges, as he interrogates her on the exact details of the passage of a military regiment to Agra (301). The ultimate transformation and domestication of Lalun's threat, however, occurs when she introduces the narrator to Khem Singh, a native mutineer, and the narrator deduces through Khem Singh's abject state that the threat of native rebellion is indeed past and that the memory of the Mutiny can finally be laid to rest.

To Be Filed for Reference: Desire in Abeyance

> You will treat it brutally, I know you will. Some of it must go; the public are fools and prudish fools. I was their servant once. But do your mangling gently—very gently. It is a great work and I have paid for it in seven year's damnation
> —"To Be Filed for Reference," *Indian Tales*

To conclude, my effort in this essay has been to situate Kipling's fiction at the edge of several critical crises in the colonial management of India. While I have argued that Kipling repeatedly attempts to organize centers of chaos such as the memory of the Mutiny, the existence of female characters, and colonial homosociality into contained narratives of everyday Anglo-Indian life, it is important to bear in mind that his fiction is also simultaneously haunted by the very fears he attempts to exorcise. At the heart of Kipling's *Indian Tales* is a story that literalizes the narrative strategies I have been addressing thus far. "To Be Filed for Reference" maps the genesis of a friendship between McIntosh Jellaludin (the only Kipling character to have successfully "gone Fantee" and passed into the hybrid, sullied space of Eurasian identity) and the ubiquitous male narrator. The friendship and the story culminate in the form of a literary transaction, an exchange of a strange body of narratives, a "hopeless muddle" of jumbled tales that Jellaludin bequeaths to the narrator on his deathbed.

The narrator first stumbles on the drunken McIntosh Jellaludin one dark night and befriends him with the enticement of tobacco and books, in exchange for what he ironically calls "the materials of a new Inferno that should make me greater than Dante" (377). Borne out of the drunken erudition of McIntosh Jellaludin, the "hopeless muddle" that Jellaludin finally hands over to the narrator never quite reaches the smooth surface of narrative completion. We are told, with foreboding irony, "If the thing is ever published, some one may perhaps remember this story, now printed as a safeguard to prove that McIntosh Jellaludin and not I myself wrote the Book of Mother Maturin" (383–84). "To Be Filed for Reference" thus begins with expectation, a promise of vicarious narrative discovery, but ends with a tale held in abeyance, as Jellaludin dies and the narrator leaves the jumbled tales unpublished. We never learn the complete contents of this mysterious "Book of Mother Maturin," except for brief allusions to it as a "bundle" that needed much expurgation and was "full of Greek nonsense" (383). Stephen Arata signals the importance of this story by reminding us that "Jellaludin is the only character in all of Kipling's Indian stories who is learned—the only character whose literary education matches Kipling's own." Yet unlike Kipling, Jellaludin's erudition produces chaos, disorder, and an undecipherable body of work that can only be "filed for reference" (*Fictions of Loss*, 167). Also, Kipling, like Jellaludin, was rumored to have labored for years on the definitive opus on his experiences in India, a book that he too called the "Book of Mother Maturin," a book that similarly never saw the light of publication.

For my purpose in this essay, Jellaludin's "uncompleted narrative" recalls my earlier invocation of Leo Bersani's different narrative order of things. Here, the script of heterosexuality and narrative closure surrenders to the pleasures of Bersani's "cock-telling," of a narrative that "lingers" over the possibility of a text that can live only in its reference rather than in its publication. Jellaludin writes through his body, paid in the scars of "damnation" that he refers to constantly. Such damnation comes also over the body of the native woman, the quiet wife who cooks and buffers Jellaludin from collapsing under the stress of cultural passing, much like the enabling role that Lalun, the native prostitute, plays in "On the City Wall." "That book will make you famous," Jellaludin poignantly adds, and in a gesture reminiscent of a parting between lovers, Jellaludin hands over his "only baby" to the narrator, as his native wife "bears witness" and approves of this transaction. Like all of Kipling's stories, the game ends grimly with colonial secrets intact, and the site of narrative bliss bequeathed to a new line of male narrators.

Notes

This essay was conceived and written in 1999 through the generous support of Smith College. Many thanks to Geeta Patel, Anindyo Roy, David DeLaura, Lynda Hart, and Lucy Mae San Pablo Burns for a series of critical conversations and interventions that helped me think through the multiple thorny dimensions of this essay.

1. Andrew Lang, *Essays in Little*, January 1891, in *Kipling: The Critical Heritage*, ed. Roger Lancelyn Green (London: Routledge and Kegan Paul, 1971), 71.

2. S. R. Crockett, "On Some Tales of Mr. Kipling's," *Bookman* (London) 7 (February 1895): 39–40, in *Kipling: The Critical Heritage*, 182.

3. Robert Buchanan, "The Voice of the Hooligan," *The Contemporary Review* 86 (December 1899): 774–89, in *Kipling: The Critical Heritage*, 236.

4. Gilbert Frankau, "Rudyard Kipling," *London Magazine* 61 (August 1928): 130–34, in *Kipling: The Critical Heritage*, 365.

5. Andrew Lang, review of *Plain Tales from the Hills*, *Daily News* (2 November 1889), in *Kipling: The Critical Heritage*, 47.

6. J. M. Barrie, "Mr. Kipling's Stories," *Contemporary Review* 59 (March 1891): 364–72, in *Kipling: The Critical Heritage*, 82.

7. *The Times*, 25 March 1890, in *Kipling: The Critical Heritage*, 52.

8. Virginia Woolf, *A Room of One's Own* (London: Panther, 1984), 97.

9. Frances Adams, "On Rudyard Kipling," *Fortnightly Review* 56 (November 1891): 686–700, in *Kipling: The Critical Heritage*, 153.

10. Teresa Hubel, *Whose India?: The Independence Struggle in British and Indian Fiction and History* (Durham: Duke University Press, 1996), 1.

11. George Orwell, "Rudyard Kipling," in *Kipling and the Critics*, ed. Elliot L. Gilbert (New York: New York University Press, 1965), 83–120.

12. Ali Behdad, *Belated Travelers: Orientalism in the Age of Dissolution* (Durham: Duke University Press, 1994), 75.

13. Stephen Arata, *Fictions of Loss in the Victorian Fin de Siècle* (New York: Cambridge University Press, 1996), 158–60.

14. Sinha adds that "Britain's unfavorable balance of trade with the rest of the world—a result of protectionist policies of many of Britain's trading partners in the second half of the century—was financed through India's export surplus with other countries. The transfer of surplus from India to Britain was managed through the complex system of 'home charges' for civil and military expenditures, guaranteed interest on railways, interest on the India Debt accumulating in England, and charges for such 'invisible services' as shipping, insurance, and so on; early Indian nationalists aptly termed this process as the 'drain of wealth.' . . . Imperial banks in India handled British overseas trade, 'coolie' labor from India was used as cheap labor on British economic concerns in different parts of the British Empire, and Indian troops, paid for by the Indians, were used to secure and extend British control overseas." (*Colonial Masculinity: The Manly Englishman and the "Effeminate Bengali" in the late Nineteenth Century* [Manchester: Manchester University Press, 1995], 24.)

15. Jenny Sharpe, *Allegories of Empire* (Minneapolis: University of Minnesota Press, 1993), 85–97.

16. Edward Thompson, *The Other Side of the Medal* (London: Hogarth Press, 1925).

17. Lewis D. Wurgaft, *The Imperial Imagination: Magic and Myth in Kipling's India* (Middletown: Wesleyan University Press, 1983), 75.

18. The complete invocation reads thus: When he comes to the room I am in, he stops, puts the *purdah* aside and looks at me. I am sure of it, for when I turn, the *purdah* has always just fallen. He must be the man who takes so impertinent an interest in my breakfast. But he will never face me and tell me what he wants. He is always in the next room. Though I have hunted him through the house again and again, he is always in the next room. "The House of Shadows," in Thomas Pinney, ed., *Kipling's India: Uncollected Sketches, 1884–88* (New York: Schocken Books, 1986).

19. Rudyard Kipling, *Indian Tales* (New York: Dodge Publishing Co., 1899), 7. All references in the text will hereafter be cited as *Indian Tales.*

20. *The Collected Works of Rudyard Kipling: Life's Handicap: Being Stories of Mine Own People* (New York: AMS Press, 1970), xvi. All references in the text will be to *Life's Handicap.*

21. Ali Behdad argues that such narrative gestures are fueled by "the opposing poles of orientalist representation: obscurity surrounding the object of representation and an insatiable desire for unveiling inherent in representation practice" (*Belated Travelers,* 19).

22. Emily Apter, *Feminizing the Fetish: Psychoanalysis and Narrative Obsession in Turn-of-Century France* (Ithaca: Cornell University Press, 1991), xiv.

23. Freud, "The Sexual Abberations," in *Three Essays on the Theory of Sexuality,* trans. James Strachey (New York: Vintage, 1962), 14.

24. Leo Bersani, *The Freudian Body: Psychoanalysis and Art* (New York: Columbia University Press, 1986), 32–33.

25. Rudyard Kipling, "The Ballad of East and West," *Barrack-Room Ballads and Other Verses* (London: Methuen, 1892), 75. The complete stanza reads: "Oh, East is East, and West and West, and never the twain shall meet, / Till Earth and Sky stand presently at God's great Judgement Seat; / But there is neither East nor West, Border, nor Breed, nor Birth, / When two strong men stand face to face, though they come from the ends of the earth!"

26. It is similarly significant that the two adult novels Kipling wrote, *Naulahka* and *The Light that Failed,* both deal rather centrally with the issue of male-to-male collaboration. *Naulahka* was coauthored by Kipling and the American writer Wolcott Balestier, while *The Light that Failed* has a major subplot that focuses on the intensely homoerotic dynamic between the older Torpenhow and Dick, the main protagonist. Christopher Lane points out that in the writing of *The Light that Failed* Kipling vacillated between two very different endings. In the first, "Dick Heldar dies in the arms of his closest male friend Torpenhow; in the second, amended version, Heldar forms a precipitous marriage to Maisie, a woman who has from the novel's outset expressed almost unmitigated hostility to him." (*The Ruling Passion: British Colonial Allegory and the Paradox of Homosexual Desire* [Durham: Duke University Press, 1995], 19.)

27. Eve Kosofsky Sedgwick, *Between Men: English Literature and Male Homosocial Desire* (New York: Columbia University Press, 1985), 198.

28. Foucault in the preface to his *Madness and Civilization* argues that the silencing of madness, irrationality in the constitution of current systems of knowledge emerge as a "great motionless structure; this structure is one of neither drama nor knowledge; it is the point where history is immobilized in the tragic category

which both established and impugns it." (*Madness and Civilization: A History of Insanity in the Age of Reason,* trans. Richard Howard [New York: Vintage Books, 1965], xii.)

29. John Kucich, *Repression in Victorian Fiction* (Berkeley: University of California Press, 1987), 3.

30. The age of consent to sexual intercourse for native women was fixed at ten in 1860, and raised to twelve in 1891. For more details, see Kenneth Ballhatchet, *Race, Sex, and Class under the Raj* (New York: St. Martin's Press, 1980), 44–50.

31. Deirdre David, *Pax Britannia: Women, Empire, and Victorian Writing* (Ithaca: Cornell University Press, 1995), 158.

32. Gayatri Chakravorty Spivak, "Can the Subaltern Speak?," in Cary Nelson and Laurence Grossberg, eds., *Marxism and the Interpretation of Culture* (Chicago: University of Chicago Press, 1988), 271–313.

33. Inderpal Grewal, *Home and Harem: Nation, Gender, Empire, and the Cultures of Travel* (Durham: Duke University Press, 1996), 49.

34. Phillipa Levine, "Venereal Disease, Prostitution, and Politics of Empire: The Case of British India," *Journal of the History of Sexuality* 4, no. 41 (1994): 586.

CHAPTER FIVE

Fantasies of "Lady Pioneers," between Narrative and Theory

Christopher Lane

Women Travelers, Feminist Critics

"The truth is," writes Simon Gikandi in *Maps of Englishness*, "students of colonial discourse and postcolonial theory do not know what to do with the women of empire—whether these women are European or native."[1] The problem arises, he argues, because we "want to read woman as the absolute other in the colonial relation" so that we can investigate imperial narratives and their associated ideologies. But when we define white women as "figures of colonial alterity," as he puts it, we deny "their cultural agency" and the important institutional role they played in "the dominant discourse[s] of empire" (122).

The observation is astute, and the dilemma it points up is telling. Uncomfortable with the way Elspeth Huxley and others celebrated such "lady pioneers" as Gertrude Bell, Mary Kingsley, and Elizabeth Sarah (Nina) Mazuchelli by emphasizing their verve and indomitable spirit,[2] many feminist scholars tried in the 1980s and early 90s to downplay this praise while still representing these women as pursuing "the only real alternative to domestic imprisonment" (Gikandi, *Maps of Englishness*, 123).[3] The latter critics' conclusions vary almost as much as the material they interpret. According to Susan Blake, Mary Hall maintained an "implicitly anti-imperial relationship to Africa" in *A Woman's Trek from the Cape to Cairo* (1907), because she tried "to achieve reciprocity, both on the trail and in the text."[4] Immediately after quoting Hall telling readers that "the porters by this time were really no trouble; like children they were quick to see that I meant what I said," Blake asserts that "the sub-

stitution of a sense of class superiority for racial superiority undermines the premises of empire," an argument that is baffling as evidence
of reciprocity.[5] Interpreting similar material, Shirley Foster draws a
parallel conclusion: "while revealing some traits of 'orientalism,' female
observers may seek to establish familiarity and mutuality, qualities of cultural or moral relativity which permit new insights and understanding."[6]

As such assumptions are widespread, Nupur Chaudhuri and Margaret Strobel are unusual in acknowledging that women travelers "complicate" our hope of "find[ing] resistance when, often, we actually face
complicity."[7] Critics appeal more often to mitigating circumstances. Indeed, according to Sara Mills and many other critics, the "transgressive
possibilities" of women's travel writing—including its irony and parody—are "potentially extremely subversive" in "violating" existing conventions.[8] A question nonetheless hangs on the meaning we give this
"potential," especially if critical theory is used "to do the work of semi-
exculpating its author."[9] "Complexity can best function to exonerate
when it is placed in contrast to some guilty simplicity," remarks James
Buzard, who points out that ambiguity is rarely exculpatory and that
indeterminacy often absolves nothing politically.[10]

Because Kingsley (1862–1900) was Britain's most influential nineteenth-century female traveler who in the late 1890s became a leading
authority on West African affairs, feminist critics have often returned to
select parts of her work, steering a course similar to that of Blake and
Mills. Although Kingsley's complicity with imperialism is apparent in
Travels in West Africa (1897), they concede, her wry observations on
gender differences in West African tribes helped dismantle imperialist
ethnography by bringing Europe and Africa into startling proximity.[11]

Creating a predictable deadlock, this complicity/resistance model has
begun to wear a little thin. It comes down to debating whether Kingsley
and her contemporaries had sufficient agency to undermine cultural
constraints or whether their ethnographic concerns finally shored up
the aims of Victorian imperialism. If we feel a sense of déjà vu about
these arguments, moreover, it's because similar disputes occurred in the
nineteenth century concerning men and women's outlooks on imperialism. "There are peculiar powers inherent in ladies' eyes," Florence
Dixie claimed in 1845 with some self-promotion,[12] a notion the *Times
Literary Supplement* upheld in 1907 when claiming that women travelers
are "unquestionably more observant of details and quicker to receive

impressions" than their male counterparts. "Their sympathies are more alert, and they get into touch with strangers more readily."[13] Still, most Victorian commentators mocked these ideas, voicing concern about women's exposure to colonial matters and their apparent loss of purity. Ironically, our debates today retain a flavor of these arguments. Granted, we're more inclined to ask whether it's possible to celebrate the provocative insights of these women without countenancing their frequently colonial judgments.[14] But the bid to attach radical significance to marginalized experience still generates interpretive paralysis, especially when individual judgments are viewed relative to a larger racist context.

Given our tendency to view individuals as representatives of their race and gender, it's easy to see why this deadlock would occur, and why, to many readers, a white woman traveling in West Africa is necessarily an avatar of British imperialism. Such emphasis views Europeans' identifications as static and self-evident; and it presents writers as a subset of their nation's imperialist beliefs, which they reproduce unthinkingly. More sophisticated approaches to European imperialism evince similar expectations through an ingenious but still inadequate compromise: they address agency whenever it voices female defiance but not racism. At such moments—and Conradians will hear a comparable echo in recent accounts of his fiction—the author becomes a mouthpiece of Victorian discourse.

Aside from its intentionalist assumptions (fictional characters apparently ventriloquize their authors), this interpretive strategy downplays the contradictions that make Kingsley and Conrad interesting.[15] I mean by this a tension in their writing signaling what is most intractable and least sophisticated about their work, rather than what is most conducive to its political salvation. Focusing on this tension, I hope to do more than obviate calls to "rescue" Kingsley or show why her work can't stand metonymically for British colonial discourse. Pinpointing instead what escapes conventional accounts of identity, I want to examine what falls between colonial narrative and postcolonial theory.

Accordingly, this essay examines what is surplus to colonial discourse and to European and African identity, both factors blocking facile reductions of history to subjectivity. My approach to travel writing takes from psychoanalytic and queer theory the assertion that what escapes identity (whether individual, collective, or national) is frequently as important, politically, as what is invoked in the name of that identity.

Though later sections of the essay will assess the colonial repercussions of this gap between identity and desire, what matters overall is our willingness to accept that writers don't have absolute control over language and ideology. It might be convenient to call ambiguity exculpatory, but it's inadequate to view memoir as a purely expressive credo, as though authors throughout their lives maintain a single perspective on dynamic issues. Neither ambiguity nor alleged transparency will take this argument far enough. If we're to engage with Kingsley's varied arguments without condemning or condoning her politics, themselves partly independent of Britain's imperialist ideology, then we need a different approach.

Mary Kingsley: Difference or Otherness?

> Of course the reason for my getting into hot water is that I have said that the African is *different,* which is a statement I stick to; it is that word *different* that gets me into trouble every time.
> —Mary Kingsley, *West African Studies*

Kingsley's *Travels in West Africa* has multiple, often contradictory aims. As John Flint declares in his introduction to this seven-hundred-page work, Kingsley "did more than any other writer to produce in Europe a willingness to try to understand African behaviour, and it was from her views that the system of indirect rule, directed towards preventing a wholesale break-up of traditional society, gained strength."[16] Paradoxically, indirect rule also helped her posit a clear racial hierarchy. "The great inferiority of the African to the European," she insisted, "lies in the matter of mechanical idea. I own I regard not only the African, but all coloured races, as inferior—inferior in kind not in degree—to the white races, although I know it is unscientific to lump all Africans together...."[17] Such beliefs led Kingsley to argue, in "The Negro Future" (1895), "if Africa does not rise under this 'fairly tried influence of the higher race,' Africa will only have herself to blame. My opinion is not hopeful; but we shall see."[18]

Although it's difficult to detect much irony in these statements, a complex set of beliefs underwrites them. Kingsley's claims about racial difference indicate that she believed strongly in white superiority,[19] though she still came to identify with Africans, calling them "my people." Her happiness apparently lay not in "London society, politics, that gateway into which I so strangely wandered—into which I don't care a hairpin if I never wander again," but with "mangrove swamps, rivers, and the sea and so on."[20] We reach an impasse here if we expect to find consistency or to pronounce Kingsley a radical. It seems more accurate to concede, as Flint has, that "Mary Kingsley was not a balanced thinker, that her object was not to harmonize conflicting interests, that to treat her theories on a purely philosophical level is to miss their significance, and that in fact she was completely partial and extreme."[21]

Kingsley was also ambitious and shrewd, "shap[ing] her theories to suit concrete political demands."[22] She doubtless knew her peers would heed her comments on white superiority and may have developed this position partly to secure a platform for indirect rule. Still, the political and psychic are not seamless elements in her work. The very incongruousness of her promoting Britain's imperial ideal while identifying with the colonized may have helped her transform a relation to both groups into full allegiance to neither. "I cannot be a bushman and a drawing roomer," she told Hatty Johnson, her Cambridge friend in January 1896, "and so I get worried and bored."[23] Alternating in imaginary terms between England and Africa, she often chose an interesting third option: nothingness or—more precisely—the sublime, an emphasis to which I will return.

Granted, Kingsley later described as "strange," "unpleasant," and "dangerous" a "distinct outbreak of anti-Imperialism" in England and feared that Britain's ambition for global domination was greater than its "spirit," apparently unequal to the task.[24] She also feared Kipling's "White Man's Burden" was "a factor in encouraging anti-Imperialism to spread in the heart of the Empire."[25] Nevertheless, she explained to Edmund Morel in February the same year (1899), "it is the black man's burden that wants singing for the poor wretch has to put up with a lot of windey headed [sic] fads and foolishness no good to him or the white man, and a jest for the Gods."[26] It is difficult to combine these statements into a single vision (or critique) of British imperialism, and almost impossible to find the sentiment of this last quotation even three years earlier in Kingsley's work.[27]

Since the range of Kingsley's arguments is neither heroic nor exemplary, it's easy to agree with Flint that she "was attempting to re-create and fossilize the conditions of the 1880s, when government was rudimentary, and the traders untrammelled by taxation, regulations, and official control. She liked the African as he was, and wished to shield him from all change."[28] Yet Kingsley's ideas and fantasies surpass what seems straightforwardly evidential, and her writing doesn't faithfully record her political beliefs.[29] Kingsley's fantasies are most edifying when her identifications (as male, as nonhuman, and even as otherworldly) are incommensurate with her identity as a woman, making it imperative that we consider her philosophical and psychic perspectives, too. Sometimes abrogating conventional ideas of personhood, Kingsley revised many of the identifications that her contemporaries associated most rigidly with gender and domesticity.

Colonialism and Fantasy

> The African you have got in your minds up here, that you are legislating for and spending millions on trying to improve, doesn't exist; *your* African is a fancy African.
> —Mary Kingsley, *West African Studies*

Since appealing to historical context softens but doesn't resolve these problems, I want to develop a different approach, ultimately considering how the Victorians responded to nineteenth-century women's travel memoirs, and how critics today grapple with problems of agency and political overdetermination. To amplify these concerns, we must first ask what fantasy—Kingsley's, the Victorians', and ours—adds to existing summaries of her observations. That is especially pressing because Kingsley's and other women's ecstatic renunciation of identity can generate a sense of sublime freedom in their writing that partly releases them from orthodox conduct. Complicating matters further, Kingsley's fascination with West African women voices a demand for intimacy escaping some of the "containment" strategies of colonial discourse. Accordingly, her fantasies push us beyond existing interpretive deadlocks, rendering prominent the mental life of an imago "*between perception and consciousness.*"[30] As Jean Laplanche and Jean-Bertrand Pontalis explain in their oft-cited formulation, "Fantasy... is not the object of desire, but its setting. In fantasy the subject does not pursue the object or its sign: he appears caught up himself in the sequence of images."[31] Because psychic reality is counterintuitive, following desires that are inconceivable in empirical terms, a person's mental imagoes may be enhanced, rather than diminished, by the extent to which they contradict external reality.

Given this argument, the idea that women travelers were more successful than men in "establish[ing] familiarity and mutuality" with indigenous populations appears highly implausible, ignoring these women's relationship to fantasy.[32] Circumscribing Europeans' encounters with indigenous tribespeople were *imagoes* whose meaning is irreducible to ideology and political reality. As James Fernandez observes, describing male and female travelers alike: "The explorer's fancies, if dispelled by the eye, were still supported by the imagination *and* by Fang willingness to feed the fantasies of their visitors."[33] Such dynamics recur in noncolonial contexts, to be sure, but the fact that Kingsley "could converse [only] in trade English, a kind of pidgin" doubtless intensified this dynamic, granting more freedom to speculation and projection.[34] Far from suggesting greater "mutuality" with indigenous people than their male counterparts, women travelers often indicate the irrelevance of indigenous people to their own experience of freedom.

Fantasy conveys partly unconscious aspirations that trouble, and sometimes confound, the very idea of cross-cultural exchange. Complicating the suggestion that "lady pioneers" aimed only to support their nations' rapacious policies, these aspirations point up the fallacy of approaching Victorian travel narratives in literal or crudely psychologistic ways. In this respect, we still have much to learn from Freud, who told Wilhelm Fliess in September 1897, eight months after Kingsley's *Travels* became an instant bestseller, "there are no indications of reality in the unconscious, so that one cannot distinguish between the truth and fiction that has been cathected with affect."[35] Freud's stress on the impossibility of distinguishing truth from fiction in the unconscious helps explain why the fantasies of "lady pioneers" fall between evidential analysis and colonial theory. This will be clearer when we consider Kingsley's preoccupation with nothingness and the sublime—phenomena undermining our and the Victorians' identitarian assumptions about women travelers by confounding sense and sex. The resistance of both elements to meaning indicates why even the best feminist and textual scholars sometimes misconstrue these travelers' claims.[36]

"I went down to West Africa to die," Kingsley told Matthew Nathan, perhaps her most intimate confidant, in 1899.[37] Kingsley, then thirty-six and nursing an unrequited love for Nathan, was dead within a year. But like many of her claims, distorted for dramatic or comic effect, the statement isn't entirely true. We could as easily say she went to West Africa to live more expansively; to advance her career as a writer, in the wake of her famous uncle, Charles; to mourn the death of her parents, who died ten weeks apart; to recover from the shock of discovering her near-illegitimacy; and to destroy a set of identifications that had thwarted her in England.[38] "West Africa amused me . . . and did not want to kill me just then," she told Nathan in the same letter, five years after returning from her second trip to the French Congo. "I am in no hurry [to die]. I don't care one way or the other, for a year or so."

These remarks contradict Kingsley's earlier claim that in *Travels* she was "not bent on discoursing on my psychological state, but on the state of things in general in West Africa."[39] They also establish a context for her calling a 1897–98 studio photograph of herself "the melancholy picture of one who tried to be just to all parties." As Victorian reviewers repeatedly confirmed, Kingsley's psychological insights are frequently more arresting than her ethnographic analysis. "Unless you . . . fall under its charm," she tells us, "African forest life . . . is the most awful life in death imaginable. It is like being shut up in a library whose books you cannot read, all the while tormented, terrified, and bored. And if you do fall under its spell, it takes all the colour out of other kinds of living."[40]

The phrase "life in death" implies that African forests sustain life precariously among death. Kingsley credits them—and Africa itself—with a kind of life-robbing ecstasy, one reason she calls African psychology a "mind forest."[41] Yet while anticipating—and even apparently desiring—death, she discovers, paradoxically, that submitting to Africa's "awful life in death" gives her "a sense of growing power," culminating in a heady feeling of impersonality. Her sense of freedom stems, as well, from her temporarily renouncing identification with Britain.

"The majesty and beauty of the scene fascinated me," Kingsley explains in an evocative moment,

> and I stood leaning with my back against a rock pinnacle watching it. Do not imagine it gave rise, in what I am pleased to call my mind, to those complicated, poetical reflections natural beauty seems to bring out in other people's minds. It never works that way with me; I just lose all sense of human individuality, all memory of human life, with its grief and worry and doubt, and become part of the atmosphere. If I have a heaven, that will be mine, and I verily believe that if I were left alone long enough with such a scene as this . . . I should be found soulless and dead; but I never have a chance of that. (*Travels*, 178)

Kingsley's subsequent remarks to Nathan strengthen her interest in this peculiar exhilaration, implying that West Africa is a powerful setting for her fantasies. Shedding her roles as an ethnographer, ichthyologist, explorer, writer, and dutiful daughter, she imagines for herself a type of desubstantiated existence stemming from anthropomorphic amnesia: "The fact is I am no more a human being than a gale of wind is. I have never had a human individual life. . . . It is the non-human world I belong to myself."[42] In one sense this claim shouldn't surprise us, for "in fantasy the subject does not pursue the object or its sign: he appears caught up himself in the sequence of images."[43] In another sense, this assertion recasts Kingsley's arguments about Britain and West Africa, making us wonder if her fantasy of anonymity isn't also a precondition for her conceptual, even "ethical" approach to British imperialism. At such moments, Kingsley favors a depersonalized understanding of universality over the stronger political advantages of her British identity.

Geography and Some Explorers

> We should, indeed, be far from recommending solitary travel in Africa, or in similarly barbarous regions, to any woman—even to the New Woman. . . . For a white female to go alone among these wild races and hideous solitudes appears a risk to something more than life.
>
> —*Daily Telegraph*, 3 December 1895

Although this feeling of ecstatic freedom punctuates works by other "lady pioneers," the meaning they gave this joy varies dramatically in their writing. When Elena Ghika reached the top of the Swiss Alps in 1855, she described her awe, conventionally, as religious ecstasy: "The image of the Infinite presented itself to my mind in all its formidable grandeur. . . . I conceived such an idea of God that it appeared to me I had never before that day given him sufficient place in my heart."[44] Others, such as Bell, represented this joy in Emersonian tones, closer to Kingsley's: "Behold! the immeasurable world . . . you feel the bands break that were riveted about your heart as you enter the path that stretches across the rounded shoulder of the earth."[45]

"We have reached the point at which all that is habitable and familiar comes abruptly to an end," declared Amelia Edwards similarly in 1874. "But for the telegraphic wires stalking, ghost-like, across the desert, it would seem as if we had touched the limit of civilisation, and were standing on the threshold of a land unexplored."[46] Such observations ask us to consider whether Edwards and her counterparts viewed sublimity as self-enhancing or as self-shattering. If deeming her experiences compensatory—as "fill[ing] . . . the great void," in Margaret Fountaine's words,[47] and thus enhancing her identity—then a traveler logically would perceive other cultures differently from one viewing travel as an opportunity to sweep away existing identifications in order to confront something closer to an enigma, or abyss, in being. These contrasting perspectives on travel and self-estrangement also have different political implications. Self-repletion arguably is faithful to European colonialism, replicating experiences that are comforting and familiar, whereas self-shattering undermines existing identificatory structures, leaving nothing in their place.[48] Leaning toward self-repletion, Bell imagined "that which is me" as "an empty jar" that travel could "fill" in a way England could not. By contrast, Mary Hall experienced in travel "a feeling of unreality. . . as if I had lost my identity."[49] "The scale is too vast," Edwards wrote similarly about Karnak temple in Egypt, "the effect too tremendous; the sense of one's own dumbness, and littleness, and incapacity, too complete and crushing. It is a place that strikes you into silence; that empties you."[50]

When placed beside these examples, Kingsley's fantasy of belonging to "the non-human world" renders doubtful any suggestion that travel only enhanced her identity; like Hall and Edwards, she views such defamiliarizing moments as emptying, putting psychic and geographical space between Britain and herself. Such radical estrangement made clear to her that cultural and psychic symbols are perforated, revealing "'holes' in . . . meaning," an idea to which I'll return when discussing the colonial relevance of Freud's theory of the uncanny.[51] In the opening pages of *Travels,* for instance, Kingsley distinguishes between ignorance, which one can diminish, and emptiness of being, which one cannot: "My ignorance regarding West Africa was soon removed. And although the vast cavity in my mind that it occupied is not even yet half filled up, there is a great deal of very curious information in its place" (1–2).

Quoting this passage, Gikandi reaches a conclusion different from mine, asserting, "Kingsley's Africa is seen as a discursive object that can fill 'the vast cavity' in the observer's mind" (*Maps of Englishness,* 147). But Kingsley is making a more interesting, provocative point: The "cavity" persists despite her expectations to the contrary; she can combine all existing knowledge of Africa and it still won't yield substance. Here,

Kingsley is closer to Conrad than even Gikandi seems to realize. In "Geography and Some Explorers" (1924), Conrad too moves from the psychic to the geographical and back again, in the end suggesting Europeans' "melancholy," "lonely" response to African "emptiness" ("the white heart of Africa") shapes their perception of the continent, *despite* obvious empirical rebuttals that the continent was well-populated at the time.[52] Designating where sex and nationality cease to make sense, Kingsley highlights an interest in West Africa's sublime, impersonal elements that is at odds with many other approaches to imperialism, then as now. In effect, what is truly "marginal" in her account prevails at the expense of material considerations such as tasks, roles, and conferred identifications.

The gap Kingsley represented was rarely a source of ecstasy. In July 1895, she dwelled on African melancholia when writing Johnson, her Cambridge friend, concluding with a callous assessment of suicide:

> The malignant melancholy these Africans suffer from is very strange. You would think with their happy-go-lucky indifferentism, their want of the deeper passions, or interest in facts underlying life, and the ease of their physical conditions, they would be the last people to suffer from *weltschmertz,* but every now and again they seem to get a glimpse behind the veil and turn sick with the horror of it and kill themselves. When you question them about it, all you can get out of them is "I no fit to live," and off they start hanging themselves and cutting their throats all over the place.[53]

Though Kingsley's interest in "malignant melancholy" and "world-pain" prevails in this letter, her tone elsewhere is more measured, doubtless because those works were written for publication. Fascinated by West African spirits, rites, and witchcraft, Kingsley declares in "Black Ghosts" (1896) that "real ghosts fairly swarm . . . on the West African coast." "I have found them such a dreadful hindrance and nuisance," she adds, "that I really feel I cannot tell you whether they were any safer or pleasanter to deal with than repentant suicides."[54]

This allusion to death beside what cannot—or will not—die recalls Kingsley's letter to Nathan. More important, Kingsley sometimes gives herself an ethereal status, as though she were colonialism's revenant—"part of the atmosphere"—and thus an observer of humanity, to which ostensibly she no longer belongs (*Travels,* 178). "Apparitions are by no means of human soul origin," she writes, and "Black Ghosts" amplifies this idea by trying to summarize how West African tribes classify "the souls of the living . . . 1. The soul that survives. 2. The bush soul. 3. The dream soul. 4. The shadow on the path."[55] All these elements surface haphazardly in her work. Moreover, as Fernandez notes, "many missionaries shared [her] view that African 'spirituality' contrasted with the materialism of the European."[56] At other times, Kingsley seems more clearly aligned with the latter group, representing herself as a diplomat for England, a humble member of a group of celebrated male explorers, and an apprentice ethnographer with "orders" from Cambridge (*Travels*, 368, 141).[57]

Certainly, Kingsley never broke conclusively with Victorian Britain. She later told the *Daily Telegraph* that she "did not do anything . . . without the assistance of the superior sex," a self-protective lie designed to thwart ridicule that she'd become a "New Woman."[58] Additionally, one of the most incongruous moments in *Travels* is her admission that, after reaching the summit of Mungo Mah Lobeh, in the Cameroons, she left her visiting card among the rocks "as a civility" to the mountain, as though she were visiting an acquaintance in London (594). Evidence also abounds in *Travels* that Kingsley identified with Victorian manhood, as well as with death and the ineffable. She named herself an "Englishman" and eventually liked being called "Sir" by her canoers, whom she dubbed "boys" as a group and individually as "Gray Shirt," "Singlet," "Silence," "Pagan," and "Passenger" (550; 298–99; 238; and 237, 251).

As apparent proof that this identification pleased her, Kingsley came thereafter to identify with such male explorers as Paul du Chaillu, Heinrich Barth, Joseph Thomson, and David Livingstone, while following in the wake of her predecessors Henry Morton Stanley and Pierre de Brazza (*Travels*, 368).[59] She occasionally "forgot I was a woman" and seemed untroubled when Macmillan said she did not write like one, instead using the judgment to sharpen her prose.[60] "I really cannot draw the trail of the petticoats over the Coast of all places," she replied, "neither can I have a picture of myself in trousers or any other excitement of that sort added. I went out there as a naturalist not as a sort of circus. . . . But if you would like my name [on the book] will it not be sufficient to put *M. H. Kingsley*?"[61]

Among Victorian travelers, Kingsley wasn't alone in so defining her relation to the world. After Ménie Muriel Dowie traveled through Poland dressed as a boy, she wrote: "if a woman's clothing offered any conveniences superior to their own, we should find men of sense desirous of imitating women."[62] And in *Woman's Position, and the Objects of the Women's Franchise League* (1891), Dixie argued "that my sex was the barrier that hid from my yearning gaze the bright fields of activity, usefulness, and reform . . . Child as I was, I resolved to defy those unnatural laws."[63] But rather than advancing, with Kingsley, a broader intellectual argument against identity per se, most of these women limited their critique to gender politics. And though it's easy to see why their courage and irreverence would garner our respect, Kingsley's fascination with sexlessness and impersonality pushes feminist commentary into a more nebulous but conceptually interesting encounter with colonial sublimity.

A Crisis at the Heart of Victorian Culture

> She died at last a woman's death in a centre of civilisation, but . . . she had lived like a man in strange countries where civilisation had not gained the mastery.
> —Obituary for Mary Kingsley, *The Lady* (London), 21 June 1900

Sometimes branded "masculine" and "manly," lady pioneers such as Bell, Marianne North, and Kingsley wrote contemptuously of the suffrage and women's political movements. "I have no use for . . . these androgines," Kingsley declared, though her books nonetheless stress the allure of a terrain where biological sex is irrelevant. North went further, castigating "the wild women in the world of petticoat government." Projecting "wildness" onto British feminists, she perceptually exonerated women travelers of the same charge. "Another thing struck me," North added: "how ugly all those strongminded females and their pet parsons are! They ought always to be kept down."[64]

Viewed relative to contemporary criticism, these examples indicate that our difficulty in situating "lady pioneers" isn't new. Kingsley's obituary in *The Lady*, reproduced as this section's epigraph, implies that her dying "at last a woman's death in a centre of civilisation" extenuates that "she had lived like a man in strange countries where civilisation had not gained the mastery."[65] According to this and related assessments, Victorian culture was torn between grudging admiration for female travelers' acuity and widespread disdain that they returned to England not as ladies or even masculine women, but as something else entirely.[66] There is, in other words, fascinating congruency between Kingsley's and her culture's concerns about the displacement of gender.

When the Royal Geographical Society declared in mid-1893 that it was inexpedient "to admit ladies," because "their sex and training render them equally unfitted for exploration,"[67] *Punch* announced the decision with glee. Pretending to pose a set of questions to the "Admirals, who brave for us the battle and the breeze," the journal asked: "what meaneth all this hitching of your trousers?" One of them responds "gloom[ily]": "Avast there with your fooling; there's a lady in the case, / A lady whom they want to make a Fellow." The journal counters with a ditty:

> A lady an explorer? a traveller in skirts?
> The notion's just a trifle too seraphic:
> Let them stay and mind the babies, or hem our ragged shirts;
> But they mustn't, can't, and shan't be geographic.[68]

The complaint that these women were "a trifle too seraphic" surpasses the ascetic ideal of missionaries (a profession Kingsley repeatedly spurned),[69] instead touching on the pantheism she avowed and the sublimity framing her fantasies of insubstantial existence. Ironically, the "seraphic" lies beyond domestic chores (motherhood and mending) and literal place (it "shan't be geographic").[70] Such judgments predate by a century Sara Mills's claim that women travelers almost fell out of symbolization in Victorian culture, having "few discursive places within western colonial institutions."[71] As Mills puts it, these women "display a tension between the negotiation of two groups of discourses, neither of which completely overrides the other."[72]

In literal terms, Mills's claim about "discursive places" is misleading. Speaking little French and almost no Fang, Kingsley wrote for and lectured to Britons keen to hear about her adventures. Her two-dozen essays appeared in such prestigious journals as the *Cornhill Magazine,* the *National Review,* the *British Empire Review,* and the *Spectator.* Further, it was Britons—not Africans—who turned *Travels* into a bestseller and Kingsley into a celebrity, a sign she succeeded very well in being heard. (Five months after the book's publication, it was already in its fifth printing.) Still, it matters to ask how Kingsley gained an audience and whether her popularity translated into lasting cultural authority over what she called the "haut politique."[73] Mills's argument is in this respect more plausible, suggesting that Kingsley's deft strategies for participating in Britain's imperial discourse softened but never eclipsed its remarkable hostility to women speaking publicly about matters they apparently couldn't understand ("they mustn't, can't, and shan't be geographic").[74] If we add that these travelers allegedly returned to Britain too otherworldly, moreover, it is to juxtapose Kingsley's and others' interest in sublimity with a cultural judgment that they had repudiated sexual difference entirely. Falling out of sense, sublimity accents the very "cavity [of the] mind" that Kingsley encountered when traveling and that Freud designated as unconscious (*Travels*, 1). In short, Kingsley highlights the identificatory dilemma of women travelers keen to receive national praise for their contributions as "ladies" while experiencing sensations and fantasies that betrayed their culture's expectations of them, and, profoundly, its very conception of personhood.

"Malignant Mourning" Revisited

Kingsley's interest in sublimity recurs in her writing beside passages voicing fascination with West Africans' "malignant mourning." I refer once more to her July 1895 letter to Hatty Johnson, as traveling in West Africa arguably was her way of glimpsing "behind the veil." In doing so, she noted the limits of Victorian symbols as they opened onto something extrasymbolic—the real or sublime—that offered her excitement and trauma. Behind the veil, meaning trails off into silence and nothingness, a point reminding us why we can't simply view her memoirs as examples of expressive theory.[75] Elsewhere, African women apparently intercede between Kingsley and sublimity. Describing such women as "comely," she imbues them with the allure of a fetish, as if they were one step removed from the sublime, one means of protecting her from the joy and distress of abrogating identity.

The adjective "comely" derives from the Middle English *cumelich*, meaning "fair, pleasant to look at," itself modifying the Old English *cymlíc:* "glorious," almost seraphic. This etymology would be unremarkable if in *Travels* Kingsley didn't use the adjective so often when admiring African women. "The women indeed are very comely," she writes of the Bubis tribe; "their colour is bronze and their skin the skin of the Bantu" (63). The comment gels with one describing the arrival, on the boat, of a beautiful woman: "I am taken possession of by a very comely-looking brown young lady..." (420; see also 152).[76]

Kingsley applies the adjective to women only; she says that her male crew comprises "a miscellaneous lot of M'pongwe, black but not comely" (383). Hence, perhaps, her informing readers, in what Mills calls "an extremely bizarre statement": "I chaperoned my men while among the ladies of Esoon—a forward set of minxes—with the vigilance of a dragon" (296).[77] "I...decreed," she adds, "like the Mikado of Japan, 'that whosoever leered or winked, unless connubially linked, should forthwith be beheaded,' have their pay chopped, I mean; and as they were beginning to smell their pay, they were careful, and we got through Esoon without one of my men going into jail" (296). Why, we might add, would a British "lady pioneer" compare herself to the emperor of Japan when trying to protect her African "boys" from the interests of the "lively Esoonian belle[s] who had certainly met them"? How, moreover, would we set about resolving this "bundle of contradictions"?[78]

"I know nothing myself of love," Kingsley once avowed in a "humbl[e]...confession" to Stephen Gwynne, her first biographer. "I have read about it. I see from men and women's actions that the thing exists just like I read about it in books, but I have never been in love, nor has anyone ever been in love with me."[79] As Kingsley clearly was infatuated with Nathan in the last years of her life, this statement rings false and truncates her vivid fantasy life. *Travels in West Africa* may give us few glimpses into Kingsley's feelings for men, but it conveys her fascination for tribeswomen through what she called a gentle form of "flirting" (21), a phenomenon we seem to witness in the following passage:

> The "Fanny Po" ladies are celebrated for their beauty all along the West Coast, and very justly. They are not however, as they themselves think, the most beautiful women in this part of the world. Not at least to my way of thinking. I prefer an Elmina, or an Igalwa, or a M'pongwe, or—but I had better stop and own that my affections have got very scattered among the black ladies on the West Coast, and I no sooner remember one lovely creature whose soft eyes, perfect form and winning, pretty ways have captivated me than I think of another. The Fanny Po ladies have often a certain amount of Spanish blood in them, which gives a decidedly greater delicacy to their features:—delicate little nostrils, mouths not too heavily lipped, a certain gloss in the hair, and a light in the eye.... I think I will remain, for the present, the faithful admirer of

my sable Ingrimma, the Igalwa, with the little red blossoms stuck in her night-black hair, and a sweet soft look and word for every one, but particularly for her ugly husband the "Jack Wash." (72)

Critics may be tempted to view such statements as evidence of Kingsley's "imperial gaze," her quest idealizing the tribeswomen's "exotic" appearance. True, she dwells repeatedly on these details, paying particular attention to women's bodies, skin, and hair. Such moments in her memoir explain the discomfort of Victorian reviewers, horrified not by Kingsley's racism but by moments when she compares West Africans with Europeans. Partly in the interests of comedy (and almost certainly for additional shock value), she juxtaposes Victorian ladies with bare-breasted Africans. "Oh ye shopkeepers in England who grumble at your lady customers," she adds, resuming an earlier discussion of West Africans' kleptomania: "just you come out here and try to serve, and satisfy a set of Fans!" (306). Moreover, Kingsley imagines "a herd of hippo stroll[ing] . . . out of one of the railway tunnels of Notting Hill Gate station," in West London, and compares the progress of a canoe to the Henley Regatta on the Thames (399, 244; see also 171).

These comparisons are largely a benign, *heimlich* aspect of Kingsley's travels, underscoring what she sees as interesting connections between West African and English life: both peoples shop and use canoes; and, as she adds, men in both cultures beat their wives (225). Understandably, critics emphasizing her transgressive potential focus most of their attention here. But this emphasis isn't complete and cannot offset Kingsley's related preoccupation with *unheimlich* aspects of West African life—aspects, according to Freud's 1919 essay on the subject, that arise from unexpected contrasts between the familiar and strange.[80] For instance, Kingsley writes at length about polygamy, fetishes, and—a subject she researches obsessively—cannibalism (see *Travels*, 117–18, 248, 273–74, and 329–31). She even claims one night to have been awakened by a "violent" smell, only to discover in a nearby bag "a human hand, three big toes, four eyes, two ears, and other portions of the human frame. The hand was fresh, the other only so so, and shrivelled" (273).[81]

While cannibalism evidently represents for Kingsley the most *unheimlich* aspect of the Fante tribe in the French Congo, her descriptions of West African men generally render men as a group uncanny, and women—whether French, British, or West African—almost seraphic.

Despite extolling female beauty, she remarks that one West African "looks like a genial Irishman who has accidentally got[ten] black, very black," and that his friend is "a strapping, big fellow, as black as a wolf's mouth" (232).[82] Although the Manichean logic of these fantasies makes such extremes almost inevitable, doing little to undermine Victorian racism, the fantasies themselves touch on the sublime, a phenomenon that bewilders colonial identities.

Such fantasies are embarrassing and interesting. Operating in the service of at least three incompatible aims, they fall between conventional and radical perspectives on otherness. Kingsley's fantasies shore up men and women's "separate spheres," helping her bolster and even conserve Britain's domination in *West African Studies* by superimposing aspects of Victorian culture onto tribal life.[83] Moreover, her idealization of African women seems only marginally preferable to her sometimes egregious thoughts on African men.

Nevertheless—indeed, simultaneously—Kingsley's memoir highlights a gap between identity and identification, in which outcomes can't always be predicted and political effects finally elude comfortable assessments. This gap manifests itself between her avowal, in 1897, "I regard not only the African, but all coloured races, as inferior—inferior in kind not in degree—to the white races," and her remarking two years later to Morel, that "the poor [African] has to put up with a lot of windey headed [sic] fads and foolishness no good to him or the white man, and a jest for the Gods."[84] Moreover, her emphasis confounds materialist and identitarian approaches to colonial writing, including the presumption that her work will endorse or fail her critics' political perspectives. In this respect, *Travels in West Africa* itself exceeds the interpretive value of the complicity/resistance model.

Finally, Kingsley's fantasies open an imaginary space beyond gender, where conventional identities stop making sense. Advancing these conflicts in her writing and person, she signals women travelers' simultaneous affinity with—and partial distance from—Europe's colonial aspirations. And while Anglo-American critics obviously prefer dwelling on the latter, indicating how such cross-cultural identifications preclude a white woman's full participation in imperialism, Kingsley's fascination with sublimity makes us wonder if, in advancing this preferred reading, we've accepted what her fantasies allow and are really doing justice to her varied impulses and designs.

Notes

I thank Jason Friedman, Philip Holden, Richard Ruppel, and the anonymous readers for the University of Minnesota Press for comments on an earlier draft. I am also grateful to Jason B. Jones, Dea Birkett, the Virginia Theological Seminary, Cambridge University Library, and the Royal African Society in London for assistance with the research. Many thanks, finally, to Dunbar Moodie and the audience at the Fisher Center, Hobart and William Smith Colleges, for thoughtful responses to an earlier version of this essay.

1. Simon Gikandi, *Maps of Englishness: Writing Identity in the Culture of Colonialism* (New York: Columbia University Press, 1996), 121.

2. Elspeth Huxley, "Editor's Introduction" to Mary Kingsley, *Travels in West Africa* (1897; abridged edition, London: Dent, 1987), 1–9. Similar recent perspectives on Kingsley include Mary Russell, *The Blessings of a Good Thick Skirt: Women Travellers and Their World* (London: Collins, 1986); Irena Dobrzycka, "Mary Kingsley—A Victorian Lady in the African Bush," *Kwartalnik-Neofilologiczny* (Poland) 35, no. 4 (1988): 431–44; Valerie Grosvenor Myer, *A Victorian Lady in Africa: The Story of Mary Kingsley* (Southampton, Hamps: Ashford, 1989); and Julia Keay, *With Passport and Parasol* (London: BBC Books, 1989). More sophisticated work includes Maria H. Frawley, *A Wider Range: Travel Writing by Women in Victorian England* (Cranbury, N.J.: Associated University Presses, 1994); Julie English Early, "Unescorted in Africa: Victorian Women Ethnographers Toiling in the Fields of Sensational Science," *Journal of American Culture* 18, no. 4 (1995): 67–75; Gerry Kearns, "The Imperial Subject: Geography and Travel in the Work of Mary Kingsley and Halford Mackinder," *Transactions of the Institute of British Geographers* 22, no. 4 (1997): 450–72; and Rita S. Kranidis, *The Victorian Spinster and Colonial Emigration: Contested Subjects* (New York: St. Martin's, 1999).

3. Mazuchelli may have coined the term "lady pioneers" in 1876 when publishing *The Indian Alps and How We Crossed Them . . .* "by a Lady Pioneer." Although informed by the work and experiences of Gertrude Lowthian Bell, Isabella Bird, Florence Dixie, Ménie Muriel Dowie, Amelia B. Edwards, Elizabeth Sarah (Nina) Mazuchelli, May French-Sheldon ("Bébé Bwana"), and many others, this essay focuses on Kingsley's conceptual break with various characteristics of travel narrative. For biographical and intellectual details about a wide range of Victorian and Edwardian women travelers, see Marion Tinling, *Women into the Unknown: A Sourcebook on Women Explorers and Travelers* (Westport, Conn.: Greenwood, 1989).

4. Susan L. Blake, "A Woman's Trek: What Difference Does Gender Make?," in *Western Women and Imperialism: Complicity and Resistance,* ed. Nupur Chaudhuri and Margaret Strobel (Bloomington: Indiana University Press, 1992), 31, 29.

5. Ibid., 31.

6. Shirley Foster, *Across New Worlds: Nineteenth-Century Women Travellers and Their Writings* (Hemel Hemstead, Herts: Harvester Wheatsheaf, 1990), 133.

7. Chaudhuri and Strobel, Introduction, *Western Women and Imperialism,* 3–4. Salome C. Nnoromele also voices impatience with such celebratory motifs in feminist criticism, in "Mary Kingsley and West Africa: Race, Gender, and Colonial Discourse" (Ph.D. diss., University of Kentucky, 1995).

8. Sara Mills, *Discourses of Difference: An Analysis of Women's Travel Writing and Colonialism* (New York: Routledge, 1991, 1993), 119.

9. James Buzard, "Victorian Women and the Implications of Empire," review essay, *Victorian Studies* 36, no. 4 (1993): 446.

10. Ibid.

11. See, for instance, Marianna Torgovnick, *Primitive Passions: Men, Women, and the Quest for Ecstasy* (New York: Knopf, 1997), 65–66. Strictly speaking, though, this assessment of Kingsley did not begin in the 1980s or 1990s. Dorothy Middleton begins the final chapter of *Victorian Lady Travellers* (London: Routledge and Kegan Paul, 1965) by declaring, "Mary Kingsley is the joker in the pack" (149). "It is, of course, as a voyager that she appears in [*Travels in West Africa*], gay, gallant, and shockingly tough, as impervious to discomfort and danger for herself as to the fears of the lesser mortals [*sic*] she drew into her tearing slip-stream" (150).

12. Florence Dixie, "Lady Travellers," *Quarterly Review* 76 (June 1845): 98, 99.

13. Concludes this reviewer, apparently without irony: women's "defencelessness is a passport . . ." "The Desert and the Sown," *TLS* (25 January 1907), 28.

14. See Sara Suleri, *The Rhetoric of English India* (Chicago: University of Chicago Press, 1992), 76; Inderpal Grewal, *Home and Harem: Nation, Gender, Empire, and the Cultures of Travel* (Durham: Duke University Press, 1996), 9–10.

15. Dea Birkett, *Spinsters Abroad: Victorian Lady Explorers* (Oxford: Blackwell, 1989), x–xi, and Birkett, *Mary Kingsley: Imperial Adventuress* (London: Macmillan, 1992). This essay owes much to both books.

16. John E. Flint, Introduction to Kingsley, *Travels in West Africa: Congo Français, Corisco, and Cameroons* (1897; 3rd ed., New York: Barnes and Noble, 1965), xvii–xviii. Subsequent references to Kingsley's *Travels* give pagination of this edition.

17. Kingsley, *Travels in West Africa*, 669. See also Kingsley, "The Development of Dodos," *National Review* 27 (March 1896): 67; and her editorial "On Efficiency and Empire," *Spectator*, 13 January 1900, 51–52.

18. Kingsley, "The Negro Future," *Spectator*, 28 December 1895, 931. Her obituarist in the *Spectator* put this more bluntly, without recording the full complexity of her argument: "While feeling a deep sympathy for all natives, and anxiously desiring their welfare, she was entirely free from any exaggerated notions as to the perfectibility of the negro, and did not in the least desire to favour schemes for treating black men as if they were white. In fact, her main contention was always that you must not try to raise the negroes by giving them votes and representative institutions and the like, but by studying them and finding out the form of government which suited them best. She desired as far as possible to keep the blacks and whites apart, each within their own polity." "Miss Mary Kingsley," *Spectator*, 16 June 1900, 836.

19. "I . . . feel certain that a black man is no more an undeveloped white man than a woman is an undeveloped man. The difference in the comparative level of the black and the white is very much the same as between women and men among ourselves. A great woman, mentally or physically, will excel an indifferent man, but no woman has ever equalled a truly great man." Kingsley, "The Development of Dodos," 71.

20. Kingsley to Alice Green, 11 April 1900, quoted in Katherine Frank, *A Voyager Out: The Life of Mary Kingsley* (Boston: Houghton Mifflin, 1986), 295, 296.

21. Flint, "Mary Kingsley—A Reassessment," *Journal of African History* 4, no. 1 (1963): 96.

22. Ibid., 95.

23. Kingsley to Hatty Johnson, 28 January 1896, quoted in Frank, *A Voyager Out,* 207.

24. See Kingsley, "Imperialism," in *West African Studies* (1899; 2d ed., London: Macmillan, 1901), esp. 415–16, a chapter added to the book's second edition. The citations are from the chapter's first two paragraphs.

25. Ibid., 419.

26. Kingsley to Edmund Morel, 20 February 1899, quoted in part in Birkett, *Mary Kingsley,* 138, and in full (but incorrectly identified, and with altered spelling) in Frank, *A Voyager Out,* 292. My thanks to Birkett for confirming this letter's source and peculiar spelling.

27. Alison Blunt, *Travel, Gender, and Imperialism: Mary Kingsley and West Africa* (New York: Guilford, 1994), 108–11.

28. Flint, "Mary Kingsley—A Reassessment," 104.

29. As Birkett cautions in *Mary Kingsley,* "Not all Mary Kingsley's statements of her experiences in West Africa are to be taken at face value.... In claiming to be a successor to [Paul] du Chaillu, Mary Kingsley could also be accused of the same misreporting and exaggeration: there were certainly many mistakes in her observations. She also interwove what she saw with the impressions drawn from earlier published accounts. She might even be said never to have been to the places she claims to have visited" (37, 41–42).

30. Jacques Lacan, *The Four Fundamental Concepts of Psycho-Analysis,* ed. Jacques-Alain Miller, trans. Alan Sheridan (1973; New York: Norton, 1981), 56, original emphasis.

33. Jean Laplanche and Jean-Bertrand Pontalis, "Fantasy and the Origins of Sexuality" (1964), in *Formations of Fantasy,* ed. Victor Burgin, James Donald, and Cora Kaplan (New York: Methuen, 1986), 26.

32. Foster, *Across New Worlds,* 133.

33. James W. Fernandez, *Bwiti: An Ethnography of the Religious Imagination in Africa* (Princeton: Princeton University Press, 1982), 35; original emphasis. For elaboration on this claim, see Joan Copjec, *Read My Desire: Lacan against the Historicists* (Cambridge: MIT Press, 1994), esp. 1–14. I advance this argument having read such invaluable historical accounts of the Asante and Fante states as Adu Boahen, "Politics in Ghana, 1800–1874," in *History of West Africa,* ed. J. F. A. Ajayi and Michael Crowder (New York: Columbia University Press, 1973), 2: 167–261; Kenneth S. Carlston, *Social Theory and African Tribal Organization: The Development of Socio-Legal Theory* (Urbana: University of Illinois Press, 1968); Elizabeth Isichei, *History of West Africa since 1800* (New York: Africana Publishing, 1977); and J. B. Webster and A. A. Boahen, *History of West Africa: The Revolutionary Years—1815 to Independence* (1967; New York: Praeger, 1970).

34. See Middleton, *Victorian Lady Travellers,* 160. Middleton's claim that Kingsley "was something of an expert" in "trade English" modifies Birkett's claim that she "could not possibly have held any language in common" with the tribespeople (*Spinsters Abroad,* 202). The implication of Birkett's claim is that all dialogue recorded in *Travels in West Africa* is Kingsley's invention.

35. Freud to Wilhelm Fliess, 21 September 1897, *The Complete Letters of Sigmund Freud to Wilhelm Fliess 1887–1904,* ed. and trans. Jeffrey Moussaieff Masson (Cambridge: Harvard University Press, 1985), 264. The remark precedes Freud's important thesis in *The Interpretation of Dreams* (1900–1901), that "*psychical* reality is a

particular form of existence not to be confused with *material* reality." Freud, *The Standard Edition of the Complete Psychological Works of Sigmund Freud,* ed. and trans. James Strachey (London: Hogarth, 1953–74), 24 vols., 5: 620; original emphases.

36. For amplification of this idea, to which I am indebted, see Copjec, *Read My Desire,* 204. Tim Dean advances a similarly compelling thesis about sexuality and impersonality in *Beyond Sexuality* (Chicago: University of Chicago Press, 2000).

37. Kingsley to Matthew Nathan, 12 May 1899, quoted in Frank, *A Voyager Out,* 269.

38. In *Mary Kingsley* Birkett argues convincingly that although "it is not possible to prove, in the accepted sense of biographical 'evidence,' that Mary learnt of her parents' shotgun wedding [four days before her birth] at the time of their deaths, [and] although it could not have been *concealed* from her at this time … it seems a highly likely scene, and helps to explain her leap to Africa and the intensity of her despair. She had lost more than her parents: she had lost her faith in them as well" (15, original emphasis).

39. Kingsley, *Travels in West Africa,* 101.

40. Ibid., 102.

41. Quoted in Olwen Campbell, *Mary Kingsley: A Victorian in the Jungle* (London: Methuen, 1957), 121.

42. Kingsley to Nathan, 12 May 1899, quoted in Frank, *A Voyager Out,* 269.

43. Laplanche and Pontalis, "Fantasy and the Origins of Sexuality," 26.

44. Elena Ghika, *Switzerland, the Pioneer of the Reformation; or La Suisse allemande,* by Madame La Comtesse Dora d'Istria (pseud.), trans. H. G., 2 vols. (Edinburgh: A. Fullarton, 1858), 2: 324.

45. Gertrude Bell, *Syria: The Desert and the Sown* (1907; New York: Arno, 1973), 1–2.

46. Edwards, *A Thousand Miles Up the Nile* (1877, rev. 1888; London: Darf, 1993), 320.

47. Margaret Fountaine, *Love among the Butterflies: The Travels and Adventures of a Victorian Lady,* ed. W. F. Cater (c. 1878–1913, 1980; Harmondsworth: Penguin, 1982), 54.

48. I amplify this argument, itself indebted to Leo Bersani's work, in *The Ruling Passion: British Colonial Allegory and the Paradox of Homosexual Desire* (Durham: Duke University Press, 1995) and in "'Savage Ecstasy': Colonialism and the Death Drive," in *The Psychoanalysis of Race,* ed. Lane (New York: Columbia University Press, 1998), 282–304.

49. All quotations appear in Birkett, *Spinsters Abroad,* 72.

50. Edwards, *A Thousand Miles Up the Nile,* 148.

51. Lacan, "The Subversion of the Subject and the Dialectic of Desire in the Freudian Unconscious" (1960), *Écrits: A Selection,* ed. Jacques-Alain Miller, trans. Alan Sheridan (New York: Norton, 1977), 299.

52. Joseph Conrad, "Geography and Some Explorers" (1924), in *White Man in the Tropics: Two Moral Tales,* ed. David Daiches (London: Harcourt, 1962), 116–17. See also Karen R. Lawrence, *Penelope Voyages: Women and Travel in the British Literary Tradition* (Ithaca: Cornell University Press, 1994), 135; Alison Blunt, "Mapping Authorship and Authority: Reading Mary Kingsley's Landscape Descriptions," in *Writing Women and Space: Colonial and Postcolonial Geographies,* ed. Blunt and Gillian Rose (New York: Guilford, 1994), 52; and Jules Law, "Cultural Ecologies of

the Coast: Space as the Edge of Cultural Practice in Mary Kingsley's *Travels in West Africa*," in *Nineteenth-Century Geographies: The Transformation of Space from the Victorian Age to the American Century*, ed. Helena Michie and Ronald Thomas (New Brunswick, N.J.: Rutgers University Press, 2003), 109–22. Good comparisons of both writers also include Lynn Thiesmeyer, "Imperial Fictions and Nonfictions: The Subversion of Sources in Mary Kingsley and Joseph Conrad," in *Transforming Genres: New Approaches to British Fiction of the 1890s*, ed. Nikki Lee Manos and Meri-Jane Rocheleson (New York: St. Martin's, 1994), 155–72; and Thiesmeyer, "Mary Kingsley, Joseph Conrad, and Women in Africa," *Japan Women's University Studies in English and American Literature* (26 March 1991), 99–119.

53. Kingsley to Johnson, July 1895, quoted in Campbell, *Mary Kingsley*, 132.

54. "Black Ghosts," *Cornhill* 74, no. 1 (or n.s. 3, 1.1; July 1896): 81.

55. *Travels in West Africa*, 521; "Black Ghosts," 81. Related Kingsley articles include "The Fetish View of the Human Soul," *Folk-Lore: A Quarterly Review of Myth, Tradition, Institution, and Custom* 8, no. 2 (June 1897): 138–51, and "The Forms of Apparitions in West Africa," *Proceedings of the Society for Psychical Research* 14 (Supplement; London: Kegan Paul, Trench, Trübner and Co., 1899), 331–42.

56. Fernandez, *Bwiti*, 275.

57. This helps explain her obsequious approach to the Royal Geographical Society and the Anthropological Institute. "I am not a member of the Anthropological [Institute] or for that matter of that of any society," she wrote to Professor Alfred Haddon on 8 June 1896. "They are not 'woman palaver.' I shall try and go and see if the doorkeeper will let me in." Kingsley, quoted in Birkett, *Mary Kingsley*, 66.

58. Kingsley, "Letter," *The Daily Telegraph*, 5 December 1895, 8; editorial, *Daily Telegraph*, 3 December 1895, 7.

59. Although the *Daily Telegraph* made this link in a story printed when Kingsley had returned to England, saying (with some archness) that her accomplishments "must rank her henceforward with the great dynasty of modern African travellers which commenced with Dr. Livingstone, and has been carried forward by the renowned names of Speke, Grant, Burton, Stanley, Cameron, Thomson, Johnson, Selous, and many others of whose work England has reason to be proud," it may have been echoing—whether knowingly or not—Kingsley's own desire to join this pantheon of explorers (3 December 1895, 7). Certainly, Kingsley's stated ambition for this reception preceded the fame that later was conferred on her. For a contrary, less plausible reading of Kingsley's celebrity, see Marni Stanley, "Skirting the Issues: Addressing and Dressing in Victorian Women's Travel Narratives," *Victorian Review* 23, no. 2 (1997): 147–48.

60. See Rudyard Kipling, *Something of Myself, for My Friends Known and Unknown*, ed. Robert Hampson (1936; Harmondsworth: Penguin, 1988), 79.

61. Kingsley to George Macmillan, 18 December 1894, quoted in Birkett, *Mary Kingsley*, 27.

62. Ménie Muriel Dowie, *A Girl in the Karpathians* (2d ed., London: Philip and Son, 1891), 17–18.

63. Dixie, *Woman's Position, and the Objects of the Women's Franchise League*, a Lecture Delivered in the Christian Institute, Glasgow, on Tuesday 21st April, 1891 (Dundee: John Leng, 1891), 9. In the 1860s Alexandrine Tinne "sailed around the Mediterranean with her crew dressed in Arab clothes" (Birkett, *Spinsters Abroad*,

285); she was later murdered in 1869, the first European woman attempting to cross the Sahara.

64. Marianne North, MS of autobiography, 382, deleted from the published version, quoted in Birkett, *Spinsters Abroad*, 201, 200; see also Middleton, *Victorian Lady Travellers*, 172. Mazuchelli also coined the term "lady pioneers" partly to distinguish her and others' achievements from the "asexual" quality of feminists: "I am by no means one of those strong-minded females who advocate what is mis-called 'woman's rights'; on the contrary, I believe women have tenderer, sweeter, purer, if not nobler, rights than such advocates wot of—rights best suited to the gentler nature of her sex, and hidden deep in the sweet and gentle life of home; but there are limits to the depreciation of womankind in the social scale, and in behalf of [sic] my Oriental sisters I object to the above order of ideas." Mazuchelli, *The Indian Alps and How We Crossed Them: Being a Narrative of Two Years' Residence in the Eastern Himalaya and Two Months' Tour into the Interior*, by a Lady Pioneer (New York: Dodd, Mead, 1876), 332. A likely sign of her concern to deflect criticism, Mazuchelli manages in this sentence to refer twice to women's "sweetness" and "gentleness."

65. "Far and Near," *The Lady* (London), 21 June 1900, 976; see also Russell, *The Blessings of a Good Thick Skirt*, 215–17.

66. This argument about traveling women's return to England is surely inseparable from earlier remarks at midcentury justifying women's emigration because of their "superfluous" relation to society. In "Why Are Women Redundant?," for instance, W. R. Greg argues that "there is an enormous and increasing number of single women in the nation, a number quite disproportionate and quite abnormal; a number which, positively and relatively, is indicative of an unwholesome social state" ("Why Are Women Redundant?" *National Review* 28 [April 1862]: 436). He laments the number of "old maids . . . wretched and deteriorating, their minds narrowing, and their hearts' withering, because they have nothing to do, and none to love, cherish, and obey" (436–37). See also the chronological developments in Greg, "Emigration or Manufactures," *Westminster Review* 40 (August 1843): 53–65; Isa Craig, "Emigration as a Preventive Agency," *English Woman's Journal* 2, no. 11 (January 1859): 289–97; "Emigrant-Ship Matrons," *English Woman's Journal* 5, no. 25 (March 1860): 24–36; "On Assisted Emigration," *English Woman's Journal* 5, no. 28 (June 1860): 235–40; J. Chapman, "Emigration," *Westminster Review* 102 (July 1874): 12–18; G. Noël Hatton, "The Future of Single Women," *Westminster Review* 121 (January 1884): 151–62; and Edward Tregear, "Compulsory Emigration," *Westminster Review* 130 (September 1888): 378–88.

67. George N. Curzon, Viceroy of India and future president of the RGS, "Ladies and the Royal Geographical Society," *Times*, 31 May 1893, 11.

68. "To the Royal Geographical Society," *Punch* 104 (10 June 1893): 269.

69. The "missionary-made class of man," writes Kingsley in "The Development of Dodos" (1896), "is a curse to the Coast, and you find him in European clothes, and without, all the way down from Sierra Leone to Loanda. The Pagans despise him, the whites hate him, but he thinks enough of himself to make him comfortable. His conceit is marvellous, nothing equals it . . ." (73).

70. In her later article "Celebrated Lady Travellers: I" (1901), Ethel F. Heddle suggested that Kingsley had a "madonna-like face," but that's merely the flip side of representing her as either an Amazon or a "maiden aunt," the latter a role she per-

fected for herself. Heddle, "Celebrated Lady Travellers: I, Ménie Muriel Dowie (Mrs. Henry Norman)," *Good Words* 42 (1901): 16; Kingsley, quoted in Birkett, *Spinsters Abroad,* 198.

71. Mills, *Discourses of Difference,* 106.

72. Ibid.

73. Kingsley to Green, 11 April 1900, quoted in Frank, *A Voyager Out,* 295.

74. That Flora Shaw, Kingsley's perceived enemy, was throughout these years colonial editor of the *Times* doesn't mitigate this problem but makes it more resilient and disturbing.

75. For an excellent account of Victorian literature and expressive theory, see Isobel Armstrong, "'A Music of Their Own': Women's Poetry—An Expressive Tradition?," *Victorian Poetry: Poetry, Poetics, and Politics* (New York: Routledge, 1993, 1996), 318–77.

76. Examples abound of Kingsley's use of this adjective: Adornments in the hair of Igalwa and M'pongwe women "are exceedingly becoming to these black but comely ladies, verily I think, the comeliest ladies I have ever seen on the Coast" (223). Earlier, she remarks that "Mrs. S. . . . is a comely and large black lady, an old acquaintance of mine" (77). And when noting the achievements of an African trader, she comments: "His efforts were ably seconded by his good lady, an exceedingly comely Gaboon woman, with pretty manners, and an excellent gift in cookery" (308).

77. Mills, *Discourses of Difference,* 157.

78. Buzard, "Victorian Women and the Implications of Empire," 446.

79. Kingsley to Stephen Gwynne, quoted in Huxley, "Editor's Introduction" to *Travels in West Africa,* 6.

80. See Freud, "The 'Uncanny'" (1919), *Standard Edition* 17: 217–56.

81. Birkett reminds us that the Fante tribe "knew of the rumours of their anthropophagy" and deliberately "contribut[ed] to their reputation as a ferocious people." Additionally, "Kingsley, accumulating racy stories for her future audience back home . . . lapped up such tales" (*Mary Kingsley,* 47).

82. See also French-Sheldon, *Sultan to Sultan: Adventures among the Masai and Other Tribes of East Africa* (Boston: Arena, 1892), 356–57.

83. *West African Studies,* 415–29.

84. Kingsley to Edmund Morel, February 1899, quoted in Birkett, *Mary Kingsley,* 138.

CHAPTER SIX

Redressing the Empire:
Anthony Trollope and British Gender
Anxiety in "The Banks of the Jordan"

Mark Forrester

When the *London Review* published Anthony Trollope's short story "The Banks of the Jordan" in three installments during January of 1861, the magazine seems to have been fully unprepared for the controversy that ensued.[1] Laurence Oliphant, a proprietor of the *Review*, wrote to the author to convey his own—and his partners'—sense of dismay, citing but one relatively mild example of the public's unfavorable response to Trollope's story: "You must make your election whether you will adapt your paper to the taste of men of intelligence & high moral feeling *or* to that of persons of morbid imagination *& a low tone of morals*."[2] While wringing his own hands sympathetically, Oliphant carefully absolved himself of responsibility in the affair: "I feel that I owe you an apology for not having read the tales before publication, but I felt such perfect confidence that anything from your pen would have defied any such criticism as the above that I had not looked at it until I saw it in the paper"; Oliphant proceeded to regret that Trollope's stories had not combined a "high moral tendency" with "literary merit."[3] Trollope seems to have responded calmly to Oliphant's ducking of editorial responsibility (and his sly moralistic backpedaling, disguised as fawning praise), writing across Oliphant's note: "A wonderful letter."[4] We cannot hope to recover the expression that crossed the writer's face as he scribbled that inscrutable observation.

If "The Banks of the Jordan" continues to startle us today, it is only because of the extent of its own investment in a homoerotic ruse. The story is narrated by a Mr. Jones ("I will call myself Jones on the present occasion"), who has traveled to Jerusalem in order to tour the Holy Land. At the hotel, a gentleman named John Smith approaches Jones and asks to travel with him. Although Jones eschews discussing personal matters, going so far as to deny that he is married and has children, the two men become emotionally and physically close. However, as they are nearing Jaffa, they encounter the strict uncle whom Jones's traveling companion has been seeking to escape. To his shame, Jones discovers that Smith is really Miss Julia Weston, whose uncle demands that Jones preserve his niece's honor by marrying her: because he cannot, the married Jones lingers discreetly behind while the others return to England. Although the narrator hints at his (continued or sudden) attraction to Julia Weston, the most intimate, even passionate, moments in the story occur while Jones believes he is with another man. We might expect that this homo-erotic aspect of the story caused the outrage that Oliphant reported, but such does not appear to have been the case. Apparently, it was sufficient that these scenes turned out to involve an unmarried and unprotected female in the unchaperoned company of a married gentleman.

Oliphant was not alone in his blind trust in Trollope's rectitude; just a few months after Trollope's death, after all, Henry James would aver, "With Trollope we were always safe."[5] But while it may be true that, in matters of gender, "Trollope does not overtly critique the Phallocentric order,"[6] it is also true that the author's thinking was more complicated and less static than is often assumed. Jane Nardin, while noting that Trollope's sympathy toward "the plight of dissatisfied women" increased at about the same time that he was writing "The Banks of the Jordan," argues for the complexity of the author's social philosophy, noting that "in considering Trollope's attitudes toward women, we must also remember that ambivalence and complexity characterize his moral vision and the fictional structures in which that vision is embodied."[7] Rather than providing the conventional endorsement of the Victorian "angel in the house," as Oliphant and his partners may have anticipated, Trollope presumes to question societal assumptions about patriarchy and the position of women.

Significantly, this reappraisal is set not in England but in the Middle East. During the same period that Trollope's thinking about women was growing (at least somewhat) more sympathetic and sophisticated, his "mapping" of empire and race was likewise becoming increasingly complex.[8] For Trollope, as for other Victorian writers, the colonies provided a space within which one could explore the relativism and malleability of moral attitudes and social structures without directly challenging the nation's foundation; in Trollope's worldview "the fixed rules . . . of morality are European rules and prevail only where Western civilization dominates."[9] In *Orientalism*, Edward W. Said argues that Western Europe did not merely interpret, but constructed, the Near East—"politically, sociologically, militarily, ideologically, scientifically, and imaginatively"— as a "surrogate and even underground self."[10] The Orient became an imaginative stage on which Westerners could, on the one hand, define themselves by contrast, while also enacting a transient and only quasi-illicit release from that identity, a safe distance from home. Among other things, this meant the opportunity to reinvent oneself sexually: "The Orient was a place where one could look for sexual experience unobtainable in Europe."[11] More recently, Joseph A. Boone has called attention to the heterosexual slant of Said's work, noting that "the possibility of sexual contact with and between men underwrites and at times even explains the historical appeal of orientalism as an occidental mode of male perception, appropriation, and control."[12] The ostensibly tamed foreignness of colonial space, and the governing power relations between imperial and colonized subjects, allowed such forbidden affinities to be cultivated under the penumbra of, in Eve Sedgwick's terms, "a fantasy-prone distinction between the domestic and the exotic."[13] At the margins of empire, on "The Banks of the Jordan," Trollope could more safely explore these inherent ambiguities of power, identity, and desire.

Had the readers of the *London Review* chosen—or been able—to acknowledge Trollope's homoerotics, they might have found much more to interest or offend them. From their first meeting, the relationship between the narrator and John Smith is described in terms that edge dangerously toward the sexual: "There was so much about him that was pleasant, both to the eye and to the understanding. . . . I must confess that I was attracted by John Smith at first sight" (110). Without this element of illicit attraction, their relationship would be stripped of its perceived danger, and the story could not be resolved into its proper emotional context: the validation of the blushing shame that pervades the entire text.[14]

As the relationship progresses, it becomes increasingly physical. John Smith has equipped himself with an uncomfortable "Turkish saddle," which the narrator condemns in terms of both national and religious chauvinism.

Let it be a rule with every man to carry an English saddle with him when travelling in the East. Of what material is formed the nether man of a Turk I have never been informed, but I am sure that it is not flesh and blood. . . . I was grieved to find that Smith was not properly provided. He was seated in one of those hard, red, high-pointed machines, to which the shovels intended to act as stirrups are attached in such a manner, and hang at such an angle, as to be absolutely destructive to the leg of a Christian. (112)

Jones expresses his consequent concern for the shape of his companion's body: "I explained this to him, taking hold of his leg by the calf to show how the leather would chafe him; but it seemed to me that he did not quite like my interference" (112–3). Not long after, Smith does have cause to regret his choice of saddles: "'Ah,' said I, 'that confounded Turkish saddle has already galled your skin. I see how it is: I shall have to doctor you with a little brandy—externally applied, my friend'" (118). Smith declines to have the brandy administered, and Jones arranges for his use of a good English saddle for the remainder of the excursion. When they resume their journey, the narrator continues to chide his companion for his masculine, or modest, reluctance: "'You should have let me rub in that brandy,' I said. 'You can't conceive how efficaciously I would have done it'" (119). As Trollope notes in his letters, it is these two passages—that "affair of the saddle, and that other affair of the leg"— to which his readers had particularly objected.[15]

The most physically intimate scenes, however, are not those that take place between Smith and Jones, but those in which the narrator is alone. At the Dead Sea, and again at the Jordan River, Trollope's narrator leaves Smith, strips, and bathes alone in the waters. Although his companion declines to join him, Jones's bathing seems to bring the two men to a greater level of intimacy: "We sat down together on a spot from which we could see the stream, close together, so that when I stretched myself out in my weariness, as I did before we started, my head rested on his legs" (125). As the narrator observes, a gentleman "does not take such liberties" with a new acquaintance at home. However, the soft-spoken and delicate Smith and the brasher and more self-confident narrator, who functions as "something of a self-portrait" of Trollope,[16] almost immediately achieve a startling level of intimacy, and even before they embark, Jones goes to uncharacteristic lengths to ensure himself of Smith's company.

Following a long and intimate—even tearful—conversation, Jones's earlier exertions overtake him:

> We were silent again for a while, and it was during this time that I found myself lying with my head on his lap. I had slept, but it could have been but for a few minutes, and when I woke I felt his hand upon my brow. As I started up he said that the flies had been annoying me, and that he had not chosen to waken me as I seemed weary. "It has been that double bathing," I said, apologetically; for I always feel ashamed when I am detected sleeping in the day. (128)

While this passage seems, on the one hand, to be almost a postcoital denouement, it also suggests a precoital seduction scene: "'Stay half a moment,' he said, speaking very softly, and laying his hand upon my arm, 'I will not detain you a minute'" (128). In any case, it soon becomes clear that, for Smith and Jones, the moment of greatest intimacy has already passed, whether during Jones's double bathing or in his sleep. While the two men remain companions, they are never again brought this physically close.

Upon the travelers' return to Jaffa, the wealthy uncle of John Smith, newly arrived from England, informs the narrator that his recent companion has in truth been his niece:

> It all came back upon me in a moment, and covered me with a shame that even made me blush. I had travelled through the desert with a woman for days, and had not discovered her though she had given me a thousand signs. All those signs I remembered now, and I blushed painfully. When her hand was on my forehead I still thought that she was a man! (137)

The revelation of Smith's female identity allows Trollope's narrator to escape the implications of his own homoerotic attraction, just as it has allowed Trollope as author to create that attraction. It is permissible for Trollope to suggest that one man may be physically attracted to another man, so long as the latter eventually turns out to be a woman. Jones's subsequent shame (at his own gullibility, and at his now strictly heterosexual improprieties) attempts to validate, by standing in the place of, the embarrassment that appears throughout the earlier, explicitly homoerotic moments.

The most physically aggressive encounters in "The Banks of the Jordan" occur between Jones and the foreign setting while he is bathing.

The story's final heterosexual turn, with its unmasking (or unmanning) of Julia Weston, may attempt to obscure its homoerotics by rewriting the earlier passionate attraction between the two men. However, Jones's desires elude his narrative (and psychological) control within the context of these sexually charged bathing encounters that cannot, or will not, be erased. In these scenes, the sexuality is inscribed within the landscape itself, rather than on the unstable gender identities of Trollope's characters.

There are two particularly significant instances of attempted, sexualized penetration in "The Banks of the Jordan," though neither is acted by one individual upon another. The first incident takes place when the traveling party penetrates "the subterranean chapel under the tomb" of the Virgin (114); the second is Jones's bathing, when he stops to immerse himself ritualistically, in the Dead Sea and the Jordan River. At the chapel, the English tourists demonstrate their imperial mastery by pushing aside the local supplicants in their territorial drive toward the altar. At the Dead Sea and the Jordan, however, the native waters reassert the region's control over these intruders by first thwarting Jones's attempted entry, and then aggressively penetrating and marking the English pilgrim's body.

Initially, amid the unsettling strangeness of the Middle East, Jones struggles to maintain a clear distinction between the Self and the Other. As an imperial tourist, Trollope was certainly aware of the disruptive effects that interactions between the foreign and the domestic might have on the fixity of identity: "Trollope's confidence as to his right to provide a cartography of peoples . . . contained also always within it the anxiety as to whether those peoples were really fully in place."[17] At the Church of the Holy Sepulchre, Trollope's narrator is quick to distinguish between his own (and Smith's) European nature and that of the "Eastern worshippers":

> It must be remembered that Eastern worshippers are not like the church-goers of London, or even of Rome or Cologne. They are wild men of various nations and races. . . . They savour strongly of Oriental life and of Oriental dirt. They are clad in skins or hairy cloaks with huge hoods. Their heads are shaved, and their faces covered with short, grisly, fierce beards. They are silent mostly, looking out of their eyes ferociously, as though murder were in their thoughts, and rapine. (114–5)

As Jones and Smith, who follows closely in Jones's wake, shove their way through the dense and dirty crowd, their penetration recalls a more general English progress through the colonized world; as Jones himself asks, with just a touch of ironic self-awareness, "How is it that Englishmen can push themselves anywhere?" (115).

The penetration of the crowd by the English tourists becomes, in turn, just one component of their competition with the worshippers to penetrate, and to master, the chapel itself: "One would have supposed that they were not lambs or doves, capable of being thrust here or there without anger on their part; and they, too, were all anxious to descend and approach the altar" (115). Though the worshippers are not "lambs or doves" (two symbols, of course, for the Christian faith), the narrator must imagine them as such in order to convert these "fierce-looking" Eastern men into the docile objects of his own persistent thrusting toward the altar. Within the context of Jones's narrative, they are more than compliant: "To them the occasion was very holy" (116). Just as the bodies of the "Eastern worshippers" are made a site for narrative inspection and penetration, "the body of the chapel" itself becomes sexualized: "The place was dark, mysterious, and full of strange odours..." (115). This vaginally or anally constructed altar of the Virgin is approached by the worshippers as they extend their "long tapers," a phallic self-assertiveness that is quickly preempted by the Englishmen: "We did assist them, getting lights for their tapers, handing them to and fro, and using the authority with which we seemed to be invested" (116). This expression of religious devotion and of imperial authority becomes an opportunity for the acting out of safe sexual fantasies within an authorized and protective script, in the same manner that Smith's transgendered pose provides an occasion, as well as an excuse, for the exercise of Jones's homoerotic fantasies.

While Jones's penetration of the chapel is forceful, masterful, and forgiven, his later attempt to penetrate the water of the Dead Sea is largely unsuccessful and unsatisfying. Not only does the high level of salt in the sea prevent proper bathing, but Jones himself becomes the object against which the force of the water acts:

> When I was in nearly up to my hips, the water knocked me down. Indeed, it did so when I had gone as far as my knees, but I recovered myself, and by perseverance did proceed somewhat further. It must not

be imagined that this knocking down was effected by the movement of the water. There is no such movement. Everything is perfectly still, and the fluid seems hardly to be displaced by the entrance of the body. But the effect is that one's feet are tripped up, and that one falls prostrate on the surface. (122–23)

The salt water will not allow him to fall down. Rather than being knocked down, he is in effect "knocked up," rising to fall on the surface of the water: "I then essayed to swim; but I could not do this in the ordinary way, as I was unable to keep enough of my body below the surface; so that my head and face seemed to be propelled down upon it" (123). The sexualized dynamics of the chapel scene, in which the English tourist successfully dominates the local worshippers, are neatly reversed, as Jones is now forced to submit to the native presence, the Otherness, embodied in the Dead Sea.

Victoria Glendinning has pointed out the extent to which sexuality is often "signaled topographically" in Trollope's fiction: "Chasms, rivers, torrents, waterfalls, high cliffs above the sea; falling, swimming, drowning; and bridges, stiles, passing-places. These were his metaphors for the ecstatic, engulfing, frightening surrender which was, it seems, his vision of sexual passion."[18] Trollope may feint toward what Mary Louise Pratt calls the "monarch-of-all-I-survey" trope,[19] presenting a highly aestheticized landscape that allows the imperial observer to render the foreign setting unreal, in order to first assimilate and then dominate it: "There was the lake, and there it had been before our eyes for the last two hours; and yet it looked, then and now, as though it were an image of a lake and not real water" (121–22). But Trollope's penchant for "frightening surrender" soon reverses the expected power relationship between colonizer and colonized, and the lake engulfs and then penetrates the intrusive foreign body. Even the stillness of the lake possesses an aggressive sexual force. By keeping Jones on stage alone throughout this scene, however, Trollope leaves the reader uncertain precisely where this passion connects, and in which direction (or directions) it is flowing.

The language of Jones's ineffective bathing, or his untidy baptism, is to a certain extent the language of rape—or, at the very least, the language of a forceful sexual encounter. His "feet are tripped up," he is knocked down, and he "falls prostrate." It is not unlike the language that has already been used to describe the penetration of the chapel, when the travelers "push themselves" into the crowd and "win [their] way through them" to the altar. In the context of Jones's narrative, how-ever, questions of complicity and consent become hopelessly blurred: the lines between seduction and rape, between conquest and submission, are blurred or obliterated.

In this instance, the "entrance" of, or the entrance to, Jones's body is his mouth, and it is the taste of the Dead Sea waters that he finds particularly offensive:

> Anything more abominable to the palate than this water, if it be water, I never had inside my mouth. I expected it to be extremely salty, and no doubt, if it were analyzed, such would be the result; but there is a flavor in it which kills the salt. No attempt can be made at describing this taste. It may be imagined that I did not drink heartily, merely taking up a drop or two with my tongue from the palm of my hand; but it seemed to me as though I had been drenched with it. (123)

This seminal fluid—forced into Jones's mouth by the Dead Sea, an act sanctioned by his homoerotic attraction toward John Smith, an illicit relationship authorized by their presence in this colonial space—is the true medium of this pilgrim's transformative baptism. A scene which begins with Jones's attempted (and failed) penetration of the aestheti-cized water's surface ends with that water's (successful) penetration of Jones. While his skin seems to dry normally, Jones cannot erase the wa-ter's effect: "And then my whole body was in a mess, and I felt as though I had been rubbed with pitch" (123). By becoming the object of the wa-ter's force, the narrator has put himself in the submissive position of the unclean "Eastern worshippers" at the chapel, and he carries his own un-seen mark of "Oriental dirt" in this sensation of pitch across the surface of his body. The taste, and the feel, of the Dead Sea linger in the depths and on the surface of the narrator's body and psyche.

The final outbound leg of Jones's excursion, the trip to the Jordan River itself, thus becomes an opportunity to attempt to cleanse himself of this water in which he has already bathed. Again, the experience is less than fulfilling: "I was forced to wade out through the dirt and slush, so that I found it difficult to make my feet and legs clean enough for my shoes and stockings; and then, moreover, the flies plagued me most un-mercifully" (125). The Eastern pilgrims, Jones learns, do not attempt to "go bodily" into the river; for them, "bathing in Jordan has come to be much the same as baptism has with us. It hardly means immersion" (125). But Jones's baptism into the sense of cultural and sexual Otherness afforded by this colonized territory is a near total immersion, or inversion. Apparently, his bathing at the Jordan does not even erase the film left on his skin by the Dead Sea, for after Jones emerges from the Jordan he expects its "filthy flavour" to save him from the flies and mosquitoes. And now he is marked by even more "dirt and slush" that cannot be removed, a tattooed badge of his transgressive conversion.

While Jones indulges in the questionable pleasures of his double bathing, Smith politely declines to join him. Indeed, Smith refuses to go even as far as the water's edge, preferring to remain at some distance from the shore. In retrospect, we can understand his reluctance as an appropriate, even necessary, modesty, but to Jones it must appear as an idiosyncratic stubbornness. Because he does not choose to bathe, Smith is given the responsibility of watching Jones's purse and pistols. In fact, the possession of these articles—of purses and pistols—has been contested throughout the story. When he first asks to accompany Jones, Smith offers to turn his purse over to him, and Jones refuses to accept. When Smith admits to not carrying a revolver, Jones scolds him: "A pistol hanging over your loins is no great trouble to you, and looks as though you could bite" (116–17), a suggestion that calls attention to the pistol's aggressively phallic qualities. When Smith then offers to take charge of Jones's pistol for him, the narrator once again declines, not yet willing to surrender this symbol of his masculine authority, commenting that "the tool will come readiest to the hand of its master" (116).

Clearly, the purse and the pistol represent two key aspects of power, as exercised by the institutions of British religious and secular authority. Jones's decision to turn over the guardianship of these possessions, however briefly, to Smith is a weighty one: "I confess that at this I almost suspected that he was going to play me foul, and I hesitated.... But to have kept the things now would have shown suspicion too plainly, and as I could not bring myself to do that, I gave them up" (122). Interestingly, surrendering the pistol and purse is the occurrence in the story for which the narrator expresses the most real regret: "I have sometimes thought that I was a fool to do so." When Smith's deception is revealed at the end of the story, Jones confesses his shame, while protesting his innocence, but the surrendering of his purse and pistols—an action that brings no consequences within the plot at all—becomes an occasion for a severe and ongoing self-condemnation, a condemnation that seems to go beyond the milder feelings of shame that he professes elsewhere.

If Jones's purse and pistols are safe while in Smith's custody, why does the narrator continue to consider himself a fool for having surrendered them? On the surface, it might appear to be merely because he has turned them over to a woman, although it then becomes unclear why this one aspect of the deception requires something more than the shame expressed elsewhere. One might consider, however, that while the pistol and purse represent two correlative poles of power, they are also clearly gendered as symbols. The purse is as vaginal as the pistol is phallic; as William A. Cohen observes in his analysis of Trollope's novel *The Eustace Diamonds*, "the symbolic substitution of female genitals with receptacles for valuables" (in that instance, a jewelry box) is a well-established literary and psychological trope.[20] By surrendering both items to Smith, the narrator acknowledges the ambiguousness of their relationship and the consequent tenuousness of his own sense of gendered identity, a psychic uncertainty that facilitates the shift from Jones's masterful penetration of the chapel to his rape, or seduction, at the Dead Sea.

An additional event that intercedes between the scenes at the chapel and at the Dead Sea is the party's sighting of a long procession of pilgrims, returning from the Jordan River to Jerusalem. This pilgrimage is one of an array of religious references and images. Jones has traveled to the cradle of Christianity at Eastertide, an occasion for spiritual and physical rebirth, and finds Jerusalem full of (other?) pilgrims, from Europe and Africa alike. While touring the Holy Land, the narrator and his companion debate the significance of seeing firsthand such sights as the home of Pontius Pilate and "the spot at which our Saviour is said to have fallen while bearing his cross" (114). While Jones finds these memorials somewhat irreverently bracing, Smith reacts with a more disappointed skepticism and asks, "Why seek such spots as these if they only dispel the associations and veneration of one's childhood?" (126).

In taking this trek across Palestine, Jones appears to identify with the sufferings of Christ, announcing his own determination to cross "the wilderness through which it is supposed that Our Saviour wandered for the forty days when the devil tempted him" (107). Later, while observing the column of pilgrims on the road to Jerusalem, the narrator empathizes with one agonizing member of that progress:

> He had bound himself to make the pilgrimage from Jerusalem to the river with one foot bare. He was of a better class, and was even nobly dressed, as though it were a part of his vow to show to all men that he

did this deed, wealthy and great though he was. He was a fine man, perhaps thirty years of age, with a well-grown beard descending on his breast, and at his girdle he carried a brace of pistols. But never in my life had I seen bodily pain so plainly written in a man's face. (120–21)

While Jones has been disgusted by (and yet drawn to) the filthy masses at the chapel, he is clearly drawn to (and yet repelled by) this solitary, suffering pilgrim. In terms of background and physical appearance, the pilgrim bears striking similarities to Jones (and to Trollope himself), and in that moment of self-reflection Jones begins to acknowledge a masculine (remember his "brace of pistols") craving for submission and suffering.

Clearly, Jones's earlier concern for the condition of Smith's skin suggests his homoerotic attraction to his companion. Now, Jones pays particular attention to the condition of this pilgrim's foot, "a mass of blood, and sores, and broken skin" (121). The mutilated foot of the pilgrim is not an overtly sexualized image (unlike the galled skin of Smith's thighs) but represents instead an aesthetic (or asceticism) of submissiveness to some form of authority, and even of masochism. From the opening lines of the story, Jones presents himself as subject to external control and discipline: "Circumstances *took me* to the Holy Land without a companion, and *compelled me* to visit Bethany, the Mount of Olives, and the Church of the Sepulchre alone" (107, emphasis added). At the Jordan River, the narrator's identification with Christ is also associated with self-denial, as he observes that "another also had come to this river, perhaps to this very spot on its shores, and submitted Himself to its waters" (126). Jones's identification with the suffering figure of the pilgrim is but one expression of his potentially dangerous attraction to this submissive and masochistic aesthetic.

After surrendering his pistols and his purse to Smith, Jones finds himself in just such a submissive, even helpless, posture at the Dead Sea—penetrated, rather than penetrating. This reversal of his position appears to grow not only out of his attraction to Smith, and out of his turning over of the symbols of his power, but also out of his increasing sense of identification with his own culturally structured perception of the Easterner worshippers, and with an aesthetic of submissiveness and masochism.

In her study of mutiny reports from British India, Jenny Sharpe has examined the ways in which invented stories of white women being raped by dark natives were used strategically to divert attention from the dead bodies of British males: "The reports contain no elaborate descriptions of men being dismembered, since such a fragmentation of the male body would allocate British men to the objectified space of the rape victim— a status that would negate colonial power at the precise moment that it needed reinforcing."[21] Overtly fictional, Trollope's story is perhaps somewhat freer to explore alternative strategies, or to escape the binding of official strategies altogether. Jones's attachment to a submissive aesthetic provides the possibility, if not the opportunity, to explore a fantasy of male/male rape. Standing behind Jones's metaphoric rape are all the sensations (of excitement, of fear) that accompany the unknown: "Once a European man is struck down, then anything is possible...."[22] But because Jones's companion has always been a woman, and because so much of the sexual presence is deployed through the foreign landscape, Trollope's ambiguous narrative destabilizes conventional dichotomies: male/female, dominant/submissive, colonizer/colonized.

For a patriarchal English society, the rape of a white man in the dark colonies was a far more serious threat to power and stability than was the rape of a white woman—more serious, perhaps, than the violent deaths of male colonists and British soldiers. The threat of male rape embodied the fears that the nation could not simultaneously assimilate the exotic Otherness of colonized subjects while maintaining a core sense of (white, male, heterosexual) identity: "Native subject and homosexual exist in parallel in these texts, their foundational mimicry gnawing at the foundations of the colonial bastion of a masculinized nation."[23] As Eve Sedgwick suggests in her reading of Dickens's *The Mystery of Edwin Drood,* in the nineteenth century "a partly Gothic-derived paranoid racist thematics of male penetration and undermining by subject peoples became a prominent feature of national ideology in western Europe. Its culmination is an image of male rape."[24] When Jones is penetrated by the Dead Sea, he becomes the realization of one of the Empire's greatest fears. However, in "The Banks of the Jordan," the orientalist colonizing enterprise in which the characters participate masks the role that submissive desire plays in drawing the Self toward the Other, to penetrate and to be penetrated.[25]

Rather than focusing on strategies for maintaining an intrusive presence in the foreign landscape, "The Banks of the Jordan" is largely concerned with getting back out again, the work of tourists rather than of colonists. Throughout the story, the mastery of any act of penetration is defined by the success of the subsequent act of withdrawal. At the subterranean chapel, Jones and Smith's retreat is every bit as important as their having reached the altar: "Having got so far our next object was to get out again. The place was dark, mysterious, and full of strange odours; but darkness, mystery, and strange odours soon lose their charms when men have much work before them" (115). The failure of Jones's attempts to penetrate the waters of the Dead Sea and the Jordan is marked by his inability to withdraw from them; he continues to carry the sensations of the "noisome" waters, and the dirt, on his person. In fact, Jones credits this lingering badge with having revived and altered him: "I have had my palate out of order too, but the full appreciation of flavours has come back to me" (127).

Having been changed so profoundly by these disruptive interactions, Jones is startled by the sudden appearance of Julia's uncle, Sir William Weston, another of Trollope's recurring "unpleasant baronets."[26] A stern and forbidding patriarch, Weston represents the conservative England from which Jones originates, and to which he has been anticipating his return. But as a consequence of Weston's wrath, Jones's punishment is to remain behind in Jaffa while the others leave the city on the packet boat: "My most earnest desire in the matter was to save Miss Weston from annoyance; and under existing circumstances my presence on board could not but be a burden to her.... It was better for all parties that I should remain" (142). The price that Trollope's narrator pays for having allowed himself to be deceived—the price that he pays for having penetrated the Holy Land with a young, single female—is his subsequent inability to withdraw. This paralysis seems rooted as deeply in Jones's colonial and homoerotic desires as in the uncle's accusations of his improprieties. Trollope may well have shared much of the nationalistic vision of empire, as space to be filled (and the less contact with its walls, the better), but his fear is that the reverse, in fact, will be true, a scene in which "the fluid seems hardly to be displaced by the entrance of the body." Rather than avoiding the foreign landscape, Trollope's Mr. Jones has allowed himself to become entangled in it; he penetrates—and is penetrated by—it, and he cannot (or he will not) escape it.

Of course, Jones's entanglement with the landscape is only one aspect of his increasing involvement with the Arab world. As I have already suggested, his growing identification with the pilgrims is another.

In "The Banks of the Jordan," the unwary traveler is threatened by the unspoken danger of coming too close to his field of study, and not being able to extricate himself. The feel of pitch from the Dead Sea waters, and the mud from the banks of the Jordan River, become the sign of the "Oriental dirt" that begins to mark Jones as changed, as different. No doubt his final return to London will bring him back completely, yet at the end of the story we leave him in Jaffa, professing his misery to be sure, while "eating cutlets of goats' flesh, and wandering among the orange groves" (143).

For Trollope, the colonial space traversed in "The Banks of the Jordan" provides a regenerative stage on which we can reconstruct individual and national identity, transformations that bridge the discourses of sexuality, religion, and Empire. Jones's desire for the Other draws him into this destabilizing space, with which he can never be fully engaged and from which he can never fully withdraw. Mary Louise Pratt, while describing the writings of Congo explorer Paul Du Chaillu, calls our attention to the Western traveler's tendency to convert each foreign landscape into a re-creation of the Garden of Eden, an ahistorical reiteration of history that simultaneously suggests both a new genesis and a new fall.[27] Trollope's troubled Edenic vision of this landscape is marked by both its forbidden sexualized presence and the narrator's attraction toward it. The proprietary compulsiveness of that attraction, and the extent of its self-absorption, may suggest some of the dangers that adhere to a cultural vision of empire, but for the moment attraction and denial, penetration and withdrawal, are held in a precarious balance. We are left with the conflicting, and provocative, image of a miserable Jones, suffering in the midst of the Garden, a Garden that is continually being constructed somewhere in order for our withdrawal from it to be continually reenacted.

Notes

I am grateful to William A. Cohen for first pointing me toward "The Banks of the Jordan" and for subsequently helping me find my way in. I am grateful also to Richard Ruppel and Philip Holden, whose encouragement and insightful comments have helped me to find my way back out again.

1. The three installments of "The Banks of the Jordan" were published in the *London Review* on 5, 12, and 19 January 1861; the story later appeared in Anthony Trollope's 1863 collection of *Tales of All Countries,* Second Series. The story has also

appeared as "A Ride Across Palestine," an alternate title provided by Trollope. Parenthetical citations within this essay refer to the page numbers for "The Banks of the Jordan," in *The Complete Short Stories, Volume 3: Tourists and Colonials,* ed. Betty Jane Slemp Breyer (Fort Worth: Texas Christian University Press, 1981).

2. N. John Hall, ed., *The Letters of Anthony Trollope, Volume One: 1835–1870* (Stanford: Stanford University Press, 1983), 140–41.

3. Ibid.

4. Victoria Glendinning, *Anthony Trollope* (New York: Knopf, 1993), 288.

5. Henry James, "Anthony Trollope," in *Literary Criticism: Essays on Literature, American Writers, English Writers,* ed. Leon Edel (New York: Library of America, 1984), 1333.

6. Priscilla L. Walton, *Patriarchal Desire and Victorian Discourse: A Lacanian Reading of Anthony Trollope's Palliser Novels* (Toronto: University of Toronto Press, 1995), 163.

7. Jane Nardin, *He Knew She Was Right: The Independent Woman in the Novels of Anthony Trollope* (Carbondale: Southern Illinois University Press, 1989), 1.

8. Catherine Hall, "Going a-Trolloping: Imperial Man Travels the Empire," in *Gender and Imperialism,* ed. Clare Midgley (Manchester: Manchester University Press, 1998), 187.

9. Jane Nardin, *Trollope and Victorian Moral Philosophy* (Athens: Ohio University Press, 1996), 15.

10. Edward W. Said, *Orientalism* (New York: Vintage, 1979), 3.

11. Ibid., 190.

12. Joseph A Boone, "Vacation Cruises; or, The Homoerotics of Orientalism," *PMLA* 110 (1995): 90.

13. Eve Kosofsky Sedgwick, *Between Men: English Literature and Male Homosocial Desire* (New York: Columbia University Press, 1985), 182.

14. When Smith first approaches Jones, for example, the latter notes that the young man appeared "half ashamed of what he was doing" (109), while the narrator acknowledges that he has frequently "had to blush for the acquaintances" he has chosen (110) and later confesses, "I always feel ashamed when I am detected sleeping during the day" (128).

15. Hall, ed., *Letters,* 117.

16. Richard Mullen and James Munson, *The Penguin Companion to Trollope* (London: Penguin, 1996), 436.

17. Hall, "Going a-Trolloping," 184–85.

18. Glendinning, *Anthony Trollope,* 464–65.

19. Mary Louise Pratt, *Imperial Eyes: Travel Writing and Transculturation* (London: Routledge, 1992), 201–08.

20. William A. Cohen, *Sex Scandal: The Private Parts of Victorian Fiction* (Durham: Duke University Press, 1996), 159.

21. Jenny Sharpe, *Allegories of Empire: The Figure of Woman in the Colonial Text* (Minneapolis: University of Minnesota Press, 1993), 67.

22. Ibid.

23. Philip Holden, "Love, Death, and Nation: Representing Amok in British Malaya," *Literature and History* 6, no. 1 (1997): 50.

24. Sedgwick, *Between Men,* 182.

25. Kaja Silverman's reading of the rape scene at Deraa in T. E. Lawrence's *Seven Pillars of Wisdom* offers fascinating and useful insights into the process by which masochistic desire subverts the power relations between the Englishman and his Turkish captors, redefining and repositioning Lawrence's understanding of the Self and the Other, with profound implications for his sense of individual (and nationalistic) identity. See Kaja Silverman, *Male Subjectivity at the Margins* (New York: Routledge, 1992), 328–38.

26. Mullen and Munson, *Penguin Companion,* 437.

27. Pratt, *Imperial Eyes,* 209.

Part III
Century's End: Conrad's Queer Indirections

CHAPTER SEVEN

From Mimicry to Menace:
Conrad and Late-Victorian Masculinity

Tim Middleton

> The ambivalence of colonial authority repeatedly turns from
> *mimicry*—a difference that is almost nothing but not quite—to
> *menace*—a difference that is almost total but not quite. And in that
> other scene of colonial power, where history turns to farce and
> presence to "a part" can be seen the twin figures of narcissism and
> paranoia that repeat, furiously, uncontrollably.
>
> —Homi Bhabha, *The Location of Culture*

> Fiction...demands from the writer a spirit of scrupulous abnegation.
> The only legitimate basis of creative work lies in the courageous
> recognition of all the irreconcilable antagonisms that make our life
> so enigmatic, so burdensome, so fascinating, so dangerous—so full
> of hope.
>
> —Joseph Conrad, to the *New York Times*,
> "Saturday Review," 2 August 1901

Conrad's 1897 novel was published at a time of heightened imperialist activity and in a culture where gender was a key site of contemporary debate.[1] This essay examines the representation of masculinity in *The Nigger of the "Narcissus"* and suggests that Conrad, by mimicking the ambivalence of colonial discourse in this arena, turns what might otherwise be read as a straight tale of masculine solidarity in the face of hardships and dissent into a far more troubling account of the tensions inherent in imperialist accounts of male identity in the late nineteenth century.

As an artist, Conrad, prompted by his mentor Edward Garnett, was at this time anxious to move away from the widely held view that he was merely a writer of exotic tales of far-flung places, and *The Nigger of the "Narcissus"* has been seen as his conscious attempt to reposition himself as an English author, addressing pressing English concerns.[2] Yet Conrad's firsthand experiences of colonialism—as a child his parents were exiled for political activities against the Russian invaders and as an adult in Africa he witnessed the horrors of the Belgian Congo—and the high ambitions for his fiction expressed in the "preface" to the novel prevent us from treating the text as a cynical exercise in artistic realignment.[3]

Although modernist parody can, as Rita Felski has argued,[4] be a vehicle for an insistent reinscription of the very gender hierarchies it purports to destabilize, the Bakhtinian notion of dialogism suggests that language's capacity to simultaneously carry several competing ideological positions means that "novelistic discourse is always criticizing itself."[5] Conrad's "scrupulous abnegation" informs the dialogic construction of the novel, a construction that enables it to encompass the jingoistic views of influential imperialists like W. E. Henley—the editor of the *New Review* in which the novel first appeared—while drawing in discourses highly corrosive to that worldview. As Henricksen cogently argues, "critics speak of Conrad's 'gross violation of point of view'. . . [but] this violation . . . is readable as a troping of the ideological tensions in the social life of discourse surrounding and informing the novel and as a deconstruction of the supposedly unitary self of the narrator."[6] Conrad's study of the impact of narcissism on the crew of the *Narcissus* provides him with a situation where he can mimic dominant imperialist values while suggesting their limitations. Through appearing in the *New Review* Conrad's text was immediately placed in a conservative, pro-imperialist context, but the novel's complex narrative style prevents it from being read as a simple imperialist tale.[7] By paying attention to the impact of the narcissism of Wait and Donkin on the ship's crew we are engaging with the heart of what, for its original British audience, was the text's menacing queerness[8] and can thus more fully locate the work in its dialogic context and unlock its account of the subtle but pervasive interplay between discourses of inversion and imperialism in the British fin de siècle.

The problem of narcissism—the love of the same—is particularly acute in patriarchies since they are cultures that rely on relations between men.[9] In Conrad's novel, as in British society at large in the 1890s, the women were "out of it" precisely because the feminine was that which was of necessity excluded from the homosocial bonds through which such a social order is maintained.[10] This policing of gender identity is particularly evident in the later nineteenth century in Britain when the crises of gender "were seen as emblematic of England's more general malaise.... The subversion of the social and economic structures of England by women [or, more generally, by the feminine] seemed imminent, and conservatives [like Henley] felt that it was imperative to stop women before they went too far."[11]

The widespread and at times obsessive exclusion of the feminine in the culture of fin de siècle Britain is based on the increasing turbulence surrounding gender roles (occasioned in part by the phenomenon of the New Woman) and the anxieties about the impact of this perceived cause of national decline in the (real and feared) imperialist clashes of the 1880s and '90s. At this time it was the feminine—specifically that loose and baggy monster of a gender identity, the New Woman—that emerged as a significant locus of modernity and a focus of its crises. The New Woman was a figure of fear not so much because of her revision of femininity but rather for her potential to hasten the refashioning of masculinity. As the eugenicist Charles Harper warned in 1894, "the New Woman, if a mother at all, will be the mother of a New Man, as different indeed, from the present race as possible, but how different, the clamorous females of today cannot expect.... [There is] the prospect of peopling the world with stunted and hydrocephalic children... and ultimate extinction of the race."[12] The idealization of the gentleman was central to both the new imperialism's construction of national identity along gendered lines and its rigorous policing of the border between the homosocial and homosexual. That the language of colonialism was inflected by these gender-related anxieties is borne out by the use of gendered terms in works on imperialism published at the time. For example, in the New Review for August 1897, immediately after the second installment of Conrad's novel, C. de Thierry writes an article on "Colonial Empires" in which England's "growing impotence" is a dominant theme.[13]

As Eve Sedgwick has argued, these anxieties circulating around gender identity and national mission inform the emergence of a discourse of heterosexual panic about homosexuality's capacity to destabilize dominant models of masculinity: "Because the paths of male entitlement... required certain intense male bonds that were not readily distinguishable from the most reprobated bonds, an endemic and ineradicable state of what I am calling male homosexual panic became the normal condition of male heterosexual entitlement."[14] The ideal of the gentleman promoted within the epoch's discourses of homosociality should therefore be seen as part of a wider process of containment linked to this "panic"; a process built on the ruling elite's narcissistic injunction to "be like us." This kind of appeal can also be read as an invitation to "become us"—raising fears of the dissolution of class boundaries—and while promoting this kind of strong same-sex identification is not the same as promoting homosexuality, it should be recalled that the invert was perceived as the uncanny double of the gentleman: he took the sanctioned gentlemanly traits of refinement and self-reliance and turned them into a queer excess based on a decadent self-absorption.

Literary culture in general, and fiction in particular, was a key battleground in the period's gender crisises. For an imperialist like Henley, the success of English literature was part and parcel of the nation's mission, and he used the *New Review* as a platform to issue calls for a robust and manly fiction and to trumpet the colonizing success of the English novel in securing "fresh continents of readers."[15] Conrad's desire to write a book about men for Henley might be seen as part of his move toward a Henleyesque position; as Jane Eldridge Miller has argued, the late nineteenth century saw a demand for "virile and rational" fiction by men to counter what was deemed a flood of debilitating feminine literature, in which Henley's editorship of the *New Review* plays a significant part.[16] *The Nigger of the "Narcissus"* is very self-consciously a book about men, and we might see it as Conrad's reaction to the fall from grace of the kind of lush aestheticism associated with the milieu of the *Yellow Book* (1894–97) and the figure of the effeminate dandy.[17] Certainly his pleasure at being published by the arch Tory and public face of anti-Wilde feeling suggests a desire to be on a particular side in what were heated debates about gendered identity in the later 1890s.[18]

Superficially, then, Conrad's novel might initially seem to be an example of the virile fiction that Henley promoted: it is a strongly homosocial text in which the women are truly "out of it," and many of the novel's British reviewers frequently discussed the text as a purely male work. The *Daily Mail* called it a "masculine narrative" while the *Daily Telegraph* declared that the novel had no concern for aesthetics and instead was determined to paint the facts "with exact and merciless severity"; the *Glasgow Herald* was pleased to note that there "is not a petticoat in all Mr. Conrad's pages."[19] Conrad was a little put out by the emphasis on the rough-and-ready nature of the crew, complaining in a letter to Sir Arthur Quiller Couch that his concern in writing the novel was "for the men only," however brutish or ruffianly some might find them.[20] However, the *Daily Chronicle* was critical of a tendency to indulge in what it saw as a rather inflated language (Sherry, *Critical Heritage*, 90), and it is the novel's language that, above all else at this period, may have suggested a femininity that is absent from the story itself.[21]

It wasn't only journalists who rang alarm bells over the novel's rich prose: Arnold Bennett, who praised the book, was also anxious about its overly adjectival style.[22] The novel's narration tends toward the descriptive and in its evocation of the sea could be said to lack the economy in adjectives that, for an influential critic like Quiller-Couch, was a marker of properly English masculine prose.[23] One (American) reviewer even went so far as to suggest that the novel would be a suitable gift for "young ladies about to vacation by the sea."[24] The novel's accessibility for a female reader was certainly an important factor in Constance Garnett's response, as she explains in a letter to Conrad on 30 December 1897: "your Brain does not think English thoughts . . . it is more delicate, more subtle, richer & more varied than ours . . . I feel so grateful for the insight you have given me into those sailors. It is such as they that are the everlasting fascinating masculine enigma for us women—the artist is more than half feminine."[25] The mixed responses and the competing attributions of gendered qualities from reviewers and other readers very clearly suggest the ambivalence of the period's discourse about masculinity. The ideological gap between the *Daily Mail* and Constance Garnett points up the extent to which the text was open to multiple readings at the time of its first publication. What she identifies is what today might be called the dialogic quality of a subversively queer fiction whose structure, as Bruce Henricksen suggests, "reflect[s] fault lines in the larger social text, generated by laissez-faire capitalism, between communal and individual interests" (*Nomadic Voices*, 45). That an allegedly masculine book, written in part for the tastes of the "hero" of the counterdecadence, was constructed with what, by the standards of the day, might be seen as feminine strategies can only raise further questions about Conrad's engagement with the norms of imperialist culture as they related to the representation of masculinity.[26] Given the prevailing climate of gender panic, for Conrad to write a book about men with a title that raises the notion of love of the same, only a year after Wilde's trials and imprisonment (the novel was written in 1896 but not published until 1897), can only be seen as hugely provocative, an act of mimicry that turns into a menacing account of the flimsiness of dominant norms.

It is my contention that the politics of Conrad's narrator in *The Nigger of the "Narcissus"* and the poetics that inform the novel's construction are part and parcel of what might be seen as a subtle parodic strategy that aims not just to mimic but to rigorously mix in apparently "irreconcilable antagonisms." At the level of textuality, Conrad therefore appears to be realizing the parodic potential of dialogism to critique the monologic constructs of colonial discourse. As Homi Bhabha has argued, colonial discourse relies on fixity and rigidity in its construction of the Other, and as such it is not able to accommodate the subversive potential of parody.[27] From this perspective Conrad's novel may be viewed as an example of what Bhabha terms the "menace of mimicry"; it can be read as a text that mimics values in order to critique them. As Bhabha puts it:

> mimicry... problematizes the signs of racial and cultural priority so that the "national" is no longer naturalizable. What emerges between mimesis and mimicry is a *writing*, a mode of representation, that marginalizes the monumentality of history, quite simply mocks its power to be a model.... The *menace* of mimicry is its *double* vision which in disclosing the ambivalence of colonial discourse also disrupts its authority... [mimicry] articulates those disturbances of cultural, racial and historical difference that menace the narcissistic demand of colonial authority. (*The Location of Culture*, 87–88)

Conrad's novel, via its narrator, mimics both the jingoistic class and racial hatreds and the narrow constructions of English masculinity promoted by the Henley set in order to deconstruct them. Conrad's representation of masculinity is far more fluid than the Henleyesque model of the virile hero, but in order to access his subversive depiction of masculinities it is necessary to locate the text both in the wider context of the period's accounts of male identity and also to consider the novel's probing of the relationship between narcissism and masculinity in the light of later psychoanalytic theory. Here Freud's 1914 account of narcissism, itself a product of an epoch and cultural milieu in which gender roles were key topics of debate and anxiety, can be of use in opening up the text to a reading that runs counter to the *New Review*ish beliefs of its narrator.[28] In Freud's account, during infancy we are all narcissists, but as the child develops, love of self is cathected into the ego ideal—the socially sanctioned site of desire.[29] For Freud there is a strongly homosexual element in the male's ego ideal ("On Narcissism," 90, 96)—his list of four love objects suggests that the ego ideal for a man may be:

(a) what he himself is (i.e., himself)
(b) what he himself was
(c) what he himself would like to be
(d) someone who was once part of himself
(84)

The formation of an ego ideal involves idealizing the love object; that this object contains aspects of oneself—or represents oneself as one would like to be—is central to the homosexual dimension of narcissism.

Throughout Conrad's novel there is a concern with competing and ambivalent definitions of masculinity that, in part, turn on the tension between the idealized figure of the gentleman and individual character's experience of actual examples of such a figure. The keynote is sounded early with the depiction of Singleton's avid reading of Bulwer-Lytton's *Pelham; or, The Adventures of a Gentleman*. The unlikely conjunction of the half-naked Singleton and Bulwer's tale of dandyism provokes the narrator into a digression on the reading habits of the crews of "Southern-going ships" (*Nigger of the "Narcissus,"* 6):[30]

> The popularity of Bulwer Lytton . . . is a wonderful and bizarre phenomenon. What ideas do his polished and insincere sentences awaken in the simple minds of the big children who people those dark and wandering places of the earth? What meaning their rough, inexperienced souls can find in the elegant verbiage of his pages? What excitement?—what forgetfulness?—what appeasement? Mystery! Is it the fascination of the incomprehensible beings who exist beyond the pale of life . . . (6)

The narrator's prejudices are clear—the "simple . . . children" who crew the *Narcissus* should have no truck with Bulwer-Lytton's "elegant verbiage." A clear distinction is established between the "real" men like Singleton who have braved "those dark and wandering places of the earth" and the "insincere" men who people Bulwer-Lytton's fiction: "grave surprise" seems a very limited reaction to such maxims as "always remember that you dress to fascinate others, not yourself" or "never let the finery of chains and rings seem *your own* choice; that which naturally belongs to women should appear only worn for their sake. We dignify foppery, when we invest it with sentiment,"[31] given that Singleton is reading this stripped to the waist and adorned with tattoos "like a cannibal chief." Conrad carefully chooses the intertext since it directly engages with arguments about masculinity that would have been very familiar in the 1890s.

Pelham is about the reform of a dandy and the idea of the gentleman; the novel works toward what one critic describes as a "liberal, popular, aristocratic order in which a reformed dandyism also figures."[32] The novel was a bestseller but, in its first edition, was roundly condemned by such influential commentators as Thomas Carlyle and William Hazlitt for its positive account of dandyism, and Bulwer-Lytton felt forced to make severe cuts—replacing positive references to Pelham's effeminacy—to create a revised text in which Pelham becomes, in the end, "a dull married man" (Lane, *Burdens of Intimacy,* 50). In its later editions *Pelham* becomes a satire on the folly of dandyism in which narcissism is ultimately restrained by altruism. This sequence complicates the narrator's attempts in *Nigger of the "Narcissus"* to establish Singleton as a heroic survivor of an earlier epoch of seamanship and as a figure who once embodied a virile masculinity. He is set up as one of those "men who knew toil, privation, violence, debauchery—but—knew not fear, and had no desire of spite in their hearts. Men hard to manage, but easy to inspire; voiceless men—but men enough to scorn in their hearts the sentimental voices that bewailed the hardness of their fate" (*Nigger,* 25). But the juxtaposition of Singleton and Bulwer-Lytton's "sentimental" tale suggests that even this apparent apogee of masculinity is far more complex than the narrator is prepared—or able—to acknowledge. Via this clever piece of intertextuality Conrad alerts the reader to the crew's interest in gentlemen and to the ways in which this fascination underscores the potential for inversion within imperialism's construction of masculinity. The interest in "beings who exist beyond the pale" (6) indicates a fascination with Otherness that escapes the narrator's capacity to explain. It is this slipping outside of dominant frames of reference that suggests the text's dialogic character, pointing up the limitations of the narrator's point of view and thus preventing a monologic reading.

A further scene, again early in the novel, works to reveal the crew's fascination with gentlemen and is significant in its suggestion that this role is more of a mask than a social inheritance. In chapter 2 there is a deckside debate among the crew about the characteristics of a gentleman:

One said:—"It's money as does it." Another maintained:—"No, it's the way they speak." Lame Knowles stumped up with an unwashed face (he had the distinction of being the dirty man of the forecastle), and showing a few yellow fangs in a shrewd smile, explained craftily that he "had seen some of their pants." The backsides of them—he had observed—were thinner than paper from constant sitting down, yet otherwise they looked first rate and would last for years. It was all appearance. (32)

Knowles's knowledge of gentlemen's backsides goes without comment, but clearly his association with dirt can have a double meaning here. It is also important to note that Knowles establishes a view of subjectivity as "all appearance" since this links back to the intertext of *Pelham* in which the reform of the dandy suggests the extent to which agency can conflict with social role—as Bulwer-Lytton puts it, "how a man of sense can subject the usages of the world to himself instead of being conquered by them."[33] Because this is a dialogic text multiple discourses are being deployed here, in particular the idea of gender instability associated with imperialism's anxiety over the fitness of British men to rule the empire and the fear of social hierarchies being broken down by a self-centered working class. In a typical policing gesture, the narrator, having reported this conversation about gentlemen with the same fascinated amazement he employs earlier when describing Singleton's reading, comments tetchily that "they were forgetting their toil, they were forgetting themselves" (32). There are clear connections being made here between talking inappropriately about men and a dereliction of duty.

The scene concludes with Wait emerging from his sickbed to chide the crew with their unmanly behavior—"jabbering near the door here like a blooming lot of old women" (35). This sequence is important in that it works to establish the link between self-absorption and unmanly behavior. Taken together the two sections establish a context for understanding the gentleman that includes the homosexual and, as such, provides an alternative to the narrator's views of the crew's manliness as merely active, unthinking, and selfless.[34] The dialogic character of Conrad's writing means that, from the very start of the novel, masculinity cannot be taken as a single, unified conception.

It will be recalled that the idealization of the gentleman was central to the new imperialism's construction of national identity along gendered lines, hence, given the period, perhaps we should not see the crew's investment as unusual.[35] However, such an investment, as Donkin's carping agitation suggests, can also lead to the inversion of the existing order: if the gentleman is the model of "how to be," then, by wanting to be gentlemen, the crew are encouraged to cast off their identity as workers in an act of social mobility that the novel's narrator and Henley's regatta might regard as revolutionary. As the narrator comments: "inspired by Donkin's hopeful doctrines they dreamed enthusiastically of the time when every lonely ship would travel over a serene sea, manned by a wealthy and well-fed crew of satisfied skippers" (103).

The class struggle was not unconnected with the debates around male gender identity we have been considering. The rebellious working-class hooligan was just as much a figure of disapprobation as his middle-class counterpart, the dandy: both were seen as evidence of a morbid decline of manhood and as such a threat to ongoing imperial dominance.[36] Wait's impact on the *Narcissus,* as I show below, is to make its crew effeminate, and in this he needs to be viewed with Donkin since, as Linda Dowling explains, for the period the effeminate dandy and the degenerate working-class male represented two sides of the same coin: "the empty and negative symbol[s] at once of civic enfeeblement and of the monstrous self absorption that becomes visible just at that moment at which . . . private interest begins to prevail against . . . public welfare."[37] Narcissism—as figured in the novel via the self-interested Donkin and the self-absorbed Wait—disrupts a culture's apparently clear-cut social hierarchies since the narcissistic think of themselves over and above their social milieu. In the novel the crew are initially shown to be altruistic, generously giving clothes to Donkin (12), helping Wait with his bags (19), but over the course of the voyage and through the impact of Wait's illness and Donkin's complaints we are presented with a story that details narcissism's corrosive power to destabilize habitual patterns of behavior. In the 1890s this kind of self-interested rejection of traditions and established hierarchies was to be seen, according to their critics, in both the working-class hooligan and the middle-class New Woman but, after the trials of 1895, it was most strongly identified with Oscar Wilde. As Joseph Bristow comments, Wilde came to "embody the kind of individualistic and anti-social, not to say narcissistic, characteristics that . . . [served] as a convenient representation of a repugnant otherness completely alien to all that English society believed should constitute normative manly behavior."[38] Here the complex interrelation between aesthetics and politics in late-nineteenth-century Britain are central to an understanding of just what Conrad's "scrupulous abnegation" might mean when it came to writing a book about men for Henley's review. Henley and his set were vehement in their condemnation of Wilde and, as John Gross has suggested, much of this is linked with Henley's self-image as the hero of the counterdecadence and thus to be seen as part of his wider war against modernity.[39] The problematic of Wilde and of Henley's attitude toward all that he was thought to represent should alert us to the fact that for Conrad to write a book about an all-male world, in particular a book in which narcissism undermines male friendship and solidarity, was not an innocent act. At one level, and this is the narrator's view, the impact of Wait and Donkin is offered as a warning about the potential for a debilitated manhood if such "monstrous self absorption" takes a grip. However, when seen in the wider context of debates around identity (gendered, national, and imperial) and in the wider frame of Conrad's life in the later 1890s, the text's apparent monologism gives way. That The Nigger of the "Narcissus" resonates within the context of the fears of the Henley circle perhaps tells us more about Conrad's desire to receive critical approbation than it does about his politics, textual or sexual.[40]

Wait's self-absorption links him to the dandy and, in the minds of Conrad's reader, in 1897 the dandy—par excellence—was the disgraced Oscar Wilde. Given Sedgwick's claims that the homosocial was always tinged with the possibility of the homosexual, I want now to sketch a reading of Wait's role in The Nigger of the "Narcissus" that suggests some of the links between the novel's mimetic depiction of an all-male world and the wider social panic about the menace perceived as inherent in male friendships in the aftermath of Wilde's trials and imprisonment. The novel figures Wait as a closeted, dandyesque man with a secret; in the text this centers around whether or not he is shamming but also re-lates to his relationship with death—figured in the text as a "monstrous friendship" (36).[41] It is clearly Wait's body that leads the Captain to hire him—the conversation between Creighton and Baker in chapter 1 sug-gests that he is viewed as a prime specimen "fine and large" (20) whom Baker would like to "feel...on a rope" (20). This scene offers us two officers squabbling over male bodies and is precisely the kind of homo-social scenario that, in this period, could be read as containing traces of homosexual desire; in response to Creighton's "slight bitterness" (20) Baker chides him for being "too greedy" (20) and reminds him that he has enjoyed "that big Finn in your watch all the voyage" (20). While this exchange is not dissimilar to the praise of the male physique to be found in an avowedly imperialist text like Rider Haggard's *King Solomon's Mines,* the difference is that Haggard's narrator is unselfconscious about the male body in a way that Conrad, writing in the immediate aftermath of Wilde's trials and imprisonment, cannot hope to be.[42]

In a letter to Edward Garnett (29 November 1896) Conrad distinguishes *The Nigger of the "Narcissus"* from boys' adventure stories on the basis that his work's "lack of incident" is more true to life. He also notes that this means his heroes are of necessity "incomplete" as men.[43] A further difference between Conrad's work and that of "straight" imperial fictions is that in the latter's heroes there is no discernible gap between appearance and reality whereas in Conrad the hero is likely to have some damning psychological flaw. Conrad's Wait is, unsurprisingly, only superficially a fine figure of a man. His body is diseased and its manly exterior hides a weak, corrupted interior that stops him from doing his job and leaves him languidly resting while the crew wait on him. Wait's corrupting potential echoes the depiction of Wilde in the popular press of 1895 as the corrupter of Alfred Douglas, and what the narrator has to say about Wait could equally have been said by a member of Henley's circle deliberating the impact of Wilde on the nation's virility:[44]

> Through him we were becoming highly humanised, tender, complex, excessively decadent: we understood the subtlety of his fear, sympathized with all his repulsions, shrinkings, evasions, delusions—as though we had been over civilised, and rotten, and without any knowledge of the meaning of life. . . . He influenced the moral tone of our world as though he had it in his power to distribute honours, treasures, or pain. (139)

Wait is an affront to the narrator's standards of manliness: he looks masculine but, in his morbid self-absorption, acts in ways that for the period would be seen as unmanly if not downright feminine. The narrator figures the crew's relations with Wait as those of slaves before a tyrant (3), as courtiers toward a prince (37) or, in Belfast's case, as those of a woman toward a sick man (140). By making them sentimentally concerned about his welfare Wait is regarded as causing the crew to act in ways that clearly challenge their investment in normative masculine identities; that they do this against their will suggests the narcissist's power to destabilize:

> All our certitudes were going; we were on doubtful terms with our officers; the cook had given us up for lost; we had overheard the boatswain's opinion that "we were a crowd of softies." We suspected Jimmy, one another, and even our very selves. We did not know what to do. At every insignificant turn of our humble life we met Jimmy overbearing and blocking the way, arm-in-arm with his awful and veiled familiar. It was a weird servitude. (43)

Wait's influence on the crew's masculinity becomes so pervasive that even their most heroic actions partake of the era's panic about the infection of the homosocial by the homosexual. While the rescue of Wait is an act of heroism that—for the narrator—proves the crew's manhood, it is very easy to read the same scene as a male birthing scenario in which the rescue party attack the female ship with a phallic crowbar to create a "splintered, oblong hole" (69) through which Wait emerges.

Through Wait, the crew's homosociality becomes dangerously sentimental; as the narrator sees it, through pandering to Wait they become tainted by an "accursed perversity" (45), breaking with conventions and rules in their attempts to satisfy his needs. In its focus on the debilitating effect of masculine sentimentality, the novel would seem to fit within that category of writing that Segdwick identifies in which "constructions of modern Western gay male identity tend to be . . . in a very intimately responsive and expressive, though always oblique, relation to incoherences implicit in modern male *hetero*sexuality" ·(*Epistemology of the Closet,* 145). The text's incoherence around masculinity rests on the "irreconcilable antagonisms" of debates about gender in British culture at the fin de siècle. It is the novel's ability to capture what Bhabha calls the "ambivalence" of English colonial discourse at a point in history when its "achievements" were felt to be under threat from working-class intransigence and male middle-class effeminacy that makes *The Nigger of the "Narcissus"* more than just a pat reiteration of the Henley set's proimperialist prejudices (*Location of Culture,* 91). The novel's dialogic organization—what Conrad called his "courageous recognition of . . . irreconcilable antagonisms"—means that what seems like mimicry is actually a text that turns on a menace to the very values it apes.[45] The representation of masculinity in *The Nigger of the "Narcissus"* is thus far more fluid than the narrator or Henley and his circle might have been able or willing to see. The dialogic tendency of the narration suggests that the reader can see beyond the narrator's limited grasp of events and, as we saw with the gap between readings of the novel by disparate figures like Constance Garnett and the *Daily Mail*'s reviewer, comes to shoulder the burden of interpretation.[46] The ambiguities of the novel's dialogic narrative are thus what enable Conrad to orchestrate his text in such a way that it can be read as offering "encouragement, consolation, fear, charm" ("preface," xlii) to the Henley circle while remaining capable of providing them with glimpses of other versions of Englishness and of gendered identity for which they had undoubtedly neglected to ask.

Notes

1. On the imperialist anxieties of the 1890s see, among others, Bernard Porter, *The Lion's Share: A Short History of British Imperialism, 1850–1983* (London: Longman [2d ed.], 1984), chapters 4 and 5. On the crises of gender in Britain in the later nineteenth century, see, among others, the essays in Sally Ledger and Scott Mc-Cracken, eds., *Cultural Politics at the Fin de Siècle* (Cambridge: Cambridge University Press, 1995).

2. On this see in particular Todd Willy, "The Conquest of the Commodore: Conrad's Rigging of 'The Nigger' for the Henley," *Conradiana* 17, no. 3 (1985): 163–82, and Peter McDonald, "Men of Letters and Children of the Sea: Conrad and the Henley Circle Revisited," *The Conradian* 21, no. 1 (1996): 15–56.

3. Conrad's childhood is covered by a number of critics: see especially Zdzislaw Najder, *Joseph Conrad: A Chronicle* (Cambridge: Cambridge University Press, 1983).

4. Rita Felski, *The Gender of Modernity* (Cambridge: Harvard University Press, 1995), 92. For a compelling account of Conrad's novel's centrality to early English modernism, see Michael Levenson, *A Genealogy of Modernism* (Cambridge: Cambridge University Press, 1984).

5. Mikhail Bakhtin, "From the Pre-History of Novelistic Discourse," in *The Dialogic Imagination: Four Essays* (Austin: University of Texas Press, 1981), 49.

6. Bruce Henricksen, *Nomadic Voices: Conrad and the Subject of Narrative* (Urbana: University of Illinois Press, 1992), 26–27. Further references are attributed in the text.

7. Conrad employed a similar strategy a few years later when the subtly anti-colonialist *Heart of Darkness* was serialized in the conservative *Blackwood's Magazine*.

8. Here and elsewhere in this essay I am using the term in its late-nineteenth-century sense of "strange" and in the early-twentieth-century sense of "homosexual." In pointing up this double voicing I am trying to avoid forcing a simplistic binarism onto what was far more fluid. This essay is not trying to say that Conrad's novel is secretly about homosexuality: rather it is suggesting that the homosexual was a key problematic in any account of heterosexuality in this period. For an interesting reflection

on the problems of working with queer theory on Victorian fiction, see Christopher Lane, "The Homosexual in the Text," in *The Burdens of Intimacy: Psychoanalysis and Victorian Masculinity* (Chicago: University of Chicago Press, 1999), 224–45.

9. This account of patriarchy is derived from Heidi Hartman, "The Unhappy Marriage of Marxism and Feminism: Towards a More Progressive Union," in Lynda Sargent, ed., *Women and Revolution* (Boston: South End Press, 1981), 14. It is assumed in Eve Sedgwick's *Epistemology of the Closet* (London: Penguin, 1994 [1990]), 184, from which I take this reference.

10. Joseph Conrad, *Heart of Darkness* (New York: Norton, 1988 [1898–99/1902]), 49.

11. Jane Miller, *Rebel Women: Feminism, Modernism, and the Edwardian Novel* (London: Virago, 1994), 32.

12. Cited by Sally Ledger in "The New Woman and the Crisis of Victorianism," in Ledger and McCracken, eds., *Cultural Politics*, 31.

13. C. de Thierry, "Colonial Empires," *New Review*, no. 99 (August 1897): 154.

14. Sedgwick, *Epistemology*, 185. Further references attributed in the text.

15. Anonymous, "A Warning to Novelists?," *New Review*, no. 100 (September 1897): 308.

16. Miller, *Rebel Women*, 17. On the *New Review*, see John Gross, *The Rise and Fall of the Man of Letters* (London: Penguin, 1969).

17. It is interesting to note that in the book's original title—*The Nigger: A Tale of Ships and Men*—the issue of masculinity was clearly foregrounded.

18. See Conrad to Edward Garnett, in Frederick Karl and Laurence Davies, eds., *The Collected Letters of Joseph Conrad: Volume 1: 1861–1897* (Cambridge: Cambridge University Press, 1983), 322–23.

19. Norman Sherry, *Conrad: The Critical Heritage* (London: Routledge, 1973), 83, 85, 88. Further references attributed in the text.

20. In Karl and Davies, eds., *Collected Letters*, 429–31.

21. The feminization of textuality in works by male modernist writers is discussed by Rita Felski, *Gender of Modernity*, 91–114. Also see Miller, *Rebel Women*.

22. Frederick Karl, *Joseph Conrad: The Three Lives* (London: Faber and Faber, 1979), 389.

23. Philip Dodd, "Englishness and the National Culture," in Robert Colls and Philip Dodd, eds., *Englishness: Politics and Culture, 1880–1920* (London: Croom Helm, 1986), 6. When Quiller-Couch wrote to Conrad about the novel, he praised the depiction of Singleton and the Skipper above all else as part of the work's truthful depiction of the heroism of the merchant seaman. For his letter, see J. H. Stape and Owen Knowles, eds., *A Portrait in Letters: Correspondence to and about Conrad* (Amsterdam: Rodopi, 1996), 28.

24. Cited Donald Rude and Kenneth Davis, "The Critical Reception of the First American Edition of *The Nigger of the 'Narcissus'*," *The Conradian* 16, no. 2 (1992): 53.

25. In Stape and Knowles, eds., *A Portrait in Letters*, 28–29.

26. It is interesting to note that psychoanalytic theory suggests that narcissism, as a psychological state, is strongly linked with the feminine. On this see Stephen Frosh, *Sexual Difference: Masculinity and Psychoanalysis* (London: Routledge, 1994), especially 106–07.

27. Homi Bhabha, *The Location of Culture* (London: Routledge, 1994), 66–67. Further references attributed in the text.

28. For an account of the broader European influences that shaped Freud's thinking, see Peter Gay, *The Bourgeois Experience: Victoria to Freud: Volume 1: Education of the Senses* (Oxford: Oxford University Press, 1984). See especially chapter 2, "Offensive Women and Defensive Men," 169–225.

29. Sigmund Freud, "On Narcissism: An Introduction," in *The Penguin Freud Library: Volume 11: On Metapsychology* (London: Penguin, 1991 [1914]), 87–89. Further references attributed in the text.

30. This and all subsequent quotations from and references to Conrad's *The Nigger of the "Narcissus"* are to the Oxford University Press [World's Classics] 1984[1897] edition. Further references are attributed in the text.

31. Cited in Lane, *Burdens of Intimacy*, 54. Further references attributed in the text.

32. J. W. Oakley, "The Reform of Honor in Bulwer's *Pelham*," *Nineteenth Century Literature* 47, no. 1 (June 1992): 51.

33. Cited Oakley, "Reform of Honor," 50.

34. It is worth noting that both scenes occur within the first serial episode of the novel and, as such, can be taken as part and parcel of Conrad's establishment of the key themes of the work as a whole for its first readers.

35. For some of the background to this see, for example, John Mackenzie, "The Imperial Pioneer and Hunter and the British Masculine Stereotype in late Victorian and Edwardian Times," in J. A. Mangan and James Walvin, eds., *Manliness and Morality: Middle-Class Masculinity in Britain and America, 1800–1940* (Manchester: Manchester University Press, 1987), 176–98.

36. On the hooligan, see Bill Schwarz, "Night Battles: Hooligan and Citizen," in Mica Nava and Alan O'Shea, eds., *Modern Times: Reflections on a Century of English Modernity* (London: Routledge, 1996), 101–28.

37. Dowling, cited in Joseph Bristow, *Effeminate England: Homoerotic Writing after 1885* (Buckingham: Open University Press, 1995), 4–5.

38. Bristow, *Effeminate England*, 10–11.

39. See John Gross, *Rise and Fall*, 171.

40. Indeed, many of the issues against which Henley railed—the popular press, the literary agent, decadent introversion—were things in which, in one way or another, Conrad's work would soon involve him. Given Henley's public hostility toward Wilde and literary agents, it is odd that Conrad (in September 1900) should take not just an agent but the very same agent that Wilde used; all this suggests that Conrad's desire to be associated with the Henley circle was temporary and little more than expedient.

41. For another view on Wait as dandy, see Jeremy Hawthorn, "The Incoherences of *The Nigger of the 'Narcissus*,'" *The Conradian* 11, no. 2 (1986): 98–115; 109–10.

42. See the various depictions of Sir Henry Curtis in *King Solomon's Mines* (Oxford: Oxford University Press, 1989), for example, 11, 200, 234–36.

43. In Karl and Davies, eds., *Collected Letters*, 321–22. For a fuller account of differences between Conrad and late-nineteenth-century adventure writing, see Andrea White, *Joseph Conrad and the Adventure Tradition: Constructing and Deconstructing the Imperial Subject* (Cambridge: Cambridge University Press, 1993).

44. On the press reaction to Wilde, see Ed Cohen, "Writing Gone Wilde: Homoerotic Desire in the Closet of Representation," reprinted in Lyn Pykett, ed., *Reading Fin de Siècle Fictions* (London: Longman, 1996 [1987]), 103–26; 104.

45. Karl and Davies, eds., *Collected Letters*, 348–49.

46. Such a tactic is central to Conrad's narrative style in a number of key works. See, for example, my discussion of *Lord Jim,* in "Re-Reading Conrad's "Complete Man": Construction of Masculine Subjectivity in 'Heart of Darkness' and *Lord Jim,*" in Carabine, Knowles, and Armstrong, eds., *Conrad, James, and Other Relations* (Boulder: Maria Curie-Sklodowska University Press, 1998), 261–76; 269–71.

CHAPTER EIGHT

"Girl! What? Did I Mention a Girl?"
The Economy of Desire in *Heart of Darkness*

Richard J. Ruppel

Conrad's novels and stories contain many representations of homosexual desire.[1] In *Lord Jim* (1900), the eponymous hero—though sexually passive—is desired not only by the heroine, Jewel, but also by the mill owner he works for and by Marlow himself. In *Under Western Eyes* (1911), the language-teacher narrator can be seen as a rather bitter, closeted homosexual, sexually attracted to Razumov. In Natalia Haldin, the narrator has found a "virile" young woman whom he can admire, even sexually, and the somber, disappointed tone of the novel might be attributed to his knowledge that a union between them is impossible. His attraction to her is homoerotic; he desires her because of her "male" qualities, but she remains a woman and, therefore, out of reach. In *Chance* (1913), Captain Anthony's first mate, Franklin, evinces a jealous love for his captain; Mrs. Fyne presides over a coterie of young women that has lesbian undertones; and Marlow's sexual orientation appears to be represented, once again, at least as ambivalent if not homosexual. Through Conrad's working life, the homosexual "species" came under increasing scrutiny, definition, and censure; same-sex desire was an increasingly contested issue within popular, legal, and medical discourses.[2] Conrad's fiction traces this interest, though most often in subterranean ways.

Conrad parodies the persistent intersection between homosexuality and adventure fiction in *Romance* (1903), one of his collaborations with Ford Madox Ford, as Sarah Cole ably demonstrates in this volume. Conrad's most famous work, *Heart of Darkness* (1899), deals with same-sex attractions in a very different way, however. *Heart of Darkness* illustrates how the adventure genre isolates men in opposition to women, who are represented very nearly as members of a separate species. In this economy, women may initiate the action; they may be goals to be won; they may be subtle opponents who don't play by the rules; they may even be objects of sentimental attachment, but in tales of adventure the real passions of love and hatred that men feel are most often reserved for other men.

If, as I hope to show, heterosexual desire finds little expression in the novella, potential and actual homosexual desire finds expression in several different ways: in the intensely homosocial bonding among Marlow and his audience aboard the *Nellie,* in Marlow's admiration for African men, in his obsessive desire to reach Kurtz, and in the Harlequin's role as a sexual rival to Kurtz's African mistress. When I suggest that these are expressions of "potential and actual homosexual desire," however, I am using contemporary and, therefore, slightly anachronistic terms. It would be ahistorical, even absurd, to describe any of these male characters—Marlow, Kurtz, or the Harlequin—as "gay." It is clear, however, that the acceptable range of male desire within what we would now call "normal heterosexuality" was greater in the nineteenth than in the twentieth century.[3] With some very recent exceptions, Conrad critics have imposed a heterosexual matrix on his work, where all "normal" male sexual desire is necessarily heterosexual. To argue that Marlow could have manifested no sexual interest in his friends aboard the *Nellie,* in the African paddlers and cannibals, in the Harlequin, or in Kurtz is just as ahistorical as it would be to argue that Marlow or anyone else in the novella is "gay." Instead, it might be best to think of the representation of sexuality as "queer," a dissident sexuality, one that dissents from the norms that were imposed with increasing system and rigor through the nineteenth century. In the pages that follow, I hope to delineate the key homosocial relationships in *Heart of Darkness* and the range of desires manifested in these relationships. Before I do, however, I will show how women are actively excluded from the economy of desire in the novella.

"The Women Are Out of It"

In British imperial tales of adventure, men leave England (a country ruled by a woman while the popularity of these tales was at its height) in part to get away from women. In the economy of much of this fiction, women represent and enforce respectability, decorum, and responsibility, and they disrupt male, homosocial relationships. They most often appear, therefore, as antagonists: either openly, as in Haggard's *King Solomon's Mines* and *She,* or covertly, as in Kipling's Indian tales. The negative portrayals of women in *Heart of Darkness* illustrate this quite well. In *Heart of Darkness,* with the exception of Kurtz's African mistress, women are sexually undesirable to men, but they are the real powers behind the scenes, and they provoke all the men's behavior. Their power is terrifying; they use it, both consciously and unconsciously, to sow discord and to kill. Despite Marlow's blithe assertion that "the women . . . are out of it"[4] and that women "live in a world of their own and there ha[s] never been anything like it and never can be" (16), Marlow and his doppelgänger Kurtz live in a world created for them by women. Kurtz dies in that world, and Marlow barely escapes with his life.[5] Women have roles as malevolent fates and puppeteers in the novella, almost never as objects of desire.

As the novella opens, Marlow joins the primary narrator, lawyer, accountant, and director of companies aboard the *Nellie.* They gather to relax, to get away from civilization, a civilization that forces them to perform their "monkey tricks," as Marlow puts it, on their "respective tight-ropes for—what is it? Half a crown a tumble. . . ." (36). They escape to an all-male holiday from the rigors and restrictions of civilization, and the homosocial bonds among these friends are very strong. The primary narrator introduces Marlow and the four members of his audience in highly affectionate terms. He begins with the Director of Companies, "our Captain and our host. We four affectionately watched his back as he stood in the bows. . . . He resembled a pilot which to a seaman is trustworthiness personified." The affection is general, for between them "there [is] . . . the bond of the sea," which holds their "hearts together through long periods of separation" (7). There is significant irony, then, that these men gather aboard a yacht called the *Nellie.* They can temporarily escape the workaday world and listen to Marlow's manly tale of adventure, but women frame that tale from the start.

Marlow encounters women five times in the novella: Marlow's Aunt; the receptionists outside the Company offices; Kurtz's painting of the woman with a blindfold, holding a torch; Kurtz's African mistress, and Kurtz's Intended.

Marlow's "excellent Aunt" uses her influence to have him appointed captain of a steamship trading on the Congo River. Though the man he replaces was killed in a grotesquely comic disagreement with an African chief over two black hens, the doting aunt has no misgivings,[6] and she misrepresents Marlow to the Company in ways that will have potentially deadly consequences. As Marlow discovers in his last conversation with her, she identifies him as "an emissary of light, something like a lower sort of apostle" (15). Immediately after this conversation, Marlow himself evinces some misgivings:

> In the street—I don't know why—a queer feeling came to me that I was an impostor. . . . I . . . had a moment—I won't say of hesitation, but of startled pause before this commonplace affair. The best way I can explain it to you is by saying that for a second or two I felt as though instead of going to the centre of a continent I were about to set off for the centre of the earth. (16)

His fears turn out to be well-founded, of course. The aunt's misrepresentations lead the Manager to both despise and fear him, putting Marlow in one kind of danger from the pilgrims. The brickmaker, who is also the Manager's spy, knows how the aunt has characterized Marlow to the Company. He tells Marlow, "You are of the new gang—the gang of virtue. The same people who sent [Kurtz] specially also recommended you" (28). The brickmaker warns him directly that those like Marlow and Kurtz in the "emissary of light" camp do not bear charmed lives—presumably meaning that they can be eliminated in one way or another (31). This partially accounts for Kurtz's death; Marlow suspects that the Manager deliberately wrecked the steamship to keep from relieving Kurtz, knowing he was ill.[7] The job itself was notoriously deadly. Marlow comes close to being killed, like his predecessor, in a pointless dispute with Kurtz's African followers, and later he very nearly dies of fever. It would be foolish to suggest that the innocent aunt understood all of this or that she harbored some machiavellian design on Marlow's life, but the consequences of her kindly machinations could hardly have been more dangerous to him if her intentions had been murderous. Marlow never visits her in the end, as he "totter[s] about" Brussels—what would they have said to each other?

The two women who act as receptionists outside the company director's office have none of the well-meaning naivete of Marlow's aunt.

Whether they represent the fates or something more,[8] they are ominous beings, presiding over the corruption and, sometimes, death of foolish young men.[9] Marlow imagines they have a clear understanding of the deadly workings of the trading society as they usher in new workers:

> She glanced at me above the glasses. The swift and indifferent placidity of that look troubled me. Two youths with foolish and cheery countenances were being piloted over and she threw at them the same quick glance of unconcerned wisdom. She seemed to know all about them and about me too. An eerie feeling came over me. She seemed uncanny and fateful. Often far away there I thought of these two, guarding the door of Darkness, knitting black wool as for a warm pall. . . . Not many of those she looked at ever saw her again—not half—by a long way. (14)

The director himself, whom Marlow characterizes dismissively as "a pale plumpness in a frock coat" (14), makes hardly any lasting impression on Marlow, but during the most dangerous moment for him in the tale, when Marlow is attempting to prevent Kurtz from rejoining his followers and ordering a massacre of Marlow himself and the pilgrims, the "knitting old woman with the cat obtrude[s] herself on [his] memory." Though Marlow immediately claims she was "a most improper person to be sitting at the other end of such an affair" (64), he is wrong again. Just as the women are not "out of it," as he supposes, the "knitting old woman" is the most appropriate vision for him to have as he fights Kurtz for his life. She presides like a malignant genie over the entire "affair."[10]

Marlow's third encounter with a woman, purely symbolic, occurs when the brickmaker shows him Kurtz's painting of the blindfolded woman carrying a torch. Marlow finds her a disturbing, even "sinister" image. Sandra Gilbert describes precisely how this painting represents women's controlling power in the novella, despite their marginality within the narrative: "Vaguely evoking an image of Justice, the picture disturbingly suggests the contradictions between power (the torch) and powerlessness (the blindfold) and thus it introduces the idea of the other who has been excluded and dispossessed but who, despite such subordination, exercises a kind of indomitable torchlike power."[11] The novella's depiction of women presents a persistent dichotomy: they are "out of it" and blind to "the truth" (from which they need protection), but also powerful and controlling in sinister ways.

Kurtz's mistress is the one truly powerful African in *Heart of Darkness,* the only African the harlequin fears. Other members of Kurtz's tribe are "simple people" who may be scared off, the harlequin reassures Marlow, by one blast of the steam whistle. But when Kurtz's mistress approaches the steamer, the harlequin is so frightened he claims, "If she had offered to come aboard I really think I would have tried to shoot her" (61). She is unarmed, of course, and the harlequin has a rifle. She must appear to him almost supernaturally powerful since he suggests he can only *attempt* to shoot her. When the steamship leaves the Inner Station, Marlow pulls the whistle to scatter the crowd, and only the African mistress remains standing (61). She is a threatening and formidable presence in every way. Her hair is "done in the shape of a helmet," and she wears "brass wire gauntlets to the elbow." As she approaches the steamer, Marlow describes her as "savage and superb, wild-eyed and magnificent; there was something ominous and stately in her deliberate progress." With her "bizarre" charms, the "gifts of witch men" that "glittered and trembled at every step," and her "helmet" and "brass gauntlets," her suggestive power derives both from the accoutrements of war and from her associations with the supernatural.[12]

Marlow's fifth and last encounter with a woman occurs at the end of the tale when he visits the Intended to return Kurtz's letters. As the African mistress's white counterpart, Kurtz's Intended is equally formidable. Kurtz's attraction to her, after all, proves fatal. He is driven "out there" because her family believed "he wasn't rich enough" to marry her (74). She is surrounded by images of death—dressed in black, living on "a street as still and decorous as a well-kept cemetery," in a room with a cold, white fireplace and a massive grand piano, "like a sombre and polished sarcophagus" (72).[13] She keeps Kurtz's memory alive, and this is one obvious reason that fearful images of Kurtz haunt Marlow during this interview. Marlow is also vividly aware of the great, ironic contrast between Kurtz's trading mission and the Intended's belief in his nobility of soul. But the Intended was also the impetus for Kurtz's career in Africa, so it is entirely appropriate that Marlow sees Kurtz's resultant corruption and death while visiting her. Marlow feels compelled to lie to her about Kurtz's last words, though lies, Marlow had explained earlier, have "a taint of death, a flavour of mortality" (29), and he feels the need to "escape" their last interview (76). Bruce Stark is right when he suggests that the Intended and "the horror" are one and the same.[14]

The knitting receptionists cannot be held responsible for the venal, hypocritical, and extraordinarily cruel behavior of the Company and its agents any more than Marlow's aunt can be blamed for his predicament in the Congo. And, strictly speaking, Kurtz's Intended and his African mistress are equally innocent; Kurtz bears most of the responsibility for his own deterioration in Africa. The representation of women in *Heart of Darkness* is therefore perfectly paradoxical. On the literal level, they have no power. On the symbolic level, they have all the power. One way to account for this paradox is to blame the narrator, Charlie Marlow, who proves himself such a misogynist both here and in his later incarnation in *Chance*. When he claims that the women are "out of it," he adds, "We must help them to stay in that beautiful world of their own lest ours gets worse." But in the original manuscript, he goes on: "That's a monster-truth with many maws to whom we've got to throw every year—or every day—no matter—no sacrifice too great—a ransom of pretty, shining lies" (49). Marlow appears to suggest that men sacrifice themselves daily to maintain the world as it is: fighting and dying in order to sustain the women who drive them on. Meanwhile, however, the women have no understanding of this because they force men to lie to them about the world, to create "pretty" fictions. The aunt's and the Intended's ignorance, in other words, is monstrous, and it frustrates and embitters Marlow.

So Marlow and Kurtz flee women (though they never really escape)— or they are driven out by women—to pursue homosocial bonds in the wilderness. Women have only the most problematized sexual presence, which provides yet another illustration of how "the women are out of it." This represents yet another paradox, because the two main female characters that make up the poles of the continuum along which Kurtz moves—the Intended and the African mistress—are both identified exclusively through their potentially sexual and sexual relationship to Kurtz.[15] "Intended," of course, implies eventual sexual ownership. And while Kurtz's African mistress is never identified as anything but the "woman" and "she" in the story, critics have settled on "African mistress" as an appropriate shorthand appellation. Yet both women are more formidable and frightening than attractive. Kurtz's African consort certainly comes across as a femme fatale, in the dominatrix mode, but she remains a *symbol* of threatening, female sexuality. In the one scene, discussed more fully below, that actually joins her with Kurtz, she complains bitterly about the harlequin, her erotic rival. Her sexuality is debilitating and, ultimately, deadly; Kurtz's liaison with her is the ultimate sign of his degeneration in the jungle. The Intended, whose race and class should make her an appropriate object of desire for European men, is equally untouchable. For Kurtz, the Intended is merely one of the possessions that define him: "My Intended, my station, my career, my ideas," as he puts it to Marlow (67). Readers may wish to dismiss this objectification of his fiancée as a feature of Kurtz's monstrous ego, but we must still account for Marlow's own response to "the girl." He is left with her portrait, and he acknowledges that "she struck me as beautiful," but he qualifies this immediately by adding, "I mean she had a beautiful expression" (71). Despite this "expression," despite his own youth and their shared trauma, there is no hint of sexual tension in their meeting. Instead, Marlow feels lucky to escape before, as he fancifully puts it, the building collapses in response to the lie she passively forces him to tell.[16]

In the sexual economy of *Heart of Darkness,* as in nearly all nineteenth-century British adventure fiction,[17] the women are truly out of it. The relationships between men, on the other hand, may have subtle and, sometimes, not-such-subtle erotic components.

Between Men: Kurtz and the Harlequin

The relationship between the harlequin and Kurtz presents the most obvious example of same-sex attraction in *Heart of Darkness.*[18] The harlequin is devoted to Kurtz—as his conversations with Marlow amply reveal. "They had come together unavoidably," Marlow explains, "like two ships becalmed near each other, and lay rubbing sides at last." The harlequin describes one intimate conversation: "'We talked of everything,' he said quite transported at the recollection. 'I forgot there was such a thing as sleep. The night did not seem to last an hour. Everything! Everything! . . . Of love too.' 'Ah, he talked to you of love!' [Marlow] said much amused. 'It isn't what you think,' he cried almost passionately. 'It was in general. He made me see things—things'" (55).

The harlequin's passion for Kurtz seems clear enough,[19] but why is Marlow "much amused" that the two spoke of love during their all-night tête-à-tête? We may posit three competing answers. First, Marlow may be amused that two men would be speaking of any parlor-room topic— like love—in the jungle, surrounded by danger and "savagery." The incongruity is simply amusing. This seems the obvious answer until we factor in the harlequin's protesting response to Marlow's amusement: "It isn't what you think." Marlow's amusement must appear something of an accusation to the harlequin, an accusation that would not be implicit in Marlow's believing the conversation was merely out of place. Instead, the harlequin must believe Marlow finds their talk of love somewhat transgressive, and it might have been either heterosexually or homosexually (to use our terms) transgressive. In the former case, we would have to believe that Marlow imagines some coarse, locker-room discussion of women. But this reading simply feels wrong in this novella. European women frame *Heart of Darkness* and they drive the action; they are never the subjects of male conversation or intimacy.[20] This leaves the possibility that Marlow imagines the talk had a homoerotic flavor, a possibility the harlequin feels challenged to deny.[21]

If the harlequin and Kurtz's relationship has homosexual undertones, then the harlequin takes the normatively female role.[22] A harlequin may be male or female, and Marlow's description makes the son of an Arch-Priest sound androgynous, but really more female than male:

> His clothes had been made of some stuff that was brown holland probably, but it was covered with patches all over, with bright patches, blue, red, and yellow—patches on the back, patches on the front, patches on elbows, on knees, coloured binding round his jacket, scarlet edging at the bottom of his trousers, and the sunshine made him look extremely gay and wonderfully neat withal because you could see how beautifully all this patching had been done. (53)

He takes such care to patch his clothes, the patches become decorative, even attractive. His physical features are equally feminine: "A beardless boyish face, very fair, no features to speak of, nose peeling, little blue eyes, smiles and frowns chasing each other over that open countenance like sunshine and shadow on a wind-swept plain" (53) Marlow, very male in his capacity as captain, "swore shamefully" when the harlequin warns him of a snag in the river. The swearing is natural enough, especially for sailors, one supposes, but the "shame" seems incongruous unless we remember the "beardless boyish face" onshore: Marlow responds to the harlequin as though he were a young woman in a conventional romance, and he's embarrassed to have been overheard by him. After Marlow's vulgarities, "The harlequin on the bank turned his little pug-nose up to me. . . . all smiles" (53). In most fiction, when young women turn their faces up to men and smile, they are asking to be kissed. Before 1900, however, the face turned up to the older man's could well have been that of a boy or young man.[23]

The harlequin nurses Kurtz through his illness, and his great feelings for Kurtz cause him to break down suddenly as he recounts this experience to Marlow:

> His feelings were too much for speech and suddenly he broke down. "I don't understand," he groaned. "I've been doing my best to keep him alive and that's enough. I had no hand in all this. I have no abilities. There hasn't been a drop of medicine or a mouthful of invalid food for months here. He was shamefully abandoned. A man like this, with such ideas. Shamefully! Shamefully! I—I haven't slept for the last ten nights. . . ." (58)

Unlike the Intended, whose devotion would probably not have survived the realization of Kurtz's true activities in Africa, the harlequin knows Kurtz thoroughly, and despite this, his love is far more tangible and significant than hers. He nurses Kurtz, goes without sleep, and even risks death to be near him. His love makes him self-effacing ("I have no abilities") and even, if we are to believe his account, self-sacrificing in his willingness to face death to save Kurtz. The harlequin believes that Kurtz's African mistress would harm Kurtz,[24] so he attempts to keep her away during his illness: "I had been risking my life every day for the last fortnight to keep her out of the house" (61).

This battle between the harlequin and the mistress to be near Kurtz has at least one odd feature. The harlequin imagines that she is angry with him for using trade cloth to repair his clothes. "She got in one day and kicked up a row about those miserable rags I picked up in the storeroom to mend my clothes with." Since cloth was a form of wealth, we might conclude that the mistress is merely venal, but the harlequin adds that he needed the cloth badly because, as he puts it, "I wasn't decent" (61). What is odd about this admission is its context. As he recalls his efforts to save Kurtz, why should he draw attention to the revealing tears in his trousers? The incongruity is readily explained if we see the mistress and the harlequin as romantic rivals. The mistress resents the harlequin's efforts to hide his shame and appear attractively "decent" to Kurtz.[25]

Marlow may be said to have felt some of the pull of the harlequin's attraction. After all, he is the one who provides an admiring, feminized description of him, and he admits to having been "seduced" by him, by "the absolutely pure, uncalculating, unpractical spirit of adventure" that "ruled this be-patched youth" (55). He helps him as much as he can, giving him an old pair of shoes and some cartridges at their parting, but Marlow expresses no real regrets when the harlequin flees the manager and paddles off with "three black fellows" (62–63). Instead, Marlow's fascination, like the harlequin's, is with Kurtz himself.

The Sexual Positions of Marlow and Kurtz

Critics have found several ways to explain Marlow's desire to reach Kurtz. Those who read *Heart of Darkness* as a dark journey into the soul see Kurtz as the end point of Marlow's quest for himself. The most straightforward explanation, on the other hand, might be that in Kurtz Marlow hopes to find a model for his own career in Africa—a success within the trading company who also manages to maintain his ideals and humanity. Motivations in great modern literature are always mixed, and the homoerotic subtext of the novella provides one other plausible explanation for Marlow's obsessive search for Kurtz.

Before the abortive attack on the steamer that kills the helmsman, Marlow and the pilgrims are hung up in a fog just below Kurtz's station. Marlow remarks, "The approach to this Kurtz grubbing for ivory in the wretched bush was beset by as many dangers as though he had been an enchanted princess sleeping in a fabulous castle" (44). Marlow intends an ironic simile; the venal trader "grubbing for ivory in the . . . bush" is the very antithesis of an "enchanted princess." Yet this is not the only passage where Kurtz is represented as an object of sexual desire, here equated with the archetypal object of male desire, an "enchanted princess." In the most famous passage describing Kurtz's corruption and degeneration in the jungle, Kurtz is given the passive role:

> "The wilderness had patted him on the head, and—lo!—he had withered; it had taken him, loved him, embraced him, got into his veins, consumed his flesh, and sealed his soul to its own by the inconceivable ceremonies of some devilish initiation." (49)

The sexual implication of these lines is obvious, but "the wilderness" is the active agent and seducer in the equation, not exactly the female agent that most critics have noted. Kurtz has *been* "caressed," "loved," "embraced," "consumed." His role as the passive recipient of desire is emphasized when Marlow claims Kurtz was the "spoiled and pampered favourite" of the jungle. In short, Kurtz is represented as the object of the wilderness's desire, an object that is ultimately penetrated and destroyed.

After the attack on the steamer, Marlow reacts disconsolately to his belief that Kurtz must be dead: "For the moment that was the dominant thought. There was a sense of extreme disappointment as though I had found out I had been striving after something without a substance" (47–48). What Marlow misses, he says, is the chance to talk to Kurtz, and especially to listen to his voice, his penetrating words. In this obsessive desire, which he shares with the harlequin, Marlow can be seen as displaying an overpowering sexual interest in Kurtz:

> "We are too late; he has vanished—the gift has vanished by means of some spear, arrow, or club. I will never hear that chap speak after all— and my sorrow had a startling extravagance of emotion, even such as I had noticed in the howling sorrow of these savages in the bush. I couldn't have felt more of lonely desolation somehow had I been robbed of a belief or had missed my destiny in life. . . ." (48)

This is an extravagant response. Marlow is alone and must be lonely among the pilgrims. Unlike them, he is not in Africa to steal as much ivory as he can with the least effort, and he had naturally been looking forward to meeting a man of real character working for the Company in Africa. But his response to Kurtz's supposed death is excessive, as one of his auditors suggests when he sighs and mutters "absurd."[26]

Indeed, with Marlow's words of extravagant regret and his audience's disgusted response, we have reached a revealing intersection of the colonialist and homoerotic undercurrents of *Heart of Darkness*. Earlier in the story, Marlow had acknowledged a kinship with the Africans, "hands clapping . . . feet stamping . . . bodies swaying, eyes rolling" (37), as his steamer churned up the Congo River. And one of his auditors had grunted and muttered something about Marlow going "ashore for a howl and a dance" (38). Clearly, Marlow's claim of a relationship with the Africans puts him at odds with his audience.[27] In this later passage, too, Marlow's audience objects, with surprising vehemence considering that these are all old friends, when Marlow suggests that kinship, when he claims his grief over Kurtz's death had something in common with the sorrow he'd heard in the Africans' cries. And his conservative audience will also not allow him to express his passionate sorrow at being thwarted in his attempt to reach Kurtz. Marlow's powerful desire to find Kurtz, to listen to his words, and to save him makes his listeners equally uncomfortable. They balk at the association Marlow makes between himself and the Africans, and they balk at the extravagance of his sorrow over his belief that he will never consummate his journey to Kurtz.

Their reaction might be described as a classic example of homosexual panic,[28] a probability the narrative frame would certainly suggest. As I noted above, the primary narrator and his friends aboard the *Nellie* are held together by very strong homosocial bonds, bonds that must make them susceptible to homosexual panic. When Marlow expresses excessive grief over what he believed was the death of Kurtz, at least one member of his audience feels that he has overstepped normal homosocial bonds. We know this because Marlow immediately responds to the panic and placates his audience by introducing "the girl," Kurtz's Intended. His amusing and incongruous ejaculation, "Girl! What? Did I mention a girl?" (49), is otherwise inexplicable. Marlow introduces conventional heterosexuality—Kurtz was affianced, after all, so Marlow's desire to meet him can be categorized as a "normal," heterosexual desire— to calm his frightened audience.

By the time Marlow finally finds him, Kurtz is too ill for the two men to develop the kind of intimacy the harlequin had experienced with Kurtz. But there are hints that their relationship might have been "intimate," intense, and "profound." On first seeing Marlow, Kurtz "rustle[s] one of the letters" someone had written to him about Marlow and "looking straight into [Marlow's] face [says], "'I am glad.'. . . A voice! A voice! It was grave, profound, vibrating" (59–60). When he intercepts Kurtz to prevent him from rejoining his followers, Marlow suggests that "the foundations of [their] intimacy were being laid" during this encounter. When Marlow returns the letters to the Intended, that "intimacy" stands between Marlow and the woman; the vision of a man prevents Marlow from attempting or, seemingly, desiring any intimacy with a woman.

Heart of Darkness is hardly unique in this regard. Through the whole panoply of British imperial fiction—from *Robinson Crusoe* to the works of Haggard, Stevenson, Buchan, Kipling; to Conrad, Forster, and beyond—women are kept to the margins. Adventure stories most often depict male bonding under extreme circumstances in the absence of women. The important relationships are between men, or between boys, or between boys and men, and the stories most often end before the inevitable, heterosexual marriage. *Heart of Darkness* is unusual, if not unique, however, because it is at war with the adventure genre right from the start. In what other adventure tale is the conservative fictional audience in such conflict with the fictional narrator? Where else do we find white fellow-"adventurers" treated with such disgust? What other story calls into question with such scathing irony the whole imperial project or has its hero return from his struggle at the edges of the colonial frontier to one imperial capital, Brussels, that is described as a "sepulchral city" (70) and another, London, as "an immense darkness" (76)? And, finally, in what other adventure tale are the homoerotic underpinnings of *all* adventure tales explored with such subtle penetration, with such surprising humor?[29]

Heart of Darkness is one more document that shows how culturally and historically determined our own notions of male desire always are. In its representation of the economy of desire, *Heart of Darkness* is therefore a seminal, transitional work that records male-to-male desire (which would now be labeled and in many quarters proscribed as "homosexual") at the same time that it registers and, perhaps, even parodies post-Wildean homosexual panic.

This leaves us with the question of how Conrad's representation of sexuality is related to his representation of colonialism. First, as I hope I have demonstrated above, both are presented in ways that appear to become threatening to Marlow's, and therefore Conrad's, conservative audience. Neither the men aboard the *Nellie* nor the male readers of *Maga* (where *Heart of Darkness* first appeared) wanted to be told of their kinship with "savage" Africans or reminded of how emotionally compelling the bonds between men might become. Relationships between white men and Africans and potentially homoerotic relationships between men, in other words, are treated in similar ways.

The second connection is related to the first. Like nearly all colonial adventure stories, *Heart of Darkness* represents men in a world without women. Some of these men are simply nondescript mediocrities. Some, like the Company Manager and brickmaker, are vicious in a small way. But the significant male characters appear to be seeking close bonds with other men in a male world.[30] The novella begins with a group of men aboard ship. One of them tells the story of his compelling search for another white man. Along the way he meets a number of white men who are of little account, but he expresses deep, even obsessive interest in the object of his search.

But his interest is also briefly aroused by the muscular Africans paddling their canoes off the coast (17), and he discovers a degree of fellowship with the cannibals that comprise his crew: "Fine fellows—cannibals—in their place. They were men one could work with, and I am grateful to them" (36). Later he admires their calmness in the face of the attack on the steamer by Kurtz's followers, and he has a brief conversation with the head man of the crew "just for good fellowship's sake" (42) Finally, Marlow achieves a moment of profound, if profoundly disturbing, intimacy with his pilot when the latter is stabbed with a spear during the attack. As he is dying, Marlow has "to make an effort to free [his] eyes from [the pilot's] gaze and attend to the steering" (47). Later, Marlow elaborates at some length on that intimacy:

> "I missed my late helmsman awfully—I missed him even while his body was still lying in the pilot-house. Perhaps you will think it passing strange this regret for a savage who was no more account than a grain of sand in a black Sahara. Well, don't you see, he had done something, he had steered; for months I had him at my back—a help—an instrument. It was a kind of partnership. He steered for me—I had to look after him, I worried about his deficiencies, and thus a subtle bond had been created of which I only became aware when it was suddenly broken. And the intimate profundity of that look he gave me when he received his hurt remains to this day in my memory—like a claim of distant kinship affirmed in a supreme moment." (51)

This appears to me to be another key moment in the novella, when its colonialism and homosocialism come together and help to explain each other. In a world without women, the possibility of intense and intensely satisfying relationships between men is obviously increased, even the possibility of intense fellowship with non-Europeans. In Marlow's almost homoerotic appreciation of the African paddlers—"they had bone, muscle, a wild vitality, an intense energy of movement that was as natural and true as the surf along their coast. . . . They were a great comfort to look at" (17)—in his companionable gratitude to his cannibal crew, a gratitude that includes Marlow's admission that he hoped he did not appear as "unappetising" to them as the other white men appeared to him (43), and in his admission to feeling a subtle but unforgettable bond with his helmsman, Marlow is suggesting that relationships between men can diminish racial divides. In the Ur text of colonial adventure fiction, *Robinson Crusoe*, in the works of Haggard, Buchan, Stevenson,

Kipling—as in *Heart of Darkness*—these interracial, potentially homo-erotic relationships can only exist away from England and apart from women.

As many others have observed, men and women left Victoria's England in part to escape a sexuality that was increasingly restricted, policed, controlled, and categorized: legally, medically, and socially. *Heart of Darkness* provides another imaginative case history of how that "escape" might play itself out in Africa. Marlow seeks and finds Kurtz, already in a homoerotic relationship with another man. He himself almost achieves an intense, potentially erotic relationship with Kurtz. Along the way, he very nearly confesses to the erotic attractiveness of African men. But this is a Conrad story, so both the potentially heterosexual and homosexual relationships end in failure. Marlow does not return to marry the girl; the relationship between Kurtz and the harlequin is already over before our guide, Marlow, arrives on the scene; Kurtz's last passionate act is the attempted murder of Marlow and the other whites, and Marlow's audience aboard the yacht reacts in scorn when he acknowledges the attraction of African men. In the end, we remain aboard the *Nellie*—a name straight out of the music halls—in a world of conventional thinking and morality that tolerates no queer lapses into racial or sexual eccentricity.

Notes

Special thanks to Hunt Hawkins, Carola Kaplan, Rolf Samuels, and, of course, Philip Holden, all of whom read and provided helpful criticism of earlier versions of this essay.

1. As I have attempted to demonstrate in "Joseph Conrad and the Ghost of Oscar Wilde," *The Conradian: Journal of the Joseph Conrad Society* 23, no. 1 (spring 1998): 19–36. But see Christopher Lane's *The Ruling Passion: British Colonial Allegory and the Paradox of Homosexual Desire* (Durham: Duke University Press, 1995), 99–125, and Sarah Cole's essay later in this volume to supplement and sophisticate my readings of *Victory* and *Romance*. And see *One of Us: The Mastery of Joseph Conrad* (Chicago: University of Chicago Press, 1996), by Geoffrey Galt Harpham, where he argues that "considered as a novelist of identification, Conrad qualifies as the greatest explorer of male-male attraction in the English language" (132). Harpham's analysis of the puns supporting a homoerotic reading of *Lord Jim* seems particularly convincing and astute (173–76).

2. For a brief history of the development of the homosexual "species," see "Joseph Conrad and the Ghost of Oscar Wilde," 20–22, noted above, which refers to the relevant work of Foucault, Jeffrey Weeks, Christopher Craft, and others.

3. For a convincing history of how, before the twentieth century, same-sex desire was more often a sign of acceptable hypermasculinity than a symptom of deviant sexuality, see Alan Sinfield's *The Wilde Century: Effeminacy, Oscar Wilde, and the Queer Movement* (London: Cassell, 1994). And for a fine, extended analysis of the homosocial continuum through the nineteenth century in England—traced through the lives of Victorian poets and their poetry—see Richard Dellamora's *Masculine Desire: The Sexual Politics of Victorian Aestheticism* (Chapel Hill: University of North Carolina Press, 1990).

4. *Heart of Darkness: An Authoritative Text, Backgrounds and Sources, Criticism,* 3rd ed., ed. Robert Kimbrough (New York: Norton, 1988), 49. All references in the body of the essay are to this edition.

5. Several critics have already written convincingly about the alien power of women in *Heart of Darkness*. See Rita Bode's "'They...should be out of it': The Women of *Heart of Darkness*," *Conradiana* 26, no. 1 (spring 1994): 20–34, for a discussion of how the women form "a powerful female network...which frequently takes charge and assumes control of the novella's events" (21). My own analysis follows Bode's closely, though I attribute the powerful representation of women in the novella to the pressures of the adventure genre, not, as Bode suggests, to both authorial intention and lack of authorial control (21). Bette London has written what may be the most compelling analysis of women's roles in *Heart of Darkness* in *The Appropriated Voice: Narrative Authority in Conrad, Forster, and Woolf* (Ann Arbor: University of Michigan Press, 1990). See also Johanna M. Smith's "'Too Beautiful Altogether': Ideologies of Gender and Empire in *Heart of Darkness*," in *Joseph Conrad: Heart of Darkness*, ed. Ross C. Murfin (Boston: Bedford, 1996), 169–84; Sandra Gilbert's "Rider Haggard's Heart of Darkness," in *Coordinates: Placing Science Fiction and Fantasy*, ed. George Slusser, Eric Rabkin, and Robert Scholes (Carbondale: University of Southern Illinois Press, 1983), 124–38; and Padmini Mongia's "Empire, Narrative, and the Feminine in *Lord Jim* and *Heart of Darkness*," in *Contexts for Conrad*, ed. Keith Carabine, Owen Knowles, and Wieslaw Krajka (Boulder: East European Monographs, 1993), 135–50. Most recently, in *Conrad and Masculinity* (Basingstoke: Macmillan, 2000), Andrew Michael Roberts argues that women serve to both foster and deny desire between men in *Heart of Darkness*. "Women," he writes, "by functioning as objects of exchange (literal or psychic) and of shared desire, have been used to maintain...a barrier [between intimate male relationships], male desire being channelled through women" (131). Later in the same insightful chapter on *Heart of Darkness*, Roberts adds: "Marlow's placing of the Intended as one of Kurtz's possessions, comparable to the ivory in which he traded, is revealed as part of an economy of repressed same-sex desire, complicit with both the structures of patriarchy and with the economies of empire" (136).

6. If she knows how the former captain died, then she is remarkably cavalier when she sends Marlow off advising him to "wear flannel" (16). If she *hasn't* informed herself, she is truly "out of it" (as we might say today), and her ignorance is dangerous.

7. "I did not see the real significance of that wreck at once. I fancy I see it now.... Certainly the affair was too stupid...to be entirely natural" (24).

8. In *Conrad in the Nineteenth Century* (Berkeley: University of California Press, 1979) Ian Watt thoroughly explores the receptionists' various possible symbolic roles, convincingly rejecting the persistent reading that they merely represent the fates. See 191–93.

9. In "Kurtz's Intended: The Heart of *Heart of Darkness*" (*Texas Studies in Language and Literature* 16, no. 3 [fall 1974]: 535–55), Bruce Stark demonstrates the sinister importance of the knitting receptionists (538–39).

10. In "'Too Beautiful Altogether,'" Johanna Smith accounts for Marlow's vision of the knitting receptionist in this way: "This silent figure of civilized domesticity only *seems* incongruous in the jungle; her reappearance dramatizes the futility of Marlow's attempt to separate the realm of domesticity from that of colonial adventure" (176). I would add that though the feminine—both domestic and "savage"—is a constant, brooding, and sinister presence in the novella, only the African mistress has an explicitly sexual presence.

11. "Rider Haggard's Heart of Darkness," 136–37.

12. In her brief but provocative discussion of the women in *Heart of Darkness* in *Gone Primitive: Savage Intellects, Modern Lives* (Chicago: University of Chicago Press, 1990), Marianna Torgovnick suggests, ingeniously, that the African mistress must be killed as Marlow's steamer pulls away from Kurtz's station. She is the only one who remains standing and unflinching when the pilgrims open fire on the Africans (155). This seems plausible, if extratextual, but it seems more fitting to me that only men risk death and actually die in the novella. The women, in this sense too, are "out of it."

13. See Bruce Stark's "Kurtz's Intended: The Heart of *Heart of Darkness*," cited above, for a compelling demonstration of the infernal associations surrounding the Intended and her almost diabolical power over Marlow in this final scene.

14. Ibid., 549, and James Ellis, "Kurtz's Voice: The Intended as 'The Horror.'" *ELT* 19, no. 2 (1976): 105–10.

15. As in most adventure fiction, the women in *Heart of Darkness* are presented (and valued) exclusively in their relationships with men. Homosexuality in the novel is therefore exclusively between men; lesbian homoeroticism is almost unthinkable in this sexual economy.

16. In a story by C. J. Cutcliffe Hyne, "The Transfer," on which *Heart of Darkness* seems to have been based, the Marlow figure (Cecil Gering) is a rival for the "Intended's" (Miss Kennedy's) affections, and the story ends with the Kurtz figure (Baron Caissier) dead and Gering preparing to marry Kennedy. So in what might be called the Ur text of the story, Marlow marries the Intended. This makes the frightful last scene between the two even more strikingly asexual. See my "*Heart of Darkness* and the Popular Exotic Stories of the 1890s," *Conradiana* 21, no. 1 (spring 1989): 3–14.

17. See *Empire Boys: Adventures in a Man's World* (London: HarperCollins Academic, 1991), 81, where Joseph Bristow shows that in most adventure fiction, "women remain marginal to the story, and the infrequent glimpses of women characters are hardly surprising given that these fictions focus on inward-looking all-male communities."

18. I am not the first reader to suggest a homoerotic bond between Kurtz and the harlequin. In *One of Us: The Mastery of Joseph Conrad*, Geoffrey Galt Harpham argues that the harlequin and Kurtz may have had a physical relationship. "Marlow understands . . . how the Russian's identification with Kurtz could fail to screen out a homoerotic dimension. He understands the ultimate compatibility between feelings of affinity and active desire" (131).

19. In "The Beast in the Congo: How Victorian Homophobia Inflects Marlow's *Heart of Darkness*" (*Conradiana* 32, no. 2 [summer 2000]: 96–118), Donald Wilson

comes to the same conclusion about Kurtz and the harlequin's relationship based on the same passage. See 109.

20. The wonderfully bearded boilermaker, for example, Marlow's one friend at the Central Station, has six children, but his wife is dead (31). Long beards are often associated with sexual potency, but the boilermaker is denied a female object for that potency. In the economy of desire within adventure fiction, domestic heterosexuality may serve as a frame, but it is most often excluded from the heart of the tale.

21. That possibility is strengthened when one considers that the homosexual Roger Casement was a possible model for the harlequin. See Norman Sherry's *Conrad's Western World* (Cambridge: Cambridge University Press, 1971), 35. (Thanks once again to Hunt Hawkins for drawing my attention to Sherry's identification of the harlequin.)

22. When I write of males taking female roles I mean, simply, that these male characters temporarily take on the attributes of female characters in a conventional, heteronormative sense.

23. For a compelling examination of the boy as an object of desire at the end of the nineteenth century, see Martha Vicinus's "The Adolescent Boy: *Fin-de-Siècle* Femme Fatale?," in *Victorian Sexual Dissidence,* ed. Richard Dellamora (Chicago: University of Chicago Press, 1999), 83–106.

24. We are faced, once again, with the symbolic power of women. What possible risk could the woman pose to Kurtz? Are we to imagine that she would harm him in some way? Overexcite him? Force him out of bed to steal more ivory? On a literal level, that seems absurd. On a symbolic level, however, it is not. Every woman in the novella poses a symbolic threat to a man or to men.

25. In *Men in Love: Masculinity and Sexuality in the Eighteenth Century* (New York: Columbia University Press, 1999), George Haggerty lays out a parallel situation from Dryden's *All for Love* (1677). Like Kurtz, Antony is seduced by Cleopatra (another African mistress, one might say). In the terms of the play, Dolabella, Antony's handsome young friend whom I would parallel with the harlequin, is a more acceptable and less dangerous erotic partner than Cleopatra. Antony's wife, Octavia, loses in her appeal to Antony because her appeal is merely to his sense of duty and honor. Dolabella very nearly succeeds in saving Antony, because his appeal is emotional and erotic. Haggerty demonstrates convincingly that in this play and in other Restoration drama, love between men is often ennobling, while love between a man and a woman may be debilitating. See chapter 1, "Heroic Friendships," 23–43. The situation in British adventure fiction is often quite similar.

26. Donald Wilson also notes ("Beast in the Congo," 108) that this passage shows Marlow revealing excessive grief for losing his chance to meet Kurtz and suggests that this is a sign of Marlow's homoerotic interest in Kurtz.

27. For a fuller account of how this exchange shows Marlow at odds with his conservative audience, see my "*Heart of Darkness* and the Popular Exotic Stories of the 1890s," 9–10.

28. I take the useful phrase "homosexual panic" from Eve Kosofsky Sedgwick's *Between Men: English Literature and Male Homosocial Desire* (New York: Columbia University Press, 1985), 83–90. Donald Wilson also believes that the story reflects homosexual panic in various ways, though he presses this too far, I think, when he claims that Marlow reveals a homoerotic interest and then covers that interest many times throughout his narrative. Wilson claims that the overheated rhetoric Marlow

uses to characterize Kurtz's activities reveals that panic. I disagree, however. Kurtz's "unspeakable" transgression is his loss of European racial identity in the jungle, not, as Wilson would have it, homosexuality. (See Wilson, "Beast in the Congo.")

29. One possible example of that humor comes when Marlow describes Kurtz as "grubbing for ivory in the wretched bush" (44). Might this be a reference to masturbation? In the context of colonial fiction, this would certainly be safer than anything involving women. (I am indebted to Philip Holden for suggesting this reading.)

30. The question of whether Conrad was conscious of his exploration of the homosocial continuum must remain a vexed one, of course. Harpham doesn't see Conrad's representation of homosexuality "as a triumphantly evasive declaration of sexual, especially homosexual, energy in the face of some external censoring agency." Conrad, he adds, "was surely oblivious to the systematic intimations of the homosexual embrace in his work" (*One of Us*, 178, 179). Leaving the issue of artistic consciousness aside, however, I would argue just the opposite. Because Conrad's representation of homosexuality is so pervasive through his career and, specifically in *Heart of Darkness*, his depiction of a moment of homosexual panic among the men aboard the *Nellie* seems so clear (and clearly humorous), I believe, to use Harpham's eloquent phrase, that Conrad's representation of homosexuality is *indeed* an "evasive declaration of sexual, especially homosexual, energy in the face of some external censoring agency." It is not "triumphantly evasive" because "triumphs" are so few and far between in Conrad's work.

CHAPTER NINE

Homoerotic Heroics, Domestic Discipline: Conrad and Ford's *Romance*

Sarah Cole

Empire and homoerotics—two terms that have come to be linked in the contemporary critical vocabulary. By the end of the nineteenth century, a flourishing tradition of English imperial writing, including adventure novels, travel tales, scholarly treatises, and the developing "science" of ethnography, had brought home to the metropolis a complex array of messages about the nature and effects of colonial encounters, fostering a notion of imperial travel as a seething site of erotic possibilities among men.[1] By century's end, life in the "contact zone," to borrow Mary Louise Pratt's suggestive phrase, seemed both reassuringly familiar as a field of white, masculine conquest and consistently troubling as a site of both political contest and undomesticated male desire.[2] Thus, for Joseph Conrad and Ford Madox Ford[3] in 1903 to title their collaborative novel *Romance* was immediately to conjure up a myriad of charged possibilities: the promise of a masculine adventure tale, whose antics might be expected to cover the familiar homoerotic terrain of late-century orientalism, in tandem with a chivalric love story, embedded in the quest tradition.[4] And, indeed—generically self-conscious from first to last—*Romance* delivers a dizzying configuration of heterosexual romantic tropes within a fantastical homoerotics of the high seas. The text teems with masculine desire, intrigue, and rivalry, all the while enacting a ritualistic love story, according to highly formalized outlines. A reader today, armed with insights from both queer theory and the related field of masculinity studies, and with an eye toward Conrad's habitual tendency to revel in the metaphorics of difference, might find

in this overlooked novel rich evidence of late Victorian Britain's penchant for imagining masculine eroticism under the legitimizing sign of
imperial geography.[5]

Yet what differentiates *Romance* from hosts of other narratives that
produce familiar imperialist, homosocial effects is the brutal directness
and self-consciousness with which Conrad and Ford chart a trajectory
away from the relative comfort of exotic male adventure into a harrowing form of modernity. As it yearns for a lost literary and social past,
whose disappearance is presented as a casualty of twentieth-century capitalism, the novel indicts the global reach of a new economic and national order. Two different narrative tendencies direct the action—one
involving the lure of male interaction in the colonies, the other involving the strictures of a domestic love plot—and by tracing them I hope
to show that this extremely nostalgic novel starkly depicts the emergence
of the modern, urban subject out of the death of the nineteenth-century
romance hero and thus plays an important role in demonstrating how
the idea of the "modern" was created and theorized by practitioners of
modernism. If *Romance* steers clear of the formal experimentation associated with both its authors, it engages directly—more directly, I would
suggest, than many of Conrad's and Ford's more famous texts—with
the problem of the male individual's helplessness, passivity, dejection,
and alienation under the regime of the modern English nation. For *Romance,* modernity is defined less by the authorial power to "make it
new"—much less any enlightenment ideal of democracy or progress—
than by the male subject's crippled impotence at the hands of the state.
The novel thus offers a striking picture of the culture's concerns about
the mechanisms by which contemporary capitalism obliterates not only
outdated literary forms, such as the adventure novel, but the faltering
idea of male individuality itself.[6]

The Romance of Class: Feudalism and the Erasure of History

Perhaps the most peculiar element in *Romance*'s fantasy is its elaborate
reverence for the feudal past. Beginning with simple matters of plot, the
text's own romance involves an imaginative return to a moment when a
decidedly premodern economic and social system held dominion. The
novel's narrator and protagonist is John Kemp, grandson of an earl,
who finds himself connected through his sister's marriage with an aristocratic Spanish family. It is Kemp's seduction into the Riego family's

drama of decline, as the family's status as a great economic power in Cuba comes under increasing threat, that engenders the narrative of his adventures. Kemp will eventually carry off and marry the heiress Seraphina Riego, last survivor of the old clan, after rollicking escapades involving pirates, kidnappings, incarcerations, near-starvation, and over-determined male enmities. Seraphina provides the necessary link, of course, the object of exchange that enables the English Kemp to inherit not only the family's fortune but its symbolic power.[7] The novel goes to great lengths to highlight the conventional paradigm whereby men who love one another marry the appropriate sisters or cousins, thus perpetuating international kinship networks and consolidating power within the old families. The structure of exchange showcased here, which conjoins marital ties with baldly economic motives, conforms to what Gayle Rubin has famously characterized as "the male traffic in women," and also directly to the "homosocial" structure of triangulated desire delineated by Eve Sedgwick in her classic study, *Between Men*.[8] Moreover, as critics have abundantly demonstrated, the imperial location of such forms of desire serves to naturalize excess in general and masculine eroticism in particular. In his study of male literary collaboration and homosexual "double talk," for instance, Wayne Koestenbaum offers a reading of *Romance* that stresses the compatibility of homoerotics with the imperial imagination: "Although Conrad and Ford depict empire as morally murky," Koestenbaum writes, "the ardor of the novel arises from scenes of men exerting sexual power over each other, a charismatic influence that the novel cannot say is either good or evil," and he adds that the "'Romance' that so sways [the protagonist] and his authors is a homosexual love affair, a literary genre, and a nimbus of attractive degeneracy surrounding fantasies of English power."[9]

Far from masking the process of woman-exchange that fuels the system, then, *Romance* extravagantly stages it, drawing attention to its ancient and ritualistic quality, as well as its spectacular homoerotics. Most striking for its display of both homoeroticism and economic anachronism is a resonant scene at the deathbed of Seraphina's cousin Carlos, in a fabulous Cuban palace under siege. Although in this scene Kemp technically takes an oath with Seraphina, at her cousin's behest, symbolically it is the men who are joined. Carlos, whose "unearthly fineness" casts an aura over the hushed and darkened room, places an arm around Kemp's neck, forcing him to drop Seraphina's hand. "'Like an Englishman, Juan,'" he demands, and Kemp pledges his honor to his almost-white double.[10] In the text's symbolic universe, Carlos has always represented the exotic, his appeal heightened by a sense of continuity with the feudal past, and the staging of him in his bed exaggerates both his aristocratic status and his effeminate beauty: "You might well have imagined he was a descendant of the Cid Campeador, only to look at him lying there without a quiver of a feature, his face stainlessly white, a little bluish in extreme lack of blood, with all the nobility of death upon it, like an alabaster effigy of an old knight in a cathedral. On the red-velvet hangings of the bed was an immense coat-of-arms" (129). If Carlos embodies romance and exoticism in Kemp's imagination, such otherness is partially elided by the whitening and disembodying effects of his illness, drawing the two men together not only erotically but racially. Even more importantly, racial difference in the men's relationship is bridged by a class-based ideal of chivalry and honor, revealed at the deathbed exchange in all its formality.

The novel's infatuation with an idealized and theatricalized aristocracy is bolstered by a vitriolic animosity, on the part of Kemp, for work. Given Conrad's habitual investment in "efficiency," the era's watchword for productive labor, such a violent stance against work comes as something of a surprise. Even before Kemp reaches Cuba, the text associates romance with escape from the drudgery of ordinary labor, presented as both futile and emasculating. These apprehensions in no way accord either with the standard work ethic associated with late-nineteenth century Britain nor with the conventional Victorian representation of colonial labor as an elided province that invisibly produces wealth: "I was tired; Romance had departed. [The planters] represented all the laborious insects of the world; all the ants who are forever hauling immensely heavy and immensely unimportant burdens up weary hillocks, down steep places, getting nowhere and doing nothing" (51). Of course, the young Kemp's invective against labor in part illustrates his surly adolescence, but it also establishes what will become one of the text's primary concerns: a condemnation (albeit in a tone of resignation) of the relentless dehumanization produced by capitalism. Even in these early pages, Kemp intuits capitalism as a system in which workers become insects, labor is despised, and the individual's psyche is fundamentally shaped by alienation from his own productivity.[11] By contrast, the Riego family, with its enormous contingent of slaves and servants, embodies an ideal of inherited power, sheltered from the body's labors, just as the palace presents a site of calm tranquility in the midst of chaos and political upheaval. Indeed, as the description of Carlos's deathbed suggests, an aura of somber quiet pervades the giant house, as if movement itself has been suspended, the body rendered nearly obsolete.

If an aristocratic world order is the object of Kemp's and the novel's rueful desire, such a goal is defined by its unattainability. For all the family's fading splendor, death and loss—loss of power, prestige, relevance—are the order of the day at Casa Riego. Not only are the old patriarch and his heir dying before our eyes but the extreme anachronism of the entire establishment trumpets its status as relic. For Kemp, the problem of unattainability is attached, above all, to the great dream of romance, and the text repeatedly characterizes romance as that which one constantly desires but can never realize. "Journeying in search of romance," Kemp theorizes, "is much like trying to catch the horizon" (62). More interesting than this repeated lament over romance's intangibility is the text's conflation of such nostalgia with a sense of mourning over an idealized masculine body. As Koestenbaum argues, the spaces of romantic adventure in *Romance* teem with male beauty and physicality, in vivid contrast to an England of emasculated and ineffectual men. Yet even at the very site of such seemingly virile masculinity, the space itself signifies its own death and indeed functions less as a thriving alternative to the dilapidation of Europe than as a hardened fossil: "The general effect of the place was of vitality exhausted, of a body calcined, of romance turned into stone. The still air, the hot sunshine, the white beach curving around the deserted sheet of water, the sombre green of the hills, had the motionlessness of things petrified, the vividness of things painted, the sadness of things abandoned, desecrated" (157). Kemp's language here connects the state of romance with the physical health of the body, suggesting that masculine enervation results when romance and its literary forms have declined. If the shining male body is the centerpiece of the romantic experience, and if the genre of adventure worships at its altar, then the "now" of the narrative (Kemp's writing as well as the authors') recognizes the inevitable failure and "desecration" of that ethos.

Even more than the deserted beaches of Rio Medio, where the Riego family holds its diminishing court, the city of Havana symbolizes for Kemp an imaginary, lost past of heroic and venerable masculinity:

> I penetrated into the heart of the city.
> And directly, it seemed to me, I had stepped back three hundred years. I had never seen anything so old; this was the abandoned inheritance of an adventurous race, that seemed to have thrown all its might, all its vigour, and all its enthusiasm into one supreme effort of valour and greed.... With what a fury of heroism and faith had this whole people flung itself upon the opulent mystery of the New World. Never had a nation clasped closer to its heart its dream of greatness, of glory, and of romance. (455–56)

Kemp creates out of Havana a location to embody his exact idea of romance, where the "fury" of passionate men discovers a goal that lives up to their desires, a form of work that engages, rather than erases, their manliness. Yet, as standard orientalist tropes demand, such a Havana has firmly "past [sic] and gone below the horizon" (456), and the contemporary city is presented as a pale shadow of its former self.[12] Nevertheless, if the present fails to achieve the standard set by the romantic past, the city does offer thrills of masculine community and antagonism notable even in this already steamy male saga. In Havana, Kemp's adventures reach a fevered pitch of homoerotic and homosocial complexity, as he moves from the crowded streets where men ogle, jostle, and combat one another, to a comically overdetermined prison term. In contrast to London, where the tale will conclude, the urban nature of Havana is inextricably bound both with its atavism and its fostering of homoerotic delights.

Romance then, thrives specifically as fantasy. Or, more accurately, in order for Kemp and the novel to perpetuate the ideal of romance, they must consistently repress the facts of history. Thus the novel enacts a kind of competition, in which romance consistently works to obliterate important political, economic, and social realities. On one hand, the text sketches a complex political situation, involving conflicts among English colonialists over slavery in Jamaica, the relation of Spain and Mexico to England, and, perhaps most central, the claims of Ireland against imperial England. On the other hand, Kemp repeatedly distances himself from these political disturbances in his relentless search for romance, insistin ʒ that the politics of empire hold only minimal interest for his story.

Indeed, Kemp's goal seems to be to divest the entire field of imperial difference and inequality of any reality, aestheticizing and generalizing all such troubling relations. Here, for example, is Kemp's rumination on the contact between the aged patriarch of the Riego family and his lifelong slave:

> At times he bent towards his master's ear. Don Balthasar answered with a murmur: and those two faces brought close together, one like a noble ivory carving, the other black with the mute pathos of the African faces, seemed to commune in a fellowship of age, of things far off, remembered, lived through together. There was something mysterious and touching in this violent contrast, toned down by the near approach to the tomb— the brotherhood of master and slave. (143)

While such language may seem absurd to the point of parody—and I will take up the larger question of parody a little later—Kemp's willful desire to make all relations among men into forms of aestheticized "fellowship" or "brotherhood" characterizes his entire narration. We can hear the familiar attributes of romance in the evocation of "things far off, remembered, lived through together," as if slavery itself has become the stuff of romance, one more dying form, sadly consigned to the retreating and calcifying past.

Most central in the text's aestheticizing mission is the relation between Kemp and his archrival, Patrick O'Brien. In a text that valorizes a fading aristocracy, the centrality of O'Brien's national and class identity can hardly be overstated. O'Brien's Irishness and glaring class difference from the protagonists set him off in stark outlines. He represents a new and hated form of power, achieved through piracy, ruthlessness, and deceit, rather than inheritance, and symbolized by the rag-tag horde that does his bidding. Yet, for all his villainy, O'Brien makes a compelling case for his actions on political and national grounds. Proclaiming himself a rebel and a victim of English injustice, O'Brien defiantly challenges Kemp and his associates in the name of national revenge: "'I would die happy,'" he asserts, "'if I knew I had helped to detach from you one island—one little island of all the earth you have filched away, stolen, taken by force, got by lying . . .'" (196, ellipses in original). O'Brien's trenchant critique of the hypocrisy of imperialist rhetoric would thus seem to position him as a spokesman for uncomfortable truths, perhaps for history itself. However, in keeping with its overall movement, the text, through Kemp's voice, insists on reframing O'Brien's claims as part of the larger romantic picture. His words are depleted of their specificity, dehistoricized and generalized in a way that weakens any sense of England's imperial culpability. Thus Kemp stresses eternal categories of difference, insisting that "we were cat and dog—Celt and Saxon, as it was in the beginning" (89), or again, "There we were, Irish and English, face to face, as it had been ever since we had met in the narrow way of the world that had never been big enough for the tribes, the nations, the races of man" (196).

When the text transforms the enmity between the two men from a specific instance of colonizer and colonized into a historically generalized encounter between "the races of man," it not only weakens the ideological impact of O'Brien's revolt but also reinvigorates the category of the homoerotic, which thrives in this text in the realm of fantasy rather than history. As in the "brotherhood of master and slave," the conflict between the men revives at the moment when moral complexity is eradicated (Kemp is once again the hero, O'Brien the villain). The antagonistic relation between Kemp and O'Brien comes to represent the successor to Kemp's formalized and heavily eroticized bond with Carlos, and the men's rivalry over Seraphina replaces the smooth exchange enacted earlier at Carlos's deathbed. When O'Brien dies (having been stabbed with a dagger, in a most suggestive fashion, in the soft area at the back of his neck), his status as successor to Carlos becomes explicit, as "he covered his face with his hands and began to cough incessantly, like a man dying of consumption. . . . Carlos had coughed like that. Carlos was dead. Now O'Brien!" (492). Not surprisingly, given O'Brien's status as Carlos's double, Kemp's immediate response to his enemy's death is an instinctive cry of loss, couched in the language of morality: "I almost wished him alive again—I wanted to have him again, rather than that I should have been relieved of him by that atrocious murder" (492). Kemp's visceral desire to revive his tormenter in fact represents an essential feature of their ongoing enmity. His consistent and irrational proclivity to save O'Brien's life (an otherwise puzzling feature of the narrative) is not so much a plot-generating device as a token of the text's driving impulse to generate homoerotic passions and homosocial rivalries. The suppression of history brings the homoerotic to life, and the elusive, ever-disappearing sphere of romance provides the setting.

Moreover, it is not only the text's primary rivals who are featured by such a structure; instead, a host of intertwined masculine relations, too numerous and complex to recount here, flourish under these romantic conditions. Among the many male ties that swarm around the novel's central opposition, however, one figure holds particular interest for this inquiry: the faithful servant Tomas Castro. This enigmatic, dour Spaniard, banditlike in appearance but defined by his overwhelming loyalty, comes to serve Kemp as a kind of bodyguard. As Castro resignedly explains, "'These [were] Don Carlos' orders. 'Serve him, Castro, when I am dead, as if my soul had passed into his body'" (208). In this rich transfusion of male loyalty from one body to the next is presented the epitome of a system of masculine ties that has no clear counterpart outside the sphere of romance. At the same time, Castro's fidelity in no way compromises his virile masculinity, embodied with symbolic resonance by the knife blade that lodges permanently in the place of his lost hand. To have the phallic Castro as companion is to exist at the apex of a fellowship-obsessed world, where the politics of loyalty and leadership are understood entirely in terms of contested masculine relations, essentially unmoored from other social structures.

Yet the position of Castro, whose style is as exaggerated and histrionic as his dagger-hand, inescapably brings up the question of parody. How serious, we might well ask, is any of this? Isn't the whole sphere of wildly homoerotic intrigue a kind of mock-romance, and isn't our naïve narrator an object of satire, rather than the mouthpiece for his sophisticated authors? Certainly, the text repeatedly veers toward the absurd in its characterization of the homoerotics of adventure romance. Most obvious as parody is the depiction of Kemp's stay in the Havana prison, where, as I have already indicated, the ludicrous and the homoerotic join hands. In the inner sanctum, among the prison's elite, the caricature of aristocratic ceremoniousness combined with homoerotic rhetoric reaches a fevered pitch, under the direction of a fanatical and theatrical prisoner, who repeatedly invokes his fellow inmates as "'a band of brothers'" and "'kindred spirits'" (484). Even the sentimental Kemp recognizes the extreme incongruity of the man's outsized formality, since "his gestures, made for large, grave men, were comic in him. They reduced Spanish manners to absurdity" (484). Traditional homosocial rituals of the sort elaborated in the novel up to now (lavishly homoerotic and deliberately formulaic) are here conjoined with heavy-handed aping of elevated gestures, suggesting perhaps that the whole phantasmatic of the text has likewise been parodic.

I would argue, however, that while the authors display an ironic sensibility through much of the narrative, and while at times they point the finger at Kemp for his credulity in adhering to a youthful notion of romance, nevertheless the text ultimately takes seriously the sense of nostalgia that Kemp repeatedly expresses for the loss of homoerotic, aestheticized fantasy. After all, Conrad and Ford quite self-consciously engage the issue of genre, beginning with their choice of title, and the end of the novel—indeed its literal last word—continues to hail "Romance" (541). Their idea seems to be to produce a form that they simultaneously parody and embody, a familiar modernist move. While a level of debunking remains part and parcel of this strategy, the text also generates pleasure out of its own excess, seeming to revel in its very anachronism. Biographically, we might also note that Conrad, in desperate financial straits at the time of *Romance*'s production, saw the novel as a potentially lucrative endeavor, given the continued popularity of the adventure story at the turn of the century.

More important than genre, however, in assessing the text's seriousness about its own thematics, is the increasingly desperate tone of the novel in the final section, which stages a marked shift from the depiction of imperial geography to the characterization of England as a stifling place of modern repression. Ultimately, Kemp is returned to England under compulsion, in a solitary confinement that contrasts with the sociality of the Cuban prison and prefigures his treatment at Newgate. There are, in other words, two types of narrative logic at work in the text, which ultimately conflict with one another. The first is governed by Kemp's romantic desires, which I have argued involve both homoerotic infatuation and the fantasy of an aristocratic escape from both work and history. This paradigm relies on a tendency to recast colonial power relations into an abstract, even aestheticized, narrative of masculine competition, and at times points toward the parodic. The second and oppositional logic involves the development of a textually satisfying love plot. Kemp and Seraphina must emerge as a new and dazzling couple, the product of chivalric endeavor. This second plot-line, which provides the culmination and conclusion of the text, eviscerates any sense of play or parody, functioning instead as a chastening reprimand, a repudiation of the many fantastical possibilities presented by the notion of romance.

"The Lot of Man": Domesticity and Death

Throughout the Caribbean portion of the novel, Kemp's romantic saga has held in balance two structures, a homoerotic set of entanglements and a heterosexual love story, each of which involves its own sedimented traditions. If the homoerotic fantasy depends on the complex notion of aestheticized and temporal romance, for the Seraphina story, Conrad and Ford resuscitate an even more familiar set of literary conventions: Kemp the knight must rescue the princess Seraphina; the two young lovers are like Adam and Eve; the exotic southern woman is brought to the safety and stability of England. Kemp himself frequently and overtly conjures up this literary history. "She was the first woman to me," he confesses early in their story, "a strange new being, a marvel as great as Eve herself to Adam's wondering awakening" (158). In conventional fashion, Kemp asserts that his specific passion in fact surpasses its literary forebears, since Seraphina "was more to me than any princess to any knight" (251). Finally, despite much talk of wonder and marvel, it is England that represents the ultimate home for lovers, the place where young romance can come to fruition: in Carlos's words to Kemp, "'I would like best to see you marry my cousin. Once before a woman of our race had married an Englishman. She had been happy. English things last forever—English peace, English power, English fidelity. It is a country of much serenity, of order, of stable affection . . .'" (150, ellipses in original).

Yet there are two key features that differentiate the conventional love plot from its masculine counterpart. First, Kemp is finally unwilling to give up the latter in favor of the former, requiring a form of force to tear him away from the terrain of romance. For all his protestations of desire for an English life with Seraphina, he continually thwarts that possibility, prolonging his time abroad and repeatedly sabotaging his own success. And second, while the homoerotics of empire remain fundamentally at odds with the life of home, the heterosexual, chivalric story finds an appropriate counterpart in the text's closing image of the domesticated couple. Or, to put it slightly differently, what *Romance* shows is that the onset of twentieth-century modernity forces the logic of homo-social adventure into conflict with the very narrative it is supposed to engender—the love story—and, when this rupture emerges, the romance hero must be compelled to grow up into a heteronormative, passive, English subject.

Hence Kemp is returned to England a prisoner in irons, stripped of his identity, and deposited in a miserable, solitary cell in Newgate. The contrast with colonial prison life could not be more striking. In his Caribbean adventure, Kemp's imprisonments form part of a rich phantasmatic experience; but back at home, a modern form of subjectivity is required, and it finds its institutional setting at Newgate:

> The whole of the outer world, as far as it affected me, came suddenly in upon me—that was what I meant to the great city that lay all round, the world, in the centre of which was my cell. To the great mass, I was matter for a sensation....
>
> All those people had their eyes on me, and they were about the only ones who knew of my existence. That was the end of my Romance! Romance! The broad-sheet sellers would see to it afterwards with a "Dying confession." (511)

Kemp's understanding of his own place in a national, cosmopolitan culture resembles Benedict Anderson's model of national identity as constituted by the anonymity and homogeneity of print culture.[13] Kemp senses that he is being transformed by the twin operations of textuality and incarceration, and his efforts to resist such manipulation are infused with a sense of futility.

Such a shift in the concept of national identity comes in the context of a sustained loss of paternal authority. As Koestenbaum notes, paternal power in *Romance* is in dire straits: Kemp's ineffectual, weak, and ultimately irrelevant father is symbolic of a large-scale failure in the structure of familial power. In the Caribbean portion of the novel, young men battle among themselves for the de facto leadership of an empire whose dying patriarch retires increasingly into the background. In England, it is the impersonal apparatus of the state—the British naval authorities in Cuba; the prison and its guards; the magistrate's court—that reaffirms the power of patriarchy despite the loss of paternal viability. Thus the novel stages a movement out of inherited models of filial identity, through a moment of delightfully excessive fraternal animosity and desire, and finally into a system whereby the overwhelming power of the state triumphs not only over men in their competitive activities but over the very notion of individuality.[14]

Even before the final section of the novel, ominously titled "The Lot of Man," there have been suggestions that what is finally at stake for the text is the nature of power itself, the fate of the individual at a moment when fundamental structures of economic, military, and political power are in flux. For instance, the text begins—and the romance plot gets underway—with a rather confusing depiction of the competition between an established cadre of smugglers (provocatively called "Free Traders") and the king's runners, official organs of the state. Here in County Kent in the early decades of the nineteenth century, the novel seems to suggest, the question of power has not yet firmly been decided in favor of the state, as highly organized, underground systems of economic and social order battle directly with the king's representatives. Though "of late the smugglers themselves had become demoralized" (12), and though at the time of writing the authors can take for granted the eventual triumph of the imperial state, nevertheless the novel begins with a look backward to a moment when the totality of unified national control might still have been resisted, in fantasy at any rate. Thus, if the novel cannot be said to perform a rigorous analysis of politicoeconomic development over the course of the century, it nevertheless presents in bold strokes the increasingly visible and formidable nature of consolidated power at century's end, an uprecendented system of global order that promises to remain both fearsome and totalizing.

The contest over fundamental structures of social and economic order is not confined to England itself, as suggested by the novel's preoccupation with the problem of piracy, the text's central crime. O'Brien and his pirates wreak havoc on the Admiralty's ships and men, and Kemp's indictment, for which he is nearly hanged, involves the confusion of his identity with that of a notorious pirate. Piracy provides a particularly appropriate form of outlawry for this novel, since it conjoins conventional romantic imagery with a serious consideration of the developing hegemony of the British empire abroad and the English government (firmly committed to hanging all convicted pirates) at home. Indeed piracy—with its direct assault against England's central imperial weapon, the navy—offers an interesting form of stubborn resistance against the hardening structures of imperial organization across the globe. Like romance itself, piracy is presented here as a disappearing form of rebellion against the utter dominance of the English nation-state.[15]

Such dominance makes itself known, once and for all, through the institution of the magistrate's court. The isolated and alienated prisoner faces an impersonal institution whose primary function is to uphold ideological and practical principles for safeguarding colonial trade.[16] In the face of such impersonality and capitalist motivation, Kemp turns to the central form through which the individual traditionally constitutes himself: language. "If there were to be any possibility of saving my life," he recognizes, "I had to tell what I had been through—and to tell it vividly—I had to narrate the story of my life; and my whole life came into my mind" (532). Language and the power of individuality—celebrated icons in liberal thinking, and of course in the history of the novel—contest directly against the official embodiment of state power. What goes on trial with Kemp in the final pages of the novel is not only the viability of the homoerotic romantic self but also the notion of individual protest. Gender, too, enters the court in complex symbolic shapes, as Kemp confronts figures who embody a variety of contemporary gender modes. Indeed, we might say that the liberal subject itself—gendered and textualized—is on trial, posed against a state whose driving motive has become unabashedly economic.[17]

During the trial, Kemp's mangled and bloody hands provide the most resonant symbol of his overdetermined struggle to assert both individual integrity and some form of viable masculinity. His torn body offers a palpable sign of his emasculation, of the damage perpetrated by the massive cultural forces against him, including, at one desperate moment, himself: "I smashed my hand upon the spikes of the rail in front of me, and although I saw hands move impulsively towards me all over the court, I did not know that my arm was impaled and the blood running down" (530). Despite a certain Christ resemblance in the ripped hands, Kemp's increasingly restricted and damaged physical body becomes a primary token of his feeble protest, of his vulnerable and pitiful stature in relation to the massiveness of the state's power. Further, the spike on which Kemp impales himself recalls Castro's spiked hand—the sign, I have argued, of the phallic power accompanying male companionship in a world organized by intertwined relations of comaraderie and enmity—and the shift is significant: far from controlling fidelity and male fellowship, Kemp has been forcefully removed from that promise, sacrificed to the demands of a particular legal and literary logic. Indeed, his release from prison results not from his narrative of self-exoneration but rather from the timely production of formal validation, submitted to the court by a naval officer. Far from elevating his status, Kemp's resonant performance at the trial showcases his isolated and caged position, his mutilation and impotence in the hands of a power structure that enforces its own formula for individuality and identity.

The magistrate's final words indicate what such a concept of Englishness entails: "'You have suffered much, as it seems, but suffering is the lot of us men. Rejoice now that your character is cleared; that here in this public place you have received the verdict of your countrymen" (540). In the magistrate's world, official procedure, national identity, gender differentiation, and a Christian narrative of obedience unite to constitute an idea of the self that will not be overruled. To be a man is not so much to range heroically over colonial geography, nor to narrate the self in compelling language, but to suffer complacently at the hands of the state, and to receive the stamp of masculine individuality through a ritual of public recognition. Perhaps most striking is how immediately and entirely Kemp comes to accept and internalize the court's position, notwithstanding his fitful efforts at rebellion and protest. Thus, in the last pages of the novel, Kemp echoes the magistrate, proclaiming that "suffering is the lot of man ... suffering, the mark of manhood, which bears within its pain a hope of felicity like a jewel set in iron" (541). Masculinity becomes a matter of endurance rather than an aestheticized contest among men; even the metaphoric jewel is imprisoned in iron, an image that recalls Kemp in shackles aboard the military ship.

If Kemp's theatrical performance had seemed to represent an effort to combat the hegemony of a court bent on flaunting its power to construct the individual for its own purposes and in its own image, such performativity is now rendered as obsolete as romance itself:

> I remember the intense bitterness of that feeling and the oddity of it all; of the one "I" that felt like that [resignation and despair], of the other that was raving in front of a lot of open-eyed idiots, three old judges, and a young girl. And, in a queer way, the thoughts of the one "I" floated through into the words of the other, that seemed to be waving its hands in its final struggle, a little way in front of me. (533)

As in Kemp's earlier depiction of his Newgate cell at the center of modern culture, here he offers a somewhat distanced and objective assessment of the modern self as a new product, a being whose emergence is as inevitable as it is painful. The modern "I" to emerge out of the old forms will no longer attempt to protest against its placement in the power structure that has constructed it. It welcomes its imprisonment, its passivity, even its own death.

The counterpart for the new Kemp is quite clearly a domestic Seraphina. The last paragraphs of the novel, which describe the reunion and happiness of the pair in their comfortable English life, are rife with images of death, strangulation, and lassitude and thus dramatize both Kemp's unacknowledged regret for lost homoeroticism and his complete internalization of the lessons taught by the court. Seraphina herself is characterized by a tendency to suffocate:

> The whole world, the whole of life, with her return, had changed all around me; it enveloped me, it enfolded me so lightly as not to be felt, so suddenly as not to be believed in, so completely that that whole meeting was an embrace, so softly that at last it lapsed into a sense of rest that was like the fall of a beneficent and welcome death. (541)

Heterosexual life embraces Kemp into death; its processes are silent and soporific, its future absolute. With its direct recollection of the earlier depiction of Newgate, the language here establishes an unbroken continuum from the debilitating imprisonment of mass culture to the strangulation of modern domesticity. Kemp complacently understands this continuity in stasis as "the little heap of dust that is life" (541).

One striking feature of Seraphina's position at the end of the novel is how smoothly it has been forged out of her earlier role as conventional romantic heroine. Unlike Kemp, who must be forcibly transformed from anachronistic romancer into modern subject, Seraphina's status within domestic ideology is presented as a natural outgrowth from her earlier scripted role. No doubt such continuity derives from her consistent position as object: of exchange, desire, rivalry. As we have seen, the novel follows two oppositional directives, neither of which takes much account of Seraphina as an individual in her own right. The first directive involves a masculine world of adventure, characterized by the fantasy of a lateral matrix of male connections and a nostalgically rendered feudal world order. The second substitutes state power and its institutional apparatus for the fantasy of self-made male communities and insists on a particular form of national, anti-individualist, heterosexual identity that conveniently supports an expanding capitalist economy based on trade. Although the love plot ultimately requires that the adventure romance be abandoned and the male hero returned home, Seraphina herself is strangely absent from all of these movements; she neither colludes with nor resists the cultural systems in which she exists. Indeed, as romance heroine she had essentially been acted on, in conventional fashion, and perhaps because of this, her transformation into a modern domestic woman is rather uneventful, a change of scene but not of subjectivity.

In *Romance,* the relation between lost worlds of male fellowship and twentieth-century alienation is binding. *Romance* fantasizes about an imagined past in which masculine relations of friendship, rivalry, and desire helped to shape the social order, and it posits an image of modernity in which the male individual is escorted firmly out of such a world, to be deposited instead in a national culture that makes no place for male intimacy and has no tolerance for resistance against modern capitalism. Both of these modes—the homoerotic romantic as well as the alienated modern—remain entirely male, dependent on gender differentiation and the occlusion of any sense of female subjectivity. Despite its apparent focus on the past, *Romance* fundamentally asks what it means to be modern, how to conceptualize essential categories of identity and desire under an intractable system of totalizing culture. The answer seems to coincide in important ways with a wider formula—universalizing and profoundly male-oriented—that has carried tremendous weight in the twentieth century: to be modern is to assert the masculine self paradoxically as lost, dying, anachronistic. And inevitably, the narrative logic and authority that accrues to such a paradoxical masculinity falls under the rubric of irony. It is irony then—the irony of constructing masculinity out of disempowerment, status out of depletion—that provides the only form of viable narrative authority under the bleak conditions of urban modernity.

Notes

1. For especially rich discussions of the relationship between imperialism and gender, see Anne McClintock, *Imperial Leather: Race, Gender, and Sexuality in the Colonial Contest* (New York: Routledge, 1995), Elaine Showalter, *Sexual Anarchy: Gender and Culture at the Fin de Siècle* (New York: Viking, 1990), 76–104, and Marianna Torgovnick, *Gone Primitive: Savage Intellects, Modern Lives* (Chicago: University of Chicago Press, 1990). For accounts of imperialism that provocatively refigure

critical gender terms, see Joseph Allen Boone, "Vacation Cruises; or the Homoerotics of Orientalism," *PMLA* 110, no. 1 (1995): 89–107; Christopher Lane, *The Ruling Passion: British Colonial Allegory and the Paradox of Homosexual Desire* (Durham: Duke University Press, 1995); and Sara Suleri, *The Rhetoric of English India* (Chicago: University of Chicago Press, 1992).

2. Mary Louise Pratt, *Imperial Eyes: Travel Writing and Transculturation* (London: Routledge, 1992).

3. Although *Romance* was published before Hueffer changed his name to Ford, I will refer to him in my discussion as Ford, the usual critical practice.

4. For a thorough discussion of the construction of this collaborative novel, see Raymond Brebach, *Joseph Conrad, Ford Madox Ford, and the Making of Romance* (Ann Arbor: University of Michigan Research Press, 1985).

5. Of the many studies of imperialism proliferating among critics of nineteenth- and twentieth-century Britain, several with particular resonance for *Romance* are Joseph Bristow, *Empire Boys: Adventures in a Man's World* (London: Harper, 1991), Robert H. MacDonald, *The Language of Empire: Myths of Popular Imperialism* (Manchester: Manchester University Press, 1994), J. A. Mangan, *The Games Ethic and Imperialism: Aspects of the Diffusion of an Ideal* (New York: Viking, 1985), Benita Parry, *Conrad and Imperialism: Ideological Boundaries and Visionary Frontiers* (London: Macmillan, 1983), and Andrea White, *Joseph Conrad and the Adventure Tradition: Constructing and Deconstructing the Imperial Subject* (Cambridge: Cambridge University Press, 1993).

6. For assessments of modernism that directly link modernist forms with economic and imperial modes at the turn of the century, see Ali Behdad, *Belated Travelers: Orientalism in the Age of Colonial Dissolution* (Durham: Duke University Press, 1994), Chris Bongie, *Exotic Memories: Literature, Colonialism, and the Fin de Siècle* (Stanford: Stanford University Press, 1991), Marianne DeKoven, *Rich and Strange: Gender, History, Modernism* (Princeton: Princeton University Press, 1991), Terry Eagleton, Fredric Jameson, and Edward Said, *Nationalism, Colonialism, and Literature* (Minneapolis: University of Minnesota Press, 1988), and Jameson, *The Political Unconscious: Narrative as a Socially Symbolic Act* (Ithaca: Cornell University Press, 1981). For discussion of globalization and modernity as processes that inevitably erase local difference and specificity, see Michael Valdez Moses, *The Novel and the Globalization of Culture* (New York: Oxford University Press, 1995).

7. In assessing Kemp's claims to inheritance, we should not overlook his equivocal racial position. Though repeatedly described (and self-described) as "English," Kemp's mother is Scottish, and this undertone of racial difference is never entirely suppressed in the novel. Thus when Kemp will later portray himself as "Saxon" to his enemy's "Celt" (discussed below), the racial self-identification is more willed than inherited. Perhaps it would be most accurate to say that the novel's insistence on subsuming Scottish into English simultaneously conforms to the novel's larger portrayal of the homogenizing nature of modernity and points to the continued remnants of difference that disturb such a totalizing picture.

8. Gayle Rubin, "The Traffic in Women: Notes on the 'Political Economy' of Sex," in *Toward an Anthropology of Women*, ed. Rayna R. Reiter (New York: Monthly Review Press, 1975), 157–210; Eve Kosofsky Sedgwick, *Between Men: English Literature and Male Homosocial Desire* (New York: Columbia University Press, 1985). In my discussion, I am assuming familiarity with Sedgwick's well-known account of

the homoerotic underpinnings of patriarchal homosociality. When I use the term "homoerotic," I aim to highlight the element of male desire; "homosocial" refers to the structures of patriarchal male culture that typically (a) trade on homoeroticism; (b) contribute to the continued suppression of women; and (c) promote and depend on restrictions on genital homosexuality among men.

9. Wayne Koestenbaum, *Double Talk: The Erotics of Male Literary Collaboration* (New York: Routledge, 1989), 169. Subsequent references cited parenthetically in text.

10. Joseph Conrad and Ford Madox Hueffer, *Romance* (New York: Doubleday, 1938), 178, 182. Subsequent references cited parenthetically in text.

11. Kemp's contempt for labor, as well as the text's larger preoccupation with an aristocracy that produces wealth without work, in some ways conforms to Conrad's lifelong dismissal of middle-class bourgeois striving and his infatuation with forms of work that either elude or mask their own productive engines. However, what differentiates *Romance* from such works as *Nostromo* (1904) or *Lord Jim* (1900), in this respect, is the heavy-handedness with which *Romance* presents the contrast between modern capitalism (with its drudgery and alienation) and an old order's imagined exemption from the problems of labor.

12. The tendency to discount any possibility of modernity in the "Orient"—a space defined by its obsolescence—is described by Edward Said in his classic *Orientalism* (New York: Random House, 1979).

13. See Benedict Anderson, *Imagined Communities: Reflections on the Origins and Spread of Nationalism* (London: Verso, 1983).

14. Edward Said has provocatively suggested that modernism represents a crisis in filial authority and a shift into what he terms an "affiliative" mode. See Edward Said, *The World, the Text, and the Critic* (Cambridge: Harvard University Press, 1983). For a psychoanalytic discussion of the rise of brotherhood as the dominant political and rhetorical form in the modern world, see Juliet Flower MacCannell, *The Regime of the Brother: After the Patriarchy* (London: Routledge, 1991).

15. For discussion of the development of the pirate image in the British popular imagination over several centuries, see Hans Turley, *Rum, Sodomy, and the Lash: Piracy, Sexuality, and Masculine Identity* (New York: New York University Press, 1999).

16. In its critique of the consolidating power of the imperial state, *Romance* suggests that the liberal concept of a free marketplace belongs with the swashbuckling atmosphere of "Free Traders" and Caribbean adventurers—with romance, in the text's lexicon—rather than in the real world of contemporary legal or trade policy. Without undertaking a disciplined account of economic theory, the text does address the increasing obliteration of individuality (and individual choice) as a category, subject to historical movements, and in that sense contributes to a wider turn-of-the-century discussion about the nature and consequences of modern economic forms. Though liberalism remained the dominant conceptual model of economic and political agency in England during this period, a host of competing intellectual currents, which offered real challenges to the centrality of the individualized liberal subject, were also taking shape around Conrad and Ford. For discussion of the fate of liberalism in Conrad's work, see Pericles Lewis, *Modernism, Nationalism, and the Novel* (Cambridge: Cambridge University Press, 2000), and Ursula Lord, *Solitude Versus Solidarity in the Novels of Joseph Conrad: Political and Epistemological Implications of Narrative Innovation* (Montreal: McGill-Queen's University Press, 1998).

For a discussion of Conrad's theorizing of his own labor, see John Marx, "Conrad's Gout," *Modernism/Modernity* 6, no. 1 (1999): 91–114.

17. The status of individualism in modernist literature—triumph or defeat? rise or fall?—is a topic that has preoccupied critics. For thorough treatment, see Michael Levenson, *Modernism and Individuality: Character and Novelistic Form from Conrad to Woolf* (Cambridge: Cambridge University Press, 1991). For an analysis of the complex ways in which modernism both repels and appropriates the "mass mind," see Michael Tratner, *Modernism and Mass Politics: Joyce, Woolf, Eliot, Yeats* (Stanford: Stanford University Press, 1995).

Part IV
Other Colonialisms

CHAPTER TEN

"Only Cathect": Queer Heirs and Narrative Desires in *Howards End*

Lois Cucullu

Until Fredric Jameson's perceptive rumination on the Great North Road as a spatial signifier of imperial expansion, *Howards End* was generally deemed a novel of local concerns, and with ample justification.[1] So expressive of a domestic sensibility did one early reviewer find it that its author was praised for "what appears to be a feminine brilliance of perception."[2] Subsequent readers found the inordinate investment heaped rhetorically on the ordinary spaces collected under the eponymous Howards End—house, rooms, garden, pony ring, meadow—as evidence of Forster's obsessive longing for his lost boyhood home, Rooksnest. More grandly, the yearning for these spaces has been read under the rubric "the condition of England" as a national elegy of the English people themselves for the loss of the countryside, their true ancestral home, by the population shift to the metropolis, unmistakable over the nineteenth century, and by the corresponding urban and suburban dilation as greater London encroached more and more on country space. Metropolitan agglomeration is such an accomplished fact in *Howards End* that the narrator can confidently confide: "to speak against London is no longer fashionable" and then unfashionably proceed to disparage everything from motorcars and petrol fumes to the razing of the Schlegel home at Wickham Place for the construction of what are derisively termed "Babylonian Flats," part of a piece with the shoddier construction that houses the clerk Leonard Bast in a modest basement flat with Jacky, his less than modest bride-to-be.[3] The urban pollution, sprawl, and corruption lend credence to the newspaper story Bast's neighbor recounts of Manchester's falling birthrate and of general decline, thus putting in doubt native and national well-being. For "if this kind of thing goes on," reasons the neighbor, "the population of England will be stationary in 1960" (37). These uncertainties, reported in such popular newspapers as the *Daily Mail,* led commentators like Ford Madox Ford to speculate in his trilogy on the state of England whether a fecund townsman with a rural temperament might yet evolve to answer the pressing dilemma of urban boom and rural ebb.[4]

With Jameson's highly suggestive reading, however, the deleterious effects decried by press and pundit alike no longer retain their insular valence. Alleging the real culprit of national unease to be found in the economic dislocation brought on by overseas production, Jameson argues that the spatial mystification, which such dislocation occasions, manifests itself structurally in Anglo modernism and specifically in Forster's novel, cropping up as chance encounters in *Howards End* and elsewhere in modernist texts more generally. These accidental occurrences, according to Jameson, are the motivated but unintended proofs of the breach that imperialism forces between urban indigene and organic place.[5] Coincidence, however abrupt and inexplicable on the face of it, becomes the tangible trace of the rootlessness modernity exacts, as nation *and* empire set subjects in motion. The longing for place, the dominant affect of *Howards End,* stands then in Jameson's critique for the disjunction empire produces on the human psyche.

Such a "spatial" allowance importantly situates empire squarely at the center of the novel as never before, so that any subsequent reading must perforce attend to the domestic and imperial culture of its address. Yet it does so by perpetuating the received wisdom that *Howards End* is a reactive novel and literary modernism writ large, a compensatory aesthetic movement: to wit, Forster, along with other modernists, was reacting to external stimuli of which they themselves were unconscious except as bodily sensations and over which they exerted no thought or control. Sentient but incognizant, Forster and later modernists could only seek redress aesthetically, the former provisionally, the latter more radically. The imperial domain that Jameson newly introduces for consideration so overwhelms the modernist imagination that empire emerges as an incomprehensible totality, with the unexpected result of putting out of reach the very process the critic endeavors to make legible with his deliberation on the spatial infinity augured by the Great North Road.

The logic of this obscuration, according to Laura Chrisman's careful analysis in "Imperial Space, Imperial Place," may be traced to the premises underlying Jameson's analysis.[6] Chief among them is the conceit that the economic structure of imperialism alone uniquely discloses itself in the novel. Privileging the economic, Chrisman points out, denies any role to politics or to ideology, such as the politics of representation or the ideological work of the novel form, or, for that matter, of modernist style, that might also explain spatial ambiguity. These exclusions are in turn exacerbated by another, in my view. Jameson's insistence on emphasizing the formal structure of modernism allows him to dismiss out of hand the popular literature of adventure fiction and imperial romance as the stock of marginal genres insignificant to modernist experimentation.[7] The result is that practitioner and protagonist, unaffected by popular genres and lacking agency, become the oblivious conduits of a modernist style that is decipherable only through the astute predilection of the literary expert. Style no less than the expert's critical acumen is granted agency and is in effect no less mystified.[8]

In reply, I propose pursuing a different path to *Howards End* and implicitly to Anglo modernism that takes advantage of the spatial problematic in Jameson's argument. Situating economy and empire within a broader institutional matrix and moving imperial literature and politics to the forefront, I will grant the novelist political agency and the novel form the ideological moment Jameson disallowed by arguing that what Forster attempts through his use of coincidence in this novel is to bring about a newly grounded masculine subject, and, even more, a queered metropolitan subject. To accomplish this reading, I will first take up the speech Forster delivered in the same month as the publication of *Howards End*, "The Feminine Note in Literature," which has been ignored by critics and, until just recently, remained unpublished, despite a new Norton critical edition of the novel.[9] For when Forster's preoccupation in the speech with the state of Anglo masculinity and the future of the English novel is read alongside his novel's overdetermined adulation of the countryside and vilification of the city, a more nuanced understanding emerges of the desires latent in *Howards End* and of the greater "ends" the novel advances that justifies my tweaking of Forster's famous epigraph— "Only Connect."

Using these two 1910 texts, I contend that one pressing objective is to displace the authority of the bourgeois household under the domestic woman's governance that authorized monogamous marriage and the procreative bourgeois couple, which the domestic novel, in turn, propagated—and this to enable a more central desire.[10] Drawing on R. W. Connell's lucid observation about gender—that, in the twentieth century, "masculinity organized around *dominance* was increasingly incompatible with masculinity organized around *expertise* or technical knowledge (610)"—I further contend that Forster works to supplant the model of masculinity hegemonic over the nineteenth century with that of the expert, hegemonic over the twentieth, this despite all his liberal and egalitarian professions.[11] In this reading, bourgeois subjectification no longer easily aligns with a Protestant, industrial, imperial, and procreative model but necessitates instead the intervention of expert knowledge, whether of the newer disciplines of psychology and sociology, or traditional ones of medicine and law. The form required for the economic consolidation of nation and expansion of empire in the nineteenth century, epitomized by the entrepreneurial Wilcox men and supported by domestic and imperial romance, is contested in this 1910 novel by the model required for the twentieth-century intellectual and expert, to include the literary expert and to include as well the queer expert. In making this argument, I am suggesting that so-called high modernism was not passively about existential loss and aesthetic recuperation but about employing a rhetoric of loss to engender a new class of subjects. In a quite material sense, the trope of longing in *Howards End,* read conventionally as Forster's nostalgia for his childhood at Rooksnest, read synecdochically as yearning for a romanticized past England, and read lately by Jameson as longing for the lost organicism of a pre-imperial state, also functions as a veiled homoeroticism aimed, not at the past, but at the present and future legitimization of the men of Forster's expert class and of his sexual affinity. Crucial to this legitimization, I will demonstrate, is locating this new class in space—finding for it an institutional locus, as it were, that is neither strictly imperial nor domestic in the sense of nineteenth-century institutional space. This difficulty in Forster's project speaks directly to past and recent criticism of his fiction that consistently and correctly, I believe, discloses its utopic or imaginary or subjunctive condition but then records this as aesthetic or technical or sexual equivocation, without fully accounting for the spatiotextual context intrinsic to his novels and absent from their analyses.[12]

If we understand the novelist's dilemma to legitimate the nonhetero-normative subjects of the educated bourgeoisie, then *Howards End* becomes a pivotal work that takes up the homoerotic address present in his first novel, *The Longest Journey,* and anticipates its exploration in *Maurice* and *A Passage to India* (all of which have resolutions that importantly turn on transactional space: Wiltshire countryside, greenwood, Mau jungles). *Howards End* thus bears importantly on imperial literature, modernism, and queer theory.[13] For with this text Forster presents readers with a literary model, a nascent queer model that appropriates the ideology of domestic romance and the manly affect of imperial fiction to conceive of a new form of social reproduction based on a same-sex affiliation that is—contrary to all other expert knowledge of its time—salubrious, affective, erotic, and generative. The principal problem of the novel and its one certain desire, I will be arguing, is to find and install the proper male heir to the estate Howards End, an heir who will serve as the progenitor of a new line of masculine subjects: one bound imaginatively to a mythical organic England but propagated independent of domestic romance; one cultivated and learned but not so urbane as to be bereft of human passion and of affective knowledge; and, finally, one robust and manly but abjuring the masculine model founded on dominance.[14] In short, Forster's novel imagines the queer literary expert and intellectual, an expert from whom Jameson himself, wittingly or not, will draw professional authority. It is to these ends I now turn.

"Democratic Affection"

In his journal at the end of 1910, Forster muses over imbuing his fiction with a fraternal affect that would in turn spawn a new homophilic democracy of men.[15] Only two months before, in October, as *Howards End* was gaining him repute as a novelist, he had attacked in "The Feminine Note in Literature" another version of "democratic affection," the excessive sentiment found in what he termed "the woman's book" that was engendering a decidedly feminized community. This frisson over affect in the English novel, homosexual attachment versus female sentimentality, points to Forster's conscious attempt to make the aesthetic novel count as an instrument of social mediation and political change. Indeed, as he was quite likely preparing his talk, there is this conspicuous brief in his journal: "to work out:—The sexual bias in literary criticism, and perhaps literature. Look for such a bias in its ideal, carnal form. Not in experience which refuses. What sort of person would the critic prefer to sleep with, in fact."[16] As his entry proposes, his talk "The Feminine Note in Literature" grapples with the complex sexual ideology of the novel genre by pitting domestic and imperial romance against one another before an elite of Cambridge University fellows, The Apostles, a group sympathetic to the novelist's literary and libidinal commitments.[17]

To make his argument, Forster connects the group's previous discussion of J. S. Mill's *The Subjection of Women,* on the fortieth anniversary of its publication, to issues of literary authority, representation, and merit, alleging that Mill's polemic contributed to the rise of female authority and the decline of the English novel, and hence to the feminization of culture. His disquiet is of no small import in 1910. With agitation for female suffrage entering its most militant phase on London streets, Forster upbraids the Victorian liberal Mill for excusing women of limitations that are socially imposed, which effectively justifies, indeed, encourages, in his view, their excessive literary output and a literature of excessive sentiment, both of which were furthering women's political liberation. Still more, he impugns the very ground of Mill's argument as it "cross[es] the line that divides the aesthetic critic from the legal," contending "that this man who seemed so sensible and rather cultured, is really a lawyer," and concludes: "[Mill] only thought of arguing it out, never of feeling for it."[18] In other words, untrained in affective knowledge, lawyers are not qualified to make judgments about emotional transactions, of which the novel, in Forster's view, is the exemplary cultural source and the literary artist, its expert. Embedded in his argument is the tacit corollary that art, not politics, should minister to affective and amatory relations, a point presumably not lost on Forster's audience, the first generation of men to grow up under the 1885 legislation that criminalized sodomy even as a private and consensual act.

Having challenged the Victorian logician's credentials, he takes issue with the literary lights of Mill's generation—the Brontës, Mrs. Gaskell, George Eliot—whom he holds principally responsible for the low state to which the genre had sunk by 1910. Their collective defect, he contends, their "feminine note," is what he calls "a preoccupation with personal relative worthiness": "the characters in a woman's book try not so much to be good as to be worthy of one of the other characters"; and thus, for example, in Brontë's *Villette* "we care that Lucy Snowe should learn to love Emanuel," from which he concludes, "to Charlotte Brontë a man is the standard."[19] In deprecating this attachment as the be-all and end-all of the domestic novel, Forster seems to anticipate that which literary critics have since come to identify as the social or heterosexual contract of the novel and the codes that made monogamous marriage and the bourgeois family the teleology of romance. He makes this claim on aesthetic grounds about the historically specific Victorian novel, when the cult of domesticity had, in fact, achieved hegemonic status. From his perspective, "the woman's book" ties characters to a flawed affect and then cultivates a readership who, subject to its emotional force and bound by its identificatory politics, unconsciously assents to it as well.[20] In effect, Forster argues against the gendered apparatus of social reproduction that the domestic novel constructs and disseminates under the guise of sentimentality. Sentimentality, the feminine note in literature, is the affective code bar none for the gendered Victorian novel. Its success, following Forster's logic, is the patent continuation of the heteronormative standard on which the bourgeois family rests. As such, this standard must be overturned to bring about the democracy the novelist seeks.

The remedy for the defective "women's book" and "the clearest example" of the masculine note in literature, Forster finds in the imperial adventure, Joseph Conrad's Lord Jim. This novel of empire, valued in "that the action takes place in wild countries, and that all the actors are men," offers Forster a literary model in which the homosocial bond not only persists as a licit constituent of masculinity but is aestheticized as the arbiter of manly behavior. Conrad's tale is more pleasing and more ethical, or so Forster claims, because the youthful Jim must answer to a standard superior to "the woman's book." Hence, where atoning to peers and loved ones would suffice for a George Eliot, a more resolute Conrad requires his boy hero "to expiate [his failed heroism] in his own eyes, he cannot do this, and he perishes." Thus Conrad has his young mariner sail past the marriage plot in order "to celebrate," as Charlie Marlow intones, "his pitiless wedding with a shadowy ideal of conduct."[21] Recanting the inclination to go native, by, in effect, "going Anglo," though the result is lethal, Tuan Jim importantly proves his latent masculinity as an Englishman and justifies Marlow's closing benediction: "He is one of us" (Lord Jim, 419).

The implications of the homosocial stimulus of Marlow's "one of us," given Forster's predilection for "democratic affection," reveal a highly romantic and racial masculine ethos that conforms to tropes of imperial discourse. This ethical allegiance, however aestheticized in *Lord Jim,* is, of course, blatantly ideological, inasmuch as it continues to justify imperial rule. This ethos functions, as Jameson explains of ethical prescripts in *The Political Unconscious,* as "the ideological vehicle and the legitimation of concrete structures of power and domination" (114).[22] Complementing this imperial ethos is Jim's personal allure, which admits a homoerotic suit—the ruddy good looks (fair and blue-eyed, English to the core), boyish manliness, moral simplicity, and native intelligence. This allure is affirmed by the garrulous Marlow's near complete obsession with the youth, an obsession seconded by most of his seasoned cronies and by the local Patusans' adulation of Jim. Both Tamb' Itam, the ever faithful and brave subordinate, and the princely Dain Waris, who is Jim's peer if not better, attest to the Englishman's racial and gendered superiority and thus advance the narrative's near manic homophilia.

Tied to these formulaic tropes of imperial adventure is this inconsistency, however. Jim's two defining acts are finally nonviolent and nonacquisitive and thus run counter to the imperial spirit of adventure fiction from *Robinson Crusoe* forward that rests on the "master of all I survey" conceit. While Jim's renunciation of marriage to a "local girl" has a certain seaworthiness about it, his ultimate refusal of command and commerce as Patusan's "Tuan" is heavier freight to float.[23] Here the representation of Jim's alter ego and foil, the boy-brigand Gentleman Brown, is decisive. The outcast Brown, in personifying a depraved masculinity, effectively corrupts the dominant tropes of daring and cunning that had once led to the acquisition of lucre, territory, and honor, long the signifying credentials of imperial masculinity. His avarice and ambush, at once cowardly and an insult to the mariners' code of conduct, contrast with Jim's rejection of profit and combat in presenting himself unarmed and alone before the disconsolate Dolomain to atone for Dain Waris's death and his earlier adolescent leap. Jim's fatal act, as it serves no deity, monarch, least of all a lady's honor, would seem gratuitous and insignificant, in other words nonheroic by older codes of masculine conduct, were it not for Marlow's vetting—Jim is "one of us." With this textual memorial, the artless Jim revises the dominance model of adventure fiction by offering instead a benign version of imperial masculinity *and* surpasses the parochial sentimentality of "the woman's book."

The male liberation promised by Conrad's late imperial fantasy becomes the exact condition Forster attempts to reproduce in his fiction. To narrativize this potent but benign masculinity, one that forgoes violence and plunder (however these forms of dominance are euphemized), not to mention matrimony, and yet survives outside the spatial boundaries of an imperial imaginary with its homoerotic and homosocial ethos intact, requires some *place* to unfold, some *means* to legitimate it, and some *one* to embody. As important, to be socially reproduced by the novel, this benign masculinity needs a formal or aesthetic apparatus to encode its queer affect—in the way, as Forster apparently discerned, that sentimentality helped encode the conjugal household as desirable, inevitable, and natural. Viewing Forster's investments in "The Feminine Note in Literature" from this perspective, we can better understand the representational dilemma that prompted his dismissal of the lawyerly Mill and his own misogyny over "the woman's book." As well, we can better understand Forster's insistence on the literary expert's remedy, at once aesthetic and ethical, to bring about the legitimization of a new order of subjects, sexual and intellectual.

It is on these terms, I suggest, that his 1910 novel deserves consideration. What Forster's talk proposes of the novel, *Howards End* sets forth. Nostalgizing quaint country house as an emblem of "old organic England," maligning the metropolis, and criminalizing brute masculinity mask his interests in refuting the material, affective, and ideological bases of domestic and imperial romance that the novel's hegemonic couple Ruth and Henry Wilcox epitomized for Edwardian readers. The libidinal investments of the novel thus importantly pivot on Ruth's idealization and abrupt demise, on Leonard Bast's fabled umbrella courtship and fatal *coup de livres*, and finally on the emasculation tout court of the Wilcox men—and these in order to produce a new model of affective and sexual relations that the novelist places in the highly naturalized setting of Howards End, primarily for the benefit of those who share his class and sexuality, his expertise and culture.

"Four Weddings and a Funeral"

Though the embodiment of Victorian domesticity nonpareil, the matriarch Ruth Wilcox is rather quickly disembodied and safely interred in the realm of myth. Untimely though her death appears, its logic is systematically organized. Her fatigue, mentioned first in Helen's letters,

metastasizes into her patent exhaustion over the London wedding of her
eldest son, her indifference to Henry and Evie's motor trip, her reserve
at the Schlegels' luncheon, and her weariness in that allegedly most energizing of modern female pastimes, shopping. At the level of plot, these
collectively signify her declining health and finally her death. Thematically, they connote an urban pathology, in which modernization and
mechanization act as an eviscerating disease assailing her body so that
all that finally remains of her is spirit: part faded Victorian gentility and
part worshipped earth mother (all those hay whisks clinging to her trailing gowns), a spirit wholly conflated with her ancestral home of Howards
End.[24] Under the cover of these nostalgic and maternal tropes, Ruth
Wilcox serves as the synecdoche of a mythic maternalism, on the one
hand, and, on the other, obsolescent domesticity, an institution, by implication, also enervated by modernization, for which the normative
bourgeois family will no longer answer.[25] Mustered out of the narrative
early, Ruth is, nonetheless, kept aloft as a mythic spirit meekly oversee-
ing her own ideological and material dispossession.

Nowhere in the text, therefore, are male and female relationships held
up as exemplary, thus disturbing the telos of domestic romance and, by
inference, of romantic adventure. Henry Wilcox's imperial lechery casts
his marriage to Ruth in a sordid light. The clerk Leonard does the right
thing by Jacky, but the wrong thing by Helen. Paul Wilcox's lone courtship,
that with Helen, does not survive an evening's buss, and Evie seems more
intent on breeding terriers than Cahills. Charles and Dolly's marriage
comes closest to the procreative standard if progeny alone be deemed a
reliable index, except that she is deprecated as utterly vacuous in the
text and he disgraces himself throughout with his bullying temper. The
orphaned Schlegels offer no better models. Tibby has been inoculated
early and thoroughly against human contact altogether; Helen metamorphoses from New Woman into single mother with no trace of carnal
blush; and Margaret, who notably marries for companionship, is sum-
marily reduced to family nanny. Beyond the Schlegels and Wilcoxes mésal-
liances, we are also told, by no less an authority than Dolly, of Tom
Howard's proposal spurned by the eccentric Miss Avery long ago, leaving
him distraught and the house without a direct male descendant: "Howards
End—Howards Ended!" as Dolly coyly adduces (146). All of these failed
or flawed relations point not only to the demise of the conjugal house-

hold but also to the central preoccupation of the text, finding an heir for Howards End—"The house has been empty long enough," Miss Avery declares, "it has been mistake upon mistake for fifty years" (193).

Given this nagging and protracted hiatus and given the relentless disparagement of London in the text, it should be far more remarkable than portrayed that into the abandoned rooms of Howards End arrive all the Schlegel accouterments of culture and even more remarkable that their worldly possessions fit so perfectly. Indeed, these coincidences appear greater than the mere consequence of an unconscious structural flaw in Forster's writing, as Jameson would have us think, resulting from the breach between empire and metropolis. Jameson's stress of their extraliterary provocation, although compelling, is as insubstantial as the mystification the text invites in which these coincidences seem to arise from the deceased Ruth Wilcox's uncanny "will" and the preternatural discernment of her spectral agent, Miss Avery. For both explanations fail to account for the most startling aspect of all: these urbane trappings arrive from the center of the vilified metropolis exempt from city contagion, and, for that matter, imperial contamination. In fact when it comes to the Schlegels' possessions, signifiers of their cultivation and intellect, the text affirms the value of their cultural capital, books, art, and furnishings, over and over again—the beauty and ideas they contain, the intimacy and easy repartee they engender, the poetry and the simple adventures and affection they inspire, and, moreover, the privilege they convey: the leisure to acquire and consume, the private space for exchange and display, the independence, material and intellectual, that such cultivation grants the Schlegels, is refused the aspiring Bast and goes unappreciated by the philistine Wilcoxes. While Jameson is certainly correct that this novel (and literary modernism in general) concerns "recoordinating the concept of style with some new account of the experience of space" ("Modernism and Imperialism," 54), what we are witnessing with the translocation of the Schlegels' material refinements into the hollowed-out household of Howards End *is* a new stylized account of space. It is the replacement of the depleted social and gendered model of Victorian domesticity (which Forster attacks in his talk and represents in the novel as a fifty-year lapse), with a new cultural and amative model to house the intellectual and, I would add, the expert of Forster's class and sexuality—the symbolic heirs to Howards End. Here, with the material and intellectual refurbishment of the country house, we find the spatial and institutional grounding to found a "democracy of affection."

Like its Victorian predecessor, it should be noted, Forster's modernized country house is no less ideological. Just as the Victorian household and sentimentality came to screen the class interests of the propertied bourgeoisie and the heteronormative standard that perpetuated the consanguineous family, as scholars have persuasively demonstrated of the bourgeois family and domestic novel, so here the cultural model that Forster introduces attempts to efface the evidence and interests of its own ideological production.[26] Indeed, this is the import of having the transformation at *Howards End* appear guided under the celestial navigation of Mrs. Wilcox—the import of narrative coincidence. Mythic maternal intervention coupled with the overdetermination of the country house as authentic English place conceal the transfer of power to and the legitimization of the intellectual and expert class and their specialized affective knowledge that Forster would subsequently advocate to his Apostle confreres.

Not only do the Schlegel possessions find a home in the country house and miraculously fit its rooms, but so too does the affective content of their material possessions. In *Howards End,* the affect that is first embodied in Ruth, then veiled as her ghostly management, is subsequently passed on to Margaret Schlegel, confidante and heir presumptive, as Ruth's progeny are shown to be inept stewards. Deeded to the eldest Schlegel, who is neither motherly nor desires to become one, it is aestheticized as cultural knowledge.[27] With this symbolic transfer, affect— previously advanced by the female avatar of the heteronormative standard, now advanced by a cosmopolitan woman ambiguously gendered, and, correspondingly, previously immanent to Howards End, now immanent to the new contents filling its interior—the text, in essence, makes cultural knowledge into the source of affect *and* implicitly confirms the aesthetic novel as the reservoir of both. In the text, affect thus moves along a signifying chain from the normal to the paranormal to the abnormal in an attempt to naturalize and authenticate its transfer. This, then, is the logic of nostalgizing the country house, of deposing its matriarch, and of installing the aesthetic and intellectual belongings of the urbane Schlegels. All is made ready to receive the successor to Howards End, one who will be the beneficiary of a cultural and affective model capacious enough to convey a homoerotic and homophilic address and to importune a homosexual subjectification. And here the text doesn't disappoint. To this high office, the young clerk Leonard and his pinched umbrella are summoned.

Clerkly Corpus

Leonard Bast's representation is caught thematically between the two opposing rhetorical strains of the novel, anti-urban boom and pro-rural revival, and, structurally, between two classes of masculinity, a romantic versus a dominance model. Fixed in the crosshairs of the novel's competing tropes and, yet, paradoxically the most mobile of its characters, Leonard trudges uneasily across the several social and class registers the novel hails. His precarious class standing as an insurance clerk inscribes his masculinity as equally unstable, an example of the institutional stamp occupation confers upon gender. Yet his romantic idealism leads him to chivalrous acts—marrying the bawd Jacky and atoning for his adultery with Helen—that his class and occupation make difficult to support. Out of place in the city and out of touch with the country appear to doom him to certain itinerancy if not outright ruin.

By 1910, however, the clerk Leonard would be a thoroughly recognizable figure of everyday London. Indeed, the clerk was a regular feature of nineteenth-century fiction from Dickens's *Sketches by Boz* to Poe's "Man of the Crowd," updated in the twentieth century not only by Forster but also by writers such as Eliot, Kafka, Woolf, and Joyce. What is remarkable about the figure in this period is its growth into an identifiable class of men, as Magali Sarfatti Larson and Maurizia Boscagli document.[28] This formation, as Larson points out, is tied to the depopulation of the countryside, as the imperialism that transformed London into a world financial center became responsible for drawing to the metropolis rural men who, formerly tied to local industries, now swelled the London staffs of global enterprises as clerks, firms such as the Porphyrion Fire Insurance Company, which employs Bast, and the Imperial and West African Rubber Company owned by Henry Wilcox and *fils*.

Noteworthy as well, according to Boscagli, were the class fears excited by the sheer size of this arriviste class. Concerns by the bourgeoisie over assimilating its numbers played directly, in turn, into more general anxieties over the potency of the male population and the soundness of imperial rule, anxieties referenced at the opening of this essay over urbanization, falling birthrates, the rise of female authority—anxieties exacerbated by labor protests, Irish home rule, and the Boer War debacle. Here, the clerk class, with its very visible presence in the city, was markedly vulnerable. Required to work indoors and at desks for long periods at menial tasks, clerks became the focus of studies that concluded that their sedentary occupations and mental labor were leading to their physical debility. They thus came to exemplify masculine decline and national malaise.[29] The cumulative effect of these apprehensions pointed to a widespread crisis in masculinity, the therapy for which became identified with a return to nature and a renewed interest in the classical male body as a means of rejuvenating male vitality.[30] This therapeutic shift can be traced in fiction writers from Kipling to Wells, from Hardy to Lawrence, as the manly ideal of imperial romance migrates to the English countryside where it takes up residence as the robust body of the Anglo-Saxon yeoman, producing in Boscagli's view, "an aristocracy of the blood, rather than of birth or of money."[31] Such a romantic and eugenic remedy had at first a greater effect on public attitudes than on public health. It mitigated the class differential separating bourgeois and laborer *and* policed the ascent of the clerk class. In other words, robustness, or want of it, became a check on the clerk's rise into middle-class ranks, and, at the same time, paradoxically served as a unifying trope that linked all Englishmen despite their class.

The classical male ideal, couched in the cult of the country, had, however, a cultural antecedent relevant to the narrative desires of *Howards End* and Leonard's character: the idealized body of classical Greece associated with Oxford Hellenism and championed by the aesthetes in the closing decades of the nineteenth century.[32] Though discredited at Oxford and in national culture during the trials of Oscar Wilde and thereafter, according to Linda Dowling, it nonetheless survived at Cambridge and among the Apostles of Forster's circle in the ethical philosophy of G. E. Moore. Not only did Moore's philosophy objectify Hellenic values but, as a moral science, it also perpetuated the idealized male body as an aesthetic truth and elevated male intimacy, homosocial and homosexual, to a public good. Though Forster's most transparent tribute to Moore's ideals is found in *The Longest Journey* with shepherd hero Stephen Wonham, it endures as well, however diminished, in Leonard Bast.

Thus any reading of Bast's representation and, in particular, his masculinity must take into account the complex cultural references surrounding this labile clerk figure. To be sure, this complexity involves middle-class nervousness over the clerkocracy's ascent, to include the social and cultural ambitions tied to assimilation, but it further includes the conflicting gender and sexual idioms informing the figure's masculinity. The clerk's institutional identification with depleted masculinity must be balanced against its imagined therapeutic opposite—the virile masculinity of the yeoman, from which the clerk descends. Added to this is Forster's own sexual inflection: yeoman virility and any vestigial remnant in the clerk encode for him as for his Cambridge set the homoerotic fantasy of the Greek ideal of manly love, lately revived by Moore. Bast's character, then, while bounder and bungler, is also the locus of the narrative desires the text sets out to gratify in grounding a new line of masculine subjects that will relegitimate manly love.[33]

No moment and no cultural artifact better captures the young Leonard's complex signification than the physical conversion he undergoes from bare to top-hatted head as he recalls with considerable pleasure the conversation with the Schlegels over his nocturnal walking adventure in the less-than-romantic London suburbs:

> He took off his top-hat and smoothed it thoughtfully. He had hitherto supposed the unknown to be books, literature, clever conversation, culture. One raised oneself by study, and got upsides with the world. But in that quick interchange a new light dawned. Was that "something" walking in the dark among the suburban hills?

> He discovered that he was going bareheaded down Regent Street. London came back with a rush. Few were about at this hour but all whom he passed looked at him with a hostility that was the more impressive because it was unconscious. He put his hat on. It was too big, his head disappeared like a pudding into a basin, the ears bending outwards at the touch of the curly brim. . . . Thus equipped, he escaped criticism. No one felt uneasy as he titupped along the pavements, the heart of a man ticking fast in his chest. (91)

While top hat secures his clerk identity and marks him a member of the genteel class, even if at the extreme fringe, it also puts in relief his ambiguous position in the metropolis. He no sooner dons it than his reverie ends.[34] But in his bareheaded trance, inspired by the cultivated Schlegels' rapture over his pedestrian adventure, he perceives that there is "something" ennobling about the return to nature that his walk roused. His inability to grasp its significance leaves unstated but tacit the romantic renewal the natural world of the country promises city men that is embodied in the fleeting spectacle of the hatless Leonard lost in thought. City artifice then subverts what would be his "natural self." His dormant masculinity, associated with romantic musing and nature, is stifled with his basin-sized top hat, rendering him clownish and his display mere buffoonery. Ironically, in the city, with hat in place, he is no more out of place.

Yet top hat, that old badge of aristocracy, also signals that underneath there breathes, as Margaret intuits, "a real man" (107). She confirms as well Bast's latent masculinity and the unwholesome effects of urbanization. "Hints of robustness survived in him, more than a hint of primitive good looks, and Margaret, noting the spine that might have been straight, and the chest that might have broadened, wondered whether it paid to give up the glory of the animal for a tail coat and a couple of ideas" (84–85). Contrary to urban get-up, Bast's figure evokes a purportedly bona fide English manliness, one which predates nation and empire and which lives on in him, however vestigially, a fact he later confirms when he shamefully admits to Helen that his people worked the land and, what is more, that his maternal grandfather hailed from the county full of suggestiveness for Forster's intimate circle, Shropshire (170).[35] Associating Leonard with the specific locale of A. E. Houseman's homoerotic lyrics subtly naturalizes the clerk and implies that poetry of a homophilic cast and of a pastoral simplicity is his rightful estate, an estate surrendered when his family ventured to the city. Indeed, what Leonard regards as his degrading agricultural heritage the text explicitly hails as heroic when it later praises yeomanry as "a noble stock" (229).

In fact, we have further proof of the clerk's latent manliness when at tea the thrilled Wilcox espies him as a competitor for Margaret's affections. There to present the eldest Schlegel a memento to ease his conscience on the advantage taken of her over Mrs. Wilcox's dying behest, Henry immediately and ironically takes affront at Leonard's intentions and becomes possessive when Margaret acknowledges the insurance clerk's sensitivity and manliness. As the narrator observes: "A woman and two men—they had formed the magic triangle of sex, and the male was thrilled to jealousy, in case the female was attracted by another male" (107). Henry's flash of jealousy importantly corroborates the dormant virility that is shortly to be awakened to reconstitute the male line of Howards End. This homoerotic geometry, cogently sketched in

Sedgwick's *Between Men,* not only suggests that sexual triangulation may be the conductor of homosexual desire but additionally suggests that such a libidinal configuration might arouse other desires in the text, such as authorizing a new class of men and model of social reproduction.[36]

Putting together, then, Bast's marginal class status, his poor health, latent manliness, rural ancestry, naive chivalry, and cultural aspirations alongside the text's narrative investments (the appropriation of affect and the cultural renovation of the abandoned Howards End) leads me to make this claim about the textual function of desire: In essence, Leonard, the displaced native son and peripatetic clerk, comes to serve in *Howards End* as the sperm donor par excellence—to such an extent, in fact, that the obliging Bast can be dispatched once the harvesting is done. For what the narrative desires is an offspring of the arcadian Bast line and not the clerkly article himself—this in order to found a new version of English masculinity, of authentic manhood, one linked to a native robustness and Victorian homosexualism that will accord with the position of property and social consequence conferred by the country house and its recent cultural acquisitions. Leonard contributes to the democracy of affection that Forster imagines, but his donation is costly. Here again the text deflects its class interests, in this instance onto the hotheaded Charles, who delivers the blow that brings on Leonard's fatal heart attack. Yet, however much his fate was preordained, as was Ruth Wilcox's, by urban blight (diagnosed, as befits his clerk status, as a weak heart), Bast's death warrants no special treatment, no airy afterlife, not even an epitaph once the official inquest is complete. "I ought to remember Leonard as my lover," Helen admits to Margaret. "But I cannot. It's no good pretending. I'm forgetting him" (239). And so the text encourages in this crucial instance "Only Disconnect," and thereby deftly discourages any restoration of domestic romance or return to the Victorian institutions that depended on the procreative couple. Leonard is discharged from the novel almost as cavalierly as is widow Jacky. In this way, the text produces, as if by fiat, the male child desired from the first.[37]

Queer Heirs and Imperial Types

Leonard's demise, however, not only frustrates domestic romance and rids the text of a sticky class complication (no clerks allowed in Forster's democracy for now), it also prevents the patrilineal succession that the text is equally at pains to unseat. The reason for this becomes clearer once we understand that it is this succession that authorizes the Wilcox men and perpetuates the imperial model of dominance they embody, passed down in the consanguineous family from Henry to his sons. Leonard's death, thus, also importantly disrupts its continuance and speeds the Wilcoxes' downfall.

What most succinctly characterizes their model of masculinity and their relation to the land is the trespass and appropriation associated with imperial aggression but here encountered on the roadway Jameson precipitately identified as the text's spatial confusion: "The Great North Road should have been bordered all its length with glebe," the narrator perceives. "Henry's kind had filched most of it" (236). And as if to make categorical the implications of this filching, there is this damning portrait of the Imperial type:

> Healthy, ever in motion, it hopes to inherit the earth. It breeds as quickly as the yeoman, and, as soundly; strong is the temptation to acclaim it as a super-yeoman, who carries the country's virtue overseas. But the Imperialist is not what he thinks or seems. He is a destroyer. (229)

In the comparison of yeoman and imperialist, the text insinuates as well that the aggression the Wilcoxes practiced in the colonies they have adapted to English soil. In this light, even their succession to Howards End on Ruth's death appears an act of trespass, in overruling her express instruction. Granted Howards End is home and Henry's intervention and foreign capital keep it mostly intact during his tenancy. Wilcox and his sons, however, never belong to it or to the land that surrounds it, and thus are more decisively outsiders to the "aristocracy of the blood" than even the hapless Leonard. With the figure of hay, the text confirms their discrepant masculinity that elsewhere signifies Ruth's profound attachment and the country's natural fecundity. From wisps to harvest, the allergic Wilcox men fail the hay test so utterly, an inherited defect according to the text, that the neighborhood oracle Miss Avery can mockingly summarize their history to Margaret in a single breath: "There's not one Wilcox that can stand up against a field in June" (195).

If a lack of native manliness disqualifies them and trespass defines them, the aggression required for their imperial ventures hardly compensates. The text may admire Henry for his energy as a man of action and acknowledge his shrewdness abroad as a man of business—as the narrator admits, it was, after all, men like him who brought wealth to the nation and independent incomes to the educated class from which the Schlegels spring—but in the end it disparages him for becoming no more than a philistine, for only knowing how to produce capital from afar. For all the profits the Imperial and West African Rubber Company wrings from the colonies, for all the power Henry amasses, he is faulted for having neither insight nor self-awareness, and hence no valor. It is this deficiency that Margaret attacks when Henry refuses to connect, as the epigraph instructs, his adultery and her forgiveness of him with Helen's and the forgiveness he refuses: "You shall see the connection if it kills you, Henry!" she declares. "A man who ruins a woman for his pleasure, and casts her off to ruin other men. And gives bad financial advice, and then says he is not responsible. These men are you. You can't recognize them, because you cannot connect" (219).

The inability to connect is not his alone but one that appears the worse for being passed on to sons who have neither Henry's grit nor his keenness. Indeed, Charles is proof enough of the harm that results when this dominance model is perpetuated through the bourgeois family and imperial discourse and compelled by the heteronormative standard. The clearest example, of course, is his mortal bullying of Leonard, required, he rashly concludes, to defend the family's and Helen's honor. Justified by the codes of imperial and domestic romance, Charles batters the unarmed Bast with the Schlegel family's heirloom sword that, together with the shower of books that falls down on the unprotected lover, brings on his heart failure. Charles's act is excessive, cowardly, and callous. Yet, not only does he fail to apprehend the consequences of his assault but, worse, to accept responsibility for it. His overweening male egotism leads him to misconstrue his court appearance, when he avers to his father who well understands its import: "I shall naturally be the most important witness there" (233).

Nor is Charles's cruelty to Bast an isolated act. More flagrant than his displays of temper first with the Schlegels' aunt and later with Tibby over Helen's dalliances, however, is his striking of wife Dolly, pregnant with their third child: "She deserved her scolding, and had bent before it, but her head, though bloody, was unsubdued" (133). The physical abuse that begins the scene ends on a derisive note with a family portrait of Charles, his marriage, and his patrimony: "Nature is turning out Wilcoxes in this peaceful abode, so that they may inherit the earth" (134). Like Henry's mindless production of capital, Charles's mindless production of progeny encourages readers "to connect" production and propagation as complementary ideological practices that draw on imperial and domestic romance to secure empire, in this instance, bequeathed to the Wilcox family as its Christian inheritance, an aspiration the earlier passage on the imperialist type exposed. This telos is frustrated at last with Charles's imprisonment and the family's disgrace. Here Henry seems to complete Dolly's earlier premonition when he confides to Margaret: "I'm ended" (237).

How different this community of Wilcox men, collapsed in Margaret's rebuke, "these men are you," is from Marlow's heroic elevation of Jim: "He is one of us." Closer to the ethos of Jim's benign masculinity is the idyllic one Margaret summons on an earlier and less explosive visit to Howards End: "In these English farms, if anywhere, one might see life steadily and see it whole, group in one vision its transitoriness and its eternal youth, connect—connect without bitterness until all men are brothers" (191). The cultural romanticism, implicit in Conrad's imperial adventure, *Lord Jim*, surfaces in the intellectual Margaret's vision of old organic England and has its antecedent in another imperial type, the soldier turned intellectual, her father, Ernst Schlegel. His romantic figure is surely a representation of the benign masculinity that attracted Forster to *Lord Jim*. Brave in defense of his German homeland, the elder Schlegel symbolically retires his weapon on discovering the acquisitiveness that war perpetuates in peace. In turning to the life of the mind over the sword and in cultivating the cultural knowledge that forms his children's inheritance, he presents a naturalized Englishman, in contrast to the superyeoman Henry, and, as such, becomes the spiritual father to the masculine line and benign masculinity that will shortly be inaugurated at Howards End.[38] Indeed, the endorsements of the soldier figure in the text (Ruth Wilcox should have married one; Margaret's unconventional fancy) are not only part of this idealization and of its translocation to the country house but also hint at its homoerotic address.

Apart from the soldier figure, there is also the romanticization of the intellectual that augurs an alternative of equal weight. The material capital that imperial types like Henry produce and acquire is being challenged by another form, cultural capital, befitting Ernst's interests and the emergence of an intellectual class. This transfer of capital investment to culture and the importance of this culture as knowledge to the private spaces of country house and to public civic space of the metropolis in legitimating the intellectual and expert class are congruent with the displacement of the Edwardian couple, Ruth and Henry Wilcox, and the domestic and imperial models they personify. This cultural capital, once it is valued and in circulation, as in the aesthetic novel Forster champions, offers the social means by which this new version of benign masculinity can be reproduced.

Manifest in Forster's exemplar of "the masculine note in literature," *Lord Jim,* and consistent with the multifold cultural signifiers and legal constraints complicating metropolitan masculinity and male sexuality at the opening of the twentieth century, the narrative desires of the text work to authorize a benign model of masculinity that looks forward to the brotherhood of men Margaret intuits and the homophilic democracy of affection Forster conceives. It is the model offered at the conclusion of *Howards End* and promised to Helen's and the deceased Leonard's son. Its utopic vision, naturalized by an English country house and native sire, legitimated by the cultural capital of the intellectual class, liberated from imperial dominance, domestic romance, and compulsory heterosexualism is a queer vision this native son comes to inherit as well.

With this behest, the text supplants the affective knowledge of the ethereal matriarch Ruth Wilcox and offsets the encroachments of an acquisitive and insensate imperial ethos that the philistine Wilcox family epitomize through colonial ventures and institutional monogamy. Thus it is that the Wilcox men are dishonored, depropriated, and unmanned, and by implication the procreative model made possible under the aegis of the Victorian household and its social envoy "the woman's book." At the novel's conclusion, an alternative to their dominant and oppressive masculinity is put in place. The hay harvest that keeps the allergic Wilcox pater indoors is the bountiful backdrop for the future generation of Englishmen, the heir to Howards End, Leonard and Helen's bastard son, and his garden playmate, Tom. Their queer friendship augurs a new amative alliance that the literary expert Forster hopes to inaugurate for himself and for the experts and intellectuals of his class—a male subjective and cultural economy that is at once affectional, poetic, erotic, and manly. To these ends, more recognizable at the beginning of this century but no less problematic, *Howards End* beckons in 1910.

Notes

I wish to thank The Society of Authors and the Provost and Scholars of King's College Cambridge for permission to quote from E. M. Forster's unpublished papers. I wish also to express my gratitude to The Huntington Library and Director of Research, Robert C. Ritchie, for the fellowship that allowed me to complete this essay.

1. In "Modernism and Imperialism" Jameson contends that, with the Great North Road as a representation of infinity, "a new spatial language—modernist 'style'—now becomes the marker and substitute (the "tenant-lieu," or place-holding, in Lacanian language) of the unrepresentable totality." See Fredric Jameson, "Modernism and Imperialism," in *Nationalism, Colonialism, and Literature*, ed. Terry Eagleton, Fredric Jameson, and Edward Said (Minneapolis: University of Minnesota Press, 1990), 58. Hereafter "Modernism and Imperialism."

2. See A. N. Monkhouse's initialed review in the *Manchester Guardian*, 26 October 1910, reprinted in Philip Gardner, *E. M. Forster, The Critical Heritage* (London: Routledge and Kegan Paul, 1973), 123–24. Hereafter *Critical Heritage*.

3. See *Howards End* (1910), ed. Paul B. Armstrong. Norton Critical Edition (New York: Norton, 1998), 79, 80. Unless otherwise stated, this and subsequent references to *Howards End* cite this edition and appear parenthetically in the text.

4. The unprecedented twenty-year national decline in the birthrate was shortly to be confirmed by the 1911 census. See Ford Madox Ford's sequence, *The Soul of London* (London: Alston Rivers Ltd., 1905); *The Heart of the Country, A Survey of a Modern Land* (London: Alston Rivers Ltd., 1906); and *The Spirit of the People, An Analysis of the English Mind* (London: Alston Rivers Ltd. 1907). In *The Spirit of the People*, Ford claims that one pressing matter for England is "the evolution of a healthy town-type," for the city does not tend toward increase of birthrates but just the opposite, their decline (60–61). Another commentator troubled by the state of the nation and the relation between city and countryside is C. F. G. Masterman, who declares that all classes are responsible for the decrease in the birthrate save the poor, and continues, "a nation is in a serious condition if its better stocks are producing smaller families or no families at all, and its least capable are still raising an abundant progeny." See C. F. G. Masterman, *The Condition of England* (London: Methuen, 1909), 87. Both men are convinced that sustaining the population in the countryside and its ethos is imperative.

5. Jameson is not alone in his emphasis on coincidence in *Howards End*. William Archer, writing for *The Nation* in 1910, found the novel to have "too much ingenious dove-tailing of incidents, too much of accidental happenings, too much twisting and stretching and straining of human material for *Howards End* to rank high as a work of art" (Archer is quoted in *Howards End*, vol. 4: Abinger Edition, ed. Oliver Stallybrass [London: Edward Arnold Publishers, 1973], xv). For Lionel Trilling, coincidence is the result of culture: "The Schlegels had met the Wilcoxes touring a cathedral; they meet Leonard Bast at a concert; culture comically brings the middle class together and separates it" (Trilling, *E. M. Forster* [New York: New Directions, 1943], 129).

6. I am indebted to Chrisman's reading of Jameson's essay, in particular her contention that "in Jameson we witness a dialectical approach to the production of art, which is held to preserve and sublate its social determinants, conjoined with a resolutely empiricist, categorical formulation of human bodies and economies." See Chrisman, "Imperial Space, Imperial Place: Theories of Empire and Culture," *New Formations*, ed. Fredric Jameson, Edward Said, and Gayatri Spivak, 34 (1998): 68.

7. Jameson concludes his essay: "The traces of imperialism can therefore be detected in Western modernism, and indeed are constitutive of it; but we must not look for them in the obvious places, in content or in representation" ("Modernism and Imperialism," 64). And at the opening of the essay, "[the topic] will not, in the present case, involve what can be called the literature of imperialism, since that literature (Kipling, Rider Haggard, Verne, Wells) is by and large not modernist in any formal sense, and, emerging from subcanonical genres like the adventure tale, remained 'minor' or 'marginal' during the hegemony of the modern and its ideology and values (even Conrad explicitly draws on more archaic storytelling form)" (44). Jameson's argument, as insightful as it is, seems to fall prey to a rhetoric of authentic place lost to imperial ventures, if not in terms of England, than in terms of Ireland ("Modernism and Imperialism," 52–59). With a critical terminus of not metropolitan London but colonized Dublin, Jameson is willing to sacrifice Joyce's claim to a unique style in order to grant him a more genuine and cohesive modernism.

8. There follows this greater mystification: the shopworn rhetoric of existential loss and its complement, the diasporic narrative of exile, are once again restored to a preeminent explanatory status. Pursued to their logical end, they bring us to a teleological cul de sac—the high modernism Jameson attempted to surmount returns with the stereotypes he was at pains to debunk: "its apolitical character," "its introspective pyschologization," and "its aesthetic and its ideological commitment to the supreme value of a now autonomous Art as such" (Modernism and Imperialism," 45).

9. The Norton critical edition referenced above contains a section on the background and context of the novel that includes Forster's journal entries, working notes, and letters from the period of the novel's composition through its reception. That his 1910 talk is overlooked is thus a curious omission. For the recently published version of the talk, see "The Feminine Note in Literature," ed. George Piggford (Bloomsbury Heritage Series. London: Cecil Woolf Publishers, 2001). See also my earlier essay that treats the import of Forster's speech and its neglect by critics: "Shepherds in the Parlor: Forster's Apostles, Pagans, and Native Sons," *Novel, A Forum on Fiction* 32, no. 1 (fall 1998): 22–25.

10. My reading of the institution of monogamy and the procreative couple is very sympathetic to Robert K. Martin's thematics of survival and continuity in Forster's fiction. We part company over what I consider to be an epistemic and institutional shift in bourgeois subjectivity that Forster's fiction and modernist fiction in general attempt to answer. What literary method and what language will enable the social reproduction of the sexual subject, a subject I take to be hegemoic in the twentieth century, as the Victorian novel and its sentimentality once proved the vehicle for the domestic and procreative model? A fuller response is the argument of the book-length study I am completing, "The Female Intellectual and the Modernist Clerisy." See Martin, "'It Must Have Been the Umbrella': Forster's Queer Begetting," in *Queer Forster*, ed. Robert K. Martin and George Piggford (Chicago: University of Chicago Press, 1997), 255–73.

11. As Connell tellingly observes of the twentieth century: "a split began to open in the hegemonic masculinity of the dominant classes, between a masculinity organized around interpersonal dominance and one organized around knowledge and expertise" (R. W. Connell, "The Big Picture: Masculinities in Recent World History," *Theory and Society* 22, no. 5 [1995]: 613). The challenge for literary artists, of course, is that their particular expertise treats the sphere of interpersonal relations. To assert their autonomy and their authority over this sphere is the argument Forster undertakes in his speech, as I demonstrate in what follows. As Connell also remarks: "It is not too strong to say that *masculinity is an aspect of institutions,* and is produced in institutional life, *as much as it is an aspect of personality* or produced in interpersonal transactions" ("The Big Picture," 602). It is this institutional matrix that includes the expertise of literary specialists I will pursue in my reading of desire and queer heirs in *Howards End.*

12. Michael Levenson's view of the conclusion of *Howards End* as "subjunctive allegory" is symptomatic of this tendency (Levenson, *Modernism and the Fate of Individuality: Character and Novelistic Form from Conrad to Woolf* [Cambridge: Cambridge University Press, 1991], 101). This criticism is especially relevant given his general assessment that "much of the inspiration" behind Forster's experiments in fiction "lies in the attempt to revive a dying tradition" (79).

13. I use the term "heteronormative standard" as well as the sex classifications "heterosexual" and "homosexual" advisedly. As scholars have pointed out of the literature of the period and as I argue, these terms were only beginning to gain disciplinary and epistemic currency. See, for example, Jonathan Ned Katz's contention: "Heterosexuality, I now think, is invented in discourse as that which is outside discourse. It's manufactured in a particular discourse as that which is universal. It's constructed in a historically specific discourse as that which is outside time. It was constructed quite recently as that which is very old: Heterosexuality is an invented discourse" (Katz, *The Invention of Heterosexuality* [New York: Dutton Books, 1995], 182). See also Alan Sinfield, *The Wilde Century: Effeminacy, Oscar Wilde, and the Queer Moment* (New York: Columbia University Press, 1994). Sinfield understands the homosexual as a belated identity (8). In observing Forster's quandary to find a space for nonnormative sexualities, we may also observe the epistemological conundrum of queer theory itself that wants to make possible the sexual subject in play but wants to have an institutional place from which such subjects can be constituted with authority, in other words, a hegemonic locus from which to argue for nonhegemonic sexualities.

14. Lionel Trilling asked this question of *Howards End* some forty years ago ("Who shall inherit England?") but also answered it too narrowly, missing the homoeroticism in the text and its intended beneficiary, the intellectual and expert that Trilling himself represents (*E. M. Forster,* 118).

15. "Democratic *affection*" appears in the journal entry in which he muses on a novel project that would contain young men, children, and adventure, "but no lovemaking—at least of the orthodox kind, and perhaps not even of the unorthodox. It would be interesting to make an intelligent man feel towards an intelligent man of lower class what I feel." He concludes: "My motive should be *democratic affection,* and I am not sure whether that has any strength" (19 December 1910, "The Locked Journal," E. M. Forster's Papers, King's College Modern Archive, Cambridge. Hereafter "The Locked Journal.") Edward Carpenter was one important influence for

this democracy with his utopian community of Millthrope and his poem *Towards Democracy* (London: Heywood Press, 1883). Forster later visited Carpenter and his partner George Merrill and claimed that Merrill's touch on the small of his back led to his conception of his homosexual novel *Maurice*.

16. 25 October 1910, "The Locked Journal." Still later, in 1911, he lamented in his journal, so widely quoted by critics, of "his weariness of the only subject that I both can and may treat—the love of men for women & vice versa" (P. N. Furbank. *E. M. Forster: A Life*, vol. 1 [London: Secker and Warburg, 1978], 199. Hereafter *Forster*.) Equally apparent are his attempts to arrive at some aesthetic answer that would unite sentiment and the eroticized male body. In his unpublished essay "On Pornography and Sentimentality," he considers whether the pornographer and the artist may have similar ends and differ only in degree. Finally there are his experiments in homoerotic short fiction written during this period for his own sexual pleasure, he claims, and subsequently burned with his writing of *A Passage to India* (5 April 1922, "The Locked Journal"). All point to the novelist's desire to legitimize queer protagonists and queer readers by modernizing the novel's aesthetic and sexual ideology.

17. Unpublished manuscript, E. M. Forster Papers, King's College Modern Archive, Cambridge. Forster's paper was again presented in December to the Friday Club, at the London home of Robin Mayor, a classmate and fellow Apostle, at which Vanessa Bell and Virginia Woolf, then still a Stephen, were present (Nicola Beauman, *E. M. Forster, A Biography* [New York: Knopf, 1994], 223). Forster recollects in his diary Woolf's comment afterward that "the paper was the best there had been, which pleases me" (11 December 1910, "The Locked Journal").

18. Mill begins *The Subjection of Women* by countervailing the strong emotions owing to the subject with an appeal to conduct a rational argument over one grounded in feelings (*On Liberty, with The Subjection of Women and Chapters on Socialism*, ed. Stefan Collini [Cambridge: Cambridge University Press, 1989], 119–20).

19. The Apostles at a previous meeting had discussed W. L. Courtney's 1904 critique of women writers, *The Feminine Note in Fiction*, whose sentiments Forster, in important ways, seems to echo, as in these introductory comments by Courtney: "Recently complaints have been heard that the novel as a work of art is disappearing and giving place to monographs on given subjects or else individual studies of character. If the complaint be true—and in some respects it obviously is true—the reason is that more and more in our modern age novels are written by women for women." He then continues much as does Forster in his speech: "It is the neutrality of the artistic mind which the female novelist seems to find it difficult to realize. . . . The female author is at once self-conscious and didactic" (Courtney, *The Feminine Note in Fiction* [London: Chapman and Hall, 1904], xii–xiii).

20. The literature on the ideology the novel carries is extensive. On the social contract of the domestic novel, see Nancy Armstrong, *Desire and Domestic Fiction: A Political History of the Novel* (London: Oxford University Press, 1987); on the heterosexual contract, see Monique Wittig, *The Straight Mind and Other Essays*, trans. Marlene Wildeman (Boston: Beacon Press, 1992), and Adrienne Rich, *Of Women Born: Motherhood as Experience and Institution* (New York: Norton, 1976), and "Compulsory Heterosexuality and Lesbian Existence," in *Women: Sex and Sexuality*, ed. Catharine Stimpson and Ethel Spector Person (Chicago: University of Chicago Press, 1980), 62–91; and Gayle Rubin's exploration of "obligatory heterosexuality" in "The Traffic in Women: Notes toward a Political Economy of Sex," in *Toward an*

Anthropology of Women, ed. Rayna Reiter (New York: Monthly Review Press, 1975), 157–210. (Hereafter "The Traffic in Women.") On the unstated ideology discourses convey, see Fredric Jameson, *The Political Unconscious: Narrative as a Socially Symbolic Act* (Ithaca: Cornell University Press, 1981).

21. Joseph Conrad, *Lord Jim: A Tale* (London: J. M. Dent and Sons, 1917), 419.

22. Tracy Seeley argues that it is a mistake to conflate Jim's unconscious idealism with Marlow's more mature vision and Conrad's aesthetic one. Granting the merit of her argument, I suggest that Forster's reading may not have made this distinction. See Seeley, "Conrad's Modernist Romance: *Lord Jim,*" *English Literary History* 59 (1992): 495–511.

23. See Richard Ruppel, "'They Always Leave Us': *Lord Jim,* Colonialist Discourse, and Conrad's Magic Naturalism," *Studies in the Novel* 30 (1998): 50–62. His essay is also the source for the concept of Jim's "benign masculinity" (59).

24. The scene in which Ruth interrupts the misunderstanding over Paul and Helen's romance best describes her attachment to the house and her alignment with nature: "She approached just as Helen's letter had described her, trailing noiselessly over the lawn, and there was actually a wisp of hay in her hands. She seemed to belong not to the young people and their motor, but to the house, and to the tree that overshadowed it" (*Howards End,* 18). Though Forster tended to mystify his creative process, Oliver Stallybrass opens his introduction to the manuscripts of *Howards End* by noting, to the contrary, how conscious Forster was of his creations and offers the example of Mrs. Wilcox's relation to hay as a deliberate part of her symbolic structure (*The Manuscripts of Howards End,* vol. 4a: Abinger Edition, ed. Oliver Stallybrass [London: Edward Arnold, 1973], vii).

25. Recent criticism has followed up on the implications of this shift in family relations. Jeane Olson importantly recognizes a new family structure, "the blended family," implicit in Forster's novel ("E. M. Forster's Prophetic Vision of the Modern Family in *Howards End,*" *TSLL* 35, no. 3 [1993]: 347–62). Kenneth Womack argues that the novel is Forster's therapeutic narrative for the rejuvenation of a larger family system ("'Only Connecting' with the Family: Class, Culture, and Narrative Therapy in E. M. Forster's *Howards End,*" *Style* 31, no. 2 [1997]: 255–69). By contrast, Jon Hegglund traces middle-class fears of contamination by mass culture to argue that the novel embodies a crisis of national identity and salubrity ("Defend the Realm: Domestic Space and Mass Cultural Contamination," *English Literature in Transition, 1880–1920* 40, no. 4 [1997]: 398–423).

26. In addition to Armstrong's *Desire and Domestic Fiction,* see also Mary Poovey, *Uneven Developments: The Ideological Work of Gender in Mid-Victorian England* (Chicago: University of Chicago Press, 1988). Terry Eagleton makes a similar point about the effect of culture in *Heathcliff and the Great Hunger, Studies in Irish Culture* (London: Verso, 1995).

27. Interestingly, it is the down-to-earth Margaret who affirms Ruth's supernatural powers, claiming "I feel that you [Helen] and I and Henry are only fragments of that woman's mind. She knows everything. She is the house, and the tree that leans over it" (*Howards End,* 222).

28. See Magali Sarfatti Larson, *The Rise of Professionalism: A Sociological Analysis* (Berkeley: university of California Press, 1977), and Maurizia Boscagli, *Eye on the Flesh: Fashions of Masculinity in the Early Twentieth Century* (New York: Westview Press, 1995). (Hereafter *Eye on the Flesh.*)

29. In addition to the commentaries by Ford and Masterman cited at the opening of the essay on the impotency of the city dwellers, see also Arnold White, *Efficiency and Empire* (1901), ed. G. R. Searle (Harvester Press, 1973), and Everard Digby, "The Extinction of the Londoner." *Contemporary Review*, July 1904, 115.

30. Carpenter's utopian community of Millthrope, previously mentioned, was a forerunner of this return to nature. Another manifestation was the group of neo-pagans associated with Rupert Brooke. See Paul Delaney, *The Neo-pagans: Rupert Brooke and the Ordeal of Youth* (New York: Free Press, 1987).

31. *Eye on the Flesh*, 57. As David Trotter explains, writers of imperial adventure turned homeward imaginatively to England after the Boer War to resuscitate what was widely perceived as their adventurers' flagging potency. See Trotter, "Kipling's England: The Edwardian Years," in *Kipling Considered*, ed. Phillip Mallett (New York: St. Martin's, 1989), 56–70.

32. Linda Dowling's suggestive analysis of the Hellenic movement that coalesced during the Victorian century locates a paradigmatic shift in male affiliation at Oxford that came to flourish in the last decades of the century under the sign of masculine love. Victorian homosexualism, she claims, entered national culture through Oxford Hellenism (Dowling, *Hellenism and Homosexuality in Victorian Oxford* [Ithaca: Cornell University Press, 1994], 132–45).

33. On this point, I take exception to Boscagli's otherwise careful analysis. In her claim that "Forster turns the clerk into a sentimentalized victim of the upper classes and of his own desire to 'improve himself'" she fails to account for the text's erotic and aesthetic investment (and Forster's as well) in Bast and in his offspring (*Eye on the Flesh*, 57). However attenuated, it is present in Bast's representation. Similarly, John Carey understands Forster's portrayal of Bast as unsympathetic, resulting from his anxiety over the youth's cultural airs (*The Intellectuals and the Masses, Pride and Prejudice among the Literary Intelligentsia, 1880–1939* [New York: St. Martin's Press, 1993], 18–20).

34. See Fred Miller Robinson's discussion on the iconography of haberdashery in *The Man in the Bowler Hat: His History and Iconography* (Chapel Hill: University of North Carolina Press, 1993), 21–27.

35. Indeed, Forster went on a walking tour of Shropshire in 1907 and even wrote Houseman of his admiration for the poems (Furbank, *Forster*, 1:152–53). Valued for their impassioned and forthright manliness, Houseman's lyrics were coded and enjoyed as erotic verse by Forster and his Cambridge fellows.

36. *Howards End* reminds us that what critics often push aside when analyzing this homoerotic geometry are the property and power relations that cohere in such exchanges, relations that Gayle Rubin took pains to make visible in reworking René Girard's study *Deceit, Desire, and the Novel: Self and Other in Literary Structure*, trans. Yvonne Freccero (Baltimore: The Johns Hopkins University Press, 1972). See the first chapter of Eve Sedgwick, *Between Men: English Literature and Male Homosocial Desire* (New York: Columbia University Press, 1985), and Rubin's "The Traffic in Women."

37. Understood this way, Katherine Mansfield's venomous quip—"I can never be perfectly certain whether Helen was got with child by Leonard Bast or by his fatal forgotten umbrella. All things considered, I think it must have been the umbrella"— loses some sting, if not wit (quoted in Gardner's *Critical Heritage*, 162).

38. My reading thus differs from George Thomson's, which decides that fathers

are ultimately irrelevant to narrative desire: "Forster's interest in the living continuity represented by ancestors and descendants is a general rather than a particular interest, it is universal rather than individual. That is why the same move can encompass ancestor worship, child glorification, and the admirable Margaret Schlegel. That is why it is not supremely important who fathers Helen's child, but is supremely important that there be a child" (*The Fiction of E. M. Forster* [Detroit: Wayne State University Press, 1967], 185).

CHAPTER ELEVEN

"Unarm, Eros!": Adventure, Homoeroticism, and Divine Order in *Prester John*

Maria Davidis

Of all of John Buchan's adventure books, *Prester John* (1910) most invites current reexamination, given its complex mix of racial politics and an advocacy of empire more subtle than that of many boys' books of the time.[1] The story of Davie Crawfurd's detection and suppression of a planned pan-African rebellion led by John Laputa, a black minister and self-proclaimed heir to the throne of Prester John,[2] Buchan's novel reveals itself as an effort to hold on to the promise and glory of empire in the post–Boer War era, when imperialism was held in lower esteem than it had traditionally been and when imperial anxiety was rising because the empire seemed threatened from both within and without. British global domination seemed imperiled on the one hand by internal weakness—the perceived degeneracy of British men—and on the other by external forces in the form of native rebellions and competition from other European powers such as Germany.

Buchan's solution to these anxieties lay in what he saw as a pure type of imperialism, initially introduced in his other works with African themes, the nonfictional *The African Colony: Studies in the Reconstruction* (1903), and the hybrid novel *A Lodge in the Wilderness* (1906),[3] and subsequently put into adventure story form in *Prester John*. In this paper, I argue that Buchan's African works intertwine Christianity and imperialism by figuring both as missions from God, a view reminiscent of mid-Victorian British rhetoric about bringing "light into the darkness" of Africa.[4] At bottom, the same tenets underlie Buchan's visions of religion and imperialism: both are noble homosocial (but not homo-sexual)[5] activities in which youths chosen by God take as natural their dominion over so-called inferiors and strive to adhere to Christian ways in a promised land (or Eden) that turns them into men and redeems them in the eyes of God. This activity, presented as virtuous rather than exploitative, rewards them with a material prosperity presented as almost incidental but also perceived as evidence of their worth in God's eyes. Worshipful of the purity he sees in Cecil Rhodes's brand of imperialism, Buchan not surprisingly ignores the abuses inflicted on Africans in the name of virtue and civilization, and the rapacity of the capitalism prac-ticed by Rhodes and others in South Africa.[6] In Buchan's view, imperi-alism is a force through which to better the world.

Writing in the spirit of this virtuous imperialism, Buchan shapes *Prester John*'s protagonist into a latter-day "Christian" making a pil-grimage and passing tests he encounters on his way down the "straight and narrow path."[7] For Buchan, danger arises with the possibility that Davie will "go primitive," a state presented in the novel as a perversion of religion, virtue, and imperialism and personified by John Laputa, the eponymous Prester John. Laputa's rebellion against British imperialism and in favor of pan-African autonomy is figured as a monstrous cor-ruption of all that he has learned from the Scottish missionaries who taught him and ordained him. The African priest distorts the imperial "creed" through a dangerous and misguided impulse toward a political independence that the book views as ultimately not in Africans' best interests. In addition, the religion that South African Britons perceive as providing a healthy homosocial environment is transformed by Laputa's sexual magnetism and polymorphous appeal into a stimulus of homo-erotic thoughts that jeopardize Davie's virtue. According to the novel's ideology, Davie's sexual and political submission to Laputa would be a supplication signifying not just a fall from virtue in the religious sense but also a defeat in the imperial sense. To remain manly and upright (in all of its senses), Davie must absorb the primitive and masculinizing energy created by being an imperialist in the landscape of South Africa, and through the adoption of Calvinist asceticism he must resist John Laputa's seductive pull. Davie's choice to conform to the ideology of Calvinist imperialism is presented to the reader as the reason for his de-feat of the African and for his triumphant return to Britain as the bene-ficiary of what is figured in the novel as providential wealth.

Empire's Progress: Buchan on South Africa, 1901–1910

The beliefs that underlie *Prester John* are most deeply rooted in the major interests of Buchan's youth: Calvinism and a classically influenced male camaraderie, which offered him firm moral codes and models of leadership. The son of a minister of the Scottish Free Kirk, Buchan was a staunch Calvinist, and in accord with these beliefs, his most loved childhood reading was Bunyan's *Pilgrim's Progress,* from which he quotes in both *Prester John* and his memoir, *Memory Hold-the-Door.*[8] Reflecting Bunyan's influence and, therefore, his absorption of Calvinism, Buchan began by "regard[ing] life as a pilgrimage along a straight and steep path on which the pilgrim must keep his eyes fixed."[9]

The male camaraderie that taught Buchan so much made its mark not only during Buchan's schooling in Scotland but also in his years at Oxford, when he was in his early twenties. The classical ideal of male fellowship, championed at late-Victorian Oxford, certainly accorded with Buchan's own social inclinations. The closed societies and overall masculine climate of the university appealed to Buchan's "love of romance and his strong sense of male friendship," according to Andrew Lownie.[10] "Invariably," Lownie continues, "it was male company [Buchan] sought out and relished, not least because with males he could drive himself physically as well as mentally."[11] Yet Buchan did not, as far as we know, embrace Platonism as fully as others of his time did, as a validation for homosexuality; and he states in his memoir that his "own predilection ha[d] always been for Rome" rather than Greece.[12] Although the immediate context of the remark does not seem sexual, Buchan's preference for the Roman over the Greek conformed to his belief in empire and in the austere republican virtue so antithetical to Greek love.[13]

Buchan's life with men developed further when, in 1901, at the age of twenty-six, he became one of the so-called Kindergarten in South Africa, a group of recent Oxford and Cambridge graduates with whom Lord Milner entrusted South Africa's future after the Anglo-Boer War. Buchan preferred to think of the group as a "crèche" and believed as Milner did that "there is no country in the world for turning boys, and indeed children, into men like South Africa."[14] Buchan could "imagine no nobler *cradle* for a race," a metaphor that of course suggests rebirth for Englishmen in South Africa (*Colony,* 392, emphasis added). This rebirth was so liberating because "Africa [was] still a home of the incalculable, not wholly explored or explorable, still a hinterland to which the youth of the south c[ould] push forward in search of fortune, and from which that breath of romance, which is the life of the English race, c[ould] inspire thinkers and song-makers" (392) At a time in which other areas of the globe seemed civilized and lacking in possibilities for exploration, South Africa still allowed for the construction of a life-giving quest romance that would strengthen boys, let them live out their dreams, and make them the superior Englishmen a nation expected them to be.

The anticipated transformation of boys into these superior men was particularly crucial during and after the Anglo-Boer War, when the deplorable physical condition of soldiers prompted anxieties about whether British specimens of masculinity could live up to the demands of maintaining a vast empire. As Anna Davin notes in her excellent study "Imperialism and Motherhood," "A poor military performance in the Boer War had dramatized fears of national inadequacy and exposed the poor health of the working class in Britain, from which were drawn both soldiers and sailors to defend the empire, and workers to produce goods with which to dominate the world economy."[15] This concern was symptomatic of and elided with a larger anxiety from the fin de siècle to the years after *Prester John* was published: the fear that Englishmen were becoming increasingly spiritually and sexually weak. In the words of one physician, "A healthy people pruned of its decadents by a high mortality amongst its children is better than a degenerate race weakened by the survival of its effete progeny."[16] Particularly in the wake of the Wilde trial of 1895, such words as "effete," "decadent," and "degenerate" in descriptions of the middle and upper classes signaled more than physical weakness. Physical frailty was presumably accompanied by sexual and emotional effeminacy—in a word, by homosexuality.

Buchan saw settlement in Africa as the solution to the degeneration of the populace, both for the working classes and for aristocrats; unlike some scientists, he saw the problem not as a genetic predisposition to inferiority but as a product of environmental disadvantages adhering to the overcrowded British Isles. Just before his death he wrote, "I saw in the Empire a means of giving to the congested masses at home open country instead of a blind alley."[17] The decadence and degeneracy feared to be suffered by the working classes at home could be remedied through mass settlement in the wide-open spaces of Edenic South Africa, and the aristocrats could enjoy similar possibilities outlined by Lady Flora, the ingenue in Buchan's *A Lodge in the Wilderness:*

> "Think of the numbers of young men of our class who have sufficient money to live on and nothing to do. They somehow fall out of the professions, and hang about at a loose end. But there is excellent stuff in them if they found the kind of life to suit them. They would have made good eldest sons, though they are very unsatisfactory younger ones. But out here they could all be eldest sons. They would have a Christian life, plenty of shooting, plenty of hard work of the kind they could really do well; and then they could marry and found a new aristocracy." (258)

Lady Flora translates the class-based and birth-order distinctions of home into the race-based civilization of South Africa and thereby creates a new Eden in which English aristocrats rule over all lesser mortals in the colony. In this vision the change of location allows men to realize their potential in a way that Britain does not. Again, the degeneracy of home is attributed to environmental constraints, here the rules of primogeniture that contribute to the corruption and wasted lives of younger sons who in Lady Flora's view have all of the character and leadership capabilities of their elder brothers. Race-based economic and political policy becomes papered over by the virtuous rhetoric of the Protestant capitalist ethic; nowhere does Lady Flora consider that the "redemption" of British men—the ability to realize their potential as eldest sons—is made possible not by the openness of the land but by an oppressive capitalist imperialism that guarantees white men, regardless of ability, the choicest jobs and properties in the country.

Buchan's environmental explanation enabled him to argue for British hegemony even after Africans had been fighting for their rights, as in the Ndebele and Shona rebellions of the 1890s. Although Buchan does not, like some imperialists of the day, argue that Africans are indisputably and permanently inferior to whites,[18] he does deem them inferior for the present and holds no illusions about the desired power politics his empire should maintain:

> That saying of Dogberry's, "An [sic] two men ride of a horse, one must ride behind," is a primary law not only of equitation but of politics in the treatment of a conquered country. For conquered it is, and there is little use disguising it: we have not been fighting for the love of it or for fine sentiment, but to conquer the land and give our people the mastery. The last word in all matters must rest with us—that is, with the people

of British blood and British sympathies. Both men must be on the horse, or, apart from parable, each race must have fair and ample representation. To deny this would be to sin against sound policy. But not to take measures to see that our own race has the casting vote is to be guilty of the commonest folly. "An two men ride of a horse, one must ride behind." (*Colony*, 337–38)

Although contemporary interpreters might see the horse as Africa, with the horse thief taking the original owner captive, Buchan believes in the nobility and beneficence of the British imperial enterprise: while the Englishman maintains a control and masculinity afforded him by his activities in the African landscape, the African is raised up to be allowed to ride on the horse and taken in the proper direction, that is, toward English civilization. The fact that mastery is a "gift" nonetheless cannot disguise that there must be master and mastered, domination and submission.

This mastery and domination are justified by what Buchan perceives as the divine nature of imperialism as Cecil Rhodes practiced it. An amalgam of capitalism and Calvinism akin to Weber's scheme in *The Protestant Ethic and the Spirit of Capitalism* (1904),[19] this imperialism was another ordering system that required discipline and promised the reward of Africa's redemption and prosperity; Buchan never comments on what we now view as rapacious British capitalism or the gross injustices to which Africans were subject. Of Carey, the Cecil Rhodes figure in *A Lodge in the Wilderness*, Buchan writes, "If some called his faith Imperialism, others pointed out how little resemblance it bore to the article cried in the marketplace. It was a creed beyond parties, a consuming and passionate interest in the destiny of his people" (*Lodge*, 4). Carey downplays business and profit in favor of a spiritual ideal that cannot be understood by the masses or by smaller capitalist minds. In this allegedly selfless imperialism, global capitalism works as a force for good that elevates the British race as a whole. This ideal conforms to Buchan's own summation, in his memoir, that he believes in an imperialism that is "humanitarian and international . . . an ethical standard, serious and surely not ignoble."[20]

This confession of faith recurs, emerging from the mouths of most of the characters over the book's course, until Lowenstein, a financier, declares, "'I almost think that our most urgent duty is to insist upon the spiritual renaissance at the back of everything. For, properly regarded, our creed is a religion, and we must hold it with the fervour of a convert'" (*Lodge*, 306). If we follow Lowenstein in translating imperialism into the language of religion, then imperialism acts as a missionary force that ministers not so much to those Africans viewed as God-forsaken as to those British who would normally consider themselves the saved. Englishmen who would be perceived as saints thus exchange the Churches of England and Scotland for the Church of Mammon as they note the changes occurring in their world. As Lord Appin, a Conservative former Prime Minister of England, remarks, "'The state, remember, has now taken the place of the mediæval church'" (*Lodge*, 310). We have here a new holy trinity, in which the corporatism of the state and big business melds with the Church to spread the wonders of the civilization that saves.

Prester John

In *Prester John*, Buchan turns to a more conventional and appealing generic method of conveying his capitalist-imperialist-Calvinist message. This 1910 novel popularizes Buchan's philosophy through the medium of a rousing adventure story in which the youthful Davie Crawfurd must be born again in the "cradle of Africa" and become a man by adhering to the faith outlined above. His encounters with Laputa, who is represented as a perverter of the imperialist creed and of the classical ideal of male camaraderie, serve as Davie's most difficult spiritual trials; and Davie can reach salvation only by resisting the political and sexual feminization and degradation that would occur were he in Laputa's hands. David must use what he learns to best his adversary, make money for himself and the empire, and return to Scotland to what is presented in the novel as the wholesome masculine atmosphere of the university.

Our first encounter with Laputa, in Davie's home village of Kirkcaple, Scotland, foreshadows his later activities in Africa. As Davie will do in Africa, so he and his friends here act in ways proper to the imperial hierarchy, by "tracking" the foreign man at night as if he were an animal: "Archie was on his knees in a second. 'Lads,' he cried, 'there's spoor here;' and then after some nosing, 'it's a man's track, going downward, a big man with flat feet'" (14). Although the boys' ambition runs "in Indian paths" rather than African, the occupation of man hunting remains the same: they seek to find and capture someone "trespassing on [their] preserves" (14). Never mind that this land is public land; as the British do in Africa, the boys roam at will over this area that they regard as their own and are only too eager to punish any outsider who treads on it.

That outsider is Laputa, who has demonstrated earlier in the day that he is not, in Kipling's words, "one of us."[21] The missionary-trained African, a clergyman ordained in the Scottish Kirk, has already offended the towns-people with his sermon on "how a black man was as good as a white man in the sight of God" and on how someday "the negroes would have something to teach the British in the way of civilization" (13). Specifi-cally, Laputa immediately alienates Davie's friend, Tam, who justifies his antipathy by citing the Genesis verses interpreted as meaning that "'the children of Ham [are] to be our servants'" (14). Laputa's claim for a black civilization threatens these Scots because it contravenes common British beliefs of the eternal inferiority of Africans; as David Daniell notes, his name alone recalls the visionary but twisted schemes of the Laputans in Swift's *Gulliver's Travels*.[22]

Laputa's rebellious statements of the day can only hint at what will come that night in the darkness, when the equally dark African will more fully reveal himself both literally and figuratively. The black priest's per-formance of a pagan African ritual around a fire he has built on shore reveals his duplicitous nature and a plenitude, beneath his minister's garb, of the savagery the missionaries were supposed to have expunged:

> There was something desperately uncanny about the negro, who had shed his clerical garments, and was now practising some strange magic alone by the sea. I had no doubt it was the black art, for there was that in the air and the scene which spelled the unlawful. As we watched, the circles stopped, and the man threw something on the fire. A thick smoke rose of which we could feel the aromatic scent, and when it was gone, the flame burned with a silvery blueness like moonlight. Still no sound came from the minister, but he took something from his belt, and began to make odd markings in the sand between the inner circle and the fire. As he turned, the moon gleamed on the implement, and we saw it was a great knife. (18)

Laputa apparently possesses more than just a calling to the ministry. Although the minister superficially resembles Davie's father in his pro-fession, his literal shedding of outer layers reveals to Davie an exotic, pagan, dark, and sexual side.[23] His daytime Christianity giving way to a nighttime native religion, Laputa's physical blackness merges with the evil of the "black art" he practices. The priest thus begins to signify what is savage and "unlawful" in contrast to the civilization and adherence to proper divine law and order found in the Kirk of Scotland. Materializing as a paranoid's version of Buchan's typical "native" who learns only "in a kind of parrot fashion," Laputa has used the missionaries' lessons about Christianity and civilization to pass himself off as the sincerest type of convert, one so committed to the teachings of the British that he becomes ordained as a minister (*Colony*, 309). His mysterious practices at night reveal to the boys his true perfidy.

In a kind of Conradian "fascination of the abomination,"[24] Davie cannot stop watching Laputa as he performs his rituals. Davie's voyeuristic narration conveys Laputa as both hypermasculine object and potential dominator: an almost naked and voiceless colonized subject possessed of a "great knife," he represents for the boy at once a homoerotic spectacle and a perverter of religion (18).[25] Once he is alerted to the boys' presence, though, the power dynamic changes. The great knife is no longer something to be looked at; instead, it has the power to inflict damage (Craig Smith sees it as a figurative rape) on the youthful figure now running from it.[26] Acting in self-defense, Davie throws a rock at Laputa and blackens his eye, leaving him with a physical reminder of his visit to Scotland's shores and a mental reminder of the ingenuity and will to dominate possessed by Scotland's sons (21).

The actual adventure foreshadowed in this scene begins only once Davie is on the brink of manhood, at the age of sixteen. Davie's father, the sedate Scottish minister, dies of "paralytic shock"; Buchan's book thereby provides the justification for the boy's leaving the domestic space of Scotland (25). God leads Davie to the all-male wilderness of South Africa as, "by the mercy of Providence," the boy is given a job as a trader in the wild outpost of Blaauwildebeestefontein (25).[27] A country that promises to make Davie a man and provide him a prosperous future— conforming to Buchan's theories in *The African Colony* and *A Lodge in the Wilderness*—South Africa is the Promised Land:

> The *Pilgrim's Progress* had been the Sabbath reading of my boyhood, and as I came in sight of Blaauwildebeestefontein a passage ran in my head. It was that which tells how Christian and Hopeful, after many perils of

the way, came to the Delectable Mountains, from which they had a prospect of Canaan. After many dusty miles by rail, and a weariful journey in a Cape-cart through arid plains and dry and stony gorges, I had come suddenly into a haven of green. (39)

The physical hardships, as well as the peril of hearing Laputa plotting with the evil Portuguese Henriques, resemble those of Christian, who is told that "these troubles and distresses . . . are no sign that God hath forsaken you; but are sent to try you."[28] Davie's successful passing of these tests is signaled by his ending up in what *Pilgrim's Progress* calls "Immanuel's Land," full of "gardens and orchards, the vineyards and fountains of water."[29] Like the schema delineated in *Lodge in the Wilderness,* this Calvinist-imperialist venture is posed as an act sanctioned by God. Only truly virtuous men already anointed by the Heavenly Father, such as Christian and Hopeful, persevere enough to enter this most fertile land—the chosen land for the chosen people.

Working on behalf of this civilization not only takes Davie to the Delectable Mountains, the Promised Land, but to God's original paradise. Upon arriving at Blaauwildebeestefontein, Davie says, "The fresh hill air had exhilarated my mind, and the aromatic scent of the evening gave the last touch of intoxication. Whatever serpent might lurk in it, it was a veritable Eden I had come to" (39). In prior imperial narratives of Africa, the continent is often seen as primeval—a post- rather than prelapsarian Eden. In *Heart of Darkness,* for instance, the European visitor may feel that he is "travelling back to the earliest beginnings of the world, when vegetation rioted on the earth and the big trees were kings."[30] Conrad's description points to the rottenness that sets in when God has forsaken the land and promises nothing for the future, in contrast to Buchan's description, which is full of freshness and evokes the pleasantness of both English past and Edenic imperial future—albeit one jeopardized by the inevitable serpent.[31]

The serpent is, of course, Laputa, and Davie's being in Blaauwildebeestefontein allows him the chance to carry out the promise of that night on the Kirkcaple shore when he first suspects Laputa of having a secret life (18). Davie's discovery that Laputa believes himself to be an incarnation of Prester John charged with a divine mission to amass treasure and use it in an attempt to overthrow British imperial rule gives him the motive to hunt out this glib-tongued menace to empire. This playing of "the game" provides Davie a legitimate imperialist cover for his attraction to the older man, but the boy's rhetoric reveals him. Davie marvels at Laputa's "great physique" (203) and confesses,

> As my eye fell on his splendid proportions I forgot all else in my admiration of the man. In his minister's clothes he had looked only a heavily built native, but now in his savage dress I saw how noble a figure he made. He must have been at least six feet and a half, but his chest was so deep and his shoulders so massive that one did not remark his height. He put a hand on my saddle, and I remember noting how slim and fine it was, more like a high-bred woman's than a man's. (101–02)

If Laputa is the serpent, Davie is the tempted. The attraction to Laputa occurs, as in Davie's childhood, when the African is dressed (or, by British standards, *un*dressed) in indigenous clothing that uncovers his "splendid proportions." Davie's perception of Laputa's androgynously attractive physical attributes, both his deep chest and his woman's hands, makes of Laputa both a homoerotic object and a worthy adversary, the adversarial element being part of the attraction.

Laputa is more than a typical adversary, though: his oratorical abilities in the pulpit transform him into a religious father figure Davie will have to supplant in order to become a man. When Laputa reads from the Old Testament in a secret ceremony Davie is stealthily witnessing, Davie "listen[s] spellbound as he pray[s]" and thinks, "I heard the phrases familiar to me in my schooldays at Kirkcaple. He had some of the tones of my father's voice, and when I shut my eyes I could have believed myself a child again" (127). While listening to Laputa seems comforting to Davie, it also makes him regress and fall under the almost magical power of a father figure—"he listened *spellbound*" (127, emphasis added). A Platonic relationship in which Davie is enchanted by the magical spell of the older man will not allow Davie to grow up; if he is to be the ideal heterosexual and homosocial imperialist he must open his eyes and go from romantic enchantment to reality.

The image of Laputa as both older homoerotic object and priestly father figure is intensified in Davie's envisioning of Laputa as more than just a minister. Laputa's being anointed in the secret ceremony in the cave reminds Davie, "so queer are the tricks of memory, of an old Sabbath-school book [he] used to have which had a picture of Samuel ordaining Saul as king of Israel" (122). Davie once again associates Laputa with his childhood and, significantly enough, the association he makes with this would-be first king of Africa is that of the first king of Israel.

Davie's admiration of Laputa's form mingles with a new sense of the divine ordering of human beings:

> Laputa took the necklet and twined it in two loops round his neck till the clasp hung down over his breast.... Then I knew that, to the confusion of all talk about equality, God has ordained some men to be kings and others to serve. Laputa stood naked as when he was born. The rubies were dulled against the background of his skin, but they still shone with a dusky fire. Above the blood-red collar his face had the passive pride of a Roman emperor. (126)

The Calvinist belief underlying Davie's remark here does not conform to the ideology of imperialism, as Davie neglects to distinguish kings and servants by race. Moreover, Laputa is described in a similar manner to the Cecil Rhodes figure in *A Lodge in the Wilderness:* "his magnificent throat and head rose like a bust of some Roman emperor" (17). Laputa possesses the same sort of imperial majesty and dignity that attracts *Lodge*'s narrator to Carey, but the purity of worship of Carey contrasts against the sexual undertones of this worship of Laputa, which signals the perils of the path.

Davie's wish to serve Laputa in a way that merges homoeroticism with religious supplication is incredibly dangerous because it would have him "riding behind," to use the words of Buchan's example from *The African Colony.*[32] To submit in this way is, for Davie, against all rational thought:

> My mind was mesmerized by this amazing man. I could not refrain from shouting with the rest [of the Africans watching the ceremony]. Indeed I was a convert, if there can be conversion when the emotions are dominant and there is no assent from the brain. I had a mad desire to be of Laputa's party. Or rather, I longed for a leader who should master me and make my soul his own.... I longed for such a general. (129)

Religious conversion mingles with sexual and political conversion—which we perceive as sexual inversion—and military discourse as Davie desires not an equal partnership with this physically dominant and emotionally magnetic African, but submission to a higher force. Mastery appears in this situation not as the "gift" Buchan describes in his outlining of imperialism but as a monstrous perversion whose Platonic undertones may not be intended by Buchan but are revealed to the reader in the scene's martial character and in the youth/adult partnership depicted. A desire so strong that it cannot be contained as Davie "shouts with the rest," it makes Davie want, in effect, to take a position beneath a black man. That subordinate position, whether we interpret it as military or sexual, should not occur in the "rational" world of the imperialist. Instead, as Davie's conscience reminds him, his mind should rebel against it.[33]

From the ideological standpoint of the novel, the Platonism to which Buchan was exposed in his Greats education at Oxford should not extend to the realm of love relationships, as it did for many of Buchan's fellow students at university. Davie's desire to be the youth in a martial Platonic relationship with Laputa is not only a religious offense but also a lapse into civic vice that makes Davie the *effeminatus* of classical republican theory. As Linda Dowling writes, the *effeminatus* is "the empty or negative symbol at once of civic enfeeblement and of the monstrous self-absorption that becomes visible in a society at just the moment at which . . . private interest has begun to prevail against those things that concern the public welfare."[34] By caring more about his own feelings than he does about the greater mission of his people, Davie abdicates responsibility and jeopardizes the project of empire.

In order for Davie to become an ideal British imperialist he must dominate the relationship with Laputa. A Platonic relationship in which the younger Davie acknowledges Laputa as his intellectual and sexual superior cannot be Davie's model for adulthood; Davie must instead look to the more wholesome and promising homosocial relationships in the Bible and become the David to Laputa's Saul. In doing so, however, he must not be the young David who soothes Saul with sweet music and follows the king; he must instead be the older David blessed by God when Saul is damned for having disobeyed God by taking the spoils of war and listening to the Witch of Endor. This is the David who uses his wits and bravery to lead the people of Israel—the chosen people— to victory. Remarking that Laputa believes in his "divine mission," Davie realizes about himself that "God had preserved me from some deadly perils. . . . I had a mission as clear as Laputa's. . . . I had been saved for a purpose, and unless I fulfilled that purpose I should again be lost" (194). Davie's mission to maintain British dominance over South Africa emerges as true and divinely inspired; Laputa's mission, like Saul's, is established as false, and British imperialism is infused with the breath of the Holy Spirit. By 1910, the British presence in South Africa needed to be bolstered by more than just politics, and Britain's hope lay with its manly youth. The novel's future, therefore, lies in the great and young king of the Israelites, Davie Crawfurd.

Davie's theft of Laputa's phallic snake necklet, which confers kingly power, enables the young man to usurp Laputa's position as David did Saul's. Facing the river across which he must swim to get away, Davie thinks in ways that fuse capitalist imperialism with the religious belief that God will provide for his chosen ones: "My first care was the jewels, so, feeling them precariously in my shirt, I twined the collar round my neck and clasped it.... I held the pistol between my teeth, and with a prayer to God slipped into the muddy waters" (156). Phallic jewel round his neck, phallic weapon in his mouth, Davie's entry into the river represents his baptism as a fully grown imperialist male. The baptism completed, the ritual that occurs upon Davie's emergence on the river's opposite bank signifies his coronation as the rightful alternative to an illegitimate king: "I found a dry sheltered place in the bush and stripped to the skin . . . while the Prester's jewels were blazing on my neck. Here was a queer counterpart to Laputa in the cave!" (157). Whereas the rubies were earlier "dulled against the background of [Laputa's] skin," they "blaze" on Davie's white neck (126, 157); whereas Laputa is made king in and of the darkness, in the cave and of Africans, Davie's "ceremony" takes place in the light of the natural world.

The final scene between Davie and Laputa confirms the disparity between Laputa's vision of himself as a noble and honorable ruler and, in the novel's moral code, the absence of the true virtue required for leadership. Laputa's command to Davie, "'Unarm, Eros! . . . The long day's task is done'" (219), echoes Shakespeare's Antony[35] and thereby reveals Laputa's perception of himself as another mighty leader fallen. To retain his virtue and avoid the humiliation of capture by the enemy, Laputa believes he must, like the Roman Antony, commit suicide. He therefore commands his subordinate, Eros/Davie, not to prevent him from that act; in fact, the Eros of the play kills himself just before Antony does so as to "escape the sorrow of Antony's death" (4.14.94), and Laputa expects the same of Davie.

The references to Antony and Eros, however, reveal a reality Laputa does not intend—a sensual underpinning more evocative of degenerate Greek love than Roman virtue. The Antony of Shakespeare's play has lost his empire because he has given himself over to the sensual Cleopatra instead of attending to matters of government; *Prester John* emphasizes

Laputa's sensuality as his paramount attribute and a cause of his weakness. Unlike the play, the novel contains no Cleopatra; instead, Laputa/Davie echoes Antony/Eros. The Eros of the quotation may be Antony's servant, but the name of course also refers to the Greek god of erotic love. The combination of god and powerful servant points again to a Platonic relationship in which the more powerful older man instructs the young boy, but also in which the older man worships the youth's freshness and sexual appeal. These homoerotic overtones are reinforced in the text as Davie literally finally manages to get his hands on Laputa ("I ran to him and with all my strength aided him to his feet," 218). Laputa, meanwhile, despite a fatal wound, manages once again to strip naked and display himself for Davie's and our eyes. Unlike earlier displays of the powerful and sexualized African body, the spectacle of injured nakedness here signifies the weakness and vulnerability of imminent death and contrasts against Davie's younger and abler clothed and civilized body.

This shift in the balance of power between Laputa and Davie is intensified by the language of youth and adulthood. The naked Laputa places the rubies round his neck and readies himself for his last act "with the weak hands of a *child*" (219, emphasis added). With hands now virtually emptied of power, Laputa becomes the youth in the relationship, and the fact that the rubies "burn" on his neck no longer matters; he has already been defeated. Davie, on the other hand, becomes the default adult in this always asymmetrical relationship; as he does so, his sense of what is imperially right seems to return. Davie's refusal to take up Laputa's invitation to commit suicide with him indicates his adherence to what the novel views as proper values: the ideal of Roman republican virtue over the corrupt Greek love offered by Laputa, the material reward of diamonds and gold left by the African rebels over betrayal of the British cause, the status of a "serious man" over that of a "rash boy" (238), the Christian movement toward life and redemption over suicide and eternal damnation. British imperialism's religious crusade therefore triumphs. As the story closes, homoeroticism remains a subtext—as it must—symbolized by Davie's matriculation in the socially acceptable, all-white homosocial male space of Edinburgh College, and by the all-male college Davie's friend establishes in Africa, where the expatriate Scots have wrought, in the words of another character, quite a "queer transformation" (245).

Notes

I would like to thank Richard Ruppel, Philip Holden, Maura Henry, Yoon-sun Lee, Caroline Alyea, and Patricia Lynch for their advice and comments on this essay.

1. John Buchan, *Prester John* (New York: Thomas Nelson, 1910). Page citations in this chapter are to this edition.

2. The legend of Prester John dates back to the Middle Ages, when Europeans heard of a Christian king who existed in what was otherwise a Muslim Middle East. Of that Prester John, to whose position John Laputa aspires, Buchan writes, "the Portuguese geographers divided Central Africa into Angola in the west, the kingdom of Prester John in the north (Abyssinia), and the empire of Monomotapa (Mashonaland) in the south. The real Prester John was a Nestorian Christian in Central Asia, whose khanate was destroyed by Genghis Khan about the end of the twelfth century; but the name became a generic one for any supposed Christian monarch in unknown countries" (John Buchan, *The African Colony: Studies in the Reconstruction* [Edinburgh: Blackwood, 1903], 21 fn. Hereafter *Colony*.)

3. John Buchan, *A Lodge in the Wilderness* (Edinburgh: Blackwood, 1906). Hereafter *Lodge*.

4. In his essay on *Prester John*, Craig Smith notes that in 1910 "John Buchan is writing about native policy as if it could be changed 'for the better,' even though by 1906 it seemed clear that southern Africa would be unified under Afrikaner leadership" (Craig Smith, "Every Man Must Kill the Thing He Loves: Empire, Homoerotics, and Nationalism in John Buchan's *Prester John*," *Novel* 28, no. 2 [winter 1995]: 175). Smith is correct about the anachronistic view of public policy but ignores the fact that *Prester John* is the culmination of a decade of beliefs originally formed from 1901 to 1903, when Buchan worked in the government of South Africa and when older beliefs about the efficacy of British imperialism were tenable.

5. In her ground-breaking *Between Men: English Literature and Male Homosocial Desire* (New York: Columbia University Press, 1985), Eve Kosofsky Sedgwick views homosexuality as part of the spectrum of homosocial practices. For the purposes of this essay I would like to distinguish between them, using "homosocial" to mean male camaraderie and "homosexual" to indicate practice of active erotic interest or activity.

6. The illicit diamond mining that Rhodes suspected of Africans is written into the plot of *Prester John* as one of the Africans' evil practices, but Rhodes's treatment of the miners is not. As H. J. and R. E. Simons write in *Class and Colour in South Africa, 1850–1950* (London: Penguin, 1969), "Africans were searched every day at the end of their shift. Stripped naked, they jumped over bars and paraded with arms extended before guards, who scrutinized hair, nose, mouth, ears, and rectum with meticulous care." And in a practice "firmly entrenched by 1888" and documented in books published in 1903 and 1910, "men due for discharge were confined in detention rooms for several days, during which they wore only blankets and fingerless leather gloves padlocked to their wrists, swallowed purgatives, and were examined for stones concealed in cuts, wounds, swellings, and orifices" (42). See also Stafford Ransome, *The Engineer in South Africa* (London: Constable, 1903), and John Angove, *In the Early Days: The Reminiscences of Pioneer Life on the South African Diamond Fields* (Kimberley: Handel House, 1910).

7. For an exclusively Calvinist interpretation, see David Daniell, introduction to *Prester John,* by John Buchan (New York: Oxford University Press, 1994), xxiii, where the author views *Prester John* as a novel about the eternal struggle between humility and pride, good and evil.

8. John Buchan, *Memory Hold-the-Door,* intro. David Daniell (1940; reprint, London: J. M. Dent and Sons, 1984).

9. Andrew Lownie, *The Presbyterian Cavalier* (London: Constable, 1995), 61.

10. Lownie, *Presbyterian Cavalier,* 31.

11. Ibid., 48.

12. *Memory Hold-the-Door,* 34.

13. Thanks to Caroline Alyea and Patricia Lynch for this point.

14. Milner to J. Randel, 12 January 1903, Milner Papers, quoted in Max Beloff, *Imperial Sunset,* vol. 1: *Britain's Liberal Empire, 1897–1921* (New York: Knopf, 1970), 129.

15. Anna Davin, "Imperialism and Motherhood," *History Workshop* 5 (spring 1978): 12.

16. William Butler, Presidential Address to Willesden and District Medical Society, read by request before Home Counties branch of Society of Medical Officers of Health, December 1899, and reprinted in *Public Health,* 1899, 326. Quoted in Davin, "Imperialism and Motherhood," 59.

17. *Memory Hold-the-Door,* 125.

18. Buchan writes, "Between the most ignorant white man and the black man there is fixed *for the present* an impassable gulf, not of colour but of mind," leaving open the possibility of native self-government at some future time (*Colony,* 289, emphasis added). Further, he advocates an educational requirement for franchise for all men, not just Africans, adding, "The lower type of European and the back-veld Dutchman have in their present state no equitable right to the decision, which the franchise gives, on matters which they are unable to come within a measurable distance of understanding. The fact that the fool may have a vote at home is no reason for exalting him to the same level in a country which is not handicapped by a constitutional history" (*Colony,* 340).

19. Max Weber, *The Protestant Ethic and the Spirit of Capitalism,* trans. Talcott Parsons (1904; New York: Charles Scribner's Sons, 1950).

20. *Memory Hold-the Door,* 125.

21. Rudyard Kipling, *Kim* (1901; reprint, New York: Penguin Books, 1989), 195.

22. David Daniell, *The Interpreter's House: A Critical Assessment of John Buchan* (London: Thomas Nelson, 1975), 117.

23. See Smith, "Every Man," 185.

24. Joseph Conrad, *Heart of Darkness* (1902; reprint, New York: Norton, 1988), 10.

25. Craig Smith hits on the Spanish definition of Laputa's name, "whore" *(la puta),* commenting that though the "economic aspect of whoring is absent," whoring signifies qualities such as corruption, sexuality, danger, and femininity. See Smith, "Every Man," 184.

26. Ibid., 185.

27. David Daniell notes Davie's "work-a-day Calvinism," in which Providence is "the source both of special care for his welfare and of particular chances that he has to make the most of" (*Prester John,* intro., xxiii, xxiv).

28. John Bunyan, *Pilgrim's Progress* (1688; reprint, Grand Rapids: Spire, n.d.), 149.

29. *Pilgrim's Progress,* 110. Interestingly, Buchan decries others' claims of reaching Canaan. He disdains, for example, the Boer's "Scriptural parallel" for his trek, in which "the persecuted children of Israel, in spite of the opposition of Pharaoh, had fled across the desert from Egypt and found a Promised Land" (*Colony,* 34).

30. Conrad, *Heart of Darkness,* 35.

31. In *The African Colony,* Buchan describes the Wood Bush, on which he models the landscape in *Prester John,* as a familiar paradise: "'A park-like country,' is the common travelers' phrase for the bush veld; but there the grass is rank and ugly, the trees isolated thorns, and the whole land flat and waterless. Here was a true park, like Chatsworth or Windsor, so perfectly laid out that one could scarcely believe that it was not a work of man. For surely a park is properly man's work, a flower of civilisation, which nature aids but rarely contrives. Yet when she does contrive, how far is the result beyond our human skill! For an exception the mountain-tops were free from mist; the land lay bathed in a cool morning light, and the scent of a thousand aromatic herbs—wormwood, southernwood, a glorified bog-myrtle, musk, and peppermint—rose from the wayside. Bracken was as plentiful as on a Scots moor, and the old familiar fragrance was like a breath of the sea" (117). The landscape is both new and incredibly familiar to him, a park laid out in the midst of a wilderness. This is the land which he believes suitable for other Britons and on which they can begin new, more fruitful lives.

32. When Davie is later captured by Laputa, the riding metaphor is virtually literalized as Davie is forced not even to ride but to walk "brutally gagged" behind the mounted African (185). Predictably enough, Davie uses what the novel sees as his superior British intelligence to steal Laputa's horse and thereby escape.

33. See also Smith, "Every Man," 187.

34. Linda Dowling, *Hellenism and Homosexuality in Victorian Oxford* (Ithaca: Cornell University Press, 1994), 8.

35. William Shakespeare, *Antony and Cleopatra,* 4.14.35, in *The Riverside Shakespeare,* ed. G. Blakemore Evans, intro. Harry Levin (Boston: Houghton Mifflin, 1974), 1378.

CHAPTER TWELVE

Many Lips Will I Kiss: The Queer Foreplay of "the East" in Russian Aestheticism

Dennis Denisoff

The diverse characters who populate Mikhail Kuzmin's novel *Wings* (1906) all find the time to philosophize on the relation of erotic pleasure to ethics and cultural norms. Their speeches create a refrain so familiar that Kuzmin doesn't even bother to note the identity of the orator of the following defense of "unnatural" desires:

> People go about like the blind, like the dead, when they might create for themselves a life burning with intensity in every moment, a life in which pleasure would be as poignant as if you had just come into the world and might die before the day were done. It is with such greed that we must fling ourselves upon life. Miracles crowd upon us at every step: there are muscles, sinews in the human body which one cannot look upon without a tremor! . . . Somewhere lies our ancient kingdom, full of sunlight and freedom, of beautiful and courageous people, and thither we sail, my argonauts, over many a sea, through mist and darkness. And in things yet unheard we shall descry ancient roots, in glittering visions yet unseen we shall know our own dear land![1]

In passages such as this one, Kuzmin anchors his celebration of homosexual love within the context of aestheticism. Walter Pater's infamous instruction that everybody burn with a "gem-like" intensity is coupled here with not only the usual sensuality and exoticism but also an imperialist orientalism. What starts out to be a personal quest is eventually depicted as an invitation to exploitation and domination; the speaker lays claim to a territory of desired "visions," which, albeit "yet unseen," he nevertheless preconstitutes as "our own dear land." In one light, this combination of foreignness and familiarity reflects the rhetorical maneuvering frequently used by Western Europeans to reinforce their imperialist arrogance; the Self requires the Other for its self-definition but, in order to maintain authority, categorizes the Other as subordinate. This reading of the passage changes, however, when one takes into account not only the difference between homosexual and heterosexual uses of orientalism but also Kuzmin's national identity.

The broader context of *Wings* defines the subjugated "argonauts" as an all-male community; part of the quoted monologue is later repeated and ascribed to one of the homosexual characters (77). For a turn-of-the-century European male homosexual, everyday society did not feel like a safe haven. By the same token, any foreign culture that his society constructed as disturbingly unconventional, as simultaneously foreign and familiar, would hold the potential of being recognized as uniquely accommodating, if not sanctioning, his same-sex desires. For the individual, such a culture might "belong" to him in the sense that, once located, it would be the closest thing to a welcoming home that he has ever felt. However, the Russian setting of Kuzmin's novel adds a further complication. In this context, the character's vision reveals a subjectivity whose imperialist foundation is in fact always partially destabilized because of the marginal position of Eastern Europe itself within the dominant discourse of aestheticism. I am interested in the ways in which such disturbances within transcultural positionality play out in East European colonial discourse. Focusing on Kuzmin's novel *Wings* and his poetry series *Alexandrian Songs* (1906), which were written at the same time, I wish to analyze the author's adaptation of orientalist strategies in order to permit his self-identification with a discourse that, although offering a positive reification of his sexual desires, imbued his national identity with a threatening alterity.

Just as dominant communities within systems of knowledge establish their defining boundaries in part through cultures and terms of the marginalized, these "subjugated knowledges," as Foucault calls them, do not articulate their own knowledge systems solely through relations with the dominant communities;[2] they also partake in power maneuvers among themselves and rely on a recognition of their own differences in establishing their identities. Such intramarginal dependencies suggest not simply the instability of major Western European networks of power and knowledge but the reliance of the hegemonic order on the relations among subjugated cultures. Russian aestheticism, with its mixture of classicist, orientalist, and homoerotic language, demonstrates the volatile impact of such dynamics on identity formation.

Aestheticism attained much of its authority from its roots in classical art and aesthetics, which were not seen as a clear threat to the moral tenets of the Victorian status quo. Its doctrine—first fully articulated in Walter Pater's *Renaissance* (1873)—involves an arguably essentialist notion of sensual pleasure as innately moral and unencumbered by any facile orthodox agenda.[3] This moral quality of beauty permits the sustained quest for polymorphous pleasures, while casting a skeptical eye on static conventions. Despite its reservations regarding doxa, however, aestheticism strongly advocates a recognition and celebration of artifice as a constant reminder of human diversity. Constructed articulations of pleasure and beauty support experimentation and are only contemptible when their constructedness is either forgotten or denied. For aestheticists, the essence of beauty is not in conflict with the creation of diverse pleasures. Difficulties arise only when constructed notions of pleasure and ethics threaten to replace the undefinable essence of beauty as the primary object of society's appreciation.

Such a usurpation is most apparent when people begin to demonize others' pleasures as immoral. Checking this tendency, a major component of Pater's aesthetic position is the need for sympathy. In his novel *Marius the Epicurean* (1885), for example, one of the eponymous hero's most constant concerns is the articulation of a notion of mutual sympathy and respect, until a "feeling of a responsibility towards the world of men and things, towards a claim for due sentiment concerning them on his side, came to be a part of [Marius's] nature not to be put off."[4] The novel ends with Marius believing that the world needs "a certain permanent and general power of compassion—humanity's standing force of self-pity—as an elementary ingredient of our social atmosphere, . . . a ready sympathy with the pain one actually sees."[5] Within Paterian aestheticism, sensual pleasure may be private and innate, but it is nevertheless interdependent with public sympathy and its cultural reinforcements. This philosophy, combined with Pater's use of a homoerotic discourse rooted in Greek and Roman classical culture, gave support to unconventional sexualities and attractions such as same-sex male desires. Aestheticism's views on ethics, beauty, and desire also form the background for Kuzmin's representation of sexual and gender identities in *Wings*. In the novel, sensual pleasure is depicted as essential and therefore amoral; as one character puts it, "love, whatever its nature, can never be depraved except in the eyes of a cynic" (26). Identities, conversely, are presented as constructs, as is suggested by the part-English aesthete Larion Dmitrievich Stroop's attempts to coax Vanya toward sprouting the "wings" of a homosexual. Through Vanya's clumsy, complex fashioning process, Kuzmin depicts identity formation as the gradual fitting of essential desires into preestablished categories formed by a particular cultural environment—a process that the novel implies can benefit from imaginative free play.

While Pater's coordination of desire and artifice proved attractive to Kuzmin, however, aestheticism was not free of cultural bias. As a homosexual and an aesthete, Kuzmin was part of aestheticism's extended community, but as a Russian, he was also always in a sense outside of it; not just part of an exotic signification of aestheticism's own deviation from Western European norms but an orientalized Other against which the doctrine was defined. Harish Trivedi has made the useful recommendation that we look at the colonialist encounter as "an interactive, dialogic, two-way process rather than a simple active-passive one; as a process involving complex negotiation and exchange."[6] As Trivedi's study demonstrates, this model is further complicated by historicization and contextualization. Such is the case when one attempts to address the experience of Eastern Europeans who found themselves functioning on both sides of the fabricated orientalist divide. Not clearly either Western European or Eastern (while at other times both), turn-of-the-century Russian identity is not addressed by the "back-and-forth" connotations of Trivedi's dialogic model, suggesting that the multiplicity of voices be viewed instead as polyphonic.

For similar reasons, Eastern European identification as part of the West's dominant culture cannot be theorized as a strategy of passing by which colonized or marginalized people take on the persona of their oppressor as a means to self-empowerment and enhanced social maneuverability. Eastern European countries such as Russia were already themselves partners, roughly speaking, in imperialist political, philosophical, and aesthetic systems. While defining orientalism as mainly "a British and French cultural enterprise," Edward Said acknowledges more than once Russia's participation in this form of ideological domination.[7] At the same time, he notes the ease with which the West during the twentieth century conflated the orient and Russia as the dangerous and threatening "East." Elsewhere, Said discusses the relation of European imperialism to minorities of the East such as the Russian Orthodox.[8] As Greta Slobin points out, "historically, Russia has been the 'other' for Western Europe, yet however distant, exotic and mysterious, Russia was a neighboring colonial power to be reckoned with."[9] Eastern Europe was not commonly defined, and did not define itself, as a potential site of imperialist exploitation. With conflicts such as the Crimean War as well as the increased immigration of Eastern Europeans westward during the nineteenth century, it was in fact often stereotyped by Western Europeans as an aggressor—a threat of degenerate contamination by a foreign body that, going against the main imperialist current, was forcing its alterity into the domain of orthodoxy. As Homi Bhabha has argued, however, "stereotyping is not only the setting up of a false image which becomes the scapegoat of discriminatory practices. It is a much more ambivalent text of projection and introjection, metaphoric and metonymic strategies, displacement, guilt, aggressivity."[10] The potential for Eastern Europeans to infiltrate the West enhanced the latter's anxieties regarding the deviancies that Victorian scientific and juridical institutions were locating within the West itself. Efforts to disempower Eastern Europe through orientalist exoticization reflect in part the West's efforts to displace what it saw as its own weaknesses.[11]

Despite the fact that Eastern Europeans were defining themselves in distinction from heteronormative desires that they situated elsewhere (including Western Europe), late-Victorian culture often marked them as possessing an alluring but dangerous alterity.[12] Perhaps the most famous example of aestheticism's role in this process is Bram Stoker's 1897 depiction of Dracula's disempowering eroticism. The character shares with major aestheticist personalities such as Pater, Swinburne, and Wilde an association (whether warranted or not) with dandyism, sexual unconventionality, and disinterest in industrial productivity. Similarly, in Virginia Woolf's *Orlando* (1928), heavily indebted to aestheticism, the eponymous hero/ine has a number of orientalist adventures, but the only exotic person to appear within the British context is the androgynous and sensual Russian princess Sasha. And in Vernon Lee's *Miss Brown* (1884), an extended critique of aestheticism's lack of moral sensitivity, the author chose not to embody the purest form of the doctrine's evil in the British aesthete Walter Hamlin but to project it onto his Russian cousin Sacha. Not only does this woman corrupt Walter but her exotic perfumes and affections also leave the upright heroine reeling on the edge of a deviant abyss. In fact, the Russian woman uses her passionate magnetism to seduce "every man, woman, and child, . . . every dog or cat that she came across."[13] Dracula has a similarly hypnotic effect on canines, as does George Du Maurier's demonic mesmerist, Svengali, in his novel *Trilby* (1894). The East European Svengali comes to signify an aestheticist extreme saturated with deadly corruption. According to Du Maurier's narrator, the man is the embodiment of greed, "walking up and down the earth seeking whom he might cheat, betray, exploit, borrow money from, make brutal fun of, bully if he dared, cringe to if he must—man, woman, child, or dog."[14] An example of the stereotype of the Eastern European Jew as an invading, exotic Other, Svengali demonstrates Said's insight that, in West European literature, anti-Semitism has often been conflated with orientalism.[15]

While aestheticism's supporters' demonization of Eastern Europeans is less pronounced than that of its critics, the advocates nevertheless did make use of orientalist objectification through such phenomena as *japonisme* and the penchant for collecting fans and peacock feathers. Aestheticism's admiration for Hellenic values and the tradition of *paederastia* also encouraged an exoticization of Mediterranean countries such as Italy, Greece, and Egypt. While *Wings* makes full use of Greek and Italian culture, however, it does not do so simply to idealize but also to normalize (that is, Western Europeanize) the Russian homosexual. The move emphasizes the cultural roots that Kuzmin and his protagonist, as Russians, share with the more famous aesthetes of England and France, thereby undermining the image of Eastern Europe as a signifier of aestheticism's alterity. But aestheticism's use of orientalism to emphasize its difference from the mainstream still demanded that Kuzmin establish in the novel some image of exoticism external to the Russian homosexual aesthete. Toward this end, he incorporates his own orientalist poetry cycle, the *Alexandrian Songs,* into the novel's plot. These poems also offer a far more imaginative and complex celebration of sexual diversity than the novel, envisioning the spirit of Pater's views rather than just rephrasing them.[16]

Attracted early on to theater and music, Kuzmin studied under Nikolai Rimsky-Korsakov at the St. Petersburg Conservatory during the 1890s. He then traveled in Egypt and Italy before returning to Russia where, in 1904, Georgey Chicherin introduced him to Sergei Diaghilev's *Mir iskoustva*, a community that was interested in not only the arts but also aestheticism and same-sex male desire. Kuzmin also maintained strong ties with St. Petersburg's main avant-garde literary scene. He first gained public attention when twelve of his *Alexandrian Songs* and his novel *Wings* were published in the journal *The Scales* in 1906. Over the next twenty years, Kuzmin's attention to homosexual love maintained its centrality, while the aestheticism and orientalism of his writing faded.

Much European literature of the nineteenth century turned to orientalist narratives as a source of imagined sexual liberation. Russia's position in relation to aestheticism, however, as both an active participant and an exoticized subject, resulted in Kuzmin's texts remaining dislocated, an inconclusiveness reflected in his early work's ambiguity around issues of sexual identity. Nevertheless, his stylized depictions of male-male desire and his acknowledgment of his own same-sex attractions have encouraged some critics to conclude that the author held a notably cohesive notion of his sexuality.[17] *Wings,* which instigated his earliest artistic and sexual public reputation, has been read by some as a relatively straightforward story of homosexual self-discovery. But even this early prose work reveals a complex interest in the multiple possibilities of self-fashioning.

Wings centers on the traveling education of Vanya Smurov, who—like Dorian Gray and so many handsome, young, burgeoning aesthetes before him—is an orphan. He is sent to St. Petersburg to live with the Kazanskis, friends of his cousin, but his expectations are not fulfilled by the city, with its "narrow vegetable plots behind gray palings, cemeteries which look from afar like enchanted groves, dank six-storied workers' tenements hulking over tumbledown shacks" (5). The Kazanski home is likewise marked by "steady rain, barrel organs in backyards, newspapers with morning tea, disorder and discomfort in dingy rooms" (8), and crass, bourgeois adults drinking, bickering, and plotting trysts. The middle-class tastelessness to which the Kazanski household aspires comes across in such things as the cheap rings that Anna Nikolayevna wears to breakfast (6) and Koka's cigarette case, which opens to expose the image of a naked woman (27). As Stroop points out to Vanya, however, "You live among people who have nothing to offer you—but perhaps that's for the best: at least you escape the prejudices of a life ordered by tradition, so that there's nothing to prevent you from becoming a truly free spirit, if only you wanted to" (15). It is this same quality of malleability that Lord Henry finds so attractive in Dorian Gray and that places Kuzmin's narrative within the classical Greek tradition of *paederastia*, where education and affection function as mutually supportive elements of a male-male relation.

Not fully appreciating Stroop's encouragement, Vanya hopes to invigorate his spirit by joining the Kazanskis in their summer retreat on the Volga. Abandoning the city for the pastoral countryside does not stop either the young man's development of a keen awareness of his own physical beauty or the bombardment of philosophical conversations that inadvertently encourage his sexual self-realization.[18] "That's why I envy you from the bottom of my heart, Vanya," explains his new friend, Sasha, after a lengthy monologue on the need to leave oneself open to diverse experiences, "you're not being forced to follow one single path, and you know everything and understand everything, not like me, even though we are the same age" (56). The assumption of Vanya's omniscience is doubly ironic coming as it does from a devout Christian. The naïveté of the young speaker, however, enhances the sincerity of his perception that Vanya can choose from a number of paths, thereby also adding weight to Stroop's earlier encouragement that Vanya make a similar recognition. Sasha's claim makes readers more willing to accept the possibility that the worldly-wise homosexual aesthete was speaking in the younger man's best interests.

As with St. Petersburg, Vanya becomes bored with the countryside and, after a coincidental meeting with his homosexual Greek professor, Daniil Ivanovich, agrees to join him on a trip to Italy. This third leg of the hero's travels ends with his arrival at, in a sense, a home to which he had never before been. Through the tutelage of Ivanovich and Stroop, the young man had already been introduced to European high culture, primarily the works of canonized artists such as Botticelli, Cervantes, Dante, Debussy, Marlowe, Mozart, Rameau, and Wagner. Even though

Vanya is unable to understand English well without Stroop's help, Shakespeare's *Romeo and Juliet* fills him with "a sense of beauty and pulsating life, as if something long-unglimpsed, half-forgotten, yet infinitely dear, had risen up and clasped him in a warm embrace" (59). As the echoes of Pater in Vanya's reaction to Shakespeare suggest, Stroop and Ivanovich do not only position their student within a dominant European tradition; they also ensure that he is steeped in the homoerotic classicism celebrated by the aesthetic movement.

When Stroop, sustaining the metaphor of travel as sexual awakening, tells Vanya that "whole worlds lie beyond your ken; a world of beauty too, without a knowledge and love of which no man can call himself educated," he is not discussing physical travel but the study of classical Greek (14). Through this language, Stroop explains, the "soulless doll" is replaced by "a being you can love, kiss or hate, a being with blood flowing in his veins, instinct with the natural grace of the naked body." Vanya eventually learns not only Greek but also Italian; we find him later reading Dante in the original (34). He also becomes familiar with the Greek lyric poet Anacreon and historical and mythological figures such as Marcus Aurelius, Antinous, Icarus, Dionysus, and Ganymede. Ivanovich lectures him on the sexual relations of Achilles and Patroclus and of Orestes and Pylades (26). Later the teacher depicts the statue "Running Youth" using the same homoerotic language that Pater uses in his essay "Winckelmann":

> What does it matter to us now that he is armless and headless? We can still feel the crimson blood pulsing beneath the white skin, and every muscle fills us with a heady rapture. The body itself, the physical substance, will perish, and perhaps even the creations of art—Phidias, Mozart, Shakespeare—will perish, but the idea, the form of beauty contained in them cannot perish, and this, perhaps, is the only thing of value in the changing and transient diversity of life. (85)

Ivanovich describes his plans to visit Athens, Alexandria, and Rome with similar rapture (73). Only a short while back, Vanya seems to have known virtually nothing about these Mediterranean cities, but now, in response to Ivanovich's invitation to travel, he speaks as if he had never imagined going anywhere else: "'Is it really possible—me in Rome?... I can't believe it,' gasped Vanya.... 'You're so good, so kind!' the boy burst forth" (79). In the next scene we find Vanya in Italy, looking "the dandy" and discussing opera with Ivanovich and Ugo Orsini, a seductive musician who wears a red carnation (82–84), an echo of the green carnation that functioned as a signifier in fin de siècle France and England of same-sex male desire. The transition is now complete. Through the assistance of Ivanovich and Stroop—two foreigners, one Greek and the other described sometimes as English and sometimes as half-English—Kuzmin's young Russian is introduced into an elitist community whose identity is deeply rooted in Western European high culture. "We are Hellenes," Stroop declares at one point (32). From the contemporary decadent literature of Swinburne and D'Annunzio to sartorial semiotics, Vanya is also made familiar with the coded discourse of the aestheticist homosexual.

What is distinctly absent from the young man's life experience, however, is any education or travel that addresses what Western Europeans considered "the East." This is not to say that "the East" is not mentioned. More than once, it enters conversation, either as an important facet of classical history or as a desired destination—a location described as familiar yet foreign. The narrator notes the tales of "Italy, Egypt, and India" that are told by the bachelors who visit Stroop's home (31). Orsini envisions his unwritten opera making use of the "Indian *manuels érotiques*" (109). Another character offers a gross summary of a tale from the "Thousand and One Nights" (41), and a canon tells a passionate story of Antinous drowning himself in the Nile for his love of Hadrian (105). Ivanovich dreams of visiting Alexandria and of going to Asia to explore recently excavated works by ancient writers (73), but his actual travels—to the best of our knowledge—lead him only as far as his friends and acquaintances in Italy. European culture makes up the majority of Vanya's education and his travels allow him to experience southern Europe firsthand, but "the East," despite its apparent importance with regard to homosexual identity, remains an exotic realm defined by imaginative texts that do not even function as historical artifacts since, in the novel, they are all delivered orally. This disembodied, foreign, unseen land constitutes the Other by which Kuzmin adopted the Western European aestheticist identity of the homosexual. Moreover, this absent signifier suggests—in part due to its very absence—a greater breadth of sexual potentialities.

Just as *Wings* contains no actual encounters with "the East," the novel also offers no extensive representation of Vanya's consideration of gender and sexuality, despite the centrality of his sexual awakening to the plot. What Kuzmin does do, however, is conspicuously arrest the narrative with a reference to his own poem cycle *Alexandrian Songs*, a text both set in "the East" and heavily invested in sexual identity-drag. The reference occurs when Vanya is mentally and physically on the verge of leaving the social position he held in childhood and entering the community defined by Stroop's homosocial network and its elitist cultural knowledge. On entering Stroop's home for the first time, Vanya hears a male voice singing a song about an exotic, sensual city. The sound makes Vanya hesitate, as he perhaps recognizes for a fleeting instant the shift that is about to occur and considers the possible sexual identities that are still before him, exposed through his growing sexual awareness but limited by the cultural signifiers he is only beginning to comprehend. The lyrics, which are part of the prelude to the *Alexandrian Songs*, ultimately lead the protagonist to a reconsideration of his sexuality and to his first experience of a relatively coherent homosexual identity.[19] The *Songs* thus depict what, in *Wings*, is an omnipresent absence—an imaginative zone through which Kuzmin has Vanya finally translate his essential desire into a cultural discourse.

In the *Alexandrian Songs*, Kuzmin presents characters who are for the most part constant in the direction of their attractions but who collectively signify the polymorphous desire of the narrator. Notwithstanding the fact that various descriptions in the poems make it clear that their narrator is not Vanya, the novel itself suggests that Kuzmin also envisions the songs as a principal catalyst for the sexual epiphany of *Wings*'s hero. The poems bring to mind the work of Constantine Cavafy, whose own stylized depictions of erotic attraction take place in Alexandria. Like Kuzmin, Cavafy not only wrote homosexual and heterosexual verse but also at times obscured the gender of the beloved. Peter Christensen also notes that, in many of Cavafy's poems, "the memory of the beloved seems at least as important as being with him";[20] Kuzmin's songs, which were written at roughly the same time, are likewise presented as remembrances of times past.

The major difference between the two poets' work on Alexandria is that Cavafy was writing about the city in which he was born and in which he spent much of his life, while Kuzmin describes a place he had only visited. As the context for the songs, Alexandria signifies, and apparently offers Kuzmin more opportunity for imagining, what Said calls "a different type of sexuality," an "Oriental sex."[21] However, as Joseph Boone has pointed out, Said does not address the function of same-sex eroticism in orientalist strategies. Instead, his "analyses of colonialist erotics remains ensconced in conspicuously heterosexual interpretative frameworks."[22] The *Alexandrian Songs* accord with Said's model only insofar as they form a contextual otherness for their narrator's and Vanya's exploration of sexual identity. This alterity is empowered by an orientalist potency that the author presents in *Wings* not as a threat but as a liberating expansion of possibilities for imaginative foreplay. Kuzmin's frequent challenge to normative sexual conventions is highlighted by his even more frequent obfuscation of gender categories entirely, leading to Vanya's later, more restricted act of cultural self-fashioning as a homosexual aesthete. Rather than signifying a geography that allows a momentary relaxation of hegemonic strictures or that subverts the hegemony, Kuzmin's orientalism creates a conceptual space in which multiple identities of the desiring subject could be articulated.[23]

The importance to Kuzmin of dislocation as a component of homosexual identity cannot be overemphasized. His repeated suggestions in the *Alexandrian Songs* that the principal narrator is absent from the city implies that the sections framed by the introduction and conclusion are not the products of visual recording but at best recollections. The opening and closing sections of the collection define Alexandria as a mental space whose exotic image stimulates the narrator's lyrics. In the first two poems of the prelude, it is the *sound* of the word "Alexandria" that functions as a catalyst for the narrator's description of the city, while the first poem in "Section II: Love" is inspired specifically by memories of Alexandria, just as the narrator, in the fifth poem of the section, defines memory as the source of imagery. The last of the Prelude's songs ends, "When will I see you, my dear city!" (141). These devices construct Alexandria as both foreign and familiar. The eroticized, distant land is, as for the argonauts of *Wings*, a home somewhere over the rainbow.

The amorphousness of the orientalist experience accords with an obfuscation of the characters' genders. None of the narrators or beloveds of the "Love" section of the cycle are overtly gendered feminine, while fewer than half of the narrators and only one of the beloveds are gendered masculine. Due to the grammar, the gendering of characters is harder to avoid in Russian than in a language such as English, making the lack of such signification for so many of the characters even more remarkable. There are a number of references to the "gray eyes" that Kuzmin frequently associates in his works with male same-sex desire. However, the gray eyes in the author's oeuvre are almost always accompanied by bushy eyebrows, but those in the "Love" section of the *Alexandrian Songs* are not. This absence does not only put gender into question while still signifying same-sex desire but also repeats Vanya's own gray eyes, which similarly lack the bushy brows.

Among the relations in the *Alexandrian Songs* that are gender-definable, male-male affection is implied most often. The third section of the collection, "She," is unique in this regard, because five of its six songs have a feminine-gendered narrator and four of them have a beloved who is gendered masculine. Kuzmin might have taken on an overtly female persona in order to justify to a homophobic readership his erotic depiction of men, but this maneuver is excessively cautious for somebody whose other works both offer numerous homoerotic passages and discuss homosexuality directly. Furthermore, this particular section of the *Alexandrian Songs* actually has few physical descriptions, making such a strategy unwarranted. Indeed, the most extensive description in the section occurs when the narrator of the fourth song orientalizes herself:

> Is it not true
> that I am foremost in Alexandria
> in the magnificence of sumptuous attire
> in the value of white steeds and silver harness,
> in the length of black tresses, cunningly entwined?
> Is there anyone who can
> paint her eyes more skillfully than I
> and dip each finger
> in a separate fragrance? (5–13)

An interpretation of the section "She" as heterosexual fails to address why one of the collection's most vivid descriptions of a woman is given by a female narrator. Nor does such a reading explain why Kuzmin placed his most extensive physical and psychological representations of women in the only section in which specifically female narrators discuss those they love. While the person or people who are desired in the section "She" are predominantly gendered masculine, the subjects described are more often the female narrators themselves and their sisters. Kuzmin's gender-drag, rather than covering up his interest in same-sex affection, actually emphasizes it.

Notably, the limitations of Kuzmin's adaptation of aestheticism are made apparent in the songs in "She" that suggest potential lesbian identification. At the top of the fifth poem in the section, Kuzmin notes that the piece is in imitation of Pierre Louÿs, a writer known for the lesbian erotics of his works, many of which are set in a mythical Alexandria. The author had read both Louÿs's "Chansons de Bilitis" (1894) and *Aphrodite* (1896) prior to finishing the *Alexandrian Songs*.[24] He presents lesbianism most often in "She" through images of narcissism—a strategy that he frequently uses in other works to depict male homosexuals or burgeoning homosexuals such as Vanya.[25] The fourth song of "She" has a narcissistic narrator who, while claiming to think of nothing but the one with "gray eyes beneath thick brows," nevertheless dwells on her own virtues and feminine beauty, as does the narrator of the fifth song. Louÿs employs a similar tactic in *Aphrodite,* where semi-naked, apparently heterosexual women carry on extensive conversations about the beauty of each other's bodies.[26] In the sixth song, the narrator is enamored of a man perched on her windowsill who claims to have mistaken *her* for a bird. After being coerced into kissing him, the narrator, instead of weaving the intended narcissus on her loom, absent-mindedly weaves a rose (the flower the man claimed was in his mouth). The narrator's narcissism is replaced here by heterosexual desire, which has been signified for centuries in Western literature by the highly prized rose.[27]

Only the first poem of "She" has a woman whose description of females is not overtly related to narcissism. After having the narrator describe her and her sisters' loves, wishes, and losses, however, Kuzmin has the poem end with the enigmatic couplet: "There were four of us sisters, four of us sisters there were, / but, can it be, there were not four of us, but five?" In this brief, repetitive song, there is no reference to anybody but the narrator, her three sisters, and their lovers. While the narrator refers to the three men loved by her sisters, she never once describes the person she herself loves. Even the gender of the object of her desire remains invisible. The narrator's description of her own relationship thus initially appears as self-centered as those of the more overtly narcissistic narrators, with the object of desire being virtually erased from the lover's discourse. This apparent lack draws attention to that enigmatic "fifth sister" who appears at the end of the poem.

Kuzmin's representations of female eroticism depend on conventions derived from either the heterosexual orientalization of the female body or the male homosexual language with which he was familiar. Though he attempts to create a space for lesbian maneuvering, he appears to find (or lose) himself in an imaginative void, unable to conceptualize a uniquely lesbian subject position because he lacks a language that he sees as specifically lesbian. This dilemma leads him to erase the sensual aspects of lesbianism, leaving only a trace of the gender of the beloved in the final reference to a "fifth sister," enacting what Terry Castle discusses as the tradition in art and literature of "ghosting" the lesbian into an apparitional context of secondary status.[28] Unlike Kuzmin's representation of male narcissism in such works as *Wings*, "Autumn Lake" (1912), and "The Trout Breaks the Ice" (1929), his images of female narcissism in the *Alexandrian Songs* do not conceptualize a cultural space for same-sex desire. Though allowing the women to objectify themselves, he never shows them applying their agency in relation to other individuals, and he never overtly depicts female-female affection. The lesbian-erotic songs therefore leave open the door to an orientalist, heteronormative reading of woman-as-object.

Halfway through the final song in the collection, the anonymous narrator shifts from discussing the departure from Alexandria, which, as noted earlier, is a mnemonic departure, to discussing the departure from the ambiguously gendered "you, my joy":

> Various beauty will I see
> into various eyes I shall gaze my fill,
> various lips will I kiss,
> to various curls will I give my caresses,
> and various names will I whisper
> at planned engagements in various groves.
> I will see all, but not you! (13–19)

The narrator's conclusion to the polymorphous memories of Alexandria endows the beloved with no gender-specificity. Indeed, rather than offering a final erotic blazon or even a fleeting image of the beloved left behind, the narrator becomes engrossed in the multitude of amorous possibilities that lie ahead, the repetition of the word "various" stimulating the tempo that leads to the swinging alliteration of the penultimate line: "Bozhidani svidanii v raznikh roschakh" (18). Even at the end of *Alexandrian Songs*, Kuzmin does not suggest a coherent identity for the speaker of the framing poems. By denying a resolution to his imaginative gender-drag, Kuzmin returns the reader to an occidental reality highlighting its own multiple orientations. One audience member for the poetry cycle who is influenced by this move is Vanya. The positioning of the *Alexandrian Songs* within someone's mind correlates with his own epiphanic state while he listens, transfixed, to the songs being sung in Stroop's home.

The reviews of *Wings* make it clear that the textual references to homosexuality were not beyond Kuzmin's contemporary readers. Laura Engelstein cites a number of critics who repudiated Kuzmin's work as "both politically retrograde and morally depraved."[29] For the yet wingless Vanya, however, the various innuendos of the adults among whom he circulates remain ambiguous. While the narrator tells us that, of late, "Vanya had taken to brushing his hair and paying more attention to his toilette," and that he often "examined his reflection in the little wall mirror," he himself only "gaz[ed] indifferently.... The tall, finely made, delicate-browed boy in the black blouse neither pleased nor displeased him" (7). Though unaffected by his own beauty, Vanya, when he passes the mirror later, cannot help "stare again . . . at his flushed face with its gray eyes and delicately-drawn brows" (10). Objectifying himself, noticing his own "childish pout" and "fair hair . . . curled slightly" (10), he does not consider the possibility that his burgeoning narcissism may carry sexual relevance. Nor does he address the numerous early hints that characters give him regarding Stroop's and Ivanovich's homosexuality (16, 21, 20, 30). It is not until he hears part of the *Alexandrian Songs* that the young man realizes his desire to live in Stroop's cultured, homosocial world:

> Then came the sound of men's voices in lazy conversation, and Vanya went through to the drawing room. How he loved this spacious room with its translucent greens, haunted by echoes of Rameau and Debussy, . . . these late bachelor suppers, convivial with wine and light-hearted talk; this study lined with books from floor to ceiling, where they read Marlowe and Swinburne, this bedroom with its toilet stand and its garland of terra-cotta fauns dancing on a background of bright green; this dining room with its coppery hues; these tales of Italy, Egypt, India; this ardent responsiveness to all poignantly lovely things, whatever age or clime had brought them forth; these strolls about the Islands; . . . this all-pervasive odor of *peau d'Espagne* with its hint of decay; these lean, strong fingers, barbaric with rings. . . . (31)

Although a number of readers realized that Stroop's home is homosexually coded, it remains beyond Vanya at this stage in his sexual self-fashioning. And yet, despite his lack of awareness regarding cultural knowledge, he prefers the aestheticist environment over the mainstream. The mysterious man playing the piano and singing about the "peacocks of Juno" and "pomegranates and lemons" draws Vanya from the Kazanski household to Stroop's homosexual haven, with neither realm being explicitly defined by Vanya's sexuality. In accord with Kuzmin's notion of desire as transitory, Vanya is unable to label his emotions, noting only that "he loved all this, without knowing what it was that drew him to it" (32). By referencing the *Alexandrian Songs,* however, Kuzmin counters the notion that individuals simply drift into environments that accommodate their fundamental sensibilities. Within the liminal space signified by "the piano's sonorous chords veil[ing] the voice's yearning phrases as in a mist" (31), the multiplicity of identities offered in the orientalist *Alexandrian Songs* penetrate the hero's consciousness. He then crosses the threshold into the bachelor's drawing room, choosing an identity that, while culturally constructed, offers the best fit for what he feels are his innate sensual desires.

In this essay I have argued that, while Kuzmin's *Alexandrian Songs* are a complete mnemonic cycle in themselves, they also create a crucial interstitial space in *Wings.* Through them, the novel's protagonist performs an orientalist drag during which he imaginatively tries on various sexual and gender identities. The novel's textual embedding, moreover, does not only represent the dissipation of a character's sexual uncertainty but also constitutes the author's own interrogation of sexual polyvalency.

Notwithstanding its support of Kuzmin's desires, aestheticism, because of its tendency to orientalize Eastern Europeans, still did not offer him a secure sense of belonging. Wishing to erase this tincture of orientalism, Kuzmin doused the Russian homosexuals of *Wings* in classical Western European cultural references. But in order for his Russo-friendly aestheticism to maximize its emulation of the dominant model, he still had to establish a familiar yet foreign marker of both its outer limits and its elitism in relation to the status quo. This he constructed as a mythic, sensual Egypt. Thus, rather than directly critiquing aestheticism's orientalist structure, he simply shifted its boundaries of privilege so that they more readily accommodated Russian homosexuals such as himself.

No longer envisioned as another exotic stereotype passively welcoming the aesthetes to his "own dear land," Kuzmin is now on board, rowing as one with the argonauts. But the author also inadvertently signals the limitations of this modification, most distinctly by the fact that he remains unable to advocate a self-defining lesbian persona, let alone identity. His efforts to broaden the community supported by aestheticism are, in other words, of limited success because he only questions the boundaries of its orientalism and not its exclusionist politics in general.

These shortcomings of Kuzmin's work are not especially surprising since there is little in *Wings* to suggest that his efforts were aimed at addressing orientalism. Rather, in line with aestheticist tradition, the novel's agenda is consistently depicted as that of challenging homophobia only. To this end, the text—combined with the immense impact that his writing had on Russian gay culture—did move aestheticism beyond its privileging of Western Europeans by allowing a broader range of individuals to feel a sense of community in which their inchoate sexual identities could be realized. Moreover, Kuzmin's exposure of aestheticism's Western European bias may have been limited in scope to addressing his own sense of marginalization, but it nevertheless does accord with postcolonialist aims of redressing the injustices of national and ethnic stereotyping.

Notes

1. Mikhail Kuzmin, *Wings, Prose and Poetry,* trans. and ed. Neil Granoien and Michael Green (Ann Arbor: Ardis, 1972), 33. The novel was originally published as *Wings* in 1906. Further quotations from this book will be referenced in the text. All translations of Russian texts are my own, except for quotations from *Wings,* which are taken from the above translation. While an excellent English translation of the *Alexandrian Songs* is available, I have translated the quotations from this text myself because it has been necessary on occasion to sacrifice formal elements of the poems in order to ensure the clarity or, in many cases, the ambiguity of the meaning of the original.

2. Michel Foucault, *Power/Knowledge: Selected Interviews and Other Writings 1972–77,* ed. Colin Gordon (Hertfordshire, UK: Harvester, 1980), 82.

3. Walter Pater, *The Renaissance,* intro. Kenneth Clark (Cleveland: Meridian, 1967).

4. Walter Pater, *Marius the Epicurean* (Oxford: Oxford University Press, 1986), 11.

5. Pater, *Marius the Epicurean,* 243–44.

6. H. Trivedi, *Colonial Transactions: English Literature and India* (Calcutta: Papyrus, 1993), 1.

7. Edward Said, *Orientalism* (New York: Vintage, 1979), 40; 17; 99–100; 191.

8. *Orientalism*, 26, 191.

9. Greta N. Slobin, "Revolution Must Come First: Reading V. Aksenov's *Island of Crimea*," in *Nationalisms and Sexualities*, ed. Andrew Parker, Mary Russo, Doris Sommer, and Patricia Yaeger (New York: Routledge, 1992), 246.

10. Homi Bhabha, "The Other Question: Difference, Discrimination, and the Discourse of Colonialism," in *Literature, Politics, and Theory*, ed. Francis Barker, Peter Hulme, and Margaret Iverson (London: Methuen, 1986), 169.

11. The function of colonialism as a means of categorizing and containing deviant elements within imperialist nations themselves is explored more thoroughly in Anne McClintock's *Imperial Leather: Race, Gender, and Sexuality in the Colonial Context* (New York: Routledge, 1995).

12. Nationalist accusations of sexual deviance were being thrown about Europe during the nineteenth century as if they were hot potatoes. For a summary of some of these gestures of self-empowerment, see Melanie Hawthorne's "'Comment Peut-on Être Homosexuel?' Multinational (In)Corporation and the Frenchness of *Salomé*," in *Perennial Decay: On the Aesthetics and Politics of Decadence*, ed. Liz Constable, Dennis Denisoff, and Matthew Potolsky (Philadelphia: University of Pennsylvania Press, 1999).

13. Vernon Lee, *Miss Brown* (1884; New York: Garland, 1978), vol. 2: 243. Talia Schaffer analyzes *Dracula* as a response to the Oscar Wilde trials in her essay "'A Wilde Desire Took Me': The Homoerotic History of *Dracula*," *ELH* 61 (1994): 381–425. On Lee and Woolf, see my essay "The Forest Beyond the Frame: Picturing Women's Desires in Vernon Lee and Virginia Woolf," in *Gender and British Aestheticism*, ed. Talia Schaffer and Kathy A. Psomiades (Charlottesville: University Press of Virginia, 2000).

14. George Du Maurier, *Trilby* (London: J. M. Dent, 1992), 47.

15. Said, *Orientalism*, 27–28.

16. Robert Aldrich summarizes the role of the Mediterranean in Russian homosexual culture in *Seduction of the Mediterranean: Writing, Art, and Homosexual Fantasy* (London: Routledge, 1993).

17. In "Historicity, Lyricism, and the Homosexual Imperative of the Kuzminian Text" (Ph.D. diss., University of Pennsylvania, 1991), Lindsay F. Watton, for example, states that turn-of-the-century Russian homosexuality is "the unique product of a combination of ideological discourses" (14) but then also assumes that Kuzmin was always able to act and write as a homosexual, or always chose to do so. Laura Engelstein's claim in *Keys to Happiness: Sex and the Search for Modernity in Fin-de-Siècle Russia* (Ithaca: Cornell University Press, 1992) that heterosexual relations "had little interest for Kuzmin" (397) is more accurate, although it does not address the diverse desires in such texts as the *Alexandrian Songs*. Notably, some scholars have concluded that Kuzmin's same-sex interests are a minor issue in his writing. In a discussion of the "object of [Kuzmin's] deepest longing" in the *Alexandrian Songs*, Joachim Baer refrains from alluding to homosexuality until the final paragraph, at which point he asks, "but who is the 'thee' in the last line whom he will never see.... Is it his muse, is it a real woman, or maybe even a man?" ("Mikhail Kuzmin's 'Aleksandrijskie Pesni,'" in *South Atlantic Bulletin* 41, no. 1 [1976]: 30). For Baer, the heterosexual possibility suggests a "real" woman, while the homosexual possibility comes across as less feasible. Vladimir Markov claims that "almost all of Kuzmin's homosexual poetry can

be seen as poems about the 'normal' love of a man for a woman" ("Poezia Mikhaila Kuzmina," in *Sobranie stikhotvorenij,* by Mikhail Kuzmin. Munich: Fink Verlag, 1977, 331). Despite the scare quotes, Markov suggests here that a consideration of homosexuality is not necessary for a full appreciation of Kuzmin's poetry.

18. For some of the more thorough articulations of the amorality of desire and identity formation in *Wings,* see pages 14–15, 25–26, 32–33, 41–42, and 48–50.

19. Vladimir Markov observes that Kuzmin could have modeled the pianist whom Vanya hears singing in Stroop's house on himself; see Markov's preface to *Wings, Prose and Poetry,* trans. and ed. Neil Granoien and Michael Green, xi. For a discussion of the similarities between the plot of *Wings* and Kuzmin's own life, see John E. Malmstad, "Mixail Kuzmin: A Chronicle of His Life and Times," in *Sobranie stikhotvorenij,* 42–47.

20. Peter G. Christensen, "C. V. Cavafy," in *The Gay and Lesbian Literary Heritage,* ed. Claude Summers (New York: Henry Holt, 1995), 150.

21. Said, *Orientalism,* 190.

22. Joseph A Boone, "Vacation Cruises; or, The Homoerotics of Orientalism," *PMLA* 110, no. 1 (1995): 90.

23. For discussions of orientalist representations of Alexandria in literature, see Aldrich, *Seduction of the Mediterranean,* as well as E. M. Forster, *Alexandria: A History and a Guide* (Oxford: Oxford University Press, 1986).

24. Malmstad, "Mixail Kuzmin," 73.

25. For a discussion of narcissism in Kuzmin's writing, see Irina Paperno, "Dvoinichestvo i Lyubovnii Treugol'nik: Poeticheskii Mif Kuzmina i yevo Pushkinskaya Proektsiya," in *Studies in the Life and Works of Mixail Kuzmin,* ed. John E. Malmstad (Wein, 1989), 57–82.

26. Pierre Louÿs, *Aphrodite: Moeurs antiques* (Paris: Fayard, 1927).

27. The quintessential configuration of the rose as a symbol of heterosexual love appears in the medieval French allegorical romance *Roman de la Rose,* by Guillaume de Lorris and Jean de Meun. Back-to-back depictions of the love of Narcissus and the love of the Rose appear in sections 6 and 7 of this work.

28. Terry Castle, *The Apparitional Lesbian: Female Homosexuality and Modern Culture* (New York: Columbia University Press, 1993).

29. Engelstein, *Keys to Happiness,* 391. For additional references to critical responses to Kuzmin's novel, see Neil Granoien's unpublished dissertation, "Mixail Kuzmin: An Aesthete's Prose" (Ph.D. diss., University of California, 1981).

CHAPTER THIRTEEN

Sex/Race Wars on the Frontier:
Homosexuality and Colonialism in
The Golden Notebook

Joseph A. Boone

> I have no time for people who haven't experimented with them-
> selves, deliberately tried the frontiers.
> —Anna in *The Golden Notebook*

> In the objectification of the scopic drive, there is always the threatened
> return of the look; in the identification of the Imaginary relation
> there is always the alienating other (or mirror) which crucially
> returns its image to the subject.
> —Homi Bhabha, "The Other Question"

An acute awareness of modernity, to paraphrase Linda Kauffman, runs
throughout Doris Lessing's *The Golden Notebook* (1962),[1] a novel that
imparts a sweepingly global vision of what Lessing calls "the ideological
'feel' of our mid-century" and the "great debates of our time" (xi). Con-
fronting what she sees as the cataclysmic breakdown of existing systems
of Enlightenment order, Lessing tackles a number of "major" issues and
debates, from Marxism to psychology to feminism, most of which have
been amply dissected by the Lessing industry that ran riot in the 1960s
and 1970s. I want to suggest, however, that we might find this novel worth
another look in light of certain modes of contemporary criticism that
have flourished since the heyday of Lessing's popularity—particularly
postcolonial and queer theory—for both these methods shed a revealing light on the dynamics of the "battle of the sexes" that forms the
overt subject matter of this epically proportioned attempt to find a fictional form capable of encompassing the history of the first half of the

twentieth century.[2] Indeed, I will argue that the colonialist setting highlighted in the novel's first notebook entry—the Black Notebook in which the protagonist Anna Wulf recalls the war years that she spent in the British Crown Colony of race-segregated Southern Rhodesia—is crucially connected to the specter of homosexuality that, in the latter sections of the novel, becomes the wellspring for the sexual and textual anxieties that form its psychodramatic core. The link between homosexuality, which first manifests itself in Southern Rhodesia and then stages a "return of the repressed" in Anna's London life, and the politics of racial segregation dovetails, intriguingly, with the novel's feminist politics as well: for if what we now call apartheid in Africa is the formative experience that underlies Anna's coming of age and inspires her first bestselling novel, *Frontiers of War* (an interracial love story between colonizer and colonized), this same experience creates the template for understanding male oppression that Anna brings back to England, in the form of "sexual apartheid." Just how race consciousness and heterosexual apartheid strangely metamorphose into homosexual panic will lead us squarely into the critical domains marked out by contemporary queer and postcolonial theory.

The fact that homosexuality is virtually the only issue that has gone unremarked in the vast amounts of criticism written about *The Golden Notebook* since its publication in 1962 is itself telling, especially given the curiously prominent yet "out of place" role that male same-sex desire plays in the trajectory of the novel, linking together its much more visible debates. In fact, the text is bracketed by two seemingly offhanded references to "queers" made to Anna Wulf by her best friend Molly in the first and last sections of "Free Women," the narrative that surrounds notebook entries that make up the bulk of the novel. Occurring as they do at the novel's beginning and end, these references suggest that what has been said offhandedly is perhaps of some consequence after all. What are the sexual anxieties being bracketed by these references, and what do the anxieties that they index have to do with the psychosexual and libidinal trajectories of this politically charged novel?

The first reference occurs when Molly, who is an actress, talks about what it is like returning to England after having spent time on the Continent. Currently, she is rehearsing a play in which, she jokes to Anna, "Every man in the cast is a queer but one, and he's sixteen. So what am I doing here?" (47). In this case, the "queer" reference forms a segue to

Molly's real point: the inadequacies of *heterosexual* English men, who know neither how to make women feel "like women" nor how to put women at ease sexually. The problematic heterosexual politics of nation and manhood thus come to seem the logical outcome of the stream of associations set into motion by Molly's throwaway reference to the sexual orientation of her fellow cast members but one. The second reference occurs within a page of the end of the text, when Anna asks Molly how her ex-husband's second wife (Marion) is faring now that she too has left Richard. Throughout the novel, the pathetically weak-willed, alcoholic, and helpless Marion has provided a foil to the "free women" that Anna and Molly aspire to be, and in response to Anna's inquiry Molly reveals that Marion has abandoned her latest fashionable cause—African racial politics—for another kind of chic: setting up a dress shop in Knightsbridge. Molly delivers a final twist to her putdown of Marion when she sardonically adds, "She's already surrounded herself with a gaggle of little queers who exploit her and she adores them and she giggles a lot and drinks just a *little* too much, and thinks they are ever such fun" (665). A truly "free" or independent woman, we're left to infer, does not surround herself with imitation men who serve as rich women's companions in the absence of the real thing. This portrait of Marion not only diminishes Marion's break from Richard by infantalizing her behavior as childish but also denigrates male homosexuals (note the repetition of "little" that links these men and Marion) by implying that they exploit women whom they cannot sexually satisfy, perhaps *because* they cannot satisfy them.

The common denominator in both of these instances, it seems, is less the condescending attitude that Molly and Anna display toward "queers" than the scarcity of heterosexual men willing to engage women such as themselves on a level of parity. The following argument takes up the complex and often devious routes by which the "male problem" for free women like Anna and Molly is deflected onto, as it were, other "Others"— a category that includes the victims of racial oppression with whom Anna emphatically *identifies* during her war years in Africa as well as the homosexual men in her present-day London life, with whom she and Molly strenuously try to *disidentify*. The failure of heterosexual men and women to establish non-antagonistic relationships in the mid-twentieth century, Lessing implies, is emblematic of the larger breakdown in communication that is constitutive of contemporary Western civilization and its claims to global hegemony, leading to the increasing meaninglessness, division, and disorder that informs Anna's inability to write, to love, or to maintain psychic equilibrium.

Cracking Apart, Cracking Open

The Golden Notebook begins on a note of division and fragmentation, as revealed in the first words that Anna Wulf speaks on the opening page: "the point is, that as far as I can see, everything's cracking up" (3). The topos of things falling apart extends, indeed, in all directions—Anna's disillusion with the political ideals she has invested in the British Communist party; the failure of her and Molly's various romances; the psychic divisions signaled by the nervous breakdowns and descents into madness that beset various characters; the dissolution of traditionally unifying concepts such as nation and empire. Nor is art, as Anna realizes, immune to such fragmentation. As she writes in the Black Notebook, "the modern novel has become a function of the fragmented society, the fragmented consciousness," whose manifestations are both global and individual: "Human beings are so divided, are becoming more and more divided, *and more subdivided in themselves,* reflecting the world" (61). As much as Anna dreams of writing "a book powered with an intellectual or moral passion strong enough to create order, to create a new way of looking at life" (61)—thereby aligning herself within the modernist tradition that flourished before the Second World War—she despairs that the moment for the modernist faith in imposing artistic order over chaos has been rendered obsolete by the prospects of "general annihilation" (243) augured by the political crises defining the Cold War world: the Korean War, the Suez crisis, the McCarthy hearings in the United States, Communist atrocities in Eastern Europe, A-bomb and H-bomb testings, rumors of germ warfare. In *The Golden Notebook,* the modernist worldview is shown in the process of becoming a postmodernist one, and Anna finds herself trapped in the midst of this shift, the victim of self-doubt, writer's block, and political impotence.

In attempting to give representation to this liminal moment, to capture this sense of a global order and a humanist notion of identity in the process of "crack up," Lessing creates a convoluted, fragmented narrative structure that straddles both modernist and postmodernist sensibilities. Foremost, the text is composed of excerpts from four colored Notebooks into which Anna attempts to segregate or "subdivide" the "divided" components of her life and psyche: Black for her African years and first novel *(Frontiers of War)*, Red for her political involvement, Yellow for the draft of her unfinished novel *(Shadow of the Third)*, and Blue for her diary (the fifth or Golden Notebook represents Anna's ambiguous attempt to synthesize these components into one document). These entries are interspersed with the contemporary narrative, "Free Women," which appears to be an omnisciently narrated account of Anna's life but which turns out to be a novella that Anna has written, thus comprising, in addition to *Frontiers of War* and *Shadow of the Third*, another fictionalized version of her life. The continual alternation between the notebooks and the "Free Women" novella creates a series of spatial and temporal overlaps and disjunctions that serves several purposes. First, the divided, fragmented narrative form reflects Anna's—and Lessing's—perception of a radically alienated world. Second, by offering the reader multifaceted, often contradictory portraits of Anna through various personae she creates, the narrative structure reflects a modern sense of the relativity of perception. Like a palimpsest, each narrative layer reveals a dimension of experience or fantasy obscured, omitted, repressed in the other narratives. The effect is to destabilize the hierarchy maintaining truth's superiority to fiction, and, indeed, at times certain "facts" of Anna's life are more accurately conveyed in her fiction than in the supposedly more objective narrative passages. Reading the summary of the novel *Frontiers of War* against her recollections of Rhodesia in the Black Notebook, or the incomplete novel *The Shadow of the Third* in the Yellow Notebook against her otherwise barely mentioned relationship with a lover named Michael, or the "Free Women" novella against the notebook entries documenting Anna's descent into madness with "Saul Green," who may or may not be an actual person, sets into play a series of mirroring refractions that refuse a single truth, creating a quintessentially self-conscious novel that is as much about the process—or (im)possibility—of writing modern fiction as it is about the events it "represents."[3]

The theme of "crack up" announced on the first page of the novel, then, reverberates on social, formal, and psychological levels, and all of these attest to the twentieth-century legacy of Lessing's ambitious authorial enterprise.[4] While the result for her protagonist is a state of severe artistic and emotional paralysis that manifests itself as writer's block and drives her into psychoanalysis, it is telling that Anna actually never stops writing, as the proliferation and expansion of the notebooks handily attests. This paradox leads Anna to ponder whether "my chang-ing everything into fiction is simply a means of *concealing something from myself*" (229; emphasis added). What is concealed, however, makes itself legible in furtive returns. Perhaps the most overt example of a narrative as well as a psychological return of the repressed occurs in Anna's very first entry in her Black Notebook. Under a column headed by the portentous word "Source," Anna unearths her wartime memories of Southern Rhodesia, especially the weekends she spent in the country with her leftist friends at the Mashopi Hotel—gatherings that inspired her best-selling novel *Frontiers of War*. But the actual events that Anna now remembers and records, as we will shortly see, reveal the degree to which her novel's story of colonial romance and miscegenation has cov-ered over and romanticized the homosexual nuances of its "Source" material. Just as this notebook marks Anna's recovery of this repressed history, I suggest that her African experience also functions as the "Source" underlying the textual repressions on which *the novel itself* rests. That is, entire text of *The Golden Notebook* may form a reworking and displace-ment of the catastrophic events—in which race and homophobia col-lide—revealed in this chronologically displaced narration of Anna's so-journ in Africa during the Second World War.

Practices of Apartheid, at Home and Abroad

The colonial experience of racial division that shadows Anna's past sets the terms for the uneasy relation of the personal and the political that stymies her subsequent efforts as a writer and whole human being. Grad-ually settled by British entrepreneurs in the late 1880s, Southern Rhode-sia—referred to as "the Colony" in the *Notebook*—was formally annexed by Britain in 1923 and granted the status of a British Crown Colony with the right to self-governance. Only as the grip of the British empire began to wane in the aftermath of the Second World War did the country gradually move toward a very fraught independence in the 1950s and 1960s.[5] In the novel, as in Lessing's personal experience, the war intro-duced into the racially divided colony a number of "alien influences," including not only restless, independent women like Anna (who arrives in the country on the eve of the war in 1939) but young Cambridge- and Oxford-educated RAF men filled, as Michael Thorpe puts it, with "the fresh Marxist idealism of the 'thirties"[6] and various political and intel-lectual refugees from Hitler's Europe. To the novel's exiles, the color bar in colonial Rhodesia forms an obvious political cause, and it galvanizes their formation of the Communist discussion group and weekend outings to the Masophi Hotel so pivotal to Anna's developing political consciousness. In the next section I will show how Anna's fictionalization in *Frontiers of War* of her past experience of racial segregation significantly alters these facts. What I want to emphasize here is the way in which Anna "imports" this knowledge of minority discrimination back to England, to which she returns at the end of the war, in the displaced form of sexual apartheid, the systematic oppression of women that depends on the division between and opposition of the sexes. That is, Anna's awakening to her second-class status as a woman is profoundly if largely subconsciously shaped by her prior experience of racial discrimination in Africa.

The substitutive logic that underlies this slippage from racial to sexual oppression guides Lessing's offhanded comment, in a 1966 interview with Florence Howe, that "the relationship between the sexes everywhere, not just in Western society, is so much a melting pot, that *it's like the color bar,* all kinds of emotions that don't belong get sucked in."[7] Even more to the point, we can see this and other related displacements at work in Anna's subconscious when, at the height of the "sex war" that precipitates her and Saul Green's ultimate descent into madness in the latter third of the text, she dreams of being back at the Mashopi Hotel, where she must fight to "re-enter" and reclaim her body from colonization by others. In an immediately following dream sequence, she envisions herself inhabiting "dark" skin and her "pen" transformed into a "gun" as she confronts an unknown "enemy" on a distant battlefield. At this point she realizes that she is an Algerian rebel fighting for independence against the French colonizers (600). The axis of colonizer/colonized that makes possible the dream's displacement of the pairing of Britain/Rhodesia for that of France/Algeria prefigures, as well, the conflict of man (colonizer) against woman (colonized)—and, more specifically, Saul against Anna—that frames the entire dream sequence. Anna has gone to sleep with the sex war being waged between her and Saul weighing heavily on her mind, and she awakens as Saul returns to her bed fresh from the arms of another woman, "smiling, a man conscious of his power with women." His challenge to Anna, "Why don't you fight me? Why don't you fight?," thus recapitulates the content of her dream on a sexual rather than racial level (603).

Another example of the psychic process whereby race comes to signify sexual conflict in Anna's subconscious occurs a few pages earlier as Anna, lying in bed with Saul, hallucinates that she has become the mad Charlie Themba, a black nationalist leader "hated by the white men and disowned by his comrades" (593). Shortly afterward, she feels herself metamorphosing into Charlie's antithesis, the noble South African populist Tom Mathlong: "I tried to imagine myself, *a black man in white-occupied territory,* humiliated in his human dignity" (597; emphasis added). In both cases, the stated terms of racial difference could as easily gloss Anna's perception of her minority status as a woman: for in her experience, her sex too is "hated by white men," and she too feels herself an interloper in "white, male-occupied territory." Such metaphors make explicit the connection between Anna's experience in Rhodesia and the "sex wars" that she experiences back "home" in England, experiences that transform her own "native" land into a menacing frontier, a constant battleground, and the site of her own colonization.[8]

The transformation of the sexual stakes of this war into textual ones is driven home in Anna's sadomasochistic affair with Saul Green, an out-of-work Hollywood writer (he has expatriated to London because of his leftist politics) whose aggressively self-defensive words strike Anna like bullets: "I, I, I, I—I began to feel as if the word I was being shot at me like bullets from a machine gun. For a moment I fancied that his mouth . . . was a gun of some kind" (556). As the metaphor of deathly combat indicates, this so-called war of the sexes is not an isolated problem but intrinsic to the larger schisms and hatreds hastening the disintegration and fragmentation of modern life. The responsibility for this deeply engrained antagonism, Lessing takes pains to illustrate, lies in the attitude and behavior of men who take the entitlements of masculinity for granted. All the men in the novel operate according to a socially sanctioned sexual double standard that works to confirm their sense of power over women by allowing them to cheat on their wives or lovers as often as possible, all the while condemning those women who attempt to exercise a similar freedom. Virtually every man with whom Anna has a sexual relationship is either married, relegating Anna to the position of the "third" (hence the title of the unfinished novel, *The Shadow of the Third*), or flaunts his sexual conquests with other women in front of Anna to let her know that she cannot expect an exclusive relationship with or commitment from him. Typical is the extreme "hostility and aggression" with which a casual lover, DeSilva, forces Anna to listen to his accounts of abusing other women, and to which she passively accedes with a deadened passivity and "listless terror" that frightens her (503, 501).

DeSilva's behavior, as well as the helpless response it calls forth in Anna, anticipates the harrowing depths of the sadomasochistic relationship into which Anna and Saul ultimately plunge. For Saul's "totally self-pitying, cold, calculating, emotionless" behavior (572) is simply an extreme version of the masculine front displayed by all the male lovers Anna has known. What men's sadistic behavior toward women simultaneously reveals and attempts to hide, Lessing dramatizes, is a desperate desire for mastery that coexists with the fear that any show of emotion will betray the fictitiousness of their power. The talismanic sign of this always suspect male authority, of which these men are all too aware, is the constant threat of being exposed as sexually incompetent, or worse, impotent. Molly's roguish ex-husband Richard—one of the captains of English industry—reveals he cannot get it up with his wife Marion; Anna and her Rhodesian lover, the German exile Willi, have a sexless relationship; Comrade Nelson, whom Anna knows from her Party connections, is a "sexual cripple" who hysterically browbeats himself for evincing "a mortal terror of sex" (484); Milt (who appears in the final interlude of the "Free Woman" novella as a more benign double of Saul) confesses he cannot sleep with women he *likes*. In turn, this sexual incompetence is almost inevitably projected by the men back onto the women, either for being unresponsive or for being "castrating" bitches (451), that is, "liberated" women whose sexual and financial independence challenges men on their own turf.

Understandably, such attitudes affect the self-conceptions that women such as Anna and Molly carry in their psyches. As Anna laconically notes, being a "free" woman in this society ironically doesn't mean being an autonomous self but rather being viewed as "free" sexual goods that any man thinks he has a right to fuck. This situation creates a contradictory psychological bind for women like Anna: on the one hand, it increases her hatred of the male sex as an utterly alien species, while on the other it creates the crisis of hyperfemininity typical of the 1950s—the desire to be perceived by men as a "real woman" rather than a castrator, a woman whose soft femininity will one day attract a "real man" rather than an abusive or infantile lover.[9] The burden created by this psychosexual impasse, Lessing shows, is an emotional numbness that only enforces a posture of terrorized passivity before these unrelenting male assaults: this is truly the "Cold War" brought home to the heterosexual bedroom of the 1950s with a vengeance. "The sex was cold, an act of hatred, hateful," Anna says of an encounter in which Saul virtually rapes her, turned on by her "No," even as she finds herself "obediently" bowing to this violation: "I could not have refused" (585). Given Anna's sexual experiences with men, the degree of internalized rage she feels— free but not free, having affairs but unfulfilled—is inevitable. "Sleeping with the enemy," Lessing emphasizes, is an age-old female dilemma that in the supposedly more enlightened sexual era of the postwar world proves neither the path to individual peace of mind nor social harmony.[10]

Colonial Lessons in Homophobia

What happens to this rage, however, is curious. Unable, or unwilling, to admit the utter insufficiency of heterosexual men to fulfill a modern woman's needs, Anna projects her rage onto another "species" of men, namely those nonheterosexual men who become scapegoats for what remains unspeakable about their straight counterparts. This is an effect not only of Anna's subconscious displacements but of Lessing's own blind spot in the sex wars she otherwise so incisively lays bare. A key to understanding the complicated dynamics at work in this process of projection and displacement lies—as I have already hinted—in the initial, Black Notebook's record of the events that actually occurred at the Mashopi Hotel during the war. For Anna's attempt in this notebook to recover the significance of her African experience of oppression opens the door through which the previously repressed subject of homosexuality enters both her consciousness and the text.

Crucial to this past is the group of unlikely friends—including Anna, her lover Willi, the three Oxford-educated RAF pilots, and Maryrose, a colonist born and raised in Rhodesia—who have initially bonded over their shared leftist political ideals. When they discover the Mashopi Hotel, an unbelievably "British" establishment "in the middle of the bush, all surrounded by kopjes and savages and general exotica" (84), they take to patronizing it in a spirit of camp colonial parody, filling their weekend holidays there with drink and political discussion. Beginning her recollections by describing the pilots, Anna mentions, *as if in passing*, the fact that "at Oxford these three had been homosexuals." She then confesses, "When I write the word down . . . well, I have to combat dislike and disquiet" (74). While Anna on one level seems aware of her homophobia, noting the way she has immediately qualified the term when she adds that eighteen months later the men are joking about "'our homosexual phase,'" she nonetheless collaborates in the men's rhetoric of deniability (homosexuality as only a passing phase) in her selective descriptions of their sexuality. For instance, when Paul, the charismatic object of everyone's desires, male or female (and the model for the dashing hero of Anna's novel *Frontiers*), writes off his sexual past with a quip—"I'm reluctantly coming to the conclusion that not only am I not a homosexual, but I never was" (123)—Anna conveys his verdict *as truth,* and she does this despite the fact that, as she well knows, he has at this point never put his putative heterosexuality to the test. Only when he loses his (heterosexual) virginity do we learn that this has been a "first"; and, not coincidentally, his partner in this initiation is Anna herself, who has always been infatuated with Paul and who thus has a more than vested interest in vouching for his "real" heterosexuality.[11] Of the pilot Jimmy, who is hopelessly in love with Paul, Anna claims that he, "unlike the others," is "truly homosexual, though he wished he wasn't," and paints a pathetic picture of his groveling abjection before Paul and the closeted existence he leads later in life (79). Next, Anna transforms the third pilot Ted's statement that he "sometimes said he preferred being homosexual" into a meaning that is more convenient to her narrative: "This meant he had a string of protégés" (80), young working-class men for whom he serves as mentor. Likewise Anna rather strenuously avoids reading anything unusual into her lover Willi's total lack of interest in having sex with her, though she does mention the fact that he experienced "a little conventional homosexuality at the age of thirteen" in the "decadent" (73) atmosphere of 1930s Berlin where he grew up. All Anna's closest male companions in the colony appear to have had sex with other men, yet only one is labeled a bona fide "homosexual," that word which gives rise in Anna to feelings of distaste and discomfort that she must force herself to "combat" even in the narrative present (a telling word choice, since it usually appears in the context of heterosexual and racial conflict).

Seen in one light, Anna's reluctance to label her friends' sexual preferences bespeaks a sexual fluidity that, as in many colonial narratives, is heightened by the group's sojourn in an exoticized Third World locale. For Lessing's colony provides a liminal space, a hiatus from the "real" world where freedom from old forms and customs, coupled with a devil-may-care pursuit of immediate pleasure fostered by the imminence of posting to battle for the RAF pilots, fosters a lack of restraint and makes room for the expression of nonconventional sexual behavior.[12] Africa thus provides an extension of the "time-out" from responsibility that university life previously offered the Englishmen—for we also learn that in college they partook of a "loose group of about twenty, all vaguely left-wing, vaguely literary, all having affairs with each other in every kind of sexual combination." Even if the men, other than Jimmy, now joke about their collegiate flirtations with homosexuality, they are freed by their life in the colony to laugh about their experiences without fear of judgment and indeed with a sense of gaining stature for having dabbled, Bloomsbury-style, in "*every kind of sexual combination*" (emphasis added). As with sex, so too with politics: Africa provides a safe space in which to "experiment" with radical ideas, as illustrated by the Communist reading group to which they belong. What Anna says of the young men at Oxford—"it was clear in retrospect that they were deliberately creating a mood of irresponsibility as a sort of social protest and sex was part of it" (75)—applies equally to the political and sexual community they form in exile in Rhodesia, a community whose boundaries remain fluid and open to a variety of otherwise marginalized experiences: "we were all, at various times, in love with each other" (77).

The crisis that brings the idyllic weekends spent at the Mashopi Hotel to an end overtly occurs over the issue of the color bar, when the hotel's proprietor, Mrs. Boothby, fires Jackson, her black cook of fifteen years, whom she accuses of not keeping in his place when Anna's friends attempt to befriend him. Evicted from the hotel's premises, Jackson's family wanders off on foot to one of the black townships, doomed to an uncertain future and virtual disintegration. But the trigger that allows Mrs. Boothby's racism to find permissible expression and disenables criticism of her actions, tellingly, is homophobia. Even more interestingly, this homophobia serves as the linchpin in the sequence of events that breaks up the Mashopi group of friends. Not only has its occurrence been omitted from the sanitized fictional account of these events in *Frontiers of War* but Anna herself has completely repressed the event from her memory, until the associative process of writing the Black Notebook forces it into consciousness. "*It seems I've forgotten the most important thing of all*—Jimmy's having upset Mrs. Boothby," Anna writes, then proceeds to explain that the weekend *before* Jackson's firing, Jimmy has drunkenly put his arms around Paul and kissed him in the presence of Mrs. Boothby. As Anna explains, Mrs. Boothby's shock and disgust is triggered by her realization that Jimmy's "unmanly" behavior has a name: "But the word 'homosexual' put him outside her pale. 'I suppose he's what they call a homosexual,'" she says, "using the word as if it, too, were poisoned" (146; emphasis added).

The events of the following weekend make clear the degree to which the racial contradictions of colonial power are being played out through the agency of such homophobia. Anna and her friends, who have been drinking and dancing all night, realize that Jimmy has disappeared and begin searching the hotel for him, at which point Jackson, the black cook, finds the youth curled up in drunken sleep in the hotel kitchen. As Jackson, trying to be helpful, stoops to raise him to his feet, Jimmy wakes and puts his arms around Jackson's neck, murmuring in a haze, "You love me, Jackson, don't you . . . none of the others love me" (147). It is at this unfortunate moment that Mrs. Boothby, already upset by the liberal behavior of her guests, newly initiated to Jimmy's homosexuality, and frustrated by her own unacknowledged infatuation with Paul, chooses to walk into the kitchen; in a blaze of righteous glory at this spectacle of disgust, she orders Jackson's immediate departure. The next day she apologizes to Jimmy—after all, he is a paying customer—but of Jackson and his family she can only say "Gone and good riddance" (152).

This sequence of events, moreover, is followed by another pivotal event that goes some distance in explaining the mechanisms of repression that have contributed to Anna's "forgetting" of the homophobic virulence of Mrs. Boothby's outburst. For it turns out that the one fortuitous consequence of the evening's harrowing events is that Anna has a fight with her lover Willi (whose strict Marxist ideology prohibits him from feeling sympathy for Jackson's plight—it is the black masses, not the victimized individual, who matter), then runs off into the veld with Paul, which leads to the sexual encounter that proves to be Paul's first (and only, seeing that he dies a few days later) intercourse with a woman. For Anna this experience represents a lifelong emotional apex: "I have never, in all my life, been as desperately and wildly and painfully happy as I was then . . . I remember saying to myself, This is it, this is being happy" (150).

Just how these multiple events are transformed into the seemingly anomalous *interracial* love story of *Frontiers of War* hinges on an ingenious series of displacements indicative of the repressive forces at work in Anna's unconscious. For another Marxist comrade (George) who joins the visitors at the Mashopi Hotel is having an affair with Jackson's wife, by whom he has fathered an illegitimate son. In Anna's novel, however, the miscegenation is much more romanticized; Paul's fictional prototype has a love affair with the young, beautiful, neglected wife of the hotel's African cook, one of the local agitators (neither is Jackson an agitator nor his wife neglected), and the romance ends in tragedy when the hotel's "Mistress Boothby" surprises them in a romantic rendezvous similar to the one Mrs. Boothby thinks she sees between Jackson and Jimmy. Hence, instead of the illicit embrace of *black man and white man* that unlocks the real Mrs. Boothby's race-hatred, then, the novel substitutes the more acceptably erotic interracial embrace of *black woman and white man*. But even this pairing, signifying the romance-that-should-have-been but that tragically is nipped in the bud, is *also* a displacement, for it rewrites into a full-blown love affair the *single* evening of passion shared between Paul and Anna, who, *like* Mrs. Boothby, has always been infatuated with Paul and hence never convinced of his bisexuality, despite overwhelming evidence to the contrary.[13]

This doubling of Anna and Mrs. Boothby raises the disturbing but nonetheless pertinent question of whether the Anna who returns to England has subconsciously imbibed from Mrs. Boothby a lesson in how to displace the rage she feels at others onto homosexuality. For if the bigoted hotel proprietress uses the "false" issue of same-sex desire to give voice to her racial prejudices in the firing of Jackson—as the next section demonstrates—Anna also latches onto the figure of the male homosexual, in the narrative present of "Free Women," as a convenient scapegoat for the ill feelings that she bears the sexually bigoted *heterosexual* men who repeatedly have disappointed her. And, again, eviction from the premises—Mrs. Boothby's solution—becomes, for Anna, her only recourse against what she sees as a life-threatening challenge to her "home" (again, paralleling Mrs. Boothby's defense of the honor of her hotel), to her femininity, and, ultimately, to her sanity.

Homosexual Housecleaning

The event to which I am referring—Anna's working up the courage to evict from her flat two gay boarders—occupies an inordinate amount of the dramatic action of the third and fourth sections of "Free Women" (thus falling right in the center of *The Golden Notebook*). Not coincidentally, it occurs in tandem with an acceleration in Anna's fear that she is "cracking up" (389). Although an innocuous young gay man named Ivor has been living in the extra bedroom in Anna's flat for some time without having warranted more than passing mention in the narrative, it is only in the third segment of "Free Women," as Anna's hysteria grows, that he and his boyfriend Ronnie suddenly command a degree of attention that, to put it simply, is disproportionate to the issues that have occupied the first two chapters of "Free Women." "Ivor had moved *into their lives*" (391; emphasis added), the text announces midway into the third installment of "Free Women" ("their" refers to Anna and her young daughter Janet). Not just into "their home," but into "their lives": the phrasing signals the psychodramatic intensity of the coming conflict, first as the well-meaning Ivor befriends and increasingly watches after Janet (whose adoration of Ivor exacerbates Anna's uneasy sense of having been displaced in her maternal function), then as Ronnie also moves in, which Anna considers the price she is expected to pay for Ivor's caretaking of Janet. At this point Anna begins to suffer the increasingly paranoid sensation of being trapped in her own home, unable to "move freely because *of those two*." This causes an initially expressed "dislike" of Ronnie to blossom *in the space of a page* to outright "contempt" for *both* boarders because they are not, in her terms, "real men." As Anna's anxieties increase, warping her sense of reality, she admits to feeling "off balance" in the same breath in which she attributes her mental instability to the men's presence in the flat: "I feel as if the spirit of this flat were being *poisoned,* as if a spirit of perverse and ugly spite were everywhere" (393–94; emphasis added). This reaction verbally echoes Mrs. Boothby's reaction when she is forced to use the word "homosexual" to categorize Jimmy's proclivities, "using the word as if it, too, were *poisoned*" (145; emphasis added). Anna freely admits her reaction is irrational, but irrationality is precisely the name of the game, now, and Anna 's uncontrollable disgust and almost obsessive desire to evict the two men forms the climax of the third section of "Free Women," at which point she orders Ronnie out of the flat.

When the fourth section picks up after a break of a hundred pages, however, this homosexual subplot is immediately resumed; for it appears that Ronnie has moved back into Ivor's room, at which point Anna decides "she was very likely mad" (507). In the psychodrama that is now clearly being played out, the incident signals another return of the sexually and textually repressed: neither Anna nor the text can so easily shake off the demon that Ronnie and Ivor have come to represent. The section ends with a second scene of expulsion, as Ronnie again leaves and Ivor attempts to conciliate Anna with a bunch of flowers. Anna's reaction quite chillingly brackets the psychological intensities set into motion by this subplot: "trembling with anger," she viciously strikes Ivor (who unlike Ronnie is a well-meaning person) across the face with the flowers and repeats the words of Mrs. Boothby to that British matron's despised other, Jackson: "'Get out,' said Anna. *She had never in her life been angry like this*" (523; emphasis added). In this uncanny conjunction between disparate narrative moments, the intensity of the rage that underlies the expulsion of two different minorities (colonized black; male homosexual) takes on exactly the same emotional valence, raising the question of just what scapegoating is being effected in the name of cleaning the house of these "poisonous" and "perverse" influences.

In Anna's case, at least, the source of her displaced rage is not hard to pinpoint, once the Ivor-Ronnie incident is located within the larger narrative structure. The psychological displacements enacted in Anna's homophobia, in fact, follow closely on a series of *actual* displacements that have recently occurred within the flat. Only when Anna's lover Michael leaves her (to work in Africa, no less) does she decide to rent out her vacant room to fill the psychological and physical void left by his absence. In contrast, the final leavetaking of Ronnie and Ivor at the end of section four makes way for the arrival of a new tenant, Saul Green, who becomes Anna's new lover. Within this larger schema, then, the gay Ronnie and Ivor are not only insufficient replacements for straight Michael, but are destined to be replaced themselves by another straight lover because they are not, in Anna's lexicon, "real men." This context suggests that Anna's anger toward Ronnie and Ivor is not only homophobic disgust but also an expression of the anger she feels toward the absent heterosexual lover(s) for whom Ivor and Ronnie can only be inadequate stand-ins (even as their own coupled status serves as a bitter reminder to Anna of what is missing in her own life).

That these two *gay* men have become scapegoats for the multitude of *heterosexual* men who have abused Anna over the years is also confirmed by the narrative sequencing of the specific day on which Anna's "contempt" for her gay boarders erupts. For, ironically, this strong emotion is the culmination of a series of incidents of male aggression that have plagued Anna throughout the day. This sequence begins with Molly's husband Richard summoning Anna to his office, where he verbally assaults her and implicitly comes on to her, and it culminates with a lewd man on the train who attempts to rub up against her, then follows her off the tube, "grinning in triumph" at having "humiliated [her] and triumphed" over her (390). Filled with a sense of panic and mounting hysteria, Anna leaves this psychopath on the sidewalk outside her door, only to enter her apartment and project her contempt for such menacing men on her homosexual boarders.

What makes these gay men so apt a vehicle for Anna's rage is not simply the fact of their being, so to speak, in the wrong place (Anna's flat) at the wrong time (just after she's been harassed); it has more to do with her own conflicted feelings about gender—or, more specifically, how her assumptions about what constitutes a real man ultimately impacts her understanding of her own femaleness. The first complaint Anna articulates against gay men betrays her own internalization of Freudian norms of female development. For the primary concern that Anna consciously articulates about Ivor is that her fatherless daughter Janet is growing too close to the young man and that Ivor's gayness therefore constitutes a deprivation in Janet's proper Oedipal development: "Janet needs a man in her life, she misses her father. Ivor is very kind to her. And yet because he's not a man . . . with a 'real man' there would be a whole area of tension, of wry understanding that there can't be with Ivor" (391). And when Anna decides to evict Ivor's lover Ronnie, she justifies it, ironically, in the name of Janet's future (hetero)sexual development: "By God . . . I'm going to see she grows up to recognize a real man when she meets one. Ronnie's going to have to leave" (405). Although Lessing has Anna self-reflexively ponder her distinction of heterosexual males as "real men" by initially putting the phrase in quotation marks on page 391 (see the above citation), by the latter passage on page 405 the quotes have been dropped—in part, I suspect, because Anna's views on this issue are very close to Lessing's own. For whereas Lessing is re-markably, and often brilliantly, sensitive to the oppressed status of women in modern patriarchal society—hence her feminist following—her views of femaleness become conflicted precisely when she accepts as a given the *dependence* of women's eroticism on male agency.[14]

This confusion is ironically apparent in Anna's wry acknowledgment that only "so long as she was loved by a man" is she "immune to the ugli-ness of *perverse* sex, *violent* sex" (407; emphasis added)—a circumlocu-tion that unthinkingly conflates Ivor and Ronnie's "perverse" sexuality and the "violent" sexuality of the man on the subway who has just as-saulted her. She is thinking specifically of the "new, frightened, vulnera-ble" Anna that emerged when Michael abandoned her. But, in fact, the security that she fantasizes existed with Michael was nonexistent—as the sadism of Michael's hot-cold reactions to Anna's love, always com-ing and leaving, has previously demonstrated to her. The "immunity" that Anna fantasizes, rather, is the desire to *pass as normal,* to be vali-dated as a woman who *can* be loved by a man: indeed, the only "proof" of being a "woman" at all, in the Freudian framework inherited by Anna and many women of her generation, however "liberated," is to be "made" into one by the right man—or, in Anna's terms, a "real" man. Anna's dependence on men for self-validation—even when she, like the reader, suspects that these very men are unworthy of the task—carries over into one of the text's more controversial assertions: its extended com-mentary on the superiority of vaginal over clitoral orgasm. A clitoral or-gasm may offer a "thousand [more] thrills, sensations, etc.," Anna writes in the voice of her fictional double, Ella, and a so-called vaginal orgasm may only be "emotion and nothing else," but *nonetheless* Anna categor-ically upholds the superiority of the latter as the "one *real* female orgasm," namely because "it is created by a man's need for a woman . . . everything else is a substitute, a fake" (215–16; emphasis added). The use of the ad-jective "real" to distinguish among types of orgasms echoes Anna's use of the same word to distinguish among types of men. "A woman's sexu-ality is, so to speak, contained by a man, if he is a *real* man," Ella muses, and Anna comments after her first sexual encounter with Saul Green, "I'd forgotten what making love to a *real* man was like" (455, 561; em-phasis added).

The flaw in such logic that Anna overlooks, however, is that it meas-ures a man's realness solely in terms of his sexual capacity, ignoring the fact that in her experience "real men" almost inevitably turn out to be both sexist and misogynistic. If such *real* men are seen as the sole source of women's *real* orgasms—especially if clitoral orgasm is admittedly more powerful—then it becomes clear that Anna's defense of the vaginal orgasm hinges on her desperate desire to be viewed, in the only terms society has provided her, as a "real woman." And, as a self-declared free woman, a single mother, and a professional writer of some renown, Anna subconsciously fears that she may have already passed beyond the pale, passed into the ranks of the "unfeminine" and hence the undesirable, in most men's eyes. The fear of non-normativity, when it comes to her own gender status, infiltrates and subconsciously molds Anna's very definition of erotic pleasure.

In turn, the desire to remain womanly-desirable—that is, in culture's terms, "feminine"—in order to attract the elusive real man goes some way in explaining the particularly strong antipathy Anna expresses to effeminately acting gay men. And this quality Ronnie, Ivor's boyfriend, represents with a vengeance. The first thought Anna expresses about Ronnie is that she "dislikes" him, but she attempts to keep her dislike in check since she realizes that her dislike is directed toward "the type rather than the person" (391). The "type" Anna has in mind is that of the limp-wristed, narcissistically self-involved, effeminate homosexual, which the text's hyperbolic descriptions of Ronnie go to pains to emphasize: his "charming coiffured head" is likened to that of "a boyish young girl" (393), he speaks with "winning charm" that reminds Anna of "a well brought up young girl, almost lispingly correct" (394), he gestures "with a little writhing movement of the hips that was quite unconscious" (405), he "trip[s]" rather than walks up the stairs (406), and, foremost, Anna fantasizes he is filled with jealousy and malice toward women, his "competitors" in the sexual market. Such a representation, in a text published in 1962, inevitably tilts the reader's sympathies against Ronnie, thereby paving the way for Anna's confession that she doesn't merely "dislike" Ronnie but rather that she is shamefully "disgusted" by him. This expression of what amounts to physical revulsion surfaces when Anna comes upon Ronnie toying with her cosmetics in the bathroom, in a feeble effort to appeal to her as "one girl to another" (405).

This scene, it seems to me, is key to understanding the psychic origins of Anna's extreme homophobia. Not only are gay men such as Ronnie and Ivor scapegoats onto whom she can displace the rage she feels toward "real" heterosexual men; given her stereotypical equation of gay men with effeminacy, it is also quite possible that Anna is displacing onto Ronnie the anger and anxiety she feels at the image of her own enacted femininity that the effeminate gay man mirrors back to the heterosexual woman. For seeing Ronnie making up *his* face in *her* mirror, with *her* cosmetics, uneasily reminds Anna that her own "femininity" is not a natural birthright but a masquerade that she creates out of her desire to be desired by straight men whose "masculinity" she has accepted as the indispensable complement to her sexual satisfaction and self-esteem. If women are doomed to represent "Otherness" in phallocentric culture, Lessing adds a twist to this formulation by figuring male homosexuality as the straight woman's "Other." For the feminine gay man's very imitation of female characteristics calls into question the "real" femininity that Anna needs to exude if she is to succeed in the game of heterosexual mating. Read in light of this displacement onto Ronnie of her own anxieties about "realness," the wording of Anna's climactic explosion of rage in the bathroom takes on an added resonance: "Good Lord! she thought, to be born a Ronnie! to be born like that—I complain about the difficulties of being my kind of woman, but good Lord!—I might have been born a Ronnie" (405–06). As the psychodramatic pitch of the scene reveals, the disgust that culminates in Anna's decision to evict Ronnie (and, later, even Ivor) forms an instance of the extreme heterosexual panic that is the inevitable consequence of the contradictory position Anna assumes in attempting to be "my kind of woman" in the heterosexual and misogynistic culture of 1950s England. The sex wars are indeed enough to drive one "mad."

Back to Africa

The role that male homosexuality assumes in the London section of *The Golden Notebook* as a site of displaced anxieties about heterosexual norms of masculinity and femininity is also subtly linked to the valences that have attached, via the issue of the color line, to homosexuality in Anna's memories of Africa. First, it turns out that Ronnie and Ivor are not the only boarders that Anna, in her singlehood, has desired to evict from the flat because they are "disturbing her peace of mind." In fact, as Anna remembers in a brief aside, her Mrs. Boothby-like sentiment that "Ronnie must go" is the exact feeling that she had about Jemmie, a previous student boarder from Ceylon whom she also disliked but whom she "couldn't bring herself to give... notice [to] *because he was coloured*" (404; emphasis added). One is reminded, uneasily, of Jackson's expulsion from the Mashopi Hotel. If Anna's experience of African colonialism has given her an intuitive understanding of the analogies binding women and blacks in parallel systems of apartheid, she resists the similar (if also partial) identification that exists between herself and gay men, because acknowledging it would delve too deeply not merely into her oppressed status as a woman but into the masquerade of femininity that her identification as a heterosexual woman forces her to assume.

Second, the narrative of Anna's eviction of Ronnie is immediately juxtaposed with another return of the *textually* repressed: an excerpt from the Black Notebook in which a new subterranean network of associations linking homosexuality and the African landscape rise to the surface of Anna's consciousness in the form of a forgotten incident. Tellingly, this is the only African memory related out of chronological order, long after the notebook's opening recollections. Anna opens this entry with the account of an accident she has witnessed on the London streets in which a man inadvertently kicks a pigeon to death, which she then proceeds to dream about. "It reminded me of something, I don't know what," Anna says about the dream, at which point she suddenly remembers the "something" she hasn't "thought of in years... an incident from the Mashopi Hotel week-ends" (413). This incident is a hunting trip on which Anna and her friends accompany Paul in order to shoot pigeons so that Mrs. Boothby can cook that quintessentially British dish, a pigeon pie. This invasion of the bush to satisfy colonial appetites quickly becomes an allegory of sex and death, of "natural" fecundity and "unnatural" carnage, played out against the primordial African landscape. Overtly, Lessing uses this symbolically charged tableau, as Anna sickens at the senseless killing of the pigeons, to underline the novel's critique of the British colonial presence, which has wreaked a parallel destruction on Rhodesia's indigenous populations. But, less obviously, the scene of cruelty and slaughter also provides the psychodramatic tableau for an underlying homosexual narrative, in which Paul sadistically torments the doggedly lovelorn Jimmy by ordering him to retrieve the fallen birds, despite Jimmy's nausea, then demeans Jimmy for abjectly obeying him ("'We don't need a dog, after all,' remarked Paul" [423]). Publicly baiting Jimmy like this becomes Paul's psychic mechanism for disavowing his own homosexual inclinations—a ploy that simultaneously attests to Paul's own unresolved desires by exposing his subconscious *pleasure* in prolonging the ritual of erotic domination that bonds the two men together, albeit as master and "dog."

This hitherto repressed incident, in which colonial allegory and homosexual psychodrama exist side by side, occurs, moreover, against the backdrop of the African veld, which Anna represents as a fount of boundless, mindless fecundity. On their way to the glade where the pigeons roost, the group has come across the mind-boggling sight of millions of grasshoppers copulating in the grass: "In every direction, all around us, were the insects, coupling . . . in thousands, crude green and crude red, with the black blank eyes staring—they were absurd, obscene, and above all, the very emblem of stupidity" (415). On the one hand, the narrative here momentarily falls into the orientalist stereotype delineated by Edward Said and other postcolonial critics, in which the Third World is equated with unthinking, untamed, "stupid" nature and procreative excess.[15] On the other hand, this demonstration of natural fecundity turns out to be an exposé of the concept of "natural" behavior itself. First of all, Anna and her group spot among the mating insects two grotesquely mismatched pairs. In one an overlarge grasshopper is being mounted by a "tiny ineffectual mate," and in the other the reverse is happening. Paul and Jimmy (themselves one such ineffectual coupling) attempt to separate the insects to create "two *well-matched* couples" (416–17; emphasis added), but the grasshoppers immediately revert to their previous alignments, rendering copulation an ever-desired but always impossible achievement. Second, as Jimmy sardonically notes, there is nothing at all in this orgy of "what we refer to as nature" to guarantee that these couplings are formed by male mounting female, as the group has assumed: "For all we know, this is a riot of debauchery, males with males, females with females" (417).

The snag in the "natural" scheme presented by the mismatched grasshoppers is next likened to the human scheme, as the beautiful Maryrose and handsome Paul stroll ahead of the rest of the group, to all appearances the "*perfectly matched* couple" (433; emphasis added)—a verbal echo deliberately linking these human players to the futilely mating grasshoppers a few pages earlier. Appearances to the contrary, however, Paul and Maryrose are as likely to make a perfect heterosexual fit as the mismatched grasshoppers—what with the solely incestuous nature of her desires (fixated on a dead brother), and his bisexual lean-ings.[16] Thus the backdrop of the African wild in this scene facilitates a denaturalizing of "nature" that returns the very concept of nature to its polymorphously perverse potential and disrupts the tendency to equate nature with normativity. This critique of the cultural meanings embedded in terms like "nature," "sexuality," and "couple" helps to explain why Anna has hitherto repressed this powerfully experienced incident, which returns only through the associations set into motion by a chance sighting (the London pigeon) and an elusive dream.

The event that follows this Black Notebook entry repeats these elliptical links, tying together Anna's heterosexual anxieties, the topos of male homosexuality, and Africa as mythic setting. A few pages later Anna relates with glee the deception she and a writer friend have played on two male editors by writing fake literary diaries that these editors take seriously as high art. In one such attempt, they pitch a journal they claim to have been written by a "lady writer of early middle-age, who has spent some years in an African colony" and who is writing a play with a tragic interracial love plot (white man, black woman) to illustrate "the superior spiritual status of the white man trapped by history, dragged down into the animal mud of Africa" (437, 439). This concept, which is Anna's clever parody of her own *Frontiers of War*, is designed to deceive an editor who—surprise—is gay, described by Anna as "wet, limp, hysterical, homosexual, intelligent" (437). If this description betrays a note of unconcealed contempt, its vitriol is made all the more intriguing by the fact that its language of denigration turns up in a description, two hundred pages later, of Anna's hysteria and self-loathing of her own "wet, limp, hysterical" female body. This passage occurs in the middle of Anna's psychic disintegration as she and Saul Green descend into mutual, claustrophobic madness. Sitting in bed and looking at her naked body, Anna equates the revulsion she feels toward her "*wet* sticky center" with "the *emotions of a homosexual. For the first time the homosexual literature of disgust* made sense to me" (612; emphasis added). What this very odd displacement of Anna's bodily self-disgust onto homosexuality manages to do is avert any self-recognition that her dislike of her sexual body—here rendered the proverbial "dark continent" of Freudian psychoanalysis—is itself the product of heterosexual *male* ambivalence toward women (expressed as castration anxiety) that she has in turn internalized.[17] Again, the profound ambivalences emanating from the ongoing "war" between "mismatched" men and women turn out to be the trigger for the text's overt expressions of homophobia. And to the degree that Anna's internalized self-disgust seems to echo Freud's scheme of female Oedipal development, the analogy that Gilles Deleuze and Félix Guattari make between psychoanalysis and colonialism becomes especially appropriate in light of Anna's conjoined experience of racial and sexual apartheid: "Oedipus is also colonization—pursued by other means, it is the interior colony... even here at home, where we Europeans are concerned, it is our intimate colonial education."[18]

Anna's allusion to the "homosexual literature of disgust," moreover, begs the question of what works she might have in mind. The most prominent candidate in British fiction would be Radclyffe Hall's 1928 *The Well of Loneliness,* and, intriguingly, Anna's discomfort with her body is tied closely to her ambivalent feelings about those women who, like Hall's protagonist, unambiguously desire other women's bodies: lesbians. In comparison with Lessing's use of male homosexuality as theme, subplot, and index of psychological disintegration, the novel's references to lesbianism are few. Nonetheless, these infrequent allusions shed light on the normalizing pressures imposed on Anna by her culture's systematic enforcement of compulsory heterosexuality, which causes her to shy away from those bonds with women that might otherwise be a source of self-affirmation and community outside the sex wars that pit men and women against each other. The question of the relationship between "female bonding" and "lesbianism" is especially interesting in light of the frame narrative, "Free Women," which foregrounds Anna's close friendship with Molly Jacobs. While some critics have positively interpreted this relationship as a mirroring female-female bond through which Anna finds her "female" identity, I am struck by the growing distance, gaps in communication, and even distrust that ultimately come to characterize this relationship. In fact, one could make the case that Anna's comments on lesbianism are part of a subconscious strategy to remove any possible homosexual imputations from this friendship, de-eroticizing its contours in order to render unthreatening the act with which the "Free Women" section (and *The Golden Notebook* as a whole) ends: "the two women kissed and separated" (666).[19] For in all the text's allusions to lesbians, female homosexuality is defined stereotypically as a reaction to a failed heterosexual ideal, rather than as a desire that exists independent of men.[20] Likewise, Anna's one recorded fantasy of making love to a woman depends solely on Saul's proximity. These thoughts

occur in tandem with Anna's and Saul's descent into madness, as Anna
grows obsessively jealous of the other women with whom he is sleeping.
She remembers that her former psychologist has argued that obsessive
jealousy is always partially homosexual—and, now, she begins to wonder whether she secretly wishes "to make love with that woman [Saul]
was with now." Not because she really desires the woman, however. Rather,
she has become so much a part of Saul's madness that she wants what
he wants, while simultaneously desiring to become Saul's object of desire by possessing that woman. If this jealousy amounts to "homosexual
desire," as her psychologist declares, it is entirely theoretical (sex in the
head, as D. H. Lawrence would say), produced and performed entirely,
as Anna admits, "for Saul's sake," not out of her own inclinations. Anna's
inability to conceptualize lesbian desire outside of a heterosexual frame
is not unlike the difficulty she has in thinking positively of her sexuality
unless it is "contained by man . . . a real man." "When she loved a man
again," Anna attempts to assure herself, "she would *return to normal:* a
woman, that is, whose sexuality would ebb and flow in response to his"
(455; emphasis added).

Survival Lessons in Colonial Mimicry

In these multiple allusions to same-sex desire, then, Lessing represents
homosexuality in gay men as what might be called the "other face" of
femininity (its negative mirror), and in lesbians as what might be called
the "defacement" of femininity (its erasure).[21] Crucially, Anna's unsettling
encounters with the specter of homosexuality mark her gradual disintegration and entry into the realm of the irrational. In terms of narrative structure, as the extended middle sequence in "Free Women" illustrates, the presence of Ronnie and Ivor precipitates Anna's feeling that
she is cracking up, going mad, and their eviction only clears the way for
the advent of Saul Green, whose tortured relationship with Anna pushes
her across the threshold of sanity into madness and self-destructive
masochism. Saul may or not be a "real" character, depending on one's
interpretation of Lessing's psychodramatic narrative techniques, but the
specific violence he represents is, as the text makes graphically clear, not
only internal to Anna but is an *active* force in the Cold War world that
forms the contemporary backdrop of the novel.[22] Even her descent into
madness cannot rob Anna of her intuitive knowledge of oppression as
an active force in history—one inflamed by various psychological and

ideological incitements to achieve domination over others—for, in a profound sense, that knowledge is kept alive through the uncanny images of Africa that haunt her subconscious as she lapses in and out of sanity. Simultaneously, and just as profoundly, her recollections of the struggle for political autonomy on the African continent—recovered through the agency of memories, dreams, and hallucinations—become the basis for her (and Lessing's) hope that the act of mental breakdown or "cracking apart" may in fact be the prelude to a larger "cracking open," one through which "the future might pour in a different shape—terrible perhaps, or marvelous, but something new" (473).

In particular, Anna's cross-racial fantasy in which she imagines herself as the heroic antiapartheid leader, Tom Mathlong, provides her with models both for surviving as an oppressed minority in "white-occupied territory" and for creating a new mode of being commensurate with a postcolonial world order. For Anna realizes that the self-possession Mathlong maintains in the face of overwhelming colonial opposition (unlike the black leader Charlie Thembla, who goes mad) is the result of his ability to detach himself by "perform[ing] actions, play[ing] roles, that he believed to be necessary for the good of others, even while he preserved an ironic doubt about the results of his action. It seemed to me that this particular type of detachment was something we needed very badly in this time" (597). "Performing" political action is not to disbelieve in its efficacy or necessity but to find a different way of catalyzing its possibilities.

This conflation of racial mimicry, politics, and survival calls to mind the work of an intellectual whose analysis of colonialism in Africa began appearing in the same era that Lessing was writing her novelistic account of the Third World—Frantz Fanon, whose *Black Skin, White Masks* appeared in 1951 and *The Wretched of the Earth* in 1961. Fanon's inquiry into the psychodynamics of racial identity under colonial rule provides a particularly useful theoretical template for understanding the imaginary identification that Lessing stages between Anna Wulf and Tom Mathlong, between First World woman and Third World black. In many ways, Mathlong's performative mimicry of colonial stereotypes and antistereotypes, which work both to protect himself *and* to advance his agenda, exemplifies Fanon's argument about the instability of racial identity, which, while it depends on masquerade and projection, is also the product of the colonized subject's internalization—or what Fanon calls "epidermalization"—of the gaze of the white colonizer on the "native's" bodily surface or skin. Considered from this perspective, the ironic detachment that Anna admires in Mathlong and that she imitatively incorporates as her own modus operandi is also, less positively, a product of self-division within one's consciousness and alienation from one's body. To the "man of color," Fanon writes, "consciousness of the body is solely a negating activity. It is a third-person consciousness." To put it slightly differently, as Gwen Bergner explains in an analysis of Fanon, "the white man's gaze produces a psychic splitting that shatters the black man's experience of bodily integrity."[23]

While acknowledging the dangers of indiscriminately collapsing the different histories of racial and female oppression, I find it productive to bring Fanon to bear on Lessing's novel because his analysis of the split subjectivity of the colonial subject also rings true of the psychic divisions that accompany Anna's psychic shattering and her doubled sense of her body as an occupied land overrun by enemy forces, as well as a territory that remains foreign to her, a frontier. One of Fanon's key terms, "masking," also illuminates the lesson in potentially successful resistance that Anna learns from Mathlong's mimicry of the colonial stereotype. For the collage of notebooks, journals, newspaper clippings, and fictional "outtakes" that contribute to the postmodern texture of *The Golden Notebook* are nothing less than a series of shifting masks—masks taking the form of the "third-person consciousness" of which Fanon writes, usually parading in the first-person voice—worn by the narrating Anna in order to perform the multiple roles that may, or may not, insure her survival when history "cracks open."

To this degree, then, Anna's experience of colonialism and the color line in Southern Rhodesia becomes the internal anchor that gives substance to her struggles and a context to her historical positioning as a modern woman in the Cold War West who is attempting both to be "free" and a "woman." Nonetheless, *The Golden Notebook* finally enacts a purgation of the most politically revolutionary (and hence "threatening") aspects of the polymorphous perversities unleashed by Anna's quest. The novel achieves this cleansing by rechanneling its dispersive, libidinal energies into a narrative trajectory at the very end of the text that upholds the normativity of heterosexual desire and the complementarity of gender roles, in the face of the novel's otherwise feminist call to emancipation. This rechanneling process begins in Anna's final notebook, the so-called Golden Notebook, whose purpose is to supersede the prior effort at compartmentalizing the contradictory facets of her life by gathering them into *one* narrative; the fact that the overall novel takes its title from this notebook intimates that even Lessing privileges this effort at consolidation over the various "component parts" that precede it, as if it holds some final, or at least more conclusive, answer to the novel's existential questions. The Golden Notebook thus operates, on the structural level, as a kind of reining-in of the libidinal energies, one that makes possible Anna's break from the self-destructiveness of her psychologically overdetermined relationship with Saul, her return to the world of everyday sanity, and, ultimately, the overcoming of her writing block by composing a new autobiographical novel (as the last sentences of the Golden Notebook reveal the "Free Women" text to be). Likewise, the final section of "Free Women," which follows the Golden Notebook and ends the novel, operates as a further streamlining of the narrative desires that have been in play since the opening pages of the text. First of all, this "fiction" recasts Anna's psychological descent into "mad love" in a much tamer form, replacing the notebooks' account of Anna's tormented relationship with Saul with her brief, and relatively sane, affair with an American writer in exile named Milt, thus corralling the perverse and dangerous energies into which the former relationship has tapped. Second, the resolution of the "free women" theme in this final segment represents a retreat from the more utopian social and artistic ideals of the novel overall: Anna cynically decides she is going to work at a marriage welfare center (rather than recommencing her novelistic career) and Molly decides to marry a nice bourgeois man with a house in Hampstead. "So we're both going to be integrated with British life at its roots," Molly quips, and whatever Lessing's note of irony, the novella leaves us with the two women in retreat from the greater aspirations of their professions, politics, and freedom, opting, instead, for something closer to the status quo.

Furthermore, as already mentioned, the final sentence only underlines the lengths to which the text seems willing to go at this ultimate moment of closure in order to exorcize its demons—including, by implication, the specter of homosexuality—as Lessing represents the two women chastely kissing and separating. No shadow of the lesbian here; no shadow, for that matter, of the feminist political ideal of sisterhood as a refuge from the heterosexual warfare that has ruptured every male-female bond in the text. Whatever its ironic intentions as yet one more "fictional" refraction of its protagonist Anna, this conclusion to "Free Women"—and hence to the novel as a whole—folds the text's manifold narrative energies into a single narrative line that stays all action: the women's kiss and separation. Anna the writer may not have capitulated to convention; but "Anna," the protagonist of "Free Women," may well have. And, beyond a doubt, this "Anna," as well as the narrating Anna, indeed as well as Lessing herself, remains trapped in those aspects of the gender ideology of the late 1950s that dictate a norm for heterosexual femininity that *needs,* as its scapegoat for the failures of heterosexual men, the homosexual Other whose presence it must also deny.

Thus, while Anna's projections onto racial "Others," via her experience of colonialism and institutionalized racial segregation, have given her access to a politicized knowledge of her position in Western patriarchy as a woman who by definition is seen as man's mirror and secondary refraction, this understanding comes at the expense of those simultaneous projections onto male homosexuality as femininity's "other face," or, to a lesser degree, onto lesbianism as the "defacement" of heterosexual femininity altogether—projections that also work as displacements, ultimately shielding Anna from the compromises involved in her performance of a woman's "natural," which is to say heterosexual, desire. As such, colonialism and homosexuality, first brought into conjunction in Anna's resurfacing memories of Southern Rhodesia, become evocative figures for the sexual and textual anxieties involved at the mid-century in attempting to become a free woman who possesses the authority to write a story that will express not only the cracking apart of a now defunct old order, but the cracking open of a radically new frontier of future being where, it is to be hoped, the recuperation of the self's repressed desires no longer depends on the othering of racial or homosexual Others.

Notes

Lessing, *The Golden Notebook,* with author's preface (1962; New York: Bantam, 1981). Cited by page reference throughout this chapter.

1. Kauffman, *Special Delivery: Epistolary Modes in Modern Fiction* (Chicago: University of Chicago Press, 1992), 154.

2. Lessing's novel had a catalytic effect among critics and popular readers alike when it appeared in 1962. Praised by many establishment critics as the achievement

of the decade, largely for its moral and political vision, the novel was further cata-pulted into visibility when its representation of the relation of the sexes from a woman's point of view became a rallying point for the first phase of the contempo-rary women's liberation movement. The novel was embraced, as Molly Hite writes, by an entire generation of intelligent, dissatisfied women "because of its subject matter," and it became a mainstay of women's studies courses throughout the next two decades. By 1985, no less than 59 dissertations, 300 articles, and 17 books had ap-peared on Lessing, the majority focusing on *The Golden Notebook*. The Lessing sta-tistics are reported in the introduction to *Approaches to Teaching Lessing's "The Golden Notebook,"* ed. Carey Kaplan and Ellen Cronan Rose (New York: The Mod-ern Language Association of America, 1989), 13. The Hite reference is from her "*The Golden Notebook* in a Graduate Seminar on Contemporary Experimental Fiction," in the same volume, 89. Although the novel has attained a certain canonical status that lasts to this day, it is neither written about nor read with the fervor it once aroused. In 1989 Claire Sprague commented on how few of her students "in the past two or three years had heard of, [much less] read Lessing"; and in the 1990s, se-rious criticism on the *Notebook* dropped to a minimum as Lessing's involvement in science fiction, which began in the 1980s, has moved her further from the novelistic mainstream. See Sprague, "*The Golden Notebook:* In Whose or What Great Tradi-tion?," in Kaplan and Rose, *Approaches,* 79.

3. Much Lessing criticism has been dedicated to "decoding" the complexities of the novel's puzzle-like, fragmented narrative structure, attempting to separate its representations of the "fiction" from the "facts" of Anna's experience—a process complicated by the revelation that the omnisciently narrated "Free Women" chap-ters, which the framing structure encourages the reader to accept as unmediated "fact," turn out to be another novel written by Anna. Among the numerous help-ful analyses of Lessing's splintered form and multiplying viewpoints, see Roberta Rubenstein, *The Novelistic Vision of Doris Lessing: Breaking the Forms of Conscious-ness* (Urbana: Univeristy of Illinois Press, 1979); Kauffman, *Special Delivery;* Betsy Draine, *Substance under Pressure: Artistic Coherence and Evolving Form in the Novels of Doris Lessing* (Madison: University of Wisconsin Press, 1983); Molly Hite, chapter 2: "The Future in a Different Shape: Broken Form and Possibility in *The Golden Notebook,*" in *The Other Side of the Story: Structures and Strategies of Contemporary Feminist Narrative* (Ithaca: Cornell University Press, 1989), 61–69; Patricinio P. Schweickart, "Reading a Wordless Statement: The Structure of Doris Lessing's *The Golden Notebook,*" *Modern Fiction Studies* 31, no. 2 (summer 1985): 263–79; and Joseph Hynes, "The Construction of *The Golden Notebook,*" *Iowa Review* 4, no. 3 (summer 1973): 100–13.

4. One effect of these ruptures on the political and social realms is "the break-down of me, Anna" (476), which manifests itself as psychosis and schizophrenic dissociation. Despite Lessing's reservations about certain aspects of psychoanalytic theory, the text abounds with references to psychotherapy, from Anna's declaration on her return to England, "I think I shall go to a psychoanalyst" (232), to reports of her sessions with the Jungian analyst Mrs. Marks, her frequent use of the notebooks to record and interpret her dreams, the fact that her lover Michael (the prototype of "Paul" in the Yellow Notebook) is a "witchdoctor" (Anna's word for psychoanalysts), and the states of hysteria, depression, schizophrenia, and altered consciousness that beset numerous characters. Lessing's knowledge of psychological theory and psy-

chotherapy runs deep and wide; particularly relevant are the popularization of Jung and the "antipsychiatry" school of the 1950s–60s. Lessing was reading Jung seriously before writing *Martha Quest;* she cites him throughout the *Children of Violence* series, as Draine notes (*Substance under Pressure,* 44). A useful summary of the impact of Jungian concepts on Lessing's work appears in Rubenstein, *Novelistic Vision,* 22–34. Rubenstein also reports Lessing's dissatisfaction with Freudian theory (or, more accurately, the psychiatric establishment's conservative version of his theories promulgated in the 1950s) for making the unconscious into, in a 1969 interview, a "great dark marsh full of monsters" dialectically opposed to reason. She feels that Jung, in contrast, more usefully embraces the unconscious as the repository of those archetypal, complementary forces of light and dark that create human wholeness. See "Doris Lessing at Stony Brook: An Interview by Jonah Raskin," in *A Small Personal Voice,* ed. Paul Schlueter (New York: Knopf, 1974), 67, quoted in Rubenstein, 23. While the influence of Jung can still be seen in Lessing's use of archetypes, dream material, and the interior quest motif in *The Golden Notebook,* she had also begun to question Jungian therapy by the late 1950s. Anna's satire of her Jungian therapist, Mrs. Marks, as "Mother Sugar" for sugar-coating the ills of contemporary society by referring every conflict to the primitive realm of myth and folklore makes clear this dissatisfaction. Around this period, Lessing's understanding of the psyche's relationship to the world was increasingly influenced by the philosophy of R. D. Laing, under whose supervision she experimented with hallucinogens to induce temporary psychotic states. Marion Vlastos summarizes the influence on Lessing's work of Laing's theory of the social origins of madness and schizophrenia in *The Divided Self* (1959) and *The Politics of Experience* (1967) in "Doris Lessing and R. D. Laing: Psychopolitics and Prophecy," *PMLA* 91(1976): 245–58. Kauffman's "schizoanalytic" reading of the novel in *Special Delivery* also relies on Laing's influence on Lessing. For Lessing's turn to Sufi philosophy in the 1970s as a more authentic predecessor to Jung's ideas, see Rubenstein, 230–31, and Draine, 92–93.

5. Southern Rhodesia was settled by English entrepreneurs long before Britain stepped in to make it a Crown Colony. In this role Britain attempted to mitigate the forces of white racism, through policies aimed at moderating the worst of the segregationist policies of the white colonists, who themselves opposed British rule. In the 1950s, Southern Rhodesia formed a "Federation" with Northern Rhodesia and Nyasaland that ushered in a period of prosperity, black economic advancement, and limited integration; this period was followed by a white backlash in the form of Ian Smith's explicitly apartheid Rhodesian Front party, which dissolved the Federation and declared the country's independence from Great Britain in 1965. A protracted racial and civil war followed, lasting until 1979, when Britain intervened to force the open elections that led to the election of Mugabe's socialist party and the declaration of Zimbabwe's independence in 1980. See Eve Bertelsen's summary in "*The Golden Notebook:* The African Background," in *Approaches to Teaching Lessing's "The Golden Notebook,"* 31–33, and, with special reference to Lessing's youth in Rhodesia, Michael Thorpe's account in *Doris Lessing's Africa* (London: Evans Brothers, 1978), 4–6. For two divergent readings of Lessing's complex relation to colonialism in her life and fiction, see Antony Beck, "Doris Lessing and the Colonial Experience," *Journal of Commonwealth Literature* 19, no. 1(1984): 64–73, who argues that her representation of colonialism "functions to conceal her fundamental commitment to the bedrock values she shares with the white settlers" (69), and Jenny Taylor,

"Memory and Desire in Going Home: The Deconstruction of a Colonial Radical," *Critical Essays on Doris Lessing*, ed. Claire Sprague and Virginia Tiger (Boston: G. K. Hall, 1986), which reads Lessing's 1965 autobiography, *Going Home*, as a symptomatic "speaking of the unspoken that lies beneath Lessing official fictional projection" (38). In both cases, note the shared assumption that the fiction contains a repressed content that hovers around the "problem" of colonialism and race.

6. Thorpe, *Doris Lessing's Africa*, 6, 7. The man Lessing married, Gottfried Lessing, also a communist, was one of these refugees and the model for Willi Wulf in the novel.

7. "A Conversation with Doris Lessing (1966)," in *Doris Lessing: Critical Studies*, ed. Annis Pratt and L. S. Dembo (Madison: University of Wisconsin Press, 1974), 10; emphasis added.

8. Lessing's most trenchant commentary on Anna's insights into the deeply destructive antagonism of men and women is conveyed not in Anna's own voice but in the displaced form of the new novel, *The Shadow of the Third*, that Anna is secretly writing in the Yellow Notebook. The depiction of the dance of attraction and repulsion binding the characters Ella and Paul (thinly veiled portraits of Anna and her ex-lover Michael) in an unceasingly antagonistic relationship becomes a damning critique of the operations of power and gender hierarchy that render the cliched equation of "sex" as a kind of "war" all too descriptive of the present state of male-female relationship. "Men. The enemy. They" (452), the character Ella in Anna's novel uncompromisingly declares. This language anticipates the imagery of war and revolution in the dream, cited above, in which Anna imagines herself as the dark-skinned North African soldier fighting colonial oppression by firing at an "enemy" implicitly identified with Saul. And as Ella's lover Paul says with defensive sarcasm, "My dear Ella, don't you know what the great revolution of our time is? The Russian revolution, the Chinese revolution—they're nothing at all. The real revolution is, women against men" (213).

9. It is no coincidence either that the book often credited with triggering the modern feminist movement was titled *The Feminine Mystique* or that it was published in 1962, the year that Lessing's novel appeared, for the production of the "mystique" that Betty Friedan critiques in this volume was not simply the product of centuries of oppression (although it was also that) but a very specific creation of the postwar years in which the present-time *The Golden Notebook* is set. Likewise, the psychological bind in which Anna finds herself trapped is intimately related to a crisis in masculine and feminine self-fashioning in the postwar period. In England, America, and indeed Western Europe, the sexual ideology emerging from the Cold War era of the fifties and early sixties was a particularly riven one, split by contradictions that a newly rearticulated notion of gender performance only barely managed to cover. On the one hand, the postwar, pre-Vietnam era was the beginning of the "sexual revolution." Coexisting with the era's heightened ideal of the surburban home and the planned, nuclear family—ideals held out, in a profound sense, as the "reward" of peacetime—was the heightened eroticization of both middle-class men and women as sexual agents and sexualized bodies, increasingly engaging in premarital sex and affairs outside of marriage. Women's roles were especially complicated by these changing sexual mores. Even as the end of the war forced many middle- and working-class women out of civilian jobs and back into domestic lives serving their men, the "career woman" and "city girl" also became more familiar

and accepted types. Indicative of a new class of educated, professional women for whom marriage was less an immediate necessity, women like Anna helped make possible a less virginal, sheltered conception of femininity that no longer depended exclusively on sexual purity. Yet such a formulation insidiously also recuperated a cultural belief in an essential "femininity," an emphasis that indeed *intensified,* throughout the fifties, as a certain image of essentialized femininity—performed on the accessorized female body, with push-up bras, wasp-waisted dresses, nylons, high heels—was mass-produced with a vengeance, as the photographs in *Life* and *Look* magazines vividly attest.

10. Perhaps the most damning commentary the text offers of the psychological consequences of this enmity on the thinking modern woman is the image Anna creates of her fictional double, Ella, masturbating to the "accompaniment of fantasies of hatred about men," feeling absolutely "humiliated" by her sexual dependence on men "for 'being [really] satisfied,'" even as she "uses this kind of savage phrase to humiliate herself" as she reaches orgasm alone, fantasizing her hatred of the very men she thinks she needs (455).

11. This sexual consummation, however, is entirely undercut as a swooning narrative climax when Paul meets a very unheroic death a few days later. Summoned to duty, he inadvertently walks into his airplane's moving propeller, and, in an instance of the "return of the repressed" that verges on parody, severs both legs "just below the crotch" (78), dying instantly. A symbolic castration of manhood if ever there was one, Paul's death casts a rather ironic light on the effects of his heterosexual initiation.

12. I have written more extensively on this phenomenon in "Vacation Cruises; or, The Homoerotics of Colonialism," *PMLA* 110 (January 1995): 89–107. I also discuss at greater length Lessing's African topos in comparison to Lawrence Durrell's evocation of Egypt in *The Alexandria Quartet* in chapter 6: "Fragmented Selves, Mythic Descents, and Third World Geographies: Fifties' Writing Gone Mad," in *Libidinal Currents: Sexuality and the Shaping of Modernism* (Chicago: University of Chicago Press, 1997).

13. The chain of displacements at work goes something like this: the Marxist comrade George is in love with the cook's wife (white/black), the cook's wife is married to Jackson the cook (black/black), Jackson "loves" Jimmy (so Jimmy says) (black/white), Jimmy is in love with Paul (white/white), Paul makes love to Anna (white/white). Anna's surrogate in the novel, in this scheme, thus becomes the black woman, the most oppressed "Other" who is also the most invisible character of this entire group.

14. As Mark Spilka argues, it is Anna's "asserted heterosexuality" in her relationships that brings out the more conservative, indeed in many ways Laurentian, side of an author whose sexual politics are otherwise diametrically opposed to those of Lawrence. See Spilka, "Lessing and Lawrence: The Battle of the Sexes," *Contemporary Literature* 16, no. 2 (spring 1975): 229.

15. Said, *Orientalism* (New York: Vintage, 1979), 190 and passim.

16. Thorpe, *Doris Lessing's Africa,* 92–93, also notes how this "perfect" match exposes Anna's romanticization of her material in her war novel.

17. This male ambivalence is revealed in the thoughts that immediately precede this expression of disgust, as Anna recalls Comrade Nelson's confession that "sometimes he looked at his wife's body and hated it for its femaleness.... Sometimes, he

said, he saw his wife as a kind of spider, all clutching arms and legs around a central devouring mouth" (612).

18. Deleuze and Guattari, *Anti-Oedipus: Capitalism and Schizophrenia*, trans. Robert Hurley et al. (1972; reprint, Minneapolis: University of Minnesota Press, 1983), 170; cited in Kauffman, *Special Delivery*, 157.

19. See Abel's suggestion that the writing of female bonding in the novel is a kind of *ecriture feminine* or female writing that stresses the relational, nonverbal, and gestural, in "*The Golden Notebook:* 'Female Writing' and 'The Great Tradition,'" in Sprague and Tiger, *Critical Essays*, 102–04. True enough, Anna and Molly's relationship bears many resemblances, both explicit and implicit, to a mother-child relationship; but this seems to me a parental model rooted in a more traditionally Oedipal sense of the need for separation and distance (hence the separation that follows their final kiss in the last line) rather than, in Chodorovian revisions of Freud's paradigm, the mirroring symbiosis that becomes a model for adult relationships with women.

20. The text's first allusions to lesbianism are filtered through the fictional alter egos of Ella (Anna) and Julia (Molly) in Anna's unfinished novel in the Yellow Notebook, *The Shadow of the Third*. Ella's lover jealously sees the two women's closeness as a "pact" working to exclude him, and thus he derides it by making defensive "professional jokes"—he is a psychiatrist—"about the Lesbian aspects of this friendship" (208–09). We later see Ella beginning to internalize this opinion when she decides not to continue confiding her romantic travails to Julia, because she fears that "two women, friends on the basis of criticism of men, are Lesbian psychologically if not physically" (455). Similarly, Anna writes in the Blue Notebook that the problem for "women of our time" is that their self-consciousness about the failure of men will "turn them bitter, or Lesbian, or solitary" (480).

21. My terms here are indebted to Lee Edelman's analysis of the film *Laura* in *Homographesis* (New York: Routledge, 1994), 192–241, in which he argues that the ultra-femme Laura represents "the other face" of Waldo Lydecker's effeminately gendered homosexuality. Lessing, in contrast, represents effeminate gay maleness (the Waldo position) as the other face of Anna's desired femininity (the Laura position).

22. A climactic moment of confrontation between Anna and Saul, recorded in a harrowing passage at the end of the Golden Notebook as Saul dangerously lapses in and out of his schizophrenia, illustrates the deep division and hatred on which masculine heterosexuality is founded: "back came the madman, *for now it was not only I I I I, but I against women*. Women the jailors, the consciences, the voice of society, and he was directing *a pure stream of hatred against me, for being a woman....* As I wept *I saw his prick stand up* under his jeans ... and I thought, derisive, oh so *now he's going to love me*" (630; emphasis added).

23. Gwen Bergner, "The Role of Gender in Fanon's *Black Skin, White Masks*," *PMLA* 101 (January 1995): 78; Frantz Fanon, *Black Skin, White Masks* (1952; trans. 1967; New York: Grove, 1991), 78, quoted in Bergner.

CODA

Rethinking Colonial Discourse Analysis and Queer Studies

Philip Holden

In Shyam Selvadurai's *Cinnamon Gardens* the protagonist Balendran Naveratnam is jolted from the comfort of his elite colonial lifestyle in Colombo by the sudden appearance of an English book:

> The books were in high piles on the floor, and, as he walked around them to get to his desk, Balendran noticed a copy of Edward Carpenter's *From Adam's Peak to Elephanta: Sketches in Ceylon and India* sitting on top of one pile. He picked it up. It had been a gift from Richard. He opened the book and read the dedication Carpenter had written to him, recalling the trip Richard and he had made to see Carpenter after reading his *Intermediate Sex....* There, for the first time, he learnt that inversion had already been studied by scientific men who did not view it as pathological, indeed men who questioned the whole notion that regeneration was the sole object of sex.[1]

This queer moment begins a key thread in the novel, in which Balendran's sexuality enables him to move between communities under colonialism— from the casual sex with Ranjan, an army private, on the beach by the Bambalapitiya railway station, to his relationship with Englishman Richard Howland, a key advisor to the Donoughmore Constitutional Commission investigating electoral reform. Yet it is also a moment that is quickly incorporated into a very colonial rationality, Balendran naming his sexuality as identity through the support of "scientific men."

Queerness is everywhere in *Cinnamon Gardens*—from the parodic naming of Balendran's father's house as "Brighton" to the alternative artists' community that exists in one of the elite enclave's bungalows.

Yet the various sites of exclusion of the colonial world—gender, race, community, sexuality, class, caste, religion—are always present in Selvadurai's novel, just as they are always subject to questioning and transgression. There are filiations, and alliances, but there are also oppositions—the feminism of the missionary school, for instance, is also racist—and no common narrative of emancipation emerges. At the end of the novel, Balendran has a stronger sense of self within a colonial world but expresses this only in a belated plea for friendship with his departed English lover, echoing another colonial intertext, E. M. Forster's *A Passage to India*.

One could argue that *Cinnamon Gardens* itself represents a theoretical intervention, a reinsertion of queer histories into modernization, into a colonial society reinventing itself as a nation. The irresolution of its ending, however, also suggests difficulties that might be faced by attempts to combine colonial discourse analysis and queer theory. Both queer studies and colonial discourse analysis arise from emancipatory projects: one might reasonably wish, as Christopher Lane memorably commented, to use the tool of queer theory to "shatter Britain's colonial legacy, once and for all."[2] This essay contends, however, that efforts to look critically at colonial texts through the lens of queer theory need to be informed, as *Cinnamon Gardens* is, by a sense of history, a history not only of the theoretical roots of colonial discourse analysis and queer studies but also, more crucially, of colonial modernity itself. As such, it forms a coda to our collection, revisiting the history of the development of queer theory and colonial discourse analysis and yet also suggesting possibilities for future work beyond the scope of the essays collected here.

Uneven Development? Colonial Discourse Analysis and Queer Theory

Colonial discourse analysis is, as an established critical space within the Western academy, the senior field of inquiry. Its concerns are certainly not new. The question of the relationship between colonial discourse and colonial power, of how one might modernize while preserving or regaining cultural and political autonomy, was a problem that vexed anticolonial intellectuals in the nineteenth and early twentieth centuries, and it informs the work that placed colonial discourse analysis on the critical table in the Western academy: Edward Said's *Orientalism*.

Much of our current critical vocabulary in colonial discourse analysis still comes to us through Said's mediation: discourse from Michel Foucault, hegemony from Antonio Gramsci, latent versus manifest from Freud, Same versus Other from Lacan or, confusingly, Hegel. Said's theoretical eclecticism has been thoroughly, and to some extent rightly, critiqued.[3] Perhaps more serious is his inability to theorize resistance to colonialism, not just in terms of violent insurrection but also in the manner in which orientalist tropes were taken up and transformed into albeit compromised instruments of liberation by nationalist projects in colonized areas. To rephrase Tania Modleski's criticism of gender studies as feminism without women, we risk here an anticolonialism without the colonized.[4]

In the 1980s, the conceptual space Said had cleared was occupied by two Western-based critics, Gayatri Spivak and Homi Bhabha. Spivak's work is to me most useful as a heuristic: she demands a scrupulous consideration of one's own academic location, not merely in terms of geography and community but also in terms of gender. Bhabha provides more of a methodology, and, indeed, for some years in the 1990s it was difficult to analyze a colonial text without resorting to the vocabulary he popularized: ambivalence, mimicry, and hybridity. It is sobering to realize, however, that Bhabha's and Spivak's most influential essays in the area of colonial discourse analysis were written more than a decade ago. In the 1990s Bhabha moved to studies of nationalism and migrancy, while Spivak, in her latest book, plots "a practitioner's progress from colonial discourse studies to transnational cultural studies."[5]

For colonial discourse analysis, the 1990s were a time of questioning, and reorientation. In a recent comment, Spivak has noted the danger of colonial discourse studies that "when they concentrate only on the representation of the colonized or the matter of the colonies, can sometimes serve the production of current neocolonial knowledge by placing colonialism/imperialism securely in the past."[6] For a time, it seemed as though inquiry had, as Robert Young suggested in *Colonial Desire*, "stagnated."[7] Much analysis noted the presence of mimicry or hybridity in a colonial text, produced Bhabha as a deus ex machina, and left investigation at that, implicitly privileging an enlightened postcolonial analyst over a colonial analysand. While there certainly were dissenting voices, the challenges they provided were usually dismissed. The most powerful attacks on postcolonialism in general, and colonial discourse analysis in particular, in the early 1990s were those of Aijaz Ahmad and Arif Dirlik, which rightly attempted to ask questions about the complicity of colonial discourse analysis with late capitalism. Postcoloniality, noted Dirlik, was "the condition of the intelligentsia of global capitalism."[8] For Ahmad, Bhabha and Said among others had turned away from the Marxist origins of critical theory to "theoretical . . . poststructuralism": postcoloniality arose at the time of "capitalism's global offensive and, by the later 1980s, its global triumph,"[9] and in its turning away from dialectical materialism was complicit with this offensive. The reception of Ahmad's work, in particular, was hostile—few of the responses in the special issue of *Public Culture* on *In Theory* were positive.[10]

At the same time as these boundary disputes were being fought out, however, a subtle change was coming over colonial discourse analysis. From its literary origins, colonial discourse analysis spread across traditional disciplinary boundaries into art history, anthropology, social geography, and history. This disciplinary expansion in turn prompted a more thoroughgoing engagement with the materialities of colonialism. Three broad trends can perhaps be identified. First, there was increasing recognition of the complexity of the colonial world, rather than mere concentration on a binary division between colonizer and colonized. Ann Laura Stoler's work on European colonial communities, for instance, or Kumari Jayawardena's on the feminist movement in Sri Lanka, displayed the complex mutual reliance of members of colonizing and protonationalist elites.[11] Second, resulting from this, colonial discourse analysis has developed a much more nuanced understanding of the continuities between colonial and postcolonial worlds. Just as we can no longer see the colonial world as a Manichean world—although individual subjects may well have perceived it as such[12]—so the division between colonialism and independence becomes less of an epistemic rupture. Finally, the relationship between colonialism and modernity has been much explored: colonialism and modernity came to many societies simultaneously, and it may be more strategically useful to examine colonial modernities as discrete moments of cultural development and transformation rather than to see modernization as simply an effect of colonialism. Partha Chatterjee, for instance, has emphasized how nationalism in colonized Asia should not be seen as merely a belated borrowing of European nationalisms but a distinctive cultural and political force in its own right.[13]

The conceptual widening of colonial discourse analysis has had two beneficial effects. Previous generations of anticolonial writers such as Frantz Fanon and C. L. R. James can now be read in their social and political context, rather than simply as proto-poststructuralists, and their critiques more precisely deployed.[14] And colonial discourse analysis no longer has to exclude Marxists and cultural materialists: "it has today become possible," remarks Neil Lazarus, "for the first time since the field was instituted in the early 1980s, for Marxist scholars to engage postcolonial studies on its own ground."[15] In analysis, we can now see colonialism less as a trauma we should forget, and more as a phenomenon containing within it a powerful heuristic with reference to the present. We can see Jamaica, Singapore, Hong Kong at the beginning of the last century as already postmodern and globalized. If postcolonialism has become less certain of its own explanatory force as a category of inquiry, the field of intellectual engagement around it has become correspondingly wider.

Queer theory has followed—albeit belatedly—a similar trajectory to colonial discourse analysis. Like colonial discourse analysis, the concerns of queer studies are not new: one can look back beyond Jeffrey Weeks's work in the 1970s to the fact that several nineteenth-century sexologists, who were responsible for the development of what Michel Foucault called the apparatus of sexuality, were themselves "Uranian."[16] Like colonial discourse analysis, however, queer studies crystalized into a clearly defined field through the catalysis of a founding text. Although very different in subject matter and critical assumptions from *Orientalism*, Eve Sedgwick's *Between Men* bears many surprising similarities to Said's work. It, too, is a theoretical mélange: Lacan mixes with a productive misreading of René Girard, and with Friedrich Engels and Claude Lévi-Strauss through the mediation of feminist anthropologist Gayle Rubin. Like *Orientalism*, *Between Men* surveys a large historical panorama, from Shakespeare's sonnets to late-nineteenth-century readers of Whitman. And like Said's work, its mode of analysis is largely synchronic rather than diachronic: Sedgwick imposes the geometry of the Girardian triangle on a variety of literary texts, but she does not at this point produce a coherent theory of development or change, just as Said's *Orientalism* at times suggests an unchanging binarism from Aeschylus to Acheson. The influence of Michel Foucault's *History of Sexuality* gave an impulse to greater historicization in queer studies. Sedgwick's next

book, *Epistemology of the Closet,* is much more carefully located historically, exploring the period at the end of the nineteenth century at which
the specification of the homosexual took place. Just as Bhabha's terminology has supplemented Said's, so Sedgwick's analytical vocabulary—
homosocial, triangular desire, the closet—has been supplemented by
Judith Butler's notion of performativity.

While the phrase "queer theory" seems to have been first used by Teresa
de Lauretis,[17] it was associated in the early 1990s with Sedgwick, Judith
Butler, and Diana Fuss. Butler's *Gender Trouble* and Fuss's edited collection *Inside/Out* provided substantial impetus to an expanding field. Influenced by both Foucault and Lacan, queer theorists argued that heterosexuality was not only a normalizing construct but also that it was
inherently unstable, dependent on self-differentiation from a homosexuality acknowledged a priori. Queer reading could locate moments of
slippage in the performance of sexuality and, indeed, of gender. As with
postcolonial theory, the most trenchant initial criticism came from Marxists. Donald Morton's critique of queer studies as proceeding via "ludic
(post)modernism toward a theoretically updated form of idealism and
away from historical materialism"[18] noted that the queer should itself
be "historicized as part of a systematic development connected to the
appearance in late capitalism of such notions as virtual realities, cyber-
punk, cybersex, teletheory."[19] Morton himself was for a time something
of the Aijaz Ahmad of queer studies, but the issues he raises have, in a
less obviously dialectical materialist form, now been placed firmly at
the center of much discussion of queer theory and queer studies. An article by Tim Edwards notes that queer theory has "little potential . . . for
any kind of communitarian politics,"[20] finding gay and lesbian commitments to praxis replaced with an "increasingly vacuous discourse of
diversity and radical 'anything goes' individualism."[21] More generously,
Joshua Gamson, looking at subjective identification with the categories
"queer," "gay," and "lesbian" in San Francisco, notes that the opposition
between queer and lesbian/gay reflects "the simultaneity of cultural
sources of oppression (which make loosening categories a smart strategy) and institutional sources of oppression (which make tightening
categories a smart strategy)."[22] Like postcolonial studies, queer studies is
broadening, leaving behind the skepticism toward any form of empirical inquiry that characterized the field early in the 1990s and engaging

with the material, if in a rather more eclectic manner than that which Morton proposed.

In terms of postcolonial studies, one of the most interesting developments in recent years in queer theory has been the notion of "global queering" and the connection of queer—and gay—identities to modernity and late capitalism. Dennis Altman's "Rupture or Continuity?" and "On Global Queering" provoked a charged debate, noting the growing tendency of groups worldwide to represent themselves as gay and questioning whether this represented the formation of a new transnational community, or the victory of a hegemonic Western apparatus of sexuality. Altman himself provided no ready answers, and, indeed, one might question his ready division between premodern "homosexual cultural traditions"[23] and modern gay identity, which excludes indigenous modernities that have relative autonomy from those of Europe and America. The debate around Altman's essay, however, is symptomatic of a larger concern regarding the politics of applying queer theory to societies outside Europe and North America. Given the rapid development of East Asian societies in the last three decades, much of the most exciting work has come from this geographical area. Peter Jackson's careful documentation of Thai elite discourses on homosexuality, for instance, raises important questions regarding the universalization of concepts such as homophobia[24] and argues for careful location in specific cultural practices. Many writers in other languages on queer issues, such as Taiwan's Chang Hsiao-Hung, are now being translated into English, and U.S. and European academics are having to take notice of them.[25] It is becoming less possible to produce what David Halperin terms "theory-heavy, empirically under-nourished work" in the field.[26]

Such changes have been paralleled by new concerns within the United States academy with queer diasporas, most eloquently expressed in the work of Gayatri Gopinath, Chandan Reddy, and Martin Manalansan. Noting the fact that groups such as Queer Nation frequently focus on metaphors of nation and citizenship, Gopinath, for instance, proposes a different model. "Queer diasporas," drawing on Stuart Hall's notion of diaspora as a flexible transnational identity, does not suggest, Gopinath emphasizes, "that transnational performances of South Asian queerness work to create some kind of purely liberatory space, free from the various violences effected by the disciplinary mechanisms of the state and nation." However, there are "possibilities" in "conceptualizing a diasporic or transnational South Asian queer sexuality."[27] Similarly, Manalansan explores the self-constitution of Filipino "gay" men, noting that hegemonic notions of globalizing gay liberation do not apply to indigenous notions of queer selfhood such as the category *bakla*. Filipino gay men in New York retain a sense of difference from a mainstream gay community because of their own sexual subjectivities.[28]

For analysis of colonialism, what is perhaps most interesting is the tension between diasporic cultural formations and national cultures that emerged from colonialism. Manalansan, for instance, notes attempts to create a "modern" gay identity in the Philippines that Other the *bakla* in a manner strikingly similar to the way in which nationalist discourse addresses itself to the condemnation of irrationality and superstition. Gopinath notes elsewhere that early nationalist groups in India created a normalized heterosexual home in opposition to Western "perversion": thus "the categories of 'queer' and 'diaspora' threaten the coherence of patrilineal, genealogical narratives of organic heterosexuality upon which the nation depends."[29] In a different vein, Chandan Reddy explores how the racialized family functions as an Althusserian ideological state apparatus within American modernity. The notion of the "American Standard of Living," propagated from the late nineteenth century onward, expressed wage labor as freedom. Simultaneously, its notion of a "family wage" privileged men as heads of households.[30] Women and immigrant groups with different familial structures were thus disadvantaged. Yet, for the latter, "the organization of these extended 'families' for whom the nuclear model was invalid and materially impossible and their historical exclusion from 'equality' within the State" led to "the emergence of counter-knowledges of how social relations might be imagined and practised differently from the form demanded by White patriarchal domesticity and the racial and gendered State that supports it" (366). Drawing on Jenny Livingstone's documentary of New York ball circuit and associated houses, *Paris Is Burning,* Reddy notes that

> ... "houses" are, in part, sites that are established by queers of color
> in antagonism to the ideologies and material exclusions of the home,
> whose central purpose is not necessarily, in the case of racial/ethnic
> homes, the reproduction of state racism. Yet, because queers of color are
> part of the political formation "people of color," it is these collectivities,
> in alterity to forms of antagonism articulated "directly" against racial

subordination . . . that might found an alternative logic or mapping of subjectivity that can extend our movement in the fight against the State and cultural "structure in dominance." (373)

In thinking of the cultures of colonialism, Reddy's formulation may be useful in the analysis of the disciplinary practices of both colonial and new national regimes and their reliance on the production of both gendered and heterosexual subjects and citizens.

Pioneering writing by Gopinath, Reddy, Manalansan, and others suggests provocative connections between postocolonial/diasporic studies and queer theory, further epitomized by Cindy Patton and Benigno Sánchez-Eppler's edited collection *Queer Diasporas*.[31] The challenge is to trace genealogies linking tactics of sexuality "in the gyrations of postmodernity"[32] to sites of contest and struggle in the colonial world. This may, in turn, involve a reconsideration of the manner in which queer studies and colonial discourse analysis meet, and it may indeed require us to reconsider the explanatory value of "colonial discourse" as a critical or conceptual term.

Our brief history of postcolonial and queer studies suggests, I think, two possible paths in the queering of colonial discourse analysis. The first, which has been the most common approach in the last decade, relies on similarities in methodological approaches between colonial discourse analysis and queer theory, emerging in the theoretical moment of poststructuralism. Bhabha's notion of mimicry is hauntingly similar to Butler's concept of performativity. For Bhabha, the colonized's continuous repetition and imitation of colonial discourse—"not quite/not white"[33]—introduces an instability that colonial discourse can never quite escape. If a brown Englishman can produce a successful impersonation of Englishness—which, after all, colonial discourse purports to teach him to do—Englishness as essential identity is called into question. Mimicry throws us back to the ambivalence of colonial discourse, its mixture of desire and disavowal. Needing to Other the colonized to establish his identity, the colonizer paradoxically is trapped in a perpetual need of the colonized, since the latter is an essential part of identity formation. Butler's idea of performativity works in a parallel manner. The walk on the wild side of camp or transvestism is, for Butler, a repetition of gender roles slightly off key, calling into question their naturalized immunity to critique. Perfomativity's relentless repetition—not quite/not straight—destablizes a normative sex-gender system. The heterosexual is tied to the homosexual by the same logic that binds the colonizer to the colonized. The homosexual is a necessary precondition of heterosexual identity: indeed, the word "heterosexual" comes into the language as a belated response to the coining of "homosexual." The homosexual subject must, however, be continually abjected: hence the title of Diana Fuss's groundbreaking volume of gay and lesbian studies essays, *Inside/Out*.

The similarities in methodological approaches are reflected in the use of similar spatial metaphors in both colonial discourse analysis and queer theory. The closet's hermetic sealing off of a private space has affinities with the boundaries and borders that colonial discourse analysis attempts to transgress. The growing popularity of the adjective "liminal" in colonial discourse analysis, drawn originally from anthropology, makes the parallel an even closer one: the limen may be the threshold to the closet. Yet the similarities here between heterosexuality and colonization seem to proceed very much from the theoretical moment, from the framework of analysis applied rather than the lived realities of colonialisms and sexualities. Any apparently stable sign can be revealed to be unstable through poststructuralist analysis of this kind: there seems no ready reason why "Europe" (which is habitually accorded deconstructive attention in colonial discourse analysis) or "heterosexuality" should be given special, and parallel, attention. With the turn of both queer theory and colonial discourse analysis to the material, insistence on such a parallel becomes less tenable, needing ever more inventive readings of textual aporias to make the intellectual connection.

There is, however, a second, more profound connection between colonial discourse analysis and queer studies, one that proceeds less from a theoretical than a historical context. Both find the latter part of the nineteenth century a period of radical cultural discontinuity: an epistemic break, in Michel Foucault's terms. For queer theory, the late nineteenth century is the time of both the identification of a homosexual as "a species," "a type of life,"[34] and, in response, of heterosexuality. For colonial discourse analysis, the late nineteenth century coincides with the rise of the New Imperialism, the apogee of the territorial division of the world among the industrialized powers, and the concomitant rise of modern nationalist movements, such as the Indian National Congress. And both queer theory and colonial discourse analysis draw their energy from, even as they question the basis of, emancipatory projects that gathered pace in the second half of the twentieth century: the struggle for gay and lesbian rights after Stonewall and the anticolonial struggle. Both take as their object of study, then, a process of subjectification, of individuals coming to see themselves as modern in a world that is always already globalized; both participate in a denaturalization of the modern.

While methodological similarities may prove tempting, they frequently lead to dehistoricized readings. An alternative strategy, locating filiations not in method but in the objects of inquiry themselves, would seem more fruitful and offer greater scope for historicity. Such a strategy does not, I think, necessitate the abandonment of the poststructuralist toolbox of colonial discourse analysis, nor a movement away from literary texts, but it requires greater self-awareness on the part of the theorist, critic, or cultural worker. Before we do this, however, we need to reread the studies that initially brought queer theory and colonial discourse analysis together in the light of new work on queer diasporas.

Ambivalent Marginality: Queer Theory Meets Colonial Discourse Analysis

The problems of a poststructuralist analysis merging Butler and Bhabha are evident in two initial studies that brought colonial discourse analysis and queer theory together, Jonathan Dollimore's *Sexual Dissidence* and Christopher Lane's *The Ruling Passion*. If these two studies seem wanting now, this is to no small degree a mark of their writers' success in opening up an area of intellectual debate, and Lane's essay in this volume indicates the extent to which the queering of colonial discourse has now developed.

Dollimore brings Bhabha and Butler together in a discussion late in *Sexual Dissidence*. Rather than looking for "a gay sensibility in an 'inner condition,'" Dollimore argues, "we might more usefully identify it outwardly and in relation to other strategies of survival and subversion, especially... the mimicry of the colonial subject."[35] While *Sexual Dissidence* attempts something much wider than a melding of colonial discourse analysis and queer theory, it does contain several analyses of colonial texts that draw on this identification of queer sexuality and colonial mimicry. The study is framed by the anecdote of a meeting between Wilde and Gide in Algeria, which Dollimore uses to make a distinction that will inform ensuing discussion—that between essentialist and antiessentialist ethics of transgression. Similarly, T. E. Lawrence is put forward as an example of a transgressive "obscure, marginal history where race and homosexuality converge."[36] The sexually dissident European traveler or adventurer, Dollimore argues, can open up fissures in imperial discourse: through a kind of cultural transvestism a multiplying effect is produced, and the contradictions of both heterosexuality and colonialism are subject to enhanced visibility and critique.

There are two problems with Dollimore's argument. First, he misreads Bhabha in suggesting that the agency of the mimic man is unproblematic: Bhabha does not unambiguously conceive of mimicry as an act of conscious resistance to colonial discourse. Second, the mapping of performativity onto mimicry makes the colonizing homosexual equivalent to the colonized mimic man—the "colonial subject" of his concluding analysis. This produces a pleasing theoretical symmetry, but it elides a recognition of the workings of colonial power. In the vast majority of situations, the colonial state's rule of difference would place these subjects on different sides of the colonizer/colonized binarism. The work of analysis is, of course, to deconstruct this binarism, but it should not wish it away.

To illustrate with Dollimore's own examples, it could be argued that Lawrence's sexuality was very much in service of empire. His Machiavellian genius, in this argument, was to harness a nationalist revolt in the service of British imperialism. One only has to look at the title of *Seven Pillars of Wisdom: A Triumph* to realize this. Given Lawrence's knowledge of classical and medieval history, the reference of the subtitle is clearly to the custom of granting a triumphal procession to a victorious Roman general—this is scarcely an antiimperialist statement. *Seven Pillars of Wisdom* is, of course, a fascinating and ambiguous text, one which, I think, unearths many of the anxieties that nineteenth-century frontier narratives epitomizing English masculinity strive to contain. To see it as a conscious expression of a dissident sexuality that can be aligned with resistance to imperialism is, however, surely wishful thinking.

Similarly, Dollimore's analysis of Wilde's meeting with Gide is circumscribed by a failure to deal with the materiality of colonialism. Wilde's intimacy with Gide is cemented by the exchange of an Algerian youth, Mohammed. There seem to be unmistakable echoes here of Gustave Flaubert's encounter with Kuchuk Hanem, which Said makes a focal point of *Orientalism*. Like Kuchuk, Mohammed is silent: he does not speak for himself, never represents his "emotions, presence, or history."[37] Rather, Gide and Wilde speak for Mohammed, and his exchange becomes a vehicle for Gide's self-realization. One could apply Sedgwick to this example in a manner that Dollimore has not envisioned: instead of a woman, one has the colonized at the apex of a Girardian triangle, the exchanged object in a traffic between men. Dollimore is right to point out that analysis should avoid falling into unconscious complicity with stereotypes of gay men as predatory: clearly, however, an erasure of the subject positions of Gide and Wilde and the privileges accorded them by colonialism seriously weakens his argument.

Christopher Lane's *The Ruling Passion* is a more theoretically consistent work than Dollimore's and is also more centrally concerned with colonial discourse analysis. Lane sidesteps Dollimore's difficulties with agency by a return to the Lacanian psychoanalysis underlying the work of Bhabha, Sedgwick, and Butler: he thus focuses on the "influence of unconscious identification, fantasy, and conflict" on political and social formations.[38] Homosexual desire shatters the fetishistic "national allegory" of imperial rule, for Lane, by introducing into it "unassimilable elements" (2). Historically, he notes, homosexual drives "resisted the allegedly unifying principles of colonialism by invoking suspicion, antagonism, and betrayal": in this action, they "helped to unmake some of Britain's imperialist policies by fostering a contrary interest, or counter-allegiance, with the colonized" (4).

Lane's avoidance of the problem of agency, however, leads to other difficulties. In a sense, Lane's difficulty in using Lacan reprises Bhabha's: as Robert Young notes, it is unclear at times whether Bhabha's use of Lacanian psychoanalysis is metaphorical, or whether he actually believes in the existence of universalized psychoanalytic constructions.[39] Lane's early discussion would seem to suggest that he does find psychoanalysis to have an analytic purchase and explanatory function. However, he frequently uses Freud, a contemporary of many of the writers he studies, in a manner that oscillates between analogy and analysis. Commenting on Dick Heldar's negotiation of homophilia in his relationship with Torpenhow in Kipling's *The Light That Failed*, Lane notes that in "an appropriate analogy here, Freud argued that the 'Primal Horde' of brothers had to maintain a similarly vigilant 'espirit de corps' against the legacy of their presocial and homosexual barbarism" (22).

The status of the reference to *Totem and Taboo* is problematic here: if Lane is merely claiming it exists within the same discursive field as Kipling's text, one cannot argue, but the implication seems to be that Freud's psychic structures provide a means of understanding Kipling's novel, and its thematization of homosociality and empire. The fact that both Freud and Jung drew on Rider Haggard's writings, which Lane registers (59–60), surely demonstrates the contiguity of metropolitan fiction and psychoanalysis: both are concerned with the creation of an implicitly male, modern, self-regulating subject. Psychoanalysis, Foucault notes, "cannot be dissociated from the generalization of the deployment of sexuality," which was an essential factor in the creation of the modern subject.[40] Using Lacanian psychoanalysis as a method of critique, Lane is unable to historicize and critique psychoanalysis itself, yet psychoanalysis is surely a part of a project of the creation of the modern subject that also embraces colonialism and the construction of the homosexual.[41]

Lane's use of psychoanalysis does result in a sensitivity to textual ambivalence that is a feature of all his writings, but often at the cost of some neglect of the materiality of colonialism. In his introduction, Lane warns about the dangers of seeing imperialism as a homogenous system, yet his methodology leads him, albeit unwillingly, to present it as such. His chapter on Kipling, for instance, begins with his coining the phrase "colonial impulse to power" (15); he soon moves on to discuss the "central axioms of colonial masculinity" (17), and the "psychic determinants" of imperial life (71). Yet the choice of texts is limited: Lane reads metropolitan fiction written by British men that thematizes colonialism from Kipling to Saki to reveal "condensed meanings," phrasing the issue of queerness in colonial discourse as an internal psychic struggle within the metropolitan literary text. Most actors in Lane's drama are the colonizers, "colonial" slipping easily into "colonialist." Texts written by colonized elites and nonfictional texts tend to be omitted, and the materiality of colonialism becomes occluded or is metaphorized into condensations and displacements in the metropolitan text. *The Ruling Passion* is an important study, with a foundational status similar to those of Sedgwick and Said: its methodology, however, can take us only so far.

Reinserting Power

If Lane's and Dollimore's valorization of disruptive queer marginality in colonial texts now, with the benefit of substantial hindsight, seems too utopian, the solution is surely not to reduce queer sexualities to a mere reflection, or component of, a colonial will to power. This is the strategy adopted by Elaine Freedgood writing on Forster's A Passage to India. Rather than seeing the homoeroticism of the text as in any way contesting imperialism, Freedgood views Forster's novel as promoting India as "a potential site for an eroticized and Orientalized all-male utopia,"[42] a utopia only made possible by the privileges imperialism grants to the author. For Freedgood, A Passage to India is a text explicitly encoded for a homosexual community, a fact shown in its title's references to Whitman, the description of India as a "queer nation," and the scene in which Aziz places a phallic collar-pin onto Fielding's collar. The "secret subject" of the text, the closeted homosexual, always remains on the colonizing side of the Manichean oppositions that structure colonialism (125):

> Accordingly, Forster directs his attention away from empire: Aziz and Fielding cannot finally be lovers, according to the narrative logic of A Passage, not because of the institutions and practices of the British Raj, but because of the self-involvement and cruelty of British women, because of the resistant and devouring landscape of India, and finally, because of the heterosexuality required by Indian Nationalism and the self-rule movement. (124)

Even the Carpenterian association of homosexuality with primitivity, Freedgood suggests, does not destabilize the text, since Forster clearly distinguishes between Western and Eastern varieties of primitivity: "For Forster and his readers, the Western primitive is an ideal, a prehistorical moment of noble savagery. The Eastern primitive, on the other hand, is what Forster continually refers to as a 'muddle'" (127).

Freedgood's analysis provides useful caveats against a valorization of the subversive potential of Forster's text, but in doing so it closes down the text's ambiguity and suggestiveness. As Lawrence Birken has shown, the primitive, and its association with perversion, was a site of considerable contestation in early twentieth-century sexology.[43] Colonial discourse of the late nineteenth and early twentieth centuries does view the primitive ambivalently: primitive energy is necessary for the regeneration of the race, and yet such energy must be managed through the technologies of self-discipline promoted by civilization. Adventure literature, one novelist administrator wrote, existed "for the latent barbarism of the young, with the amiable object of awakening in them a spirit of adventure which the circumstances of later life will render it impossible for the vast majority in any degree to satisfy."[44] Quite clearly, the Eastern primitive cannot be so easily marked out from the Western. The "self-involvement and cruelty of British women" is less a feature of Forster's text than it is of the majority of colonial British writing: to balance Mrs. Turton we have Mrs. Moore. Adela's attempt to "avoid . . . the mentality" of the Anglo-Indian woman, and her later comment that "I am told we all get rude after a year,"[45] show Forster's awareness of the fact that many European women throughout the British empire played out a socially constructed role that left little room for maneuver.

Freedgood's flattening out of textual ambiguities results in less than credible hypotheses concerning Colonial Office instrumentality in the deployment of homosexual civil servants:

> Officially, the British Empire reviled homosexuality; unofficially homo-sexuality and homosexuals were deployed strategically within empire, to build personal relationships that, in their intimacy and temporary equality, seemed to transcend the constraints and cruelties typical of other colonial relations. Men like Forster and Gide, T. E. Lawrence and Richard Burton, gave empire a more human face and form. (138)

Just as interracial homosexual relations were not automatically subversive, it seems unlikely that they were uniformly participatory in imperial strategy. Toward whom, one might ask, was the "human face and form" turned?

It is tempting to think that one might combine the best features of Freedgood's and Lane's work, to inject something of Freedgood's stress on the coercive nature of colonial power into the skillful registering of ambivalence that Lane's analysis provides. Without theoretical reformulations, however, and concomitant attention to the material practices of both colonialism and sexual minorities, such investigation may well find itself faced with a Sisyphean task. Joseph Allen Boone's influential essay "Vacation Cruises; or, the Homoerotics of Orientalism" is one such attempt. Sensitive to both the inequalities of power under colonialism and to the potential of homoeroticism to destabilize colonial discourse, Boone's essay begins with a wide-ranging discussion of Richard Burton, Gustave Flaubert, Lawrence Durrell, and Joe Orton. Boone concentrates on a restricted geographical area and briefly refers to a text that "speaks back" to homoerotic orientalist discourses, Mohammed Mrabet's *Love with a Few Hairs:* clearly the cultural traffic is not all one-way. The essay promises that "a series of collisions between traditionally assumed Western sexual categories...and equally stereotypical colonialist tropes" will be shown to "generate ambiguity and contradiction rather than assert an unproblematic intellectual domination over a mythic East."[46] It concludes that "the *other* other's story can unsettle the assumed hierarchy colonizer/colonized" resulting in "a crisis in male subjectivity" (104), while simultaneously suggesting that, through many homoerotic narratives, "the aegis of patriarchy" may be given renewed authority. The homoerotic colonial text becomes a palimpsest, in which authority is continually overwritten by homosexual desire in a series of textual transactions without reference to a wider discursive and material environment outside the text. The danger here is that a stress on textual ambiguity outside a social context results in one having one's critical cake and eating it: gay male subjectivity on the margins[47] is fragmented, a site of discursive rupture, but also complicit in a hegemonic imperial discourse. All literary texts are, of course, arguably both hegemonic and subversive, but the challenge for a critic is surely to illustrate how they operate within a particular discursive and material context. Without this illustration, Boone's analysis, despite its cogent individual textual readings, thus exemplifies Eve Sedgwick's criticism of applications of Butler's notion of performativity in which academic analyses struggle "to ascertain whether particular performances...are really *parodic and subversive*...or just *uphold the status quo*. The bottom line is generally the same: kinda subversive, kinda hegemonic."[48]

Sexuality, Colonialism, Modernity

Rather than returning to an original moment of symmetry between Bhabha and Butler, attempts to queer colonial discourse theory might respond to current concerns about materiality and the global in both queer and postcolonial studies. Reddy, Gopinath, Manalansan, and others, we have seen, respond by moving away from the postcolonial to diaspora studies; many contributors to the recent *Ariel* issue on queer theory and postcolonial studies wish to preserve the categories of postcolonial and colonial but also register a need for new theoretical paradigms. Terry Goldie, for instance, notes a lack of self-reflexivity in many efforts to use Butler's vocabulary to explore postcoloniality, so that every "non-white culture in the world can now be queered into a variant of the African-American."[49] Such unreflexive analysis, Rob Cover notes, may fail to account for "distinctive cultural ways of representing and understanding sexuality and non-heterosexuality in the non-Western regions of the world."[50] Yet the strategies offered to overcome these difficulties—to seek texts that offer not "an excursion into the brown world but an exploration and explanation from within the brown world"[51] or to look earnestly for "non-Western, non-bourgeois evidences of non-heteronormative sexualities"[52]—to some degree miss the point: the "brown world" is our world, whoever "we" might be, far more than we might be prepared to realize it—looking elsewhere may also be a matter of looking at ourselves.

Instead of seeing the "brown world" as Other, we might rather productively look at it as a generative site of colonial modernity, with all the uneven distributions of power that such a site might contain. We should not forget, indeed, the colonial roots of much poststructuralist theory: Derrida's and Althusser's early years were influenced by the divided world of the Algerian *colon,* while Foucault wrote *The Archaeology of Knowledge* in two years in the privileged enclave of Sidi Bou Saïd in Tunisia, a space from which it was impossible to exclude the politics of postcolonial nationalism. We need to look at sexuality and colonialism, then, as features of unevenly distributed but connected modernities.

My own theoretical preference here would be to use Foucault—eschewing the widely used and abused term "discourse" for Foucault's later concept of governmentality, following the lead of theorists of colonialism such as Partha Chatterjee, David Scott, and Nick Thomas. In a seminar given later in his life, Foucault noted that his project in the last twenty-five years had been to understand how human beings "develop knowledge about themselves" through such ways as "economics, biology, psychiatry, medicine and penology. The main point is not to accept this knowledge at face value but to analyze these so-called sciences as very specific 'truth games' related to specific techniques that human beings use to understand themselves."[53] These techniques Foucault terms "technologies"; in modern societies, these may be externally imposed by the state, or internally incited, and the "contact between the technologies of domination of others and those of the self I call governmentality."[54] The culmination of Foucault's work on the notion of the disciplinary society, governmentality is thus conceived of as a form of power in which individual subjects are not forcibly subjugated but rather encouraged to work toward their own self-improvement, to discipline themselves as citizens of a state. Thomas and Scott have noted that the colonial projects in nineteenth- and twentieth-century Ceylon and Fiji may be theorized using governmentality in that they attempted "systematic redefinition and transformation of the terrain on which the life of the colonized was lived."[55]

As Chatterjee has pointed out, however, while colonialism introduced a project of governmentality, of modern disciplinary power, it was constitutionally incapable of realizing the project's goals. Since the rationale for colonial power was based on a division between the colonizer and the colonized, "the colonial state was necessarily incapable of fulfilling the criterion of representativeness—the fundamental condition that makes modern power a matter of interiorized self-discipline rather than external correction."[56] The project was thus taken up by protonationalist elites, who engaged in community-wide disciplinary projects to create modern non-Western subjects, subjects for whom, as C. L. R. James famously remarked, "respectability was not an ideal, it was an armour."[57] Paradoxically, then, the new nation offered the possibility of fulfilling the project of governmentality of which colonialism dreamed, but which it could never realize.

Crucial to this project was gender and sexuality. In a world dominated by colonialism and increasingly global flows of capital, nationalist and pronationalist elites attempted to recreate themselves as modern subjects. National pasts were, if not invented, substantially remolded, and degenerate elements expelled: the community comprising a nation in waiting was reimagined as composed of citizens committed to self-discipline and somatic control. The private, feminized space of the home became the place of culture and tradition, opposed to the masculine modernity of the public world. Homosexuality and other non-normative sexualities became associated both with atavism—part of a decadent communal past so earnestly to be disavowed in the present—and also, paradoxically, with degeneration, as a marker of how the West had fallen away from the project of modernity. Modern disciplinary power, in this view, would be perfected not by the colonialists but by the new nations that emerged from colonialism.

Colonized and noncolonized areas that experienced European domination in the colonial world do, of course, have widely different histories, but all share in a process of becoming variously modern, and of simultaneously attempting to claim this modernity as autochthonous, rather than merely deriving from the West. Such a shared history produces surprising parallels among apparently disparate communities and projects. The Straits Chinese reform movement in the Straits Settlements in the late nineteenth and early twentieth centuries has often been thought of as complicit with colonialism, in its creation of respectable Anglophone Straits Chinese British subjects. Many of its features, however—the division of the domestic and public spheres, the elimination of "decadent" Malay cultural elements, the reinvention of Confucianism as a fulfilment of the project of Enlightenment rationality, the promotion of a *mens sana in corpore sano*—share similarities with an explicitly anticolonial project, the May Fourth Movement in China from 1919 onward. Superficially, there are important differences between the projects: the Straits Chinese sought a reform of Confucianism and a return to a rational Chinese tradition, while May Fourth Movement intellectuals sought an escape from Confucianism and the burden of Chinese tradition into a new modernity. The Straits Chinese reform movement took place in an area that was intensely colonized, and which in many senses was brought into being by colonialism: the May Fourth Movement crystallized around a continued resistance to colonialism borne of a new sense of nationalism. In the writings of both movements, however, the community is represented by a disciplined subject, differentiated from decadent tradition and also Western degeneration. The Straits Chinese community leader Lim Boon Keng[58] thus warned young men about wearing "dandy shoes or fancy hats," and avoiding "voluptuous and sensual . . . wallowing in impurity and sinking into corruption" of "wild and unnatural living."[59] Women, in contrast, were urged to leave behind the slovenly atavism of Malay culture epitomized by the "*déshabillé* aspect" of the sarong and baju.[60] In Ba Jin's novel, *Jia*,[61] a key May Fourth Movement text, the assertive heterosexuality of the protagonist Jue Hui, concerned to protect China against foreign domination, is contrasted to the queer sexuality of his grandfather, a representative of the old order, and of "Confucian Morals."[62]

The creation of modern subjects by such nationalist and protonationalist communities has profound effects on how sexuality is viewed in our contemporary world, since many modern nation-states are the result of the success, or partial failure, of such projects. Colonial discourse is thus not a nightmare that we should analyze upon waking, but rather a particular mode of power that forms the basis for other disciplinary projects in the present. Queering colonial discourse in the Straits Settlements, for instance, leads us directly to the refusal of Singapore's Register of Societies to register the sexual minorities' rights group People Like Us, or the discourses of sodomy in Malaysia that surround the fall from grace of Anwar Ibrahim.

Foucauldian analysis is not, of course, the only possible methodology. Among others, one might take a more strongly Marxist or broadly cultural materialist approach. John D'Emilio's work on the relationship between the growth of industrial capitalism and the rise of non-normative sexual identifications is surely crucial here and might be viewed not only in a European and North American but also in a global context.[63] Analysis of colonial texts through the lens of queer theory, however, will surely be most fruitful if it interrogates the epistemological assumptions of both colonial discourse analysis and queer theory and examines, without resorting to a premature reductiveness, their places within global systems of knowledge.

Such an interrogation, I think, introduces a number of caveats. First, we need to move away from the still-frequent identification of colonial and colonialist. Colonial discourse analysis often takes as its object of inquiry a very narrow range of texts, often those produced by European travelers or visitors. More attention needs to be given to texts published in the colonies, whether by European or non-European elites, and the reading practices that accompany them. Work in European languages is important, but it should ideally be supplemented by readings in other languages, and we should be aware of the presence of several public spheres, often linguistically distinct, in the colony and indeed in areas in which colonialism was peripheral. If some of the colonized actively answered back to colonialism, others carried on cultural projects that took sharply different trajectories and were not directly concerned with the colonial power at all. If the full range of colonial discourse is taken into account, much more potential for queer reading emerges, since sexualities will emerge as already "queered," already situational, read and modeled by a variety of differently positioned subjects.

Second, we need to address the fact that colonial discourse analysis often examines self-consciously literary texts and proceeds to make extrapolations from such texts about lived social realities and notions of subjectivity and community. Literary texts were important under colonialism, since their study was often used as a means of creating a hegemonic relationship with the colonized.[64] Colonized subjects might read such literary texts aberrantly or construct autonomous native literary traditions:[65] literary texts here become "portable machines" for the construction of modern subjectivities that can be applied to nationalist or community-building projects outside those of their original audience.[66] None of this, however, is self-evident—in the queering of colonial discourse, we have to think of the social function of the literary text, its circulation, and conditions of the twin processes of writing and of reading. If literary texts are to be used for analysis, they need to be carefully located in colonial and metropolitan reading communities: their literariness itself needs to be made an object of inquiry.

Third, we should recognize that we are unlikely in our analyses to find uncontaminated "non-Western, non-bourgeois evidences of non-heteronormative sexualities"[67] represented in any unmediated way within the discourses of colonial modernity. We are, for instance, more likely to find non-Western bourgeois heteronormative sexualities that themselves interpret and distance themselves from a nonheteronormative "tradition." Homophobia may at times be a key element of emancipatory national projects: struggles for gay or lesbian rights, or space, may be complicit with colonialism. Rather than merely attempting to discover exemplary social actors who combine both emancipatory projects, we should rather examine carefully the complex manner in which sexuality and colonialism overlap and gain leverage from each other.

These three caveats lead to a fourth: queering colonial discourse analysis requires an act of self-distancing from internalized North American notions of multiculturalism, a careful negotiation between universality and particularity. Peter Jackson rightfully remarks in a recent article that Thai discursive representations of sexuality cannot be theorized by merely relating them to Euro-American equivalents. Thus, we have noted, "homophobia" in many Thai contexts, for instance, should not be seen as universal but as emerging from a set of very distinct discursive practices, some class based, not all of them Western in origin.[68] Poststructuralist theory alone cannot provide this distance: Gayatri Gopinath's analysis of self-reflexive anthropology, such as the work of Susan Seizer, notes that such writing, for all its foregrounding of the anthropologist's investment in her own research process, may replicate "colonial discursive framings" in its attempt to fix an implicitly normative Western les-

bian subjectivity in contrast to an Indian Other.[69] Non-Western modernities may evolve under their own dynamics, and modernization is not
merely a process of becoming Western. At the same time, many analyses
that combine queer theory and colonial discourse analysis stop at the
door to specific cultural knowledge: the critic performs a ritual self-
reflexivity, stressing the limits of his or her ability to theorize as a cultural outsider, but then goes no further. Such critiques, in showing "sensitivity" in not engaging with the dynamics of colonial and postcolonial
cultures, in fact often accept the broad parameters of colonial epistemologies or the epistemologies of nationalist projects. Queering colonial discourse analysis must require an engagement with the specifics of
cultural practices in the colonial and postcolonial world, however challenging this engagement might be for the scholar in the Western academy: there should perhaps be a greater emphasis on genuinely collaborative work.

In conclusion, let me return to Foucault. Late in his life, when he became centrally concerned with the place of sexuality within the formation of modern subjectivities, Foucault also became concerned with
ethics, of how one might practice freedom within the confines of a disciplinary society. When asked in an interview about these concerns,
Foucault turned to decolonization, not merely as a metaphor, but as a
concrete example of the failure of the Enlightenment project of emancipation:

> I am not trying to say that liberation as such . . . does not exist: when a
> colonized people attempts to liberate itself from its colonizers, this is
> indeed a practice of liberation in the strict sense. But we know very well,
> and moreover in this specific case, that this practice of liberation is not
> in itself sufficient to define the practices of freedom that will still be
> needed if this people, this society, and these individuals are to be able to
> define admissible and acceptable forms of existence or political society.[70]

If they can work together, critical analysis of colonialism and queer
theory surely provide us with the means to assess the extent to which
we, and others connected to us by various filiations of identification and
power, experience in different ways and to different degrees the condition of living in liberation without freedom. Such assessment may also
lead us, often painfully, to begin to enact practices of freedom parallel
to those that Foucault espoused.

Notes

1. Shyam Selvadurai, *Cinnamon Gardens* (London: Anchor, 1999), 57–58.

2. Christopher Lane, *The Ruling Passion: British Colonial Allegory and the Paradox of Homosexual Desire* (Durham: Duke University Press, 1995), 13.

3. See Bart Moore-Gilbert, *Postcolonial Theory: Context, Practices, Politics* (London: Verso, 1997), 40–61, for a cogent summary (and synthesis) of many of these criticisms.

4. See Tania Modleski, *Feminism Without Women: Culture and Criticism in a "Postfeminist Age"* (New York: Routledge, 1991).

5. Gayatri Spivak, *A Critique of Postcolonial Reason: Towards a History of the Vanishing Present* (Cambridge: Harvard University Press, 1999), ix–x.

6. Ibid., 1.

7. Robert J. C. Young, *Colonial Desire: Hybridity in Theory, Culture, and Race* (London: Routledge, 1995), 164.

8. Arif Dirlik, "The Postcolonial Aura: Third World Intellectuals in the Age of Global Capitalism," *Critical Inquiry* 20 (1994): 356.

9. Aijaz Ahmad, *In Theory: Classes, Nations, Literatures* (London: Verso, 1992), 42.

10. *Public Culture* 6, no. 1 (fall 1993) contains several evaluations of Ahmad, mostly negative. The most balanced assessment is probably David Scott's in "The Aftermaths of Sovereignty: Postcolonial Criticism and the Claims of Political Modernity,'" *Social Text* 48 (1996): 1–26.

11. See in particular Stoler, *Race and the Education of Desire: Foucault's "History of Sexuality" and the Colonial Order of Things* (Durham: Duke University Press, 1995), and Jayawardena's *The White Woman's Other Burden: Western Women and South Asia During British Rule* (London: Routledge, 1995).

12. See, for instance, Cooper and Stoler's comment that they, in the study of colonialism, "are interested in understanding why Manichean dichotomies had such sustaining power in the face of such obvious hybridity and variation. Why did so many people—contemporary actors, not just latter-day historians—subscribe to divisions out of sync with the quotidian experiences that they shared?" See Ann Laura Stoler and Frederick Cooper, "Between Metropole and Colony: Rethinking a Research Agenda," in *Tensions of Empire: Colonial Cultures in a Bourgeois World*, ed. Frederick Cooper and Ann Laura Stoler (Berkeley: University of California Press, 1997), 9.

13. See Partha Chatterjee, *The Nation and Its Fragments: Colonial and Postcolonial Histories* (Princeton: Princeton University Press, 1993).

14. For a trenchant critique of efforts to produce Frantz Fanon as a poststructuralist theorist, see Henry Louis Gates Jr., "Critical Fanonism," *Critical Inquiry* 17 (1991): 457–70.

15. Neil Lazarus, *Nationalism and Cultural Practice in the Postcolonial World* (Cambridge: Cambridge University Press, 1999), 15.

16. See Joseph Bristow, *Sexuality* (London: Routledge, 1997), 179.

17. David Halperin, "A Response from David Halperin to Dennis Altman," *Australian Humanities Review* (1996), http://www.lib.latrobe.edu.au/AHR/emuse/Globalqueering/halperin.html (12 October 1999).

18. Donald Morton, "Birth of the Cyberqueer," *PMLA* 110 (1995): 369.

19. Ibid.

20. Tim Edwards, "Queer Fears: Against the Cultural Turn," *Sexualities* 1 (1998): 480.

21. Ibid., 481.

22. Joshua Gamson, "Must Identity Movements Self-Destruct?: A Queer Dilemma," in *Queer Theory/Sociology,* ed. Steven Seidman (Oxford: Blackwell, 1996), 412–13.

23. Dennis Altman, "On Global Queering," *Australian Humanities Review* (1996), http://www.lib.latrobe.edu.au/AHR/archive/Issue-July-1996/altman.html (12 October 1999). See also Altman's "Rupture or Continuity? The Internalization of Gay Identities," *Social Text* 48 (1996): 77–94.

24. Peter Jackson, "Thai Research on Male Homosexuality and Transgenderism and the Cultural Limits of Foucaultian Analysis," *Journal of the History of Sexuality* 8 (1997): 84.

25. See Hsiao-Hung Chang, "Taiwan Queer Valentines," in *Trajectories: Inter-Asia Cultural Studies,* ed. Kuan-Hsing Chen (London: Routledge, 1998), 283–298.

26. Halperin, "Response."

27. Gayatri Gopinath, "Funny Boys and Girls: Notes on a Queer South Asian Planet," in *Asian American Sexualities: Dimensions of the Gay and Lesbian Experience,* ed. Russell Leong (New York: Routledge, 1996), 120.

28. Martin M. Manalansan, "In the Shadows of Stonewall: Examining Gay Transnational Politics and the Diasporic Dilemma," in *The Politics of Culture in the Shadow of Capital,* ed. Lisa Lowe and David Lloyd. (Durham: Duke University Press, 1997), 485–505.

29. Gopinath, "Queer Diasporas: Gender, Sexuality, and Migration in Contemporary South Asian Literature and Cultural Production" (Ph.D. diss., Columbia University, 1998), 3.

30. Chandan C. Reddy, "Homes, Houses, Nonidentity: *Paris Is Burning,*" in *Burning Down the House: Recycling Domesticity,* ed. Rosemary Marangoly George (Boulder: Westview Press, 1998), 360.

31. Cindy Patton and Benigno Sánchez-Eppler, eds., *Queer Diasporas* (Durham: Duke University Press, 2000).

32. Ibid., 2.

33. Homi Bhabha, "Of Mimicry and Man: The Ambivalence of Colonial Discourse," *October* 28 (1984): 132.

34. Michel Foucault, *The History of Sexuality.* Volume 1: *An Introduction,* trans. Robert Hurley (New York: Vintage, 1990), 43.

35. Jonathan Dollimore, *Sexual Dissidence: Augustine to Wilde, Freud to Foucault* (Oxford: Clarendon Press, 1991), 312.

36. Ibid., 333.

37. Edward Said, *Orientalism* (London: Routledge, 1978), 6.

38. Lane, *The Ruling Passion,* 3.

39. See Robert Young's account in *White Mythologies: Writing History and the West* (London: Routledge, 1990), 153–54.

40. Foucault, *The History of Sexuality,* 129.

41. One of the most cogent accounts of psychoanalysis's own place within the apparatus of sexuality is Foucault's in *The History of Sexuality,* 115–31.

42. Elaine Freedgood, "E. M. Forster's Queer Nation: Taking the Closet to the Colony in *A Passage to India,*" *Genders* 23 (1996): 123.

43. Birken gives a tripartite genealogy of sexology from its origins in the nineteenth century to the present day. He notes that the association of "perversion" with primitivity popular from 1895 to 1915 contained its own contradictions and was eventually superseded by a homo/heterosexual binarism. *Consuming Desire: Sexual Science and the Emergence of a Culture of Abundance, 1871–1914* (Ithaca: Cornell University Press, 1988), 95.

44. Hugh Charles Clifford, *The Further Side of Silence* (Garden City: Doubleday, 1923), 319.

45. E. M. Forster, *A Passage to India* (London: Arnold, 1926), 146.

46. Joseph A. Boone, "Vacation Cruises; or, the Homoerotics of Orientalism," *PMLA* 110 (1995): 91.

47. The phrase is Kaja Silverman's. Her reading of T. E. Lawrence's "double mimesis" of Arab identity in *Seven Pillars of Wisdom*, while insightful in its attention to textual detail, is very much representative of this type of analysis. See Kaja Silverman, *Male Subjectivity at the Margins* (New York: Routledge, 1992).

48. Eve Kosofsky Sedgwick, "Queer Performativity: Henry James's *The Art of the Novel*," *GLQ* 1 (1993): 15.

49. Terry Goldie, "Introduction: Queerly Postcolonial," *Ariel* 30, no. 2 (1999): 21.

50. Rob Cover, "Queer with Class: Absence of Third World Sweatshop in Lesbian/Gay Discourse and a Rearticulation of Materialist Queer Theory," *Ariel* 30, no. 2 (1999): 39.

51. Goldie, "Introduction," 23.

52. Cover, "Queer with Class," 32.

53. Michel Foucault, "Technologies of the Self," in *Technologies of the Self: A Seminar with Michel Foucault*, ed. Luther H. Martin et al. (Amherst: University of Massachusetts Press, 1988), 18.

54. Ibid., 19.

55. David Scott, "Colonial Governmentality," *Social Text* 43 (1995): 205. See also Nick Thomas, *Colonialism's Culture: Anthropology, Travel, and Government* (Cambridge: Polity, 1994), 40–43.

56. Partha Chatterjee, "The Disciplines in Colonial Bengal," in *Texts of Power: Emerging Disciplines in Colonial Bengal*, ed. Partha Chatterjee (Minneapolis: University of Minnesota Press, 1995), 8.

57. C. L. R. James, *Beyond a Boundary* (Durham: Duke University Press, 1993), 8.

58. See Philip Holden, "The Beginnings of 'Asian Modernity' in Singapore: A Straits Chinese Body Project," *Communal/Plural* 7 (1999): 59–78.

59. Lim Boon Keng [as W. C. Lin], "Straits Chinese Hedonism," *Straits Chinese Magazine* 4 (1900): 108.

60. Soh Poh Thong, "Concerning Our Girls," *Straits Chinese Magazine* 11 (1907): 143.

61. *Jia* is normally translated as *Family*, but the single character carries a wider connotation in Chinese. "Family" *(jiating)* is certainly an important connotation, but the character also suggests home, and it is not insignificant that the Chinese word for nation—as opposed to state—is *guojia* (literally "state family").

62. Ba Jin [Pa Chin], *The Family*, trans. Sidney Shapiro (Beijing: Foreign Languages Press 1958), 61.

63. See John D'Emilio, *Making Trouble: Essays on Gay History, Politics, and the University* (New York: Routledge, 1992).

64. The fullest account of English literature's role in creating a colonized elite is Gauri Viswanathan's *Masks of Conquest: Literary Study and British Rule in India* (New York: Columbia University Press, 1989). Viswanathan's study has recently been disputed by both Harish Trivedi and Leela Gandhi, the latter noting that "rather than being passive objects of an authoritarian and alien pedagogy, Indian readers remained obdurately selective in their response to the English syllabus." See Leela Gandhi, *Postcolonial Theory: A Critical Introduction* (Edinburgh: Edinburgh University Press, 1998), 155, and Harish Trivedi, *Colonial Transactions: English Literature and India* (Manchester: Manchester University Press, 1995).

65. See my own account of the complicities and resistances involved in the study of English literature by elite communities in colonial Singapore: "Complicity and Resistance: English Studies and Cultural Capital in Colonial Singapore," *Kunapipi* 22, no. 1 (2000): 74–84.

66. Simon During, "Postcolonialism and Globalisation: A Dialectical Relation After All?", *Postcolonial Studies* 1 (1998):44.

67. Cover, "Queer with Class," 32.

68. Jackson, "Thai Research," 84.

69. Gayatri Gopinath, "Homo-Economics: Queer Sexualities in a Transnational Frame," in *Burning Down the House: Recycling Domesticity,* ed. Rosemary Marangoly George (Boulder: Westview Press, 1998), 114.

70. Michel Foucault, "The Ethics of the Concern of the Self as a Practice of Freedom," trans. P. Aranov and D. McGrawth, in *Ethics, Subjectivity, Truth,* ed. Paul Rabinow (New York: New Press, 1997), 282–83.

Contributors

Anjali Arondekar is assistant professor of critical race studies in the Department of Women's Studies at the University of California, Santa Cruz. She has published in the journals *Interventions, Postmodern Culture, Symploke,* and *Journal of Asian Studies,* and she is working on a book tentatively titled *A Perverse Empire: Victorian Sexuality and India.*

John C. Beynon is assistant professor of English at California State University, Fresno, where he teaches courses in eighteenth-century British literature and culture and in lesbian and gay studies. He served as assistant editor of *The Encyclopedia of Gay Histories and Cultures* and has published essays on William Beckford and John Cleland.

Joseph A. Boone is chair and professor of English at the University of Southern California, where he teaches modernism, the novel as genre, and queer theory. He is the author of *Tradition Counter Tradition: Love and the Form of Criticism* and *Libidinal Currents: Sexuality and the Shaping of Modernism,* and he has coedited *Engendering Men: The Question of Male Feminist Criticism* and *Queer Frontiers: Millennial Geographies, Genders, and Generations.* He has received Guggenheim and Rockefeller grants to work on a project about the homoerotics of colonialism, ranging from Crusader tracts to contemporary political cartoons.

Sarah Cole is assistant professor of English and comparative literature at Columbia University, where she teaches courses on twentieth-century

British literature and culture. Her book *Modernism, Male Friendship, and the First World War* is forthcoming.

Lois Cucullu is assistant professor of English at the University of Minnesota. She has published essays on Elizabeth Bishop, Virginia Woolf, and E. M. Forster, and she is completing a book on literary modernism and the cult of the expert, which draws on her research in the history and theories of the novel, the sociology of expert culture, the rise of English studies as a discipline, feminist theory, and the history of sexuality.

Maria Davidis received her Ph.D. from Princeton University. She has published articles on E. M. Forster and Kate O'Brien, and she is working on a study of gender and fantasies of youth in imperial narratives written from 1890 to 1930.

Dennis Denisoff is assistant professor of English at Ryerson University. He is the author of *Aestheticism and Sexual Parody,* the editor of *Queeries: An Anthology of Gay Male Prose,* and the coeditor of *Perennial Decay: On the Aesthetics and Politics of Decadence.* He is editing a collection of Victorian short stories and completing *Sexual Visuality from the Victorian Novel to Film Noir.*

Mark Forrester is an English instructor at the University of Maryland, College Park, where he is completing his dissertation on Frank Norris and American literary naturalism.

Terry Goldie is the author of *Pink Snow: Homotextual Possibilities in Canadian Fiction* and *Fear and Temptation: The Image of the Indigene in Canadian, Australian, and New Zealand Literatures;* he is coeditor (with Daniel David Moses) of *An Anthology of Canadian Native Literature in English.* He teaches Canadian and postcolonial literatures at York University, with particular interest in gay studies, literary theory, and drama.

Philip Holden is associate professor of English literature at the National University of Singapore. He is author of *Orienting Masculinity, Orienting Nation: W. Somerset Maugham's Exotic Fiction* and *Modern Subjects / Colonial Texts: Hugh Clifford and the Discipline of Literature in the Straits Settlements, 1895–1907.* He has written several articles on colonial and postcolonial literature and culture for periodicals such as *Literature and History, Ariel, Biography,* and *Communal/Plural.*

Christopher Lane is professor of English at Northwestern University. Author of *The Burdens of Intimacy: Psychoanalysis and Victorian Masculinity* and *The Ruling Passion: British Colonial Allegory and the Paradox of Homosexual Desire,* he is also editor of *The Psychoanalysis of Race* and coeditor of *Homosexuality and Psychoanalysis.* His next book, *Hatred and Civility: The Antisocial Life in Victorian England,* is forthcoming.

Tim Middleton is the head of English and Creative Studies at Bath Spa University College. He is co–vice chair of the Joseph Conrad Society in the United Kingdom, and he is editing a three-volume collection on modernity.

Richard J. Ruppel is professor and chair of the English department at Viterbo University in La Crosse, Wisconson. His essays on Joseph Conrad have appeared in *The Conradian, Studies in the Novel, Conradiana,* and *L'Epoque Conradienne.* He is writing a book on male intimacy in the life and works of Joseph Conrad.

Hans Turley is associate professor of English at the University of Connecticut. He is the author of *Rum, Sodomy, and the Lash: Piracy, Sexuality, and Masculine Identity* and has also written several articles on the eighteenth-century novel and eighteenth-century culture. He is coeditor of *The Eighteenth Century: Theory and Interpretation.* His next major project is a biography of Lord Rochester.

Index

Protestant sensibility, x, xiii
Puar, Jasbir, xxiv n. 3
Punch, 103

queer sexuality, 136, 139, 153, 167
queer theory, 92, 261; colonial discourse
  analysis and, 303–5, 317; development
  of, 299–303

race, 84, 92, 93, 105–6, 107, 116–17, 228,
  268, 274
Ransome, Stafford, 238 n. 6
Reddy, Chandan, 301, 302–3, 311
Rembrandt: *Danae,* 36
Reynolds, Joshua, 36
Rhodes, Cecil, 224, 228
Rich, Adrienne, 219 n. 20
Richardson, John, xvii
Rimsky-Korsakov, Nikolai, 247
Roberts, Andrew Michael, 168 n. 4
Robinson, Fred Miller, 221 n. 34
Roman de la Rose, 260 n. 27
Rome, 248
Rousseau, G. S., 43 n. 46
Rowbotham, Sheila, 62 n. 17
Royal Geographical Society, 102, 112 n. 57
Rubenstein, Roberta, 290 n. 3
Rubin, Gayle, 299; "Traffic in Women,"
  174, 219 n. 20, 221 n. 36
Ruppel, Richard J., ix–xxvi, 152–71,
  220 n. 23
Russell, Mary, 108 n. 2
Russia: and alterity, 242; polyphony, 244

Said, Edward, 282, 298, 300, 306–7, 308;
  Orientalism, 117, 190 n. 12, 245, 251–
  52, 293 n. 15, 296, 299; *The World, the
  Text, and the Critic,* 190 n. 14
Saki (Hector Hugo Munro), 308
Sánchez-Eppler, Benigno, xxiv n. 3, 303
Sapphism, xvii, xix, 21, 22, 24, 25, 28, 30,
  34, 35, 38, 40 n. 15
Schaffer, Talia, 259 n. 13
Schwarz, Bill, 150 n. 36
Schweickart, Patricinio P., 290 n. 3
Scotland, Scottishness, 189 n.7
Scott, David, 312–13, 318 n. 10
Scott, Sarah: *Millennium Hall,* 41 n. 26

Sedgwick, Eve Kosofsky, xvii, 145, 300,
  307, 308, 311; *Between Men,* xii, xx,
  45, 52, 75, 117, 127, 170 n. 28, 174, 189–
  90 n. 8, 211, 221 n. 36, 238n. 5, 299;
  Epistemology of the Closet, xii, xx, 60,
  137–38, 147, 149 n. 9
Seeley, Tracy, 220 n. 22
Seizer, Susan, 316
Selvadurai, Shyam: *Cinnamon Gardens,*
  295, 296
Shakespeare, William, 299; *Antony and
  Cleopatra,* 236; *Romeo and Juliet,* 249
Sharpe, Jenny, 70, 126–27
Shaw, Flora, 114 n. 74
Sherry, Norman, 170 n. 21
Showalter, Elaine: *Sexual Anarchy,*
  188 n. 1
Silverman, Kaja, 31, 131 n. 25, 320 n. 47
Simons, H. J.: and R. E., 238 n. 6
Sinfield, Alan, 168 n. 3, 218 n. 13
Singh, Shailendre Dhari, 71
Sinha, Mrinalini, xxiv n. 5, 70
Slobin, Greta, 245
Smiles, Samuel, xiii
Smith, Craig, 231, 238 n. 4, 239 n. 25,
  240 n. 33
Smith, Johanna M., 168 n. 4, 169 n. 10
sodomy, 24, 40 n. 12, 59
Soh Poh Thong, 320 n. 60
South Africa, 224–25, 226
Southern Rhodesia, 262, 266, 270–72,
  281–83, 287, 289, 291 n. 5
Spain, 177
Spectator (UK), 103
Spilka, Mark, 293 n. 14
Spivak, Gayatri, ix, xxiv n. 2, 80–81, 297
Sprague, Claire, 290 n. 2
Stanley, A. P., xiii
Stanley, Henry Morton, 101
Stanley, Marni, 112 n. 59
Stark, Bruce, 157, 169 n. 9, 169 n. 13
Stein, Arlene, xi
Stevenson, Robert Lewis, 166
Stoker, Bram: *Dracula,* 245, 246,
  259 n. 13
Stoler, Ann Laura, ix, 298, 318 n. 11
Stonewall, 305
St. Petersburg, 247

DH

820.
935
3
IMP